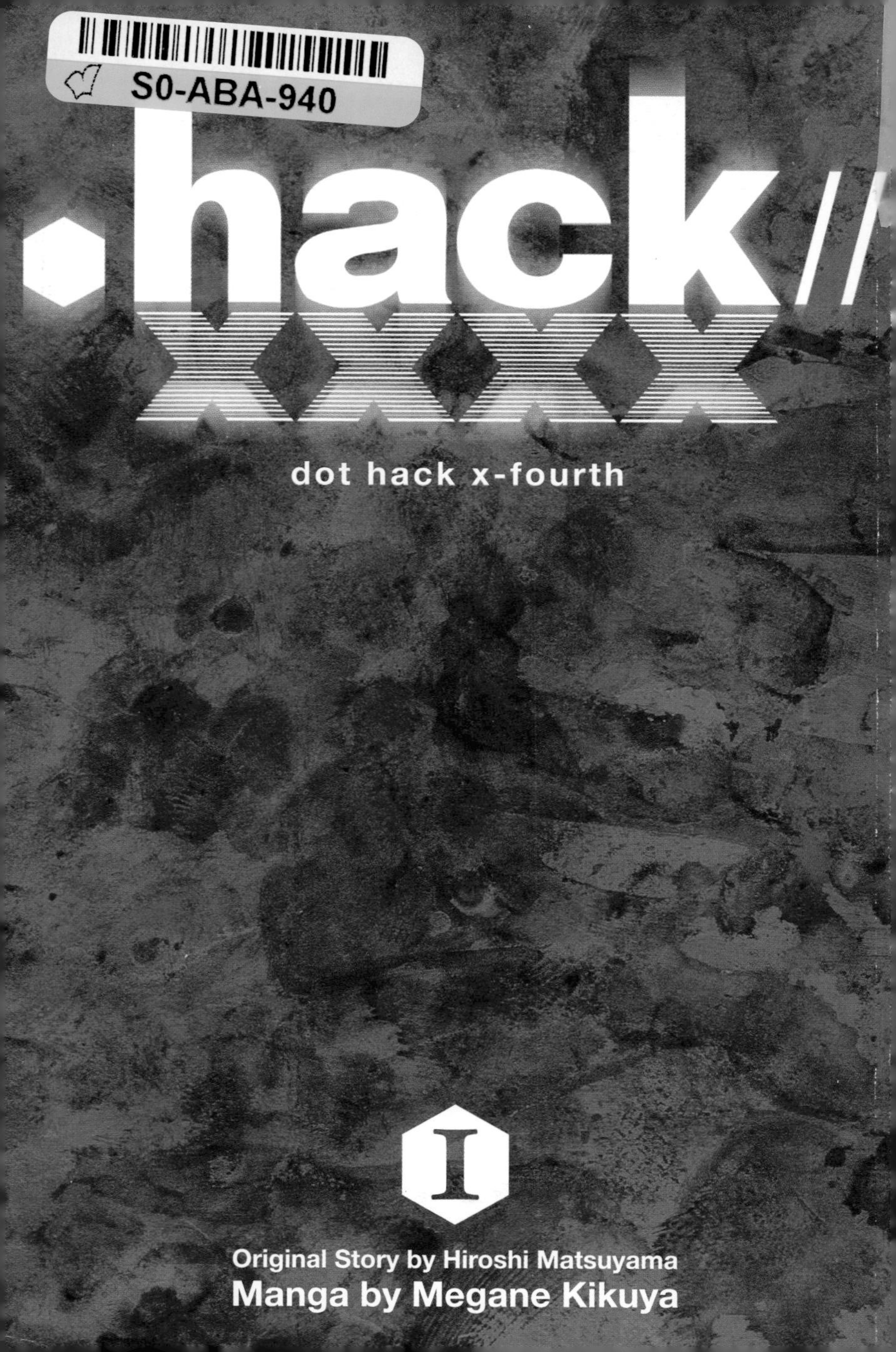
.hack//XXXX
dot hack x-fourth
I
Original Story by Hiroshi Matsuyama
Manga by Megane Kikuya

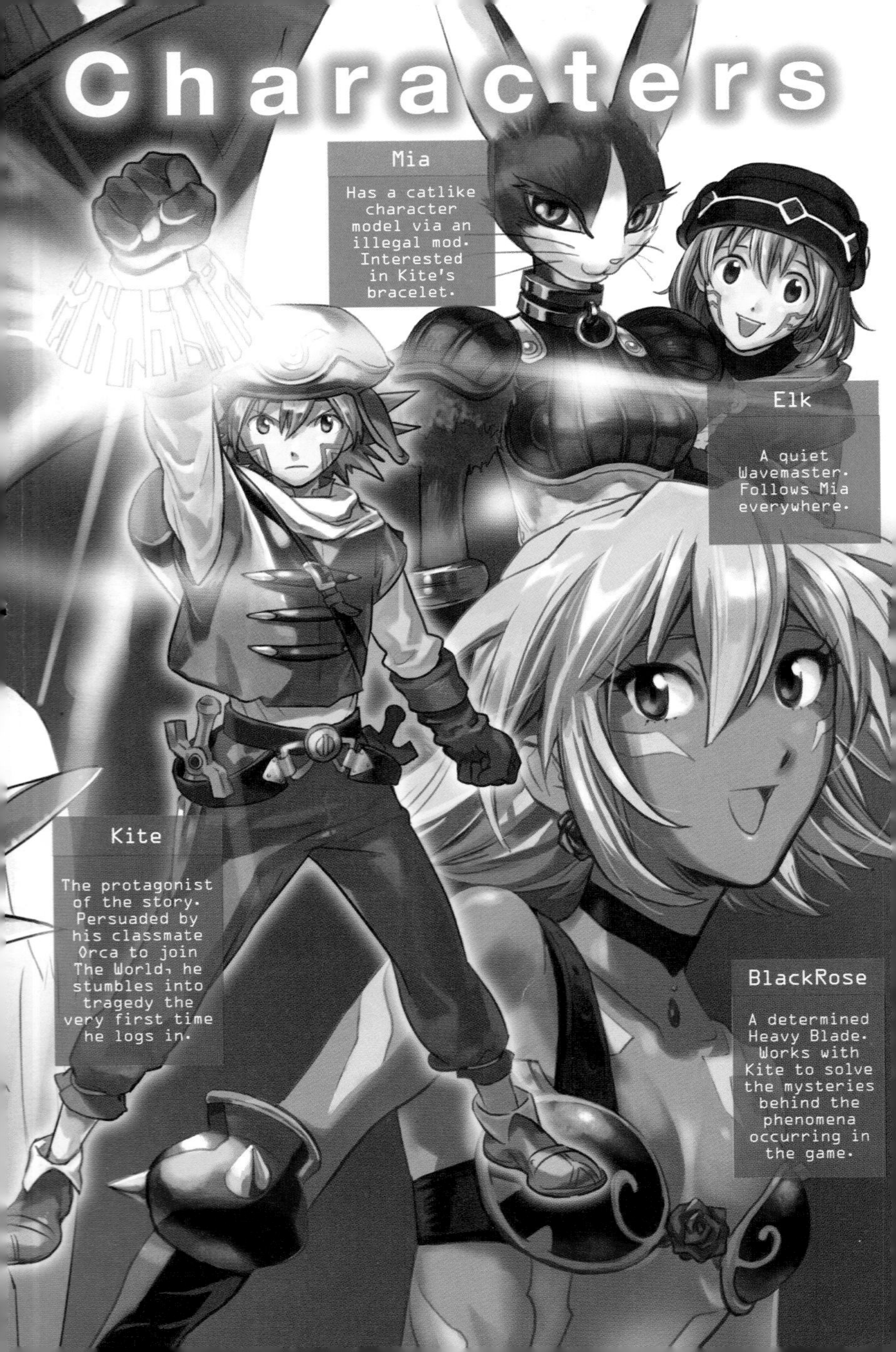
Characters
Mia
Has a catlike character model via an illegal mod. Interested in Kite's bracelet.
Elk
A quiet Wavemaster. Follows Mia everywhere.
Kite
The protagonist of the story. Persuaded by his classmate Orca to join The World, he stumbles into tragedy the very first time he logs in.
BlackRose
A determined Heavy Blade. Works with Kite to solve the mysteries behind the phenomena occurring in the game.

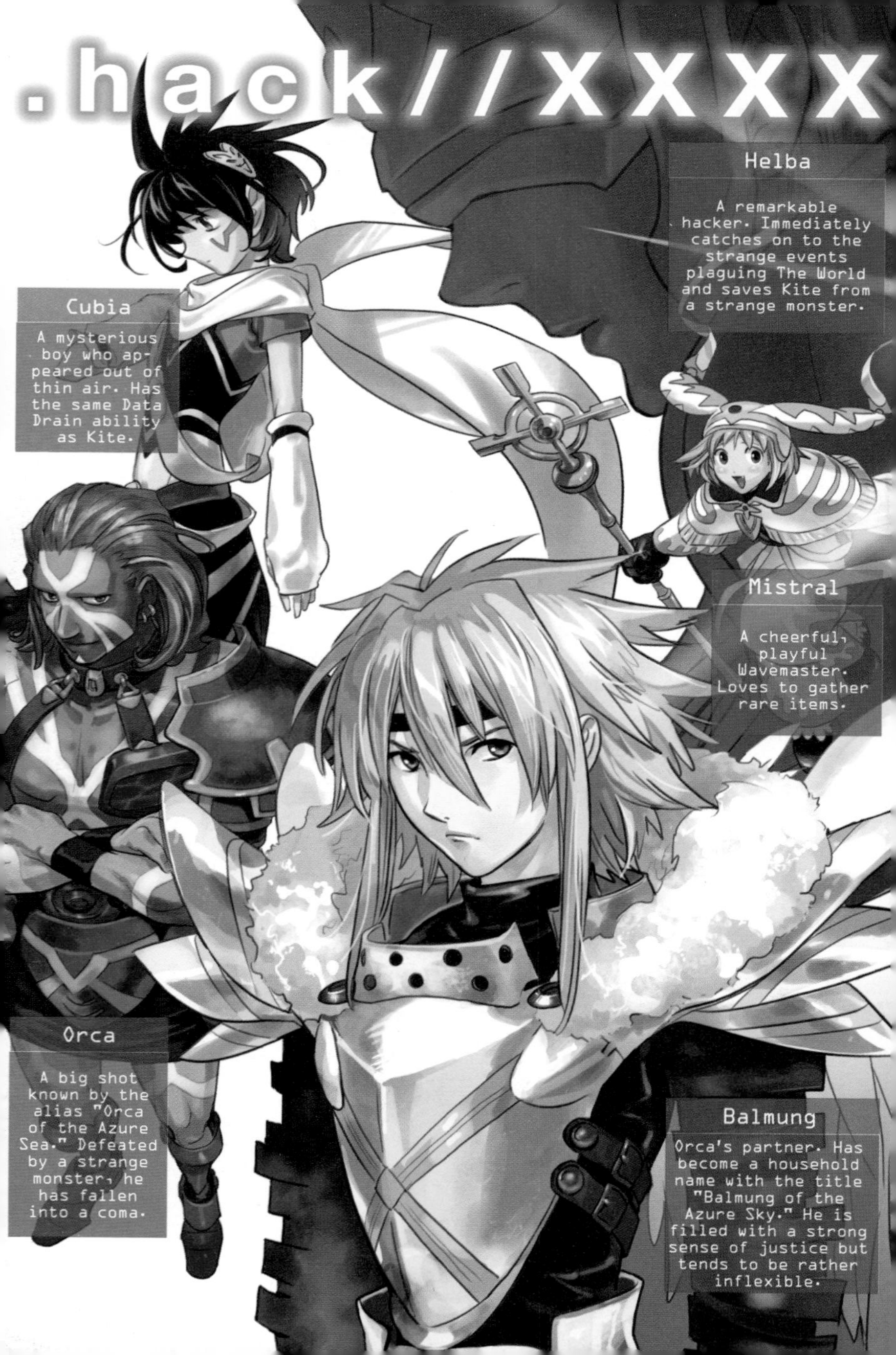
.hack//XXXX
Helba
A remarkable hacker. Immediately catches on to the strange events plaguing The World and saves Kite from a strange monster.
Cubia
A mysterious boy who appeared out of thin air. Has the same Data Drain ability as Kite.
Mistral
A cheerful, playful Wavemaster. Loves to gather rare items.
Orca
A big shot known by the alias "Orca of the Azure Sea." Defeated by a strange monster, he has fallen into a coma.
Balmung
Orca's partner. Has become a household name with the title "Balmung of the Azure Sky." He is filled with a strong sense of justice but tends to be rather inflexible.

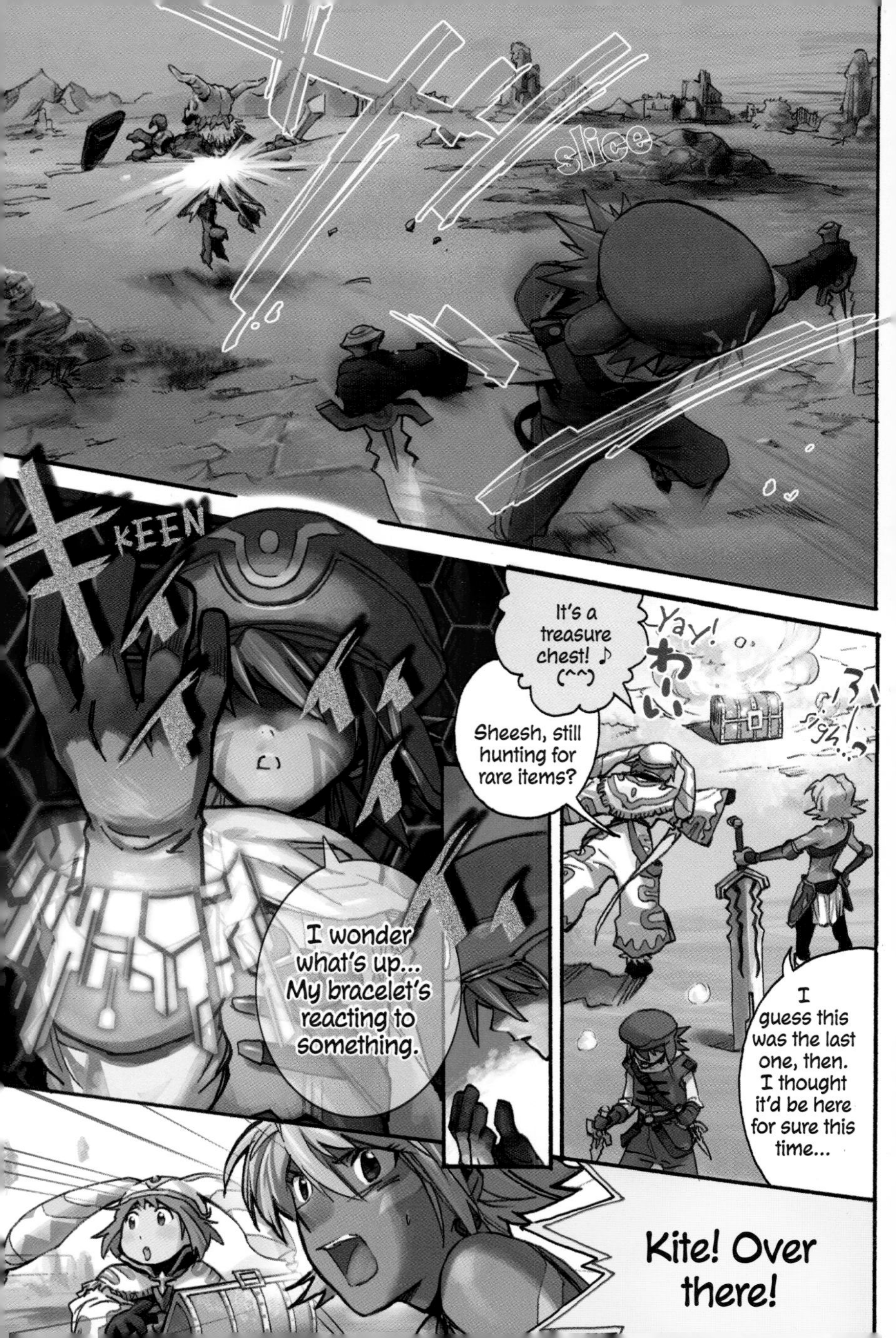
slice
KEEN
It's a treasure chest! ♪ (^^)
Yay!
わい
Sheesh, still hunting for rare items?
sigh
I wonder what's up... My bracelet's reacting to something.
I guess this was the last one, then. I thought it'd be here for sure this time...
Kite! Over there!

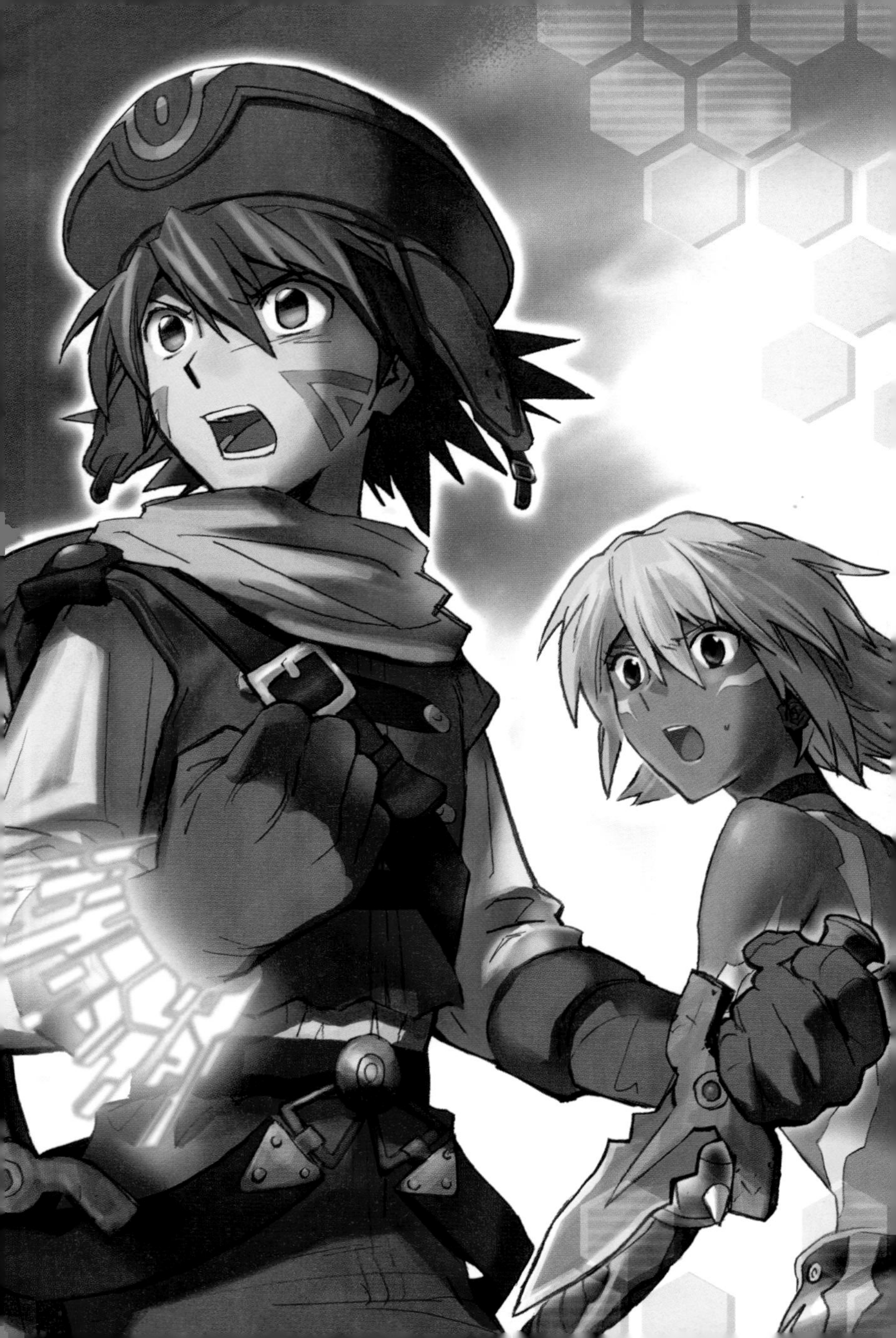

log 001

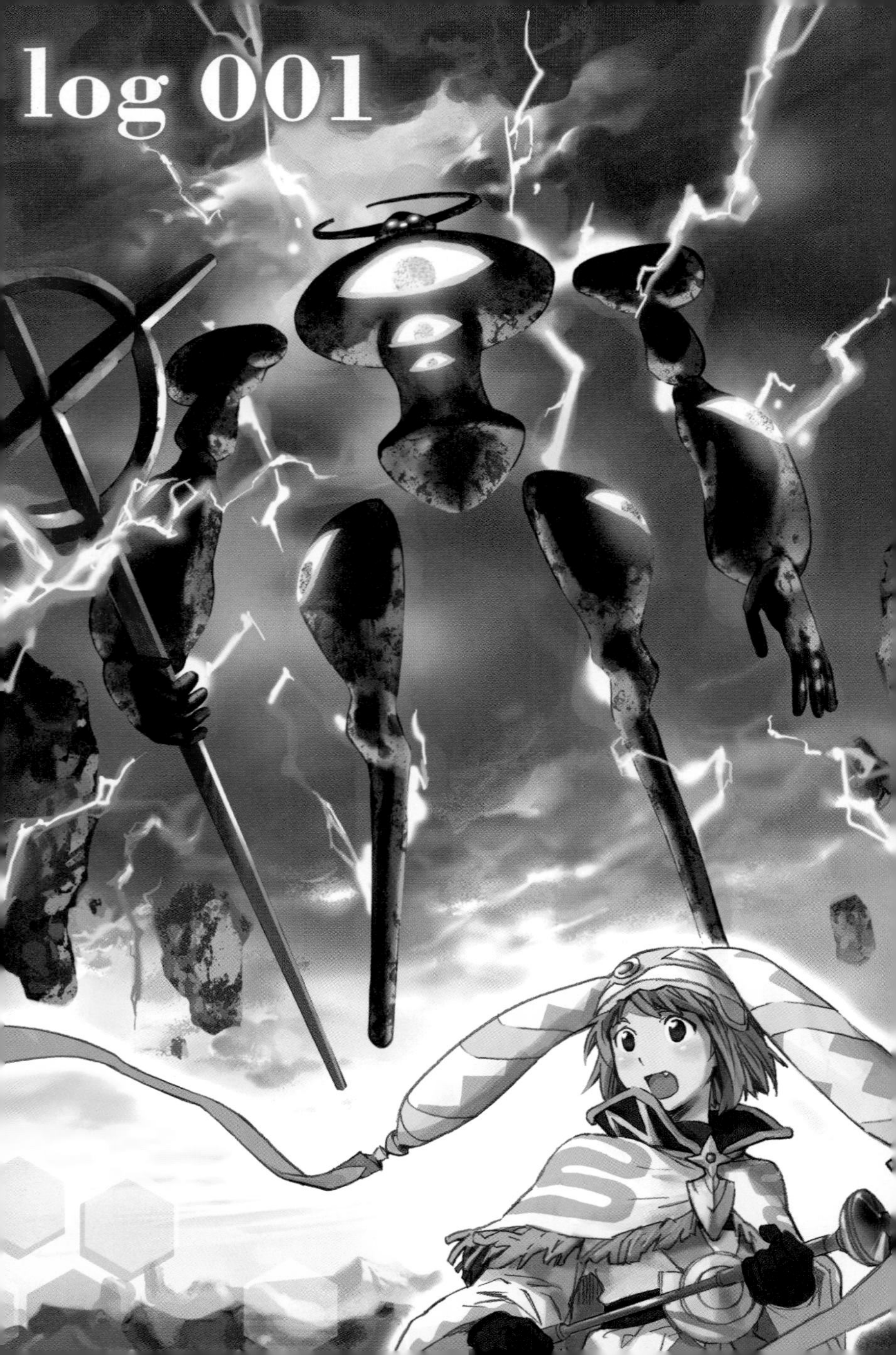

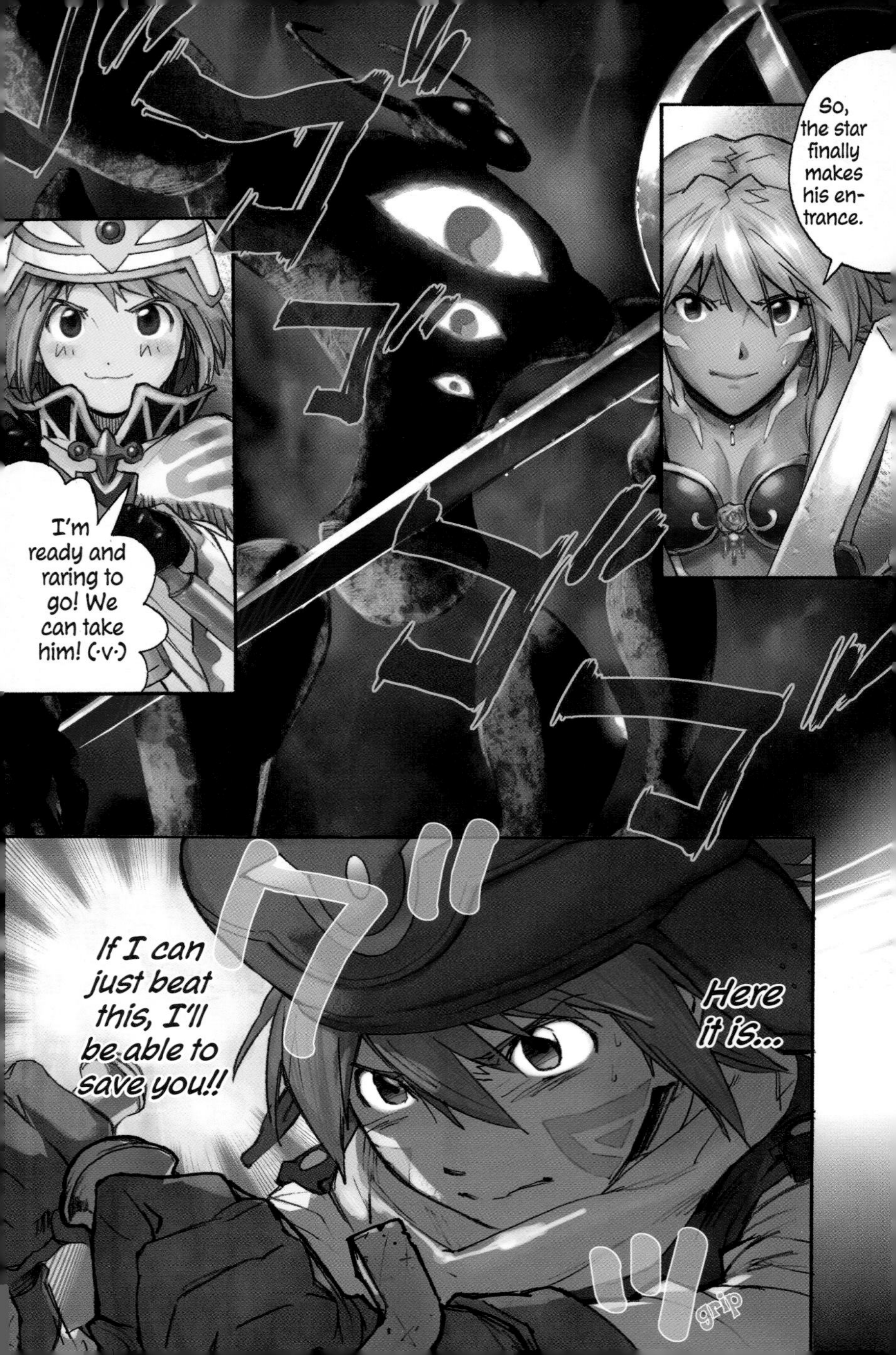
So, the star finally makes his entrance.
I'm ready and raring to go! We can take him! (·v·)
Here it is...
If I can just beat this, I'll be able to save you!!
grip

.hack// XXXX

Volume 1

Original Story by
Hiroshi Matsuyama
Manga by Megane Kikuya

TOKYOPOP®

HAMBURG // LONDON // LOS ANGELES // TOKYO

.hack//XXXX Volume 1
Original Story by Hiroshi Matsuyama
Manga by Megane Kikuya

Translation - Ryan Peterson
English Adaptation - Marc Lunden
Fan Consultants - Christopher Wagner and Colin Farrell
Copy Editor - Jessica Chavez
Retouch and Lettering - Michael Paolilli
Graphic Designer - Tina Corrales

Editor - Peter Ahlstrom
Digital Imaging Manager - Chris Buford
Pre-Production Supervisor - Lucas Rivera
Production Manager - Elisabeth Brizzi
Managing Editor - Vy Nguyen
Creative Director - Anne Marie Horne
Editor-in-Chief - Rob Tokar
Publisher - Mike Kiley
President and C.O.O. - John Parker
C.E.O. and Chief Creative Officer - Stu Levy

A  Manga

TOKYOPOP Inc.
5900 Wilshire Blvd. Suite 2000
Los Angeles, CA 90036

E-mail: info@TOKYOPOP.com
Come visit us online at www.TOKYOPOP.com

ISBN: 978-1-4278-0931-5

First TOKYOPOP printing: June 2008
10 9 8 7 6 5 4 3 2 1
Printed in the USA

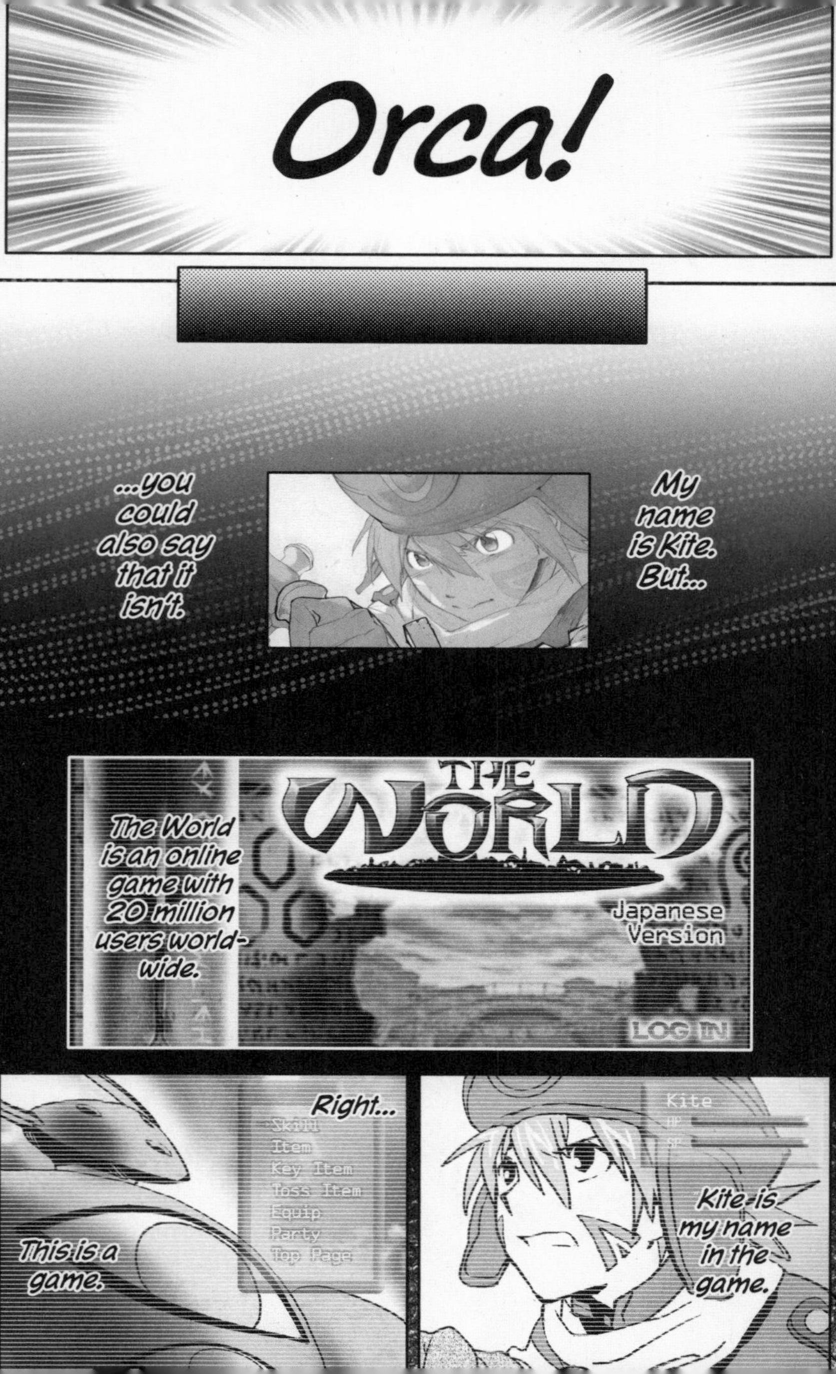

Orca!
My name is Kite. But...
...you could also say that it isn't.
THE WORLD
Japanese Version
LOG IN
The World is an online game with 20 million users world-wide.
Kite
HP
SP
Kite is my name in the game.
Right...
Skill
Item
Key Item
Toss Item
Equip
Party
Top Page
This is a game.

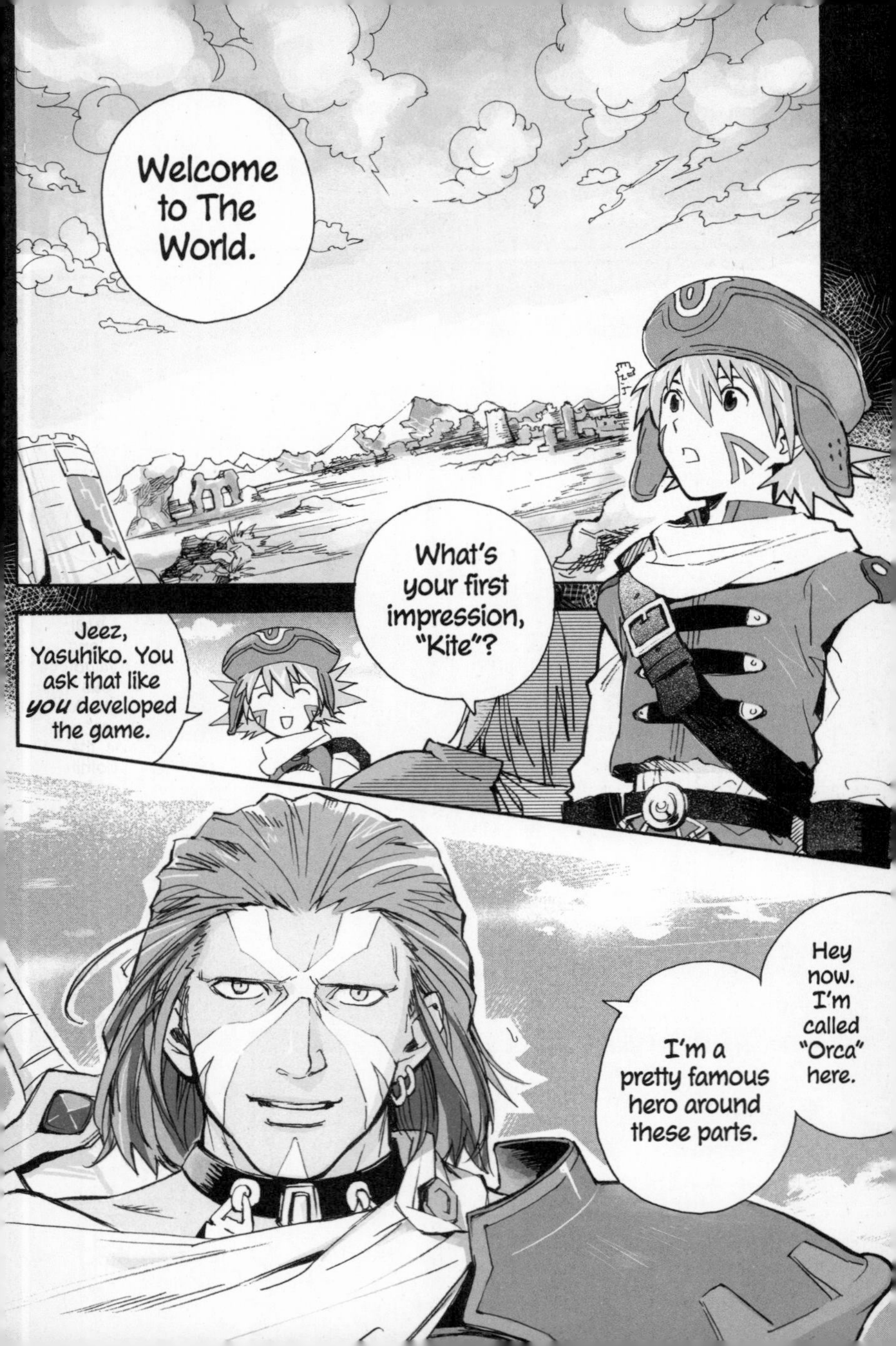
Welcome to The World.
What's your first impression, "Kite"?
Jeez, Yasuhiko. You ask that like *you* developed the game.
Hey now. I'm called "Orca" here.
I'm a pretty famous hero around these parts.

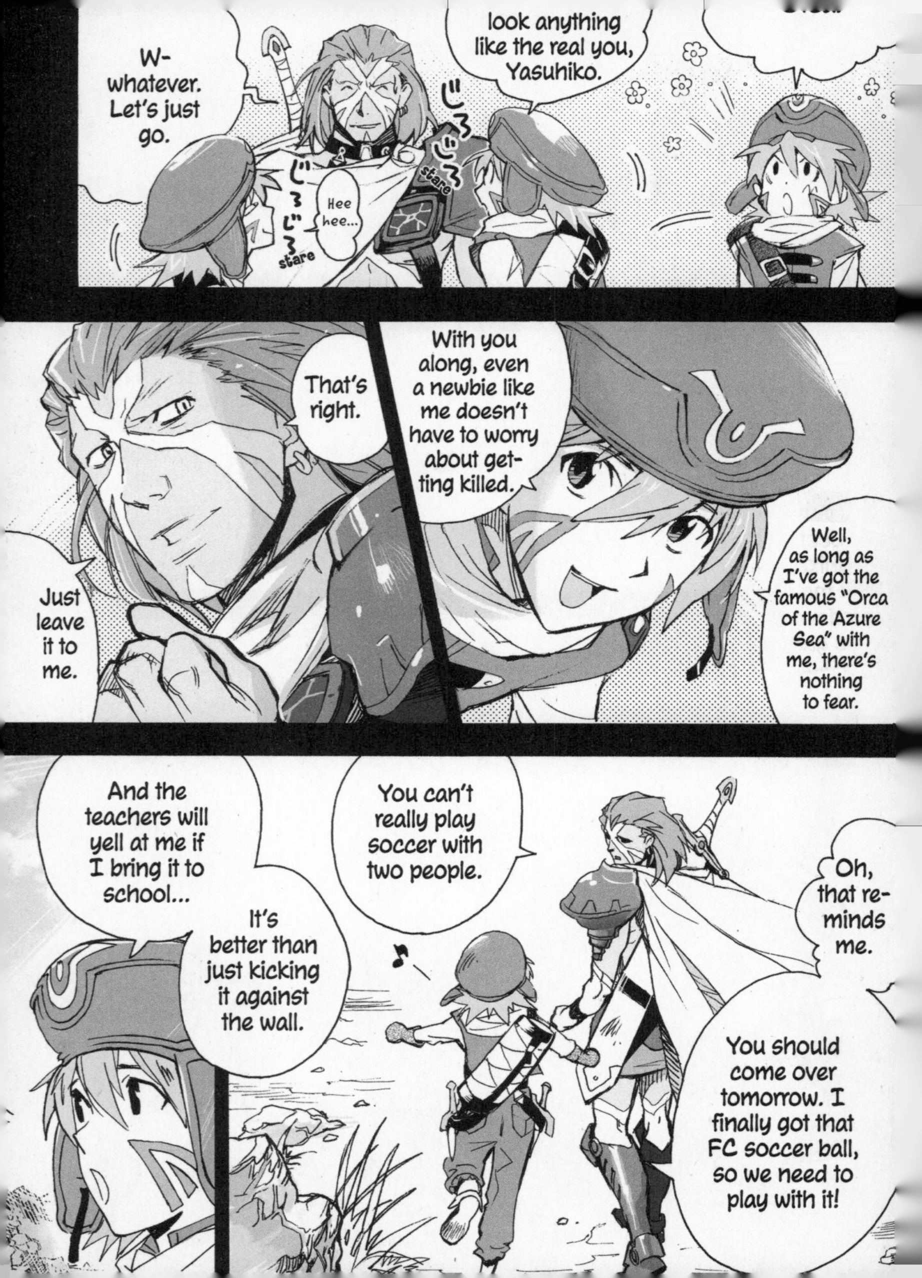

look anything like the real you, Yasuhiko.
じろじろ stare
じろじろ stare
Hee hee...
W-whatever. Let's just go.
Well, as long as I've got the famous "Orca of the Azure Sea" with me, there's nothing to fear.
With you along, even a newbie like me doesn't have to worry about get-ting killed.
That's right.
Just leave it to me.
Oh, that re-minds me.
You should come over tomorrow. I finally got that FC soccer ball, so we need to play with it!
You can't really play soccer with two people.
And the teachers will yell at me if I bring it to school...
It's better than just kicking it against the wall.

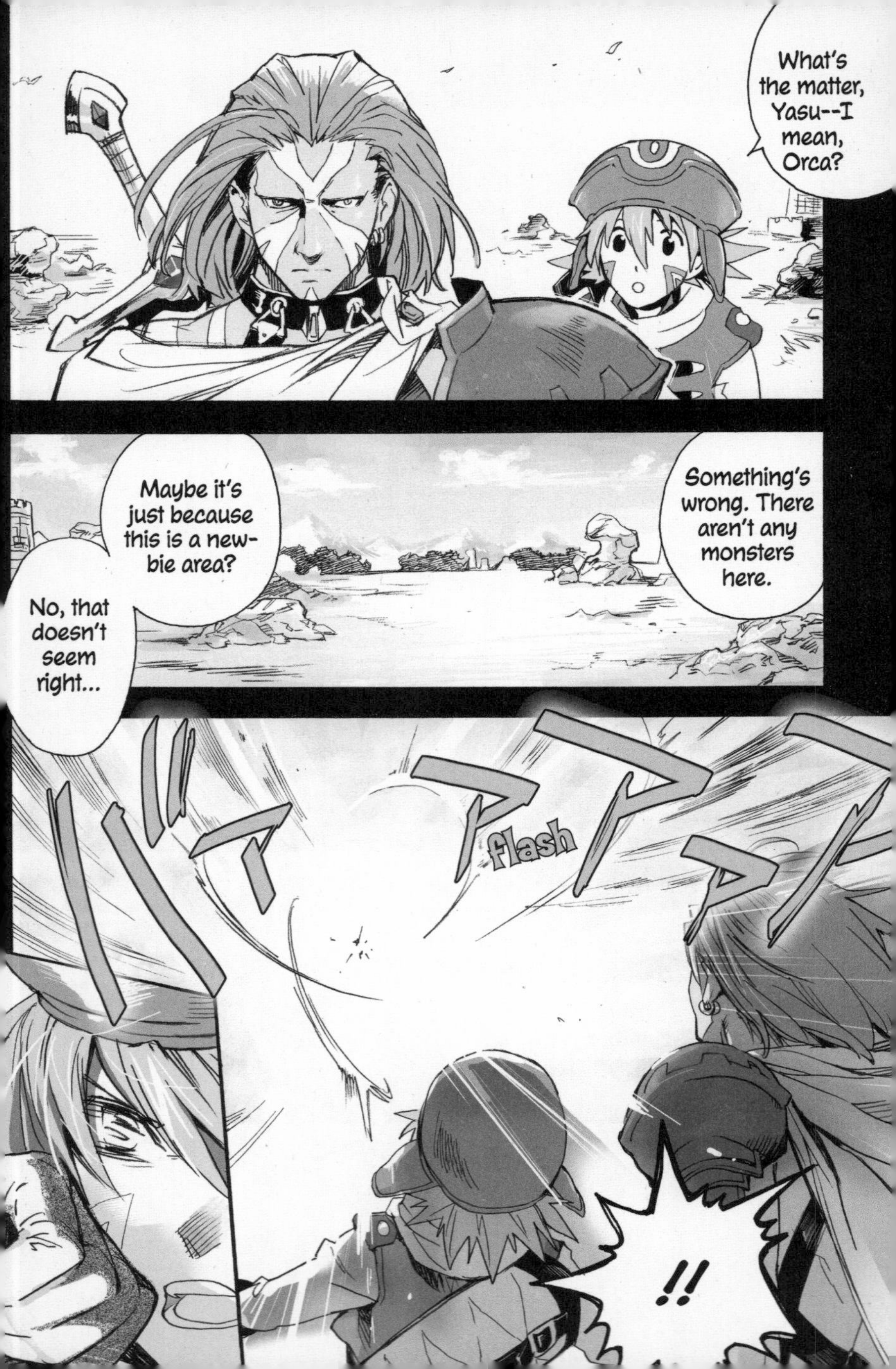
What's the matter, Yasu--I mean, Orca?
Something's wrong. There aren't any monsters here.
Maybe it's just because this is a new-bie area?
No, that doesn't seem right...
flash
!!

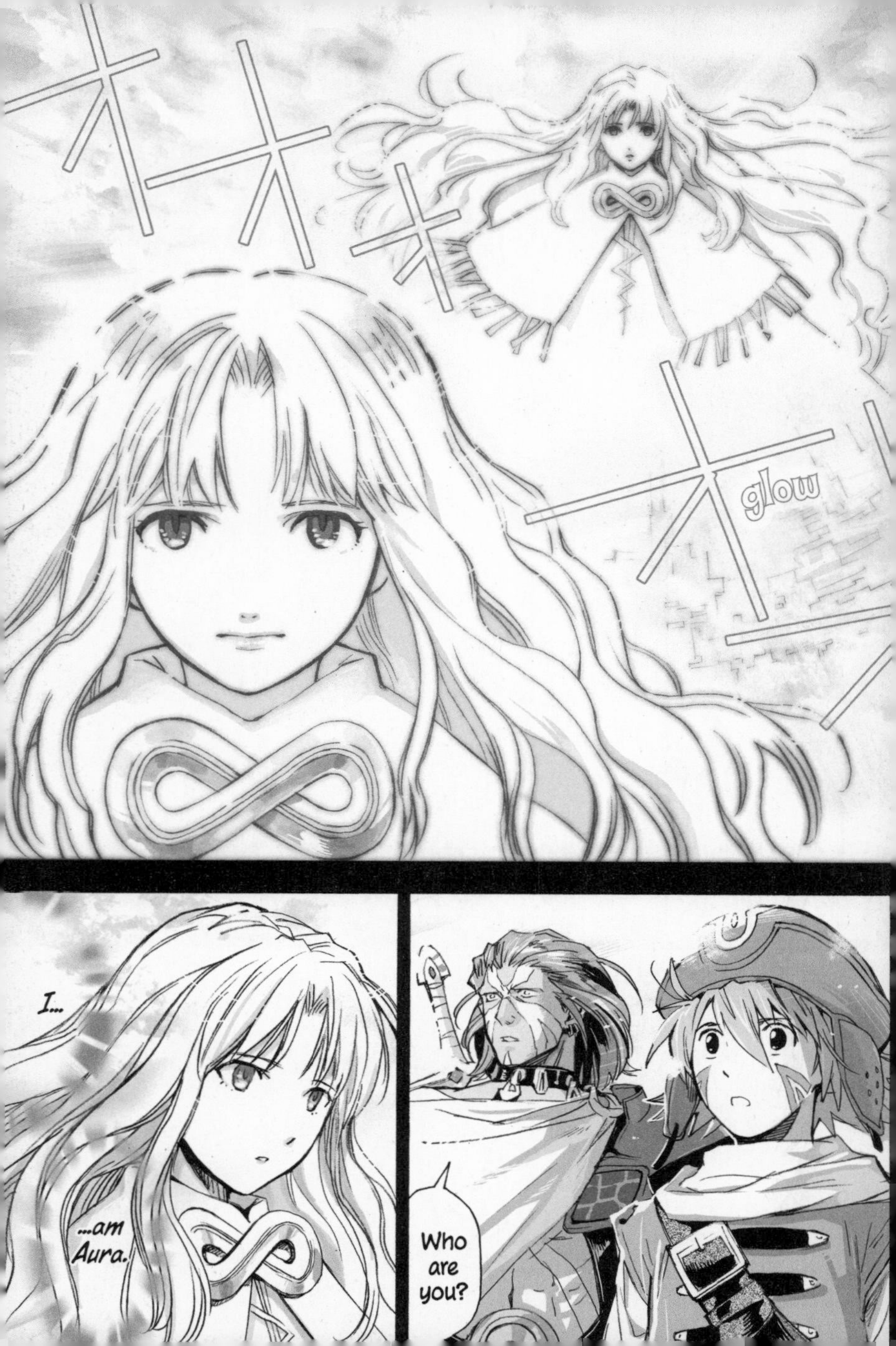
glow
I...
...am Aura.
Who are you?

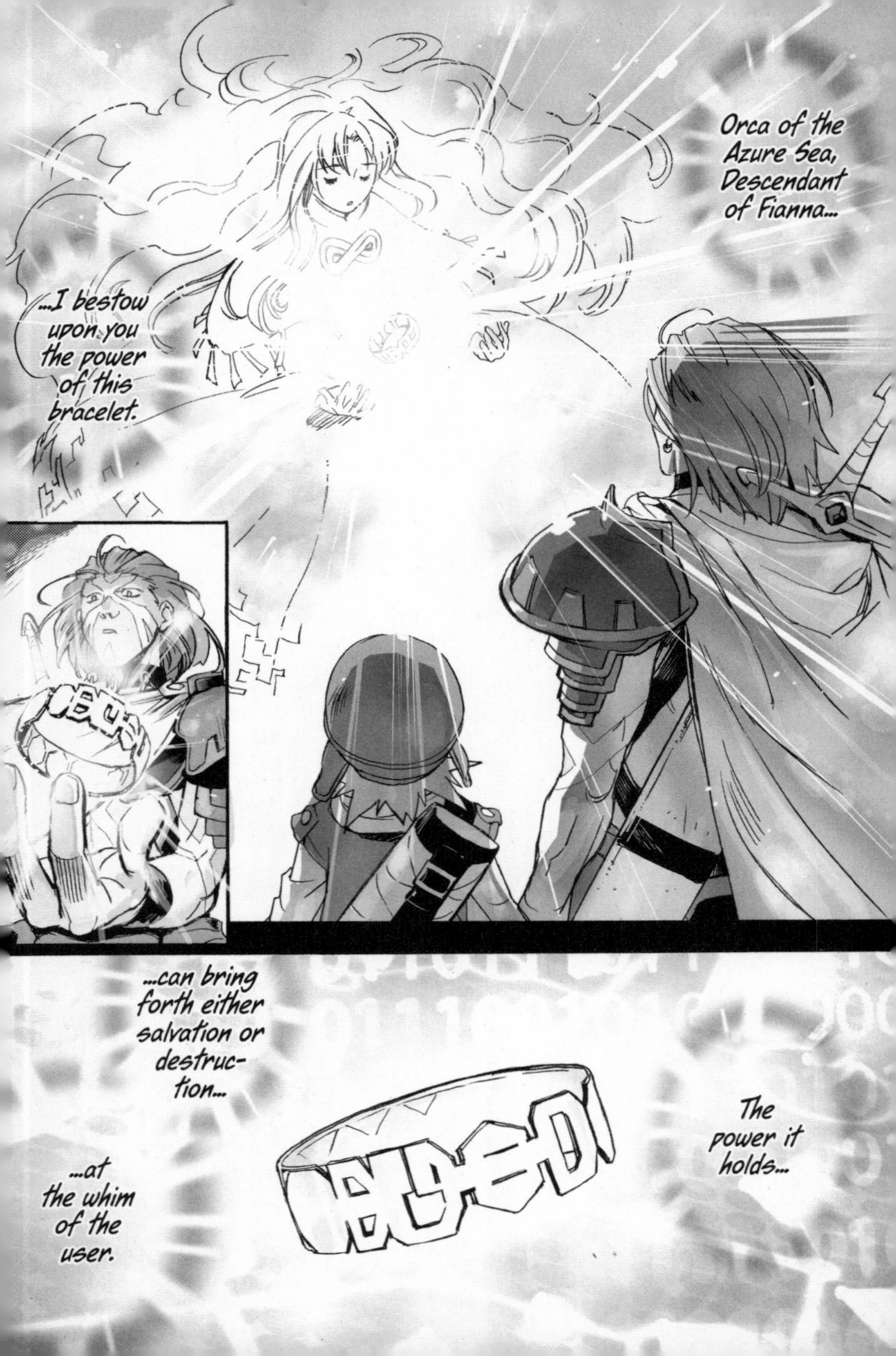
Orca of the Azure Sea, Descendant of Fianna...
...I bestow upon you the power of this bracelet.
The power it holds...
...can bring forth either salvation or destruction...
...at the whim of the user.

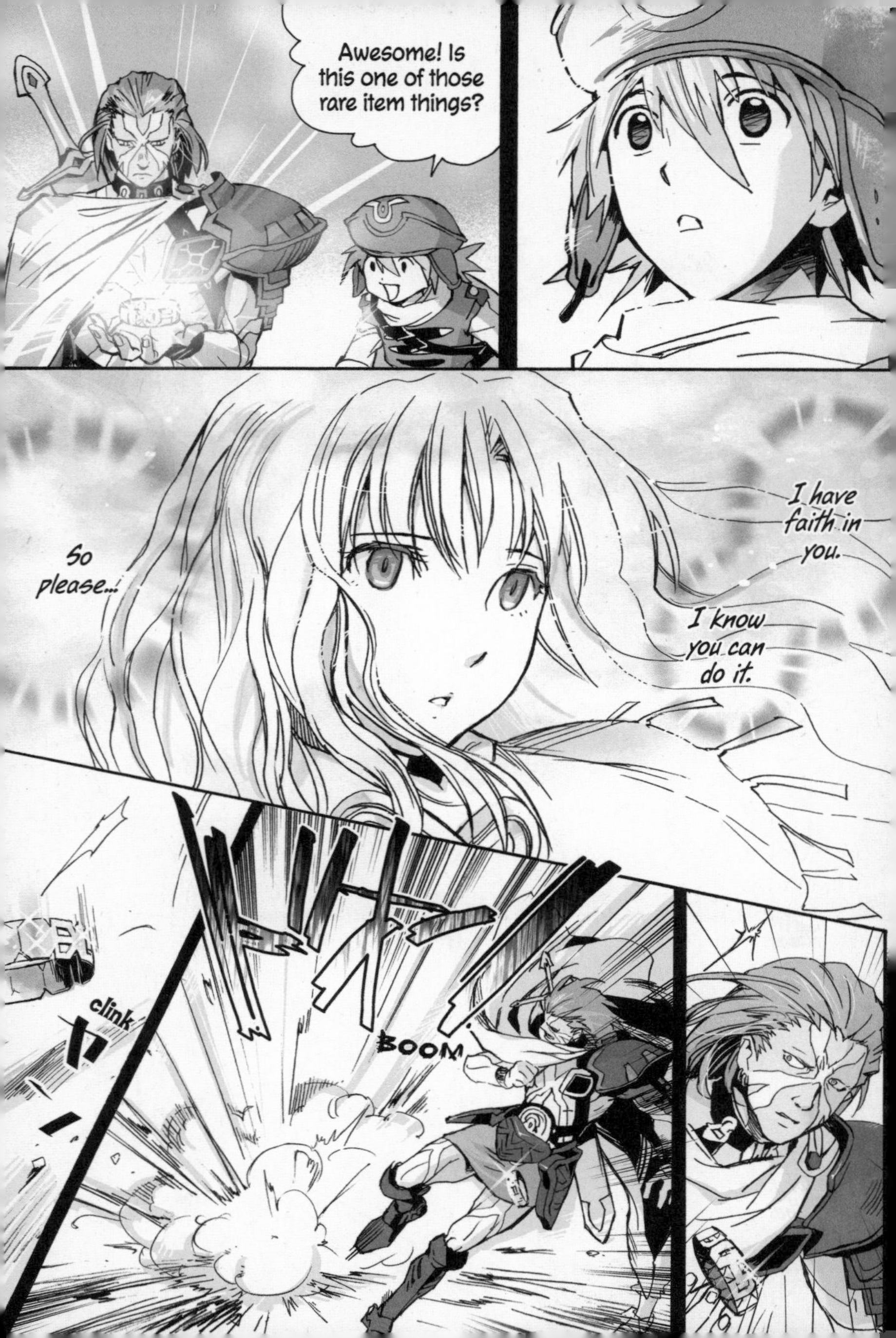
Awesome! Is this one of those rare item things?
I have faith in you.
I know you can do it.
So please...
clink
BOOM

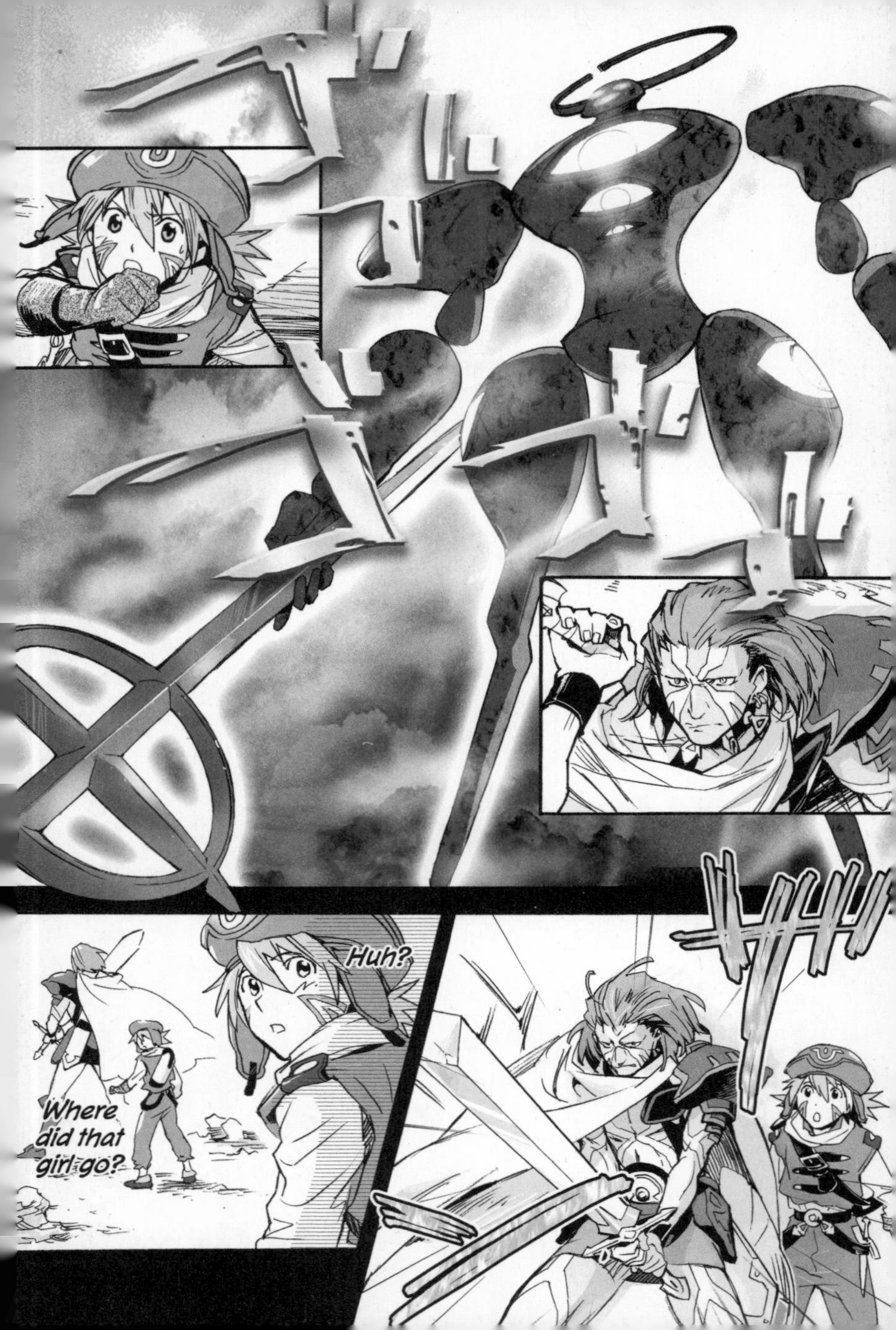
Huh?
Where did that girl go?

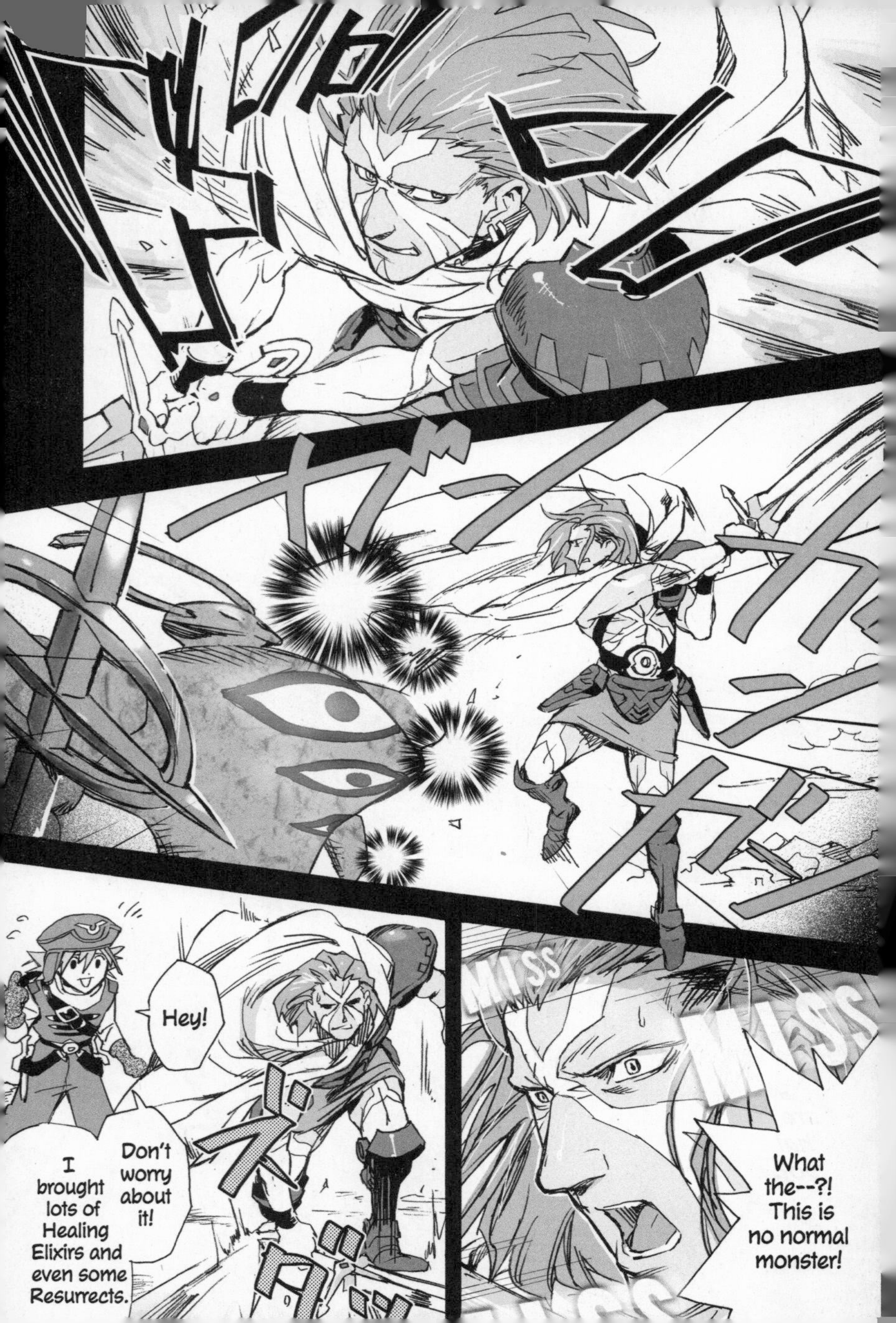
MISS
MISS
What the--?! This is no normal monster!
Hey!
Don't worry about it!
I brought lots of Healing Elixirs and even some Resurrects.

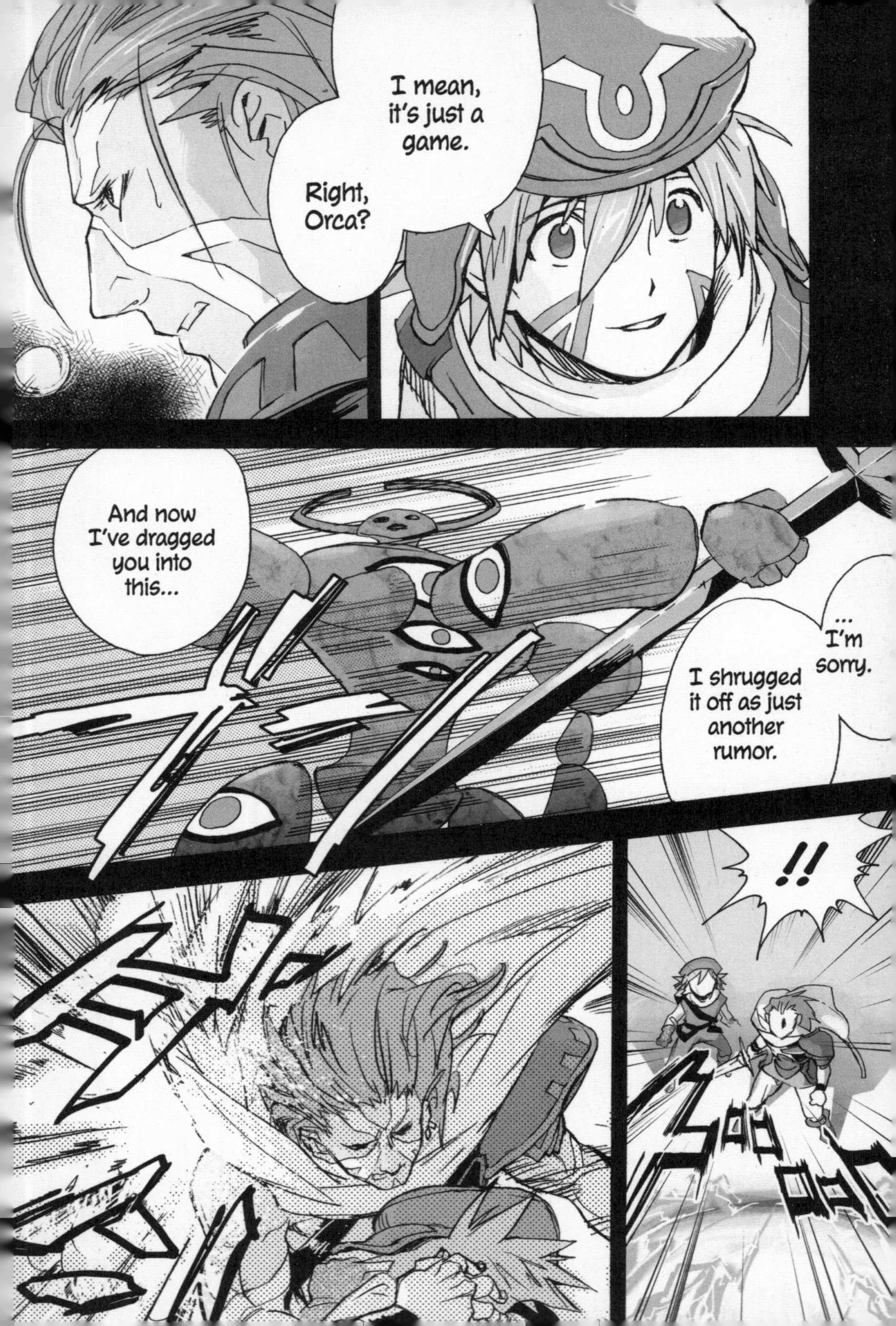

I mean, it's just a game.
Right, Orca?
And now I've dragged you into this...
... I'm sorry.
I shrugged it off as just another rumor.
!!

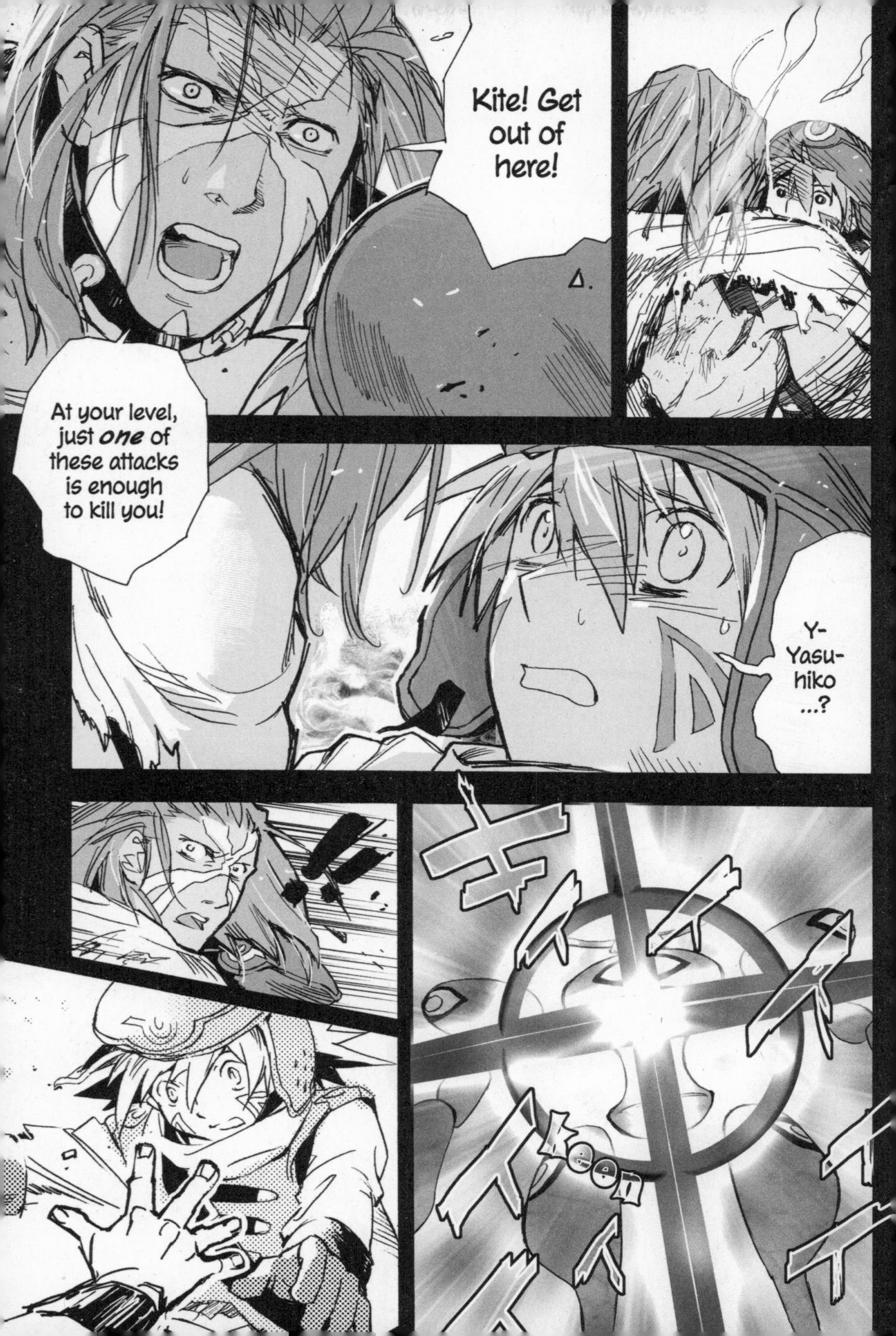
Kite! Get out of here!
At your level, just *one* of these attacks is enough to kill you!
Y-Yasu-hiko ...?

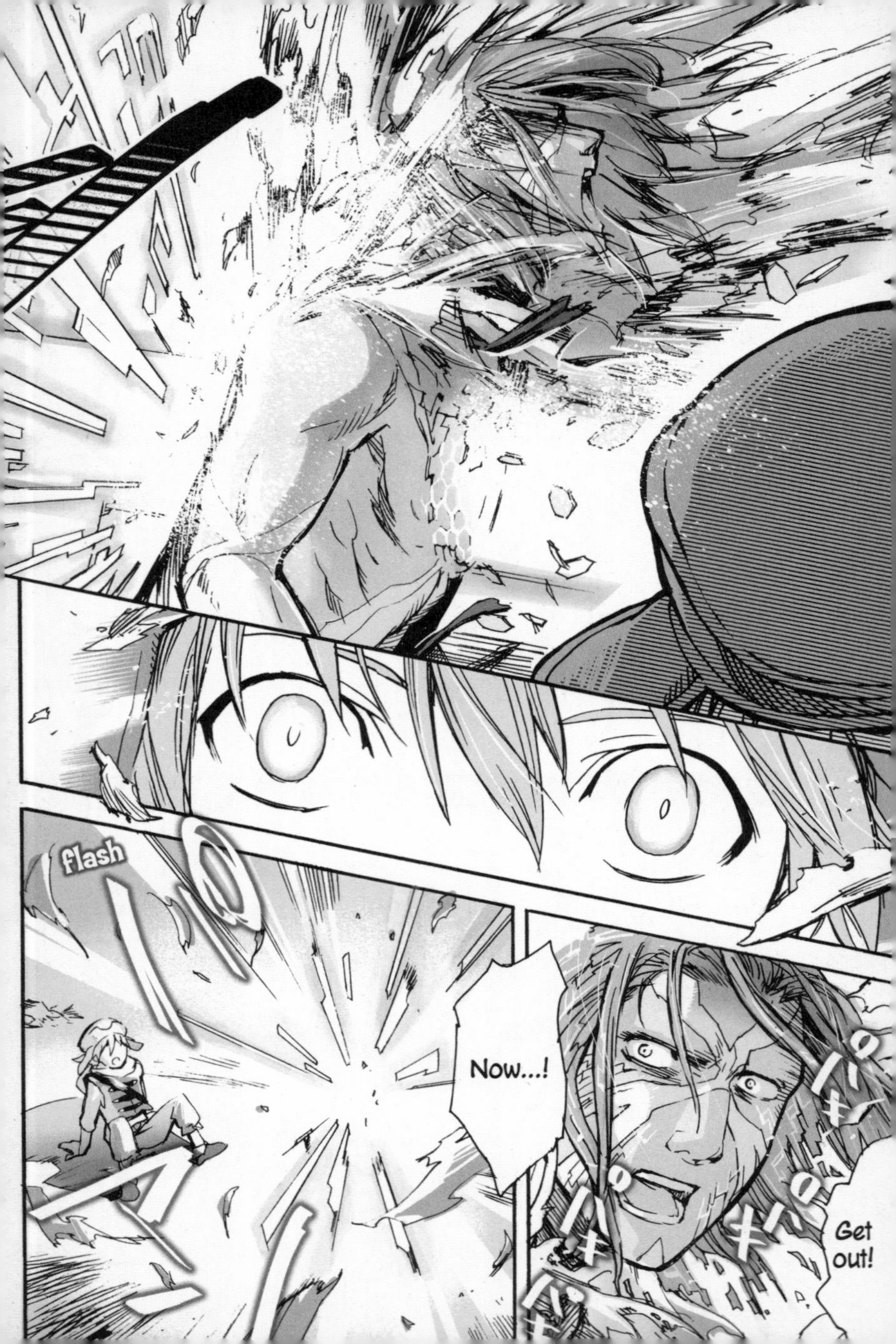
flash
Now...!
Get out!

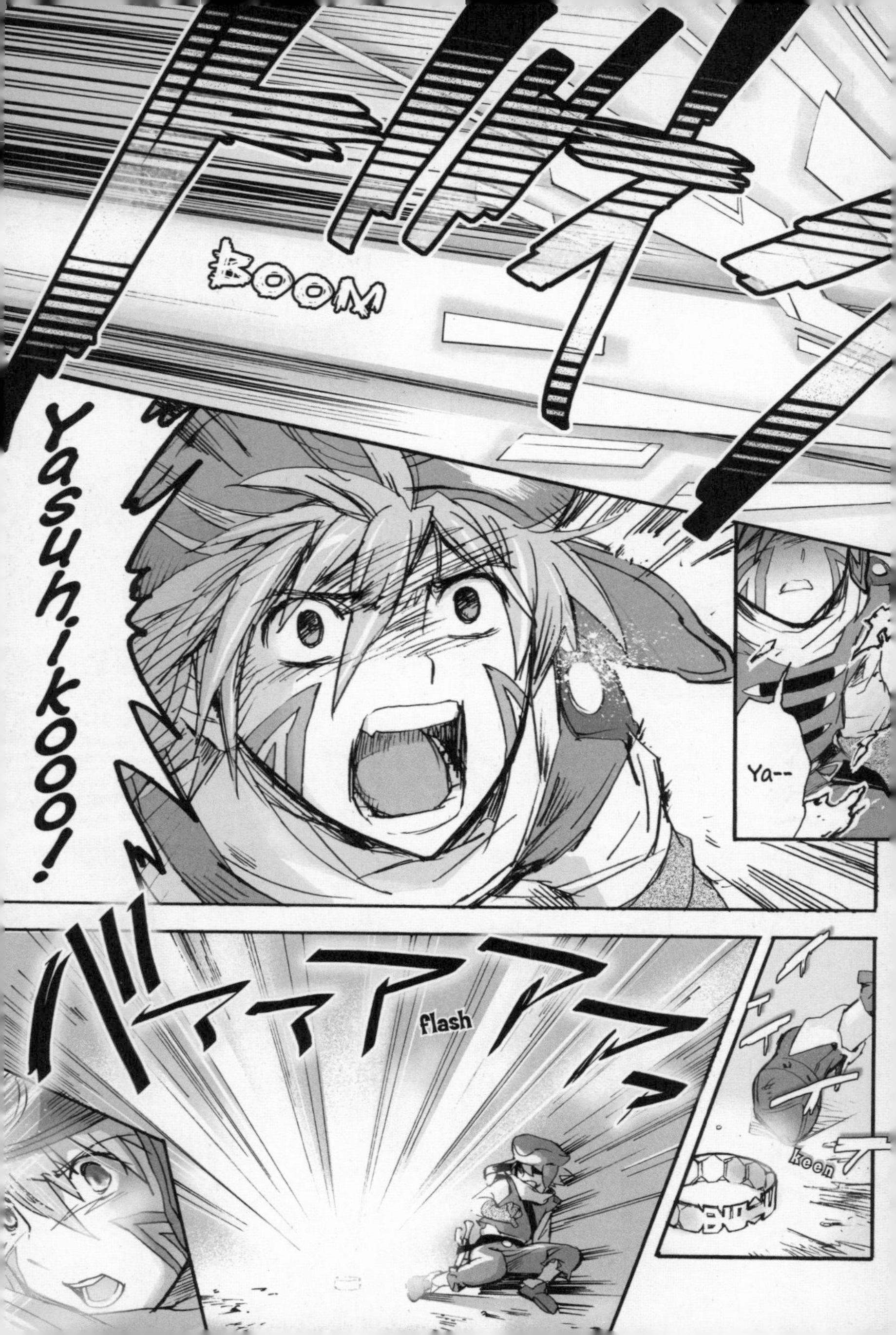
BOOM
Ya--
Yasunikoooo!
keen
flash

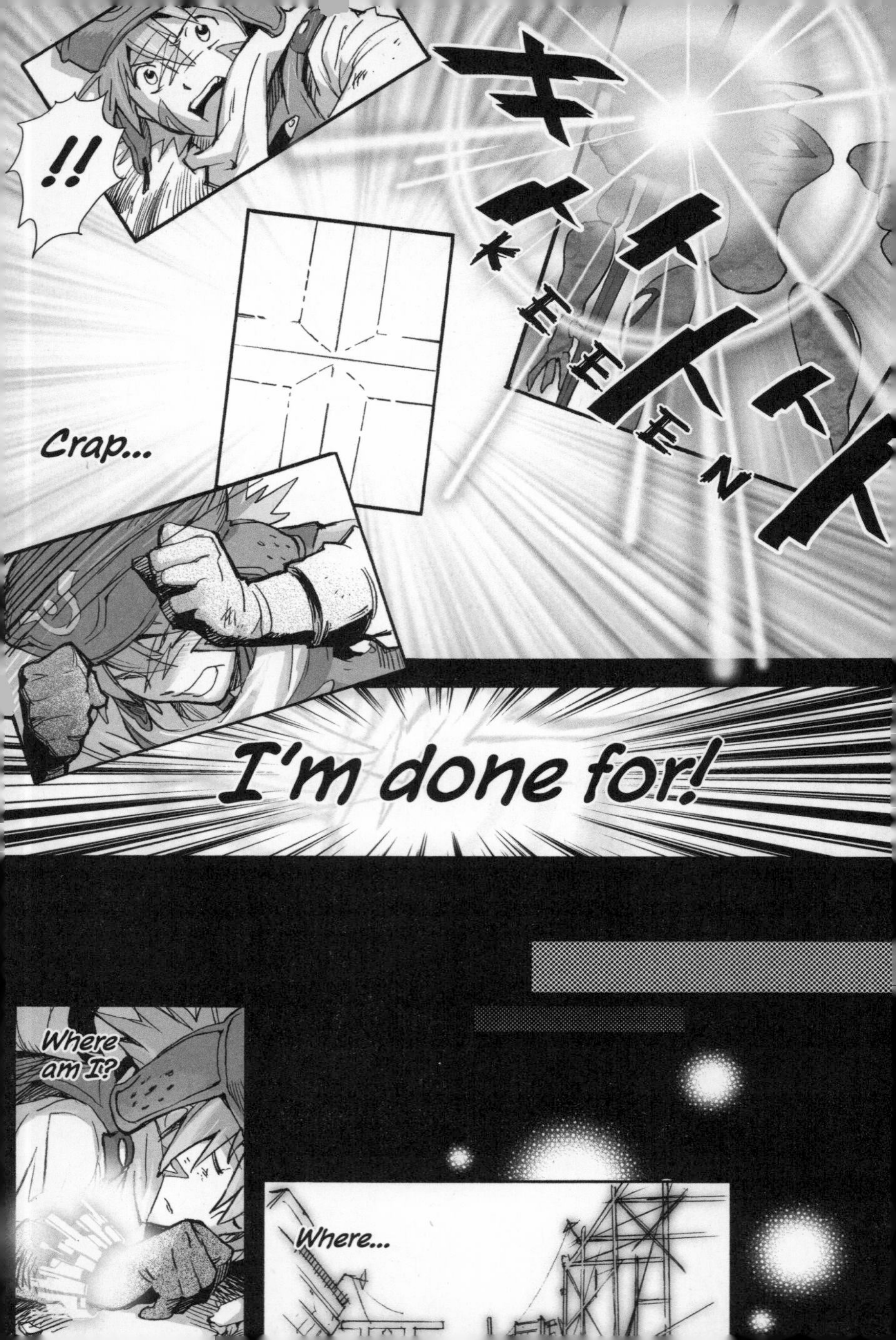
!!
KEEEN
Crap...
I'm done for!
Where am I?
Where...

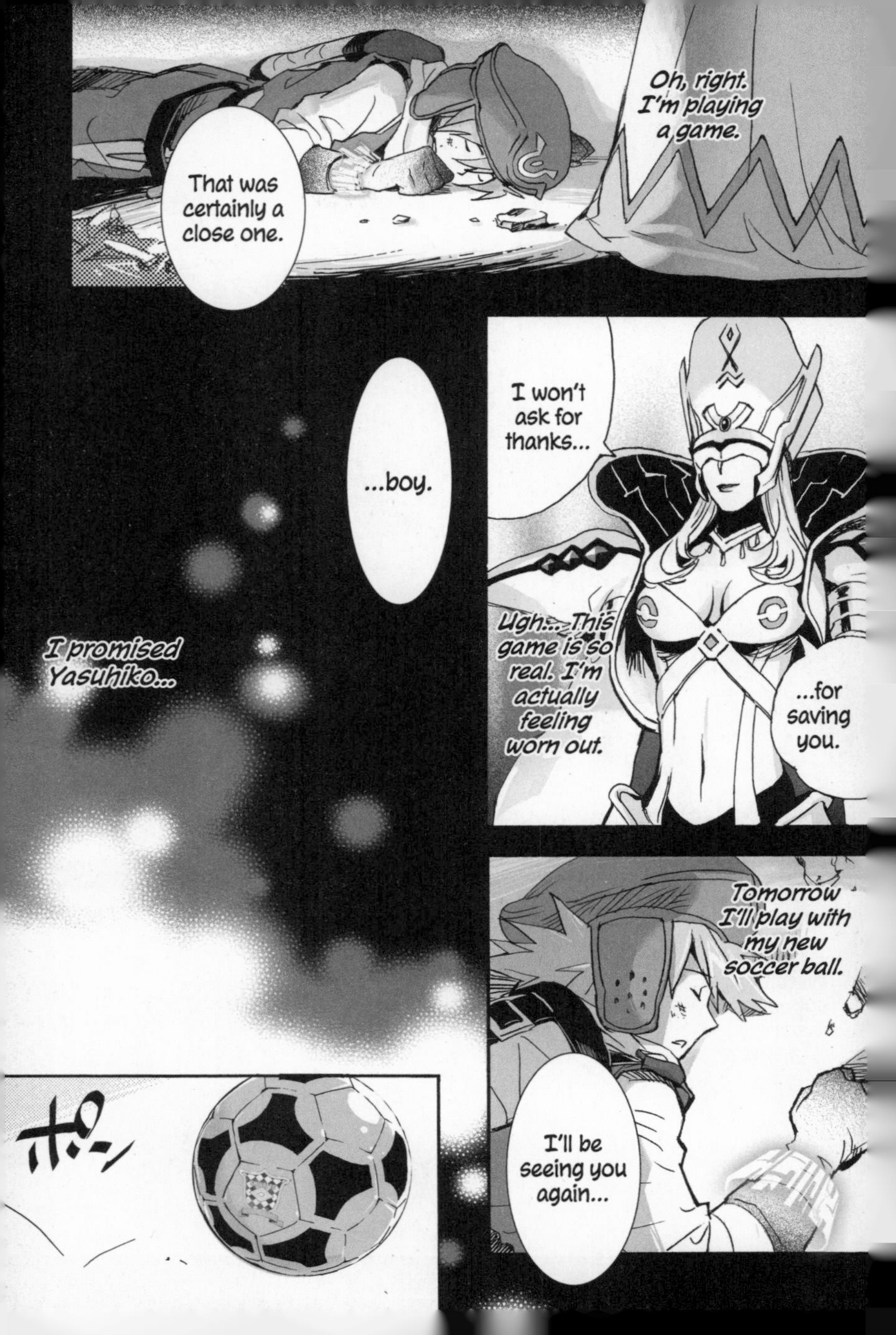
Oh, right. I'm playing a game.
That was certainly a close one.
I won't ask for thanks...
...for saving you.
Ugh... This game is so real. I'm actually feeling worn out.
...boy.
Tomorrow I'll play with my new soccer ball.
I'll be seeing you again...
I promised Yasuhiko...
ポーン

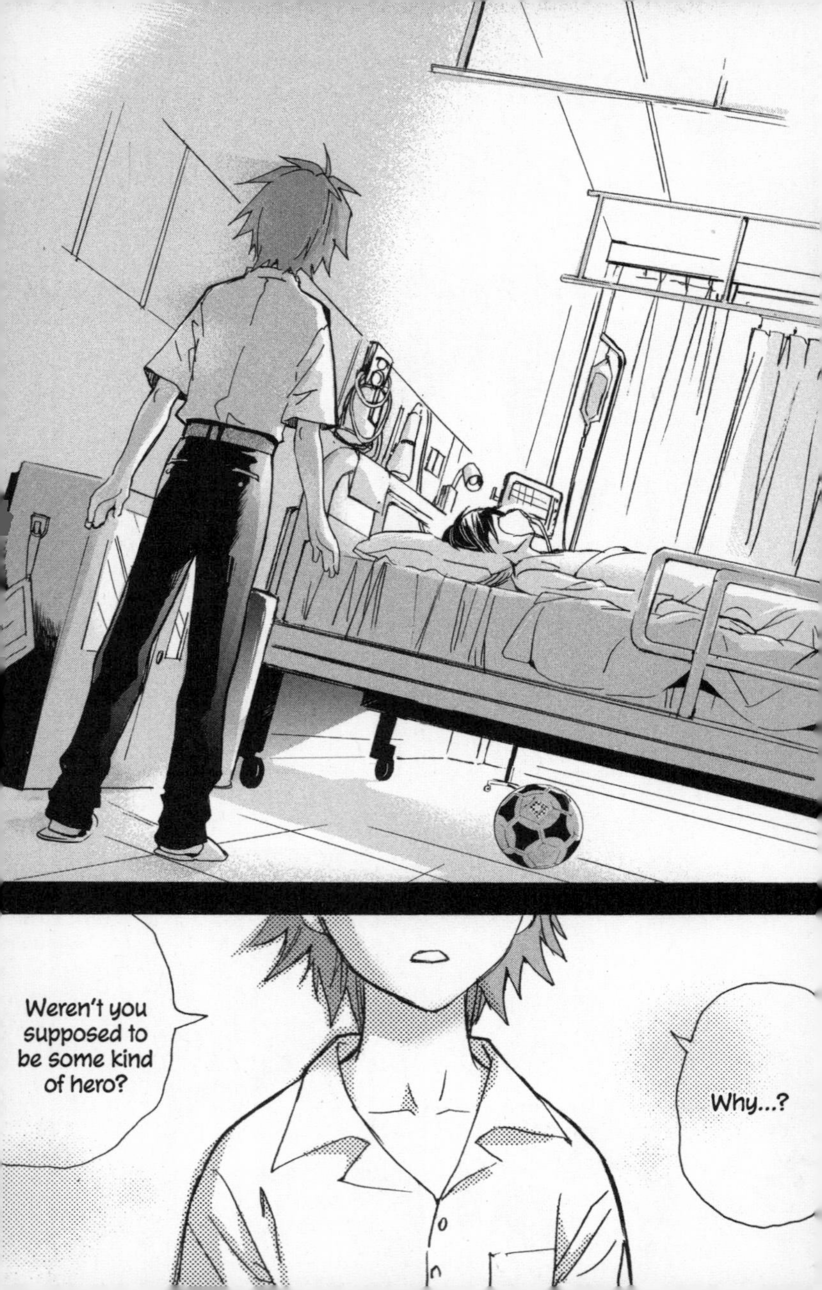
Why...?
Weren't you supposed to be some kind of hero?

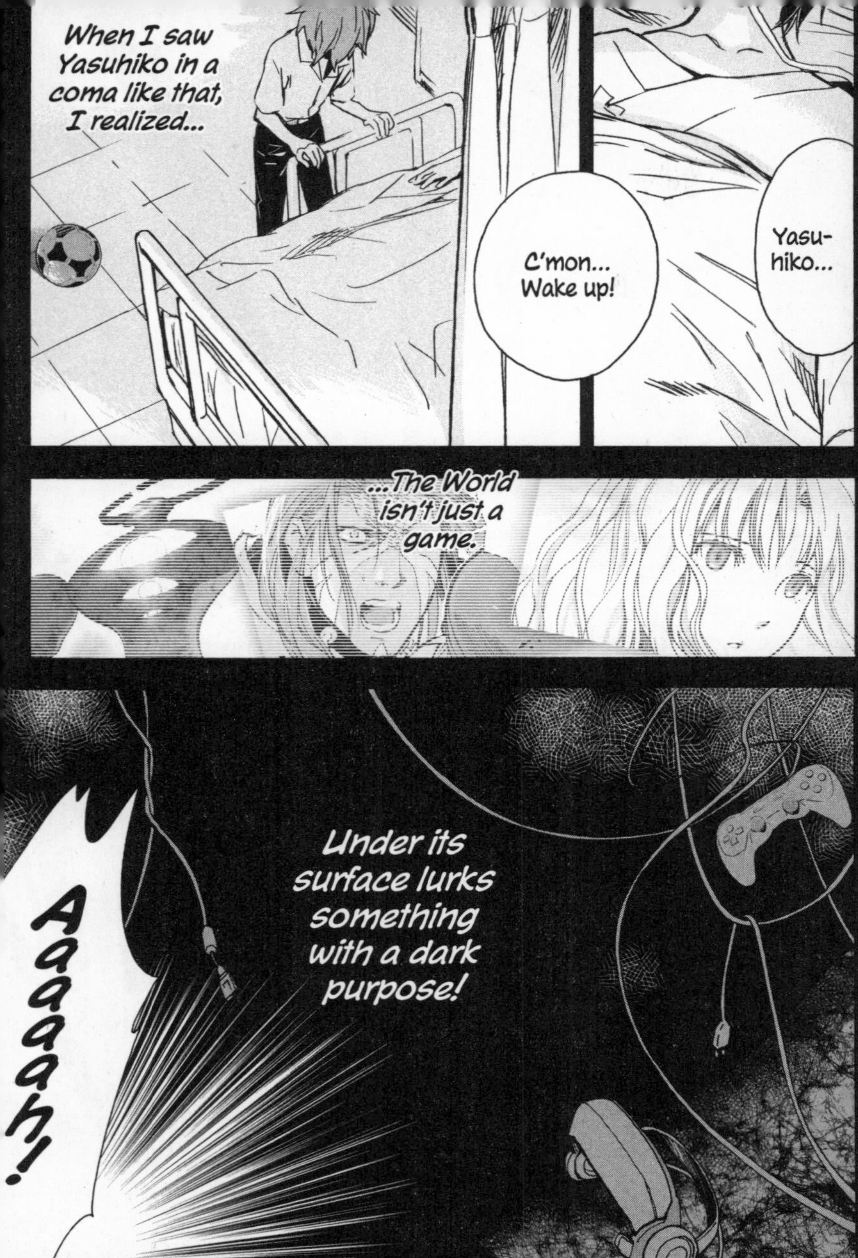
Yasu-hiko...
C'mon... Wake up!
When I saw Yasuhiko in a coma like that, I realized...
...The World isn't just a game.
Under its surface lurks something with a dark purpose!
Aaaaah!

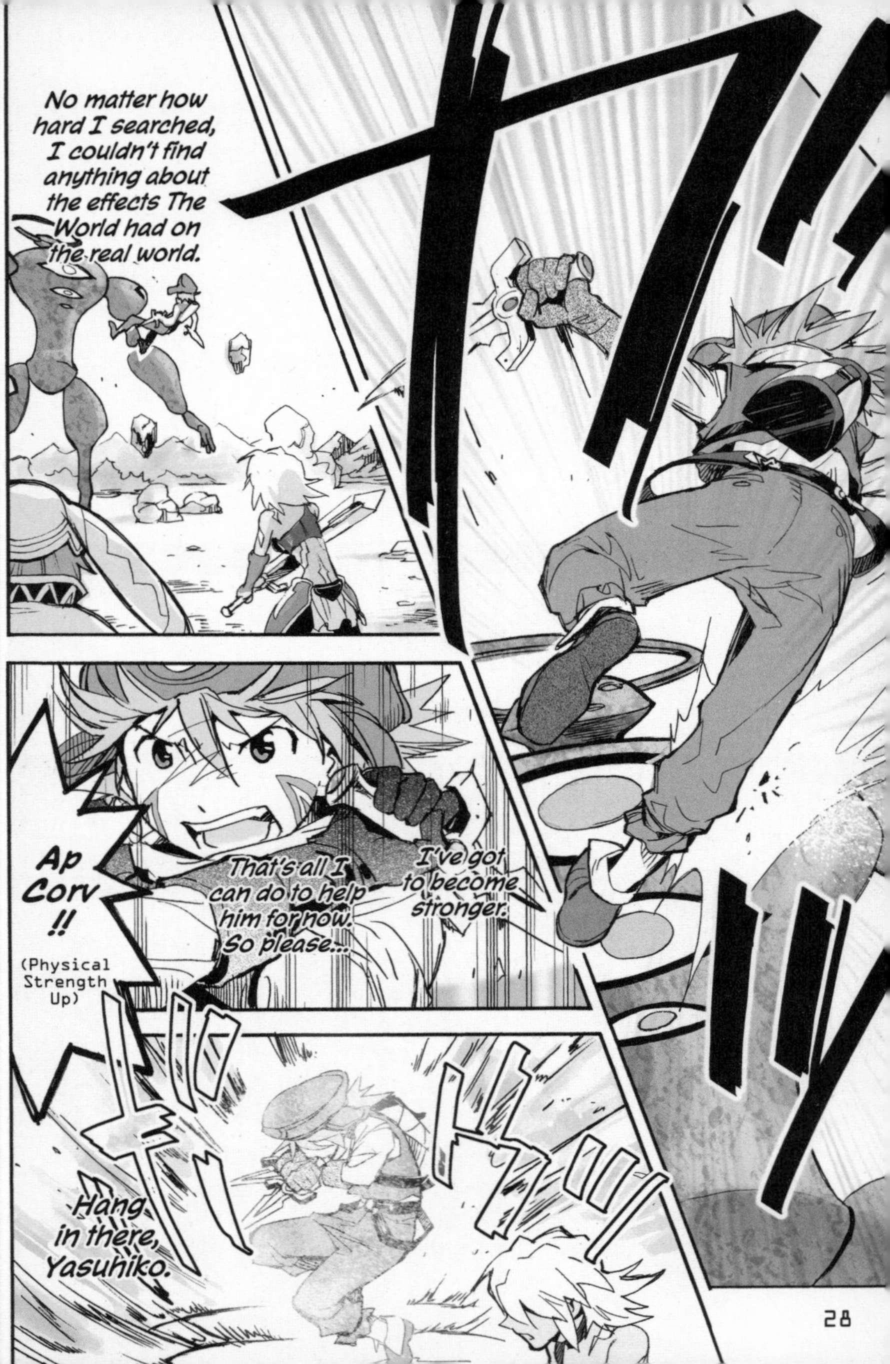
No matter how hard I searched, I couldn't find anything about the effects The World had on the real world.
Ap Corv !!
(Physical Strength Up)
That's all I can do to help him for now. So please...
I've got to become stronger.
Hang in there, Yasuhiko.

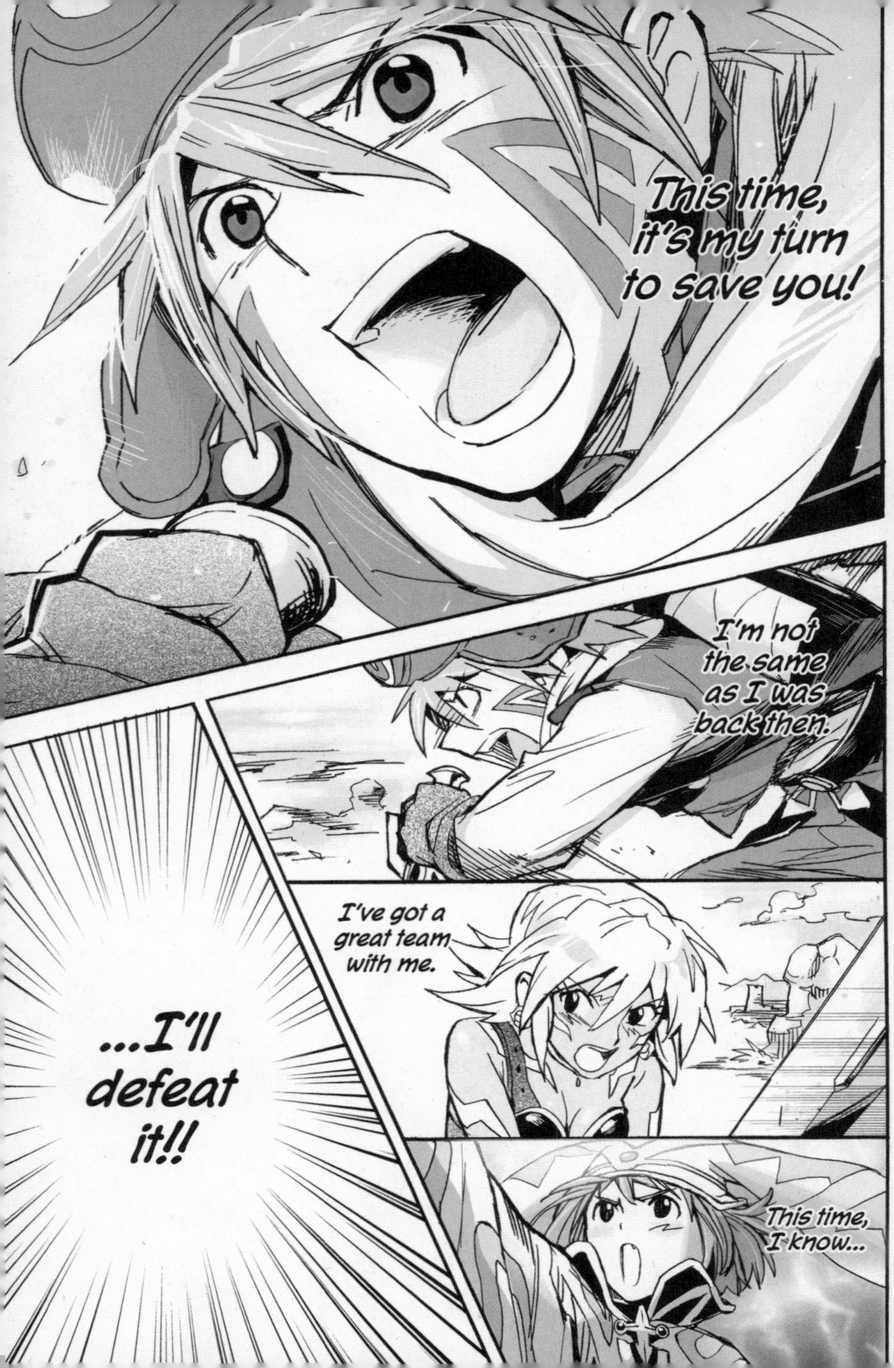
This time, it's my turn to save you!
I'm not the same as I was back then.
I've got a great team with me.
This time, I know...
...I'll defeat it!!

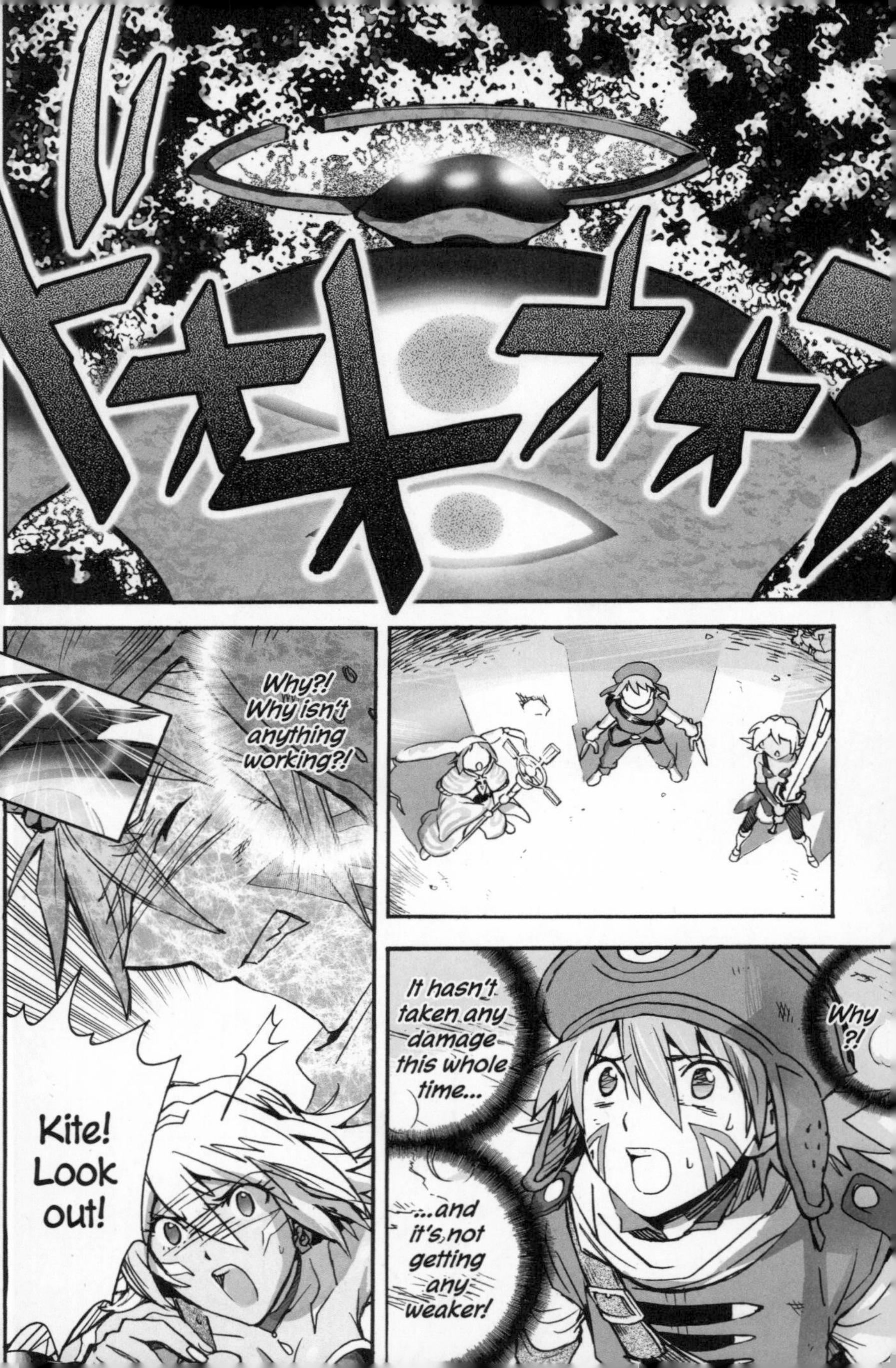

Why?! Why isn't anything working?!
Why ?!
It hasn't taken any damage this whole time...
...and it's not getting any weaker!
Kite! Look out!

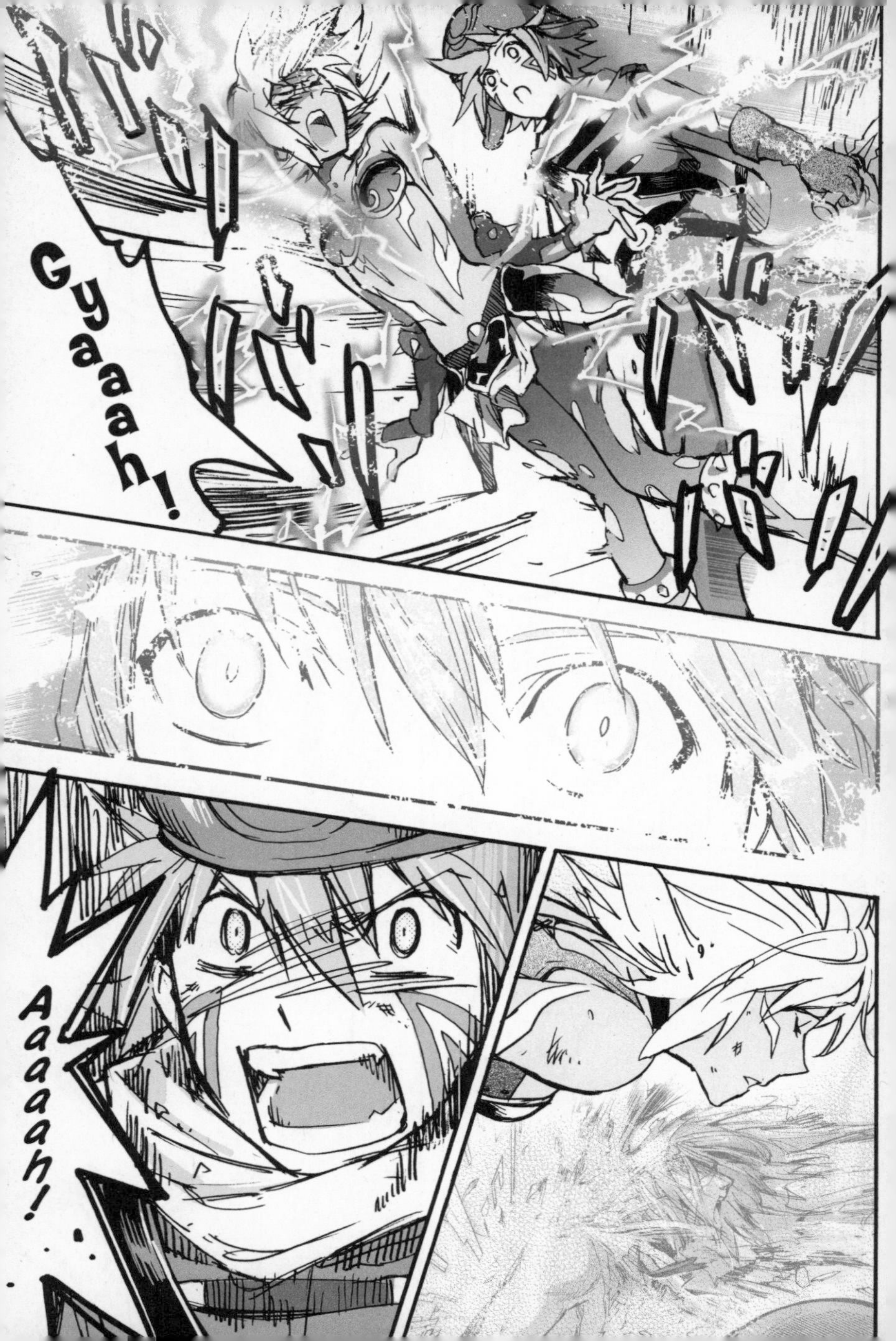
Gyaaah!
Aaaaah!

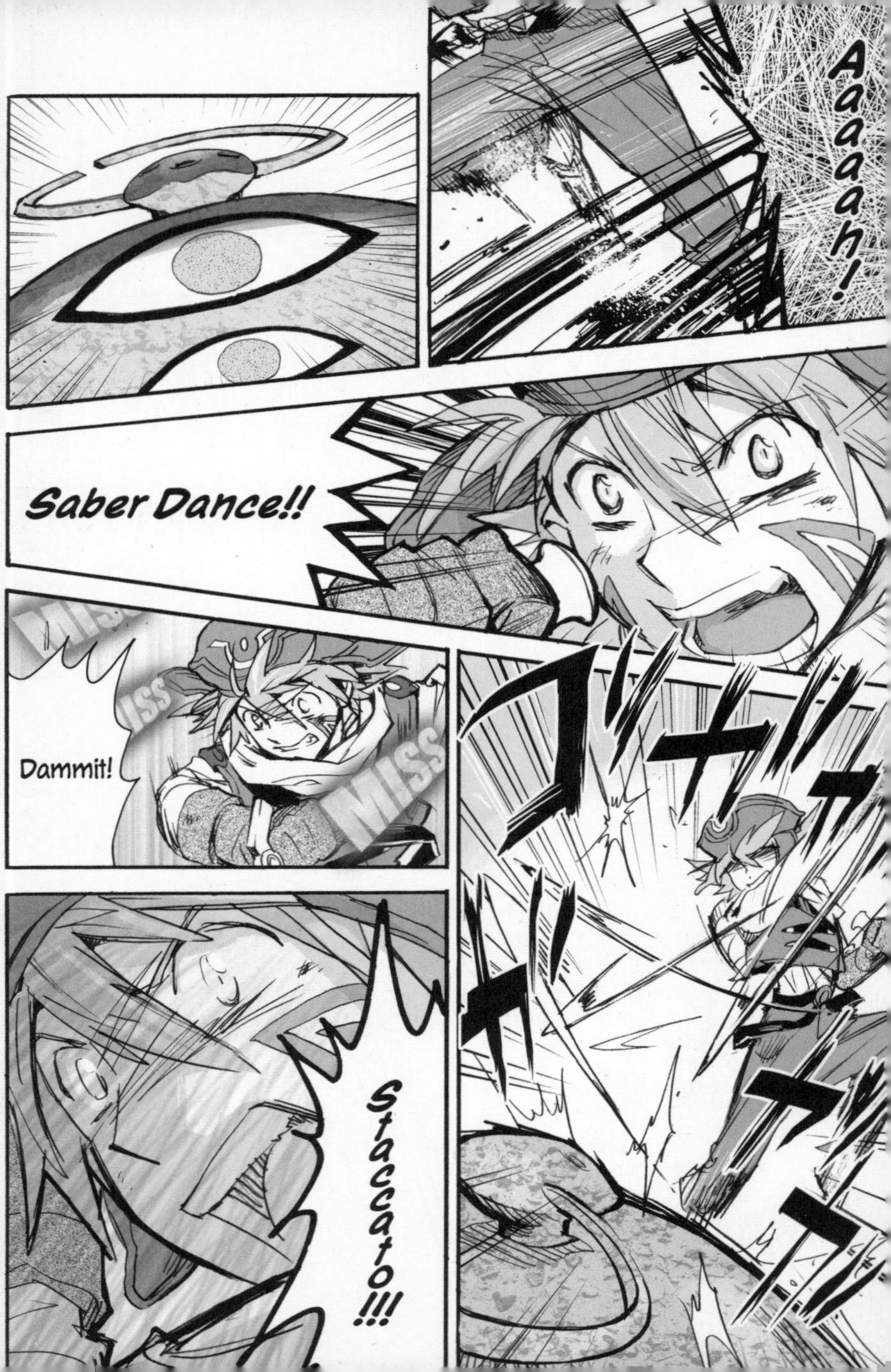
Aaaaah!
Saber Dance!!
Dammit!
MISS
MISS
MISS
MISS
Staccato!!!

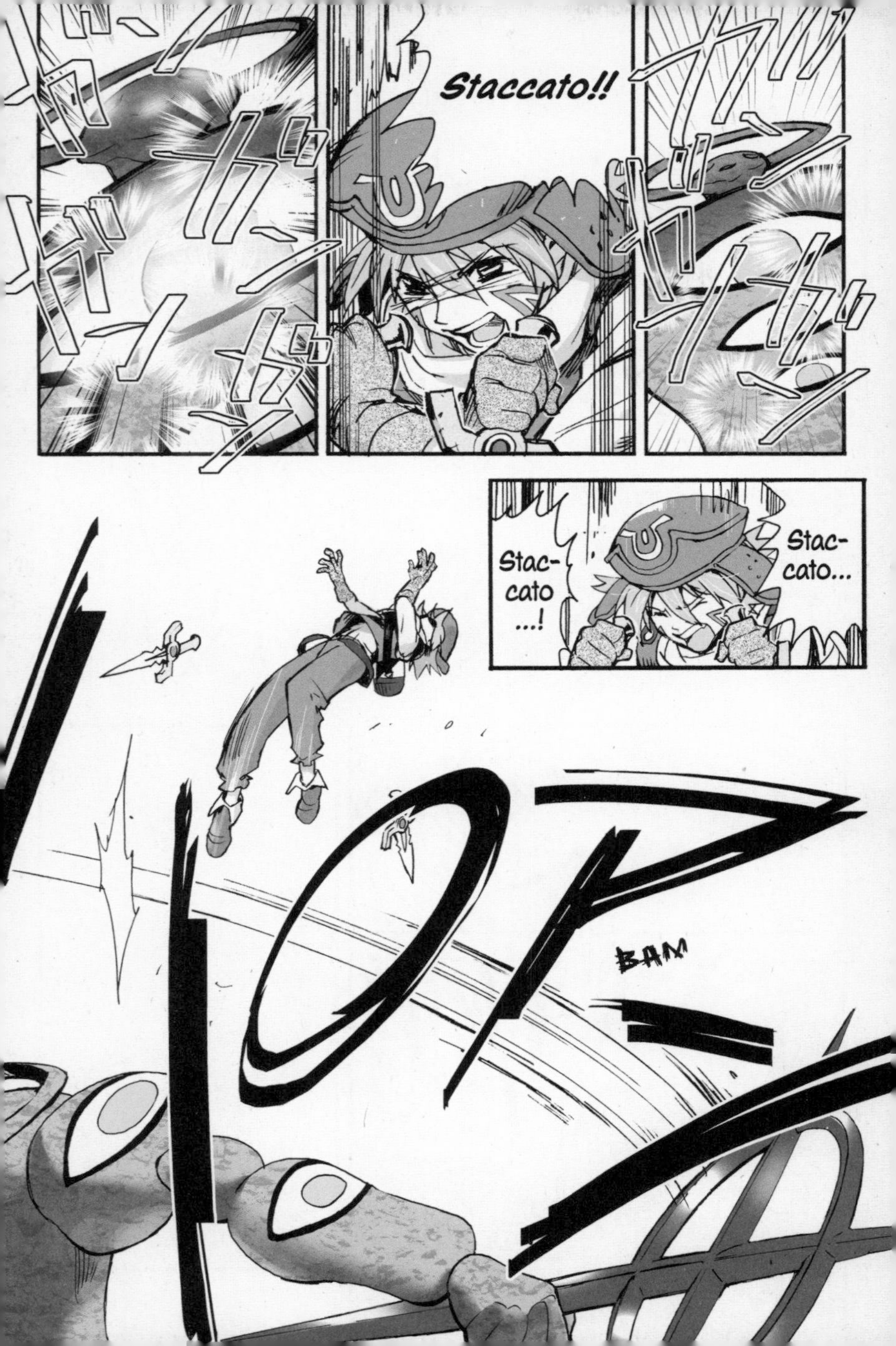
Staccato!!
Stac-cato...
Stac-cato ...!
BAM

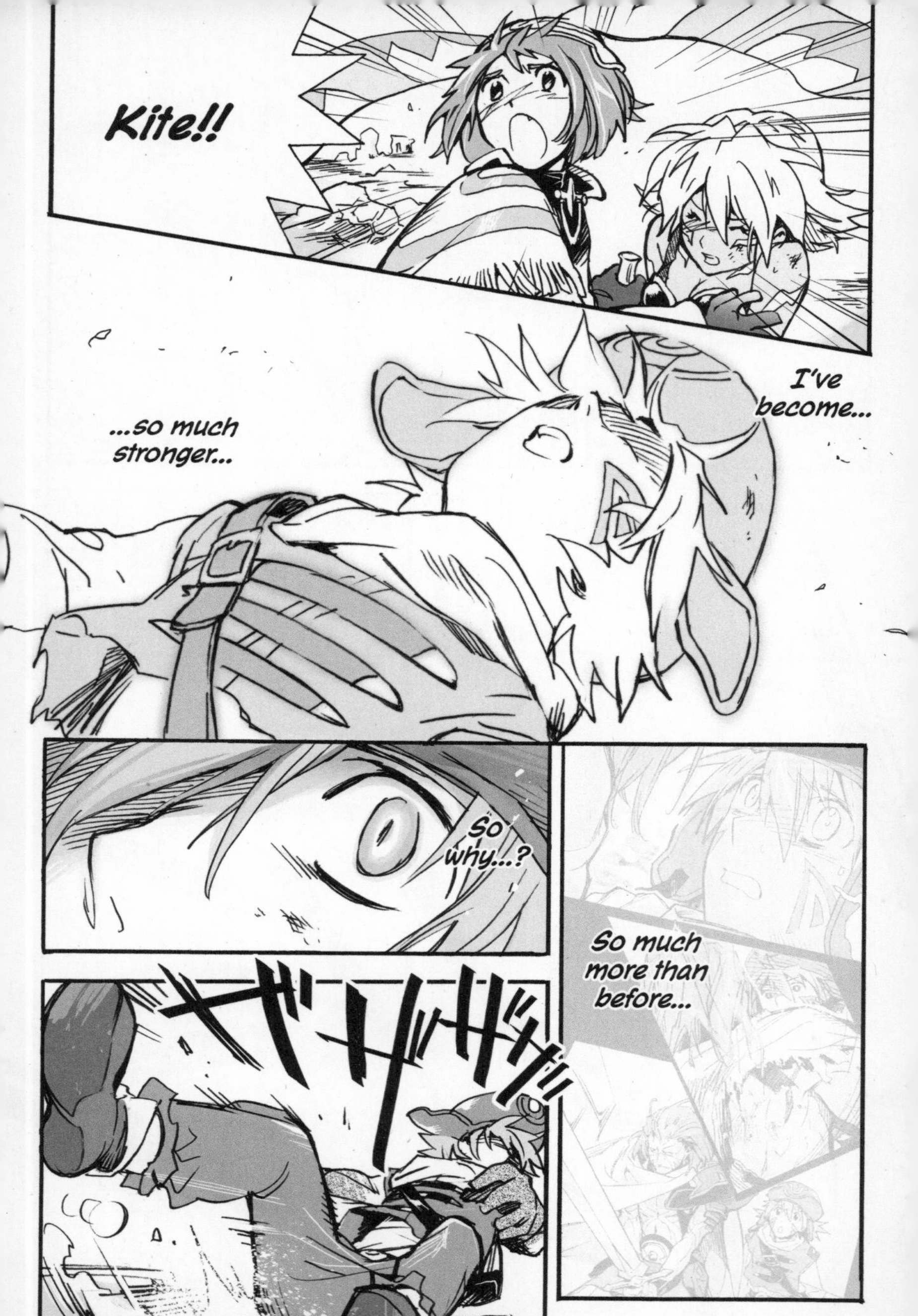

Kite!!
I've become...
...so much stronger...
So why...?
So much more than before...

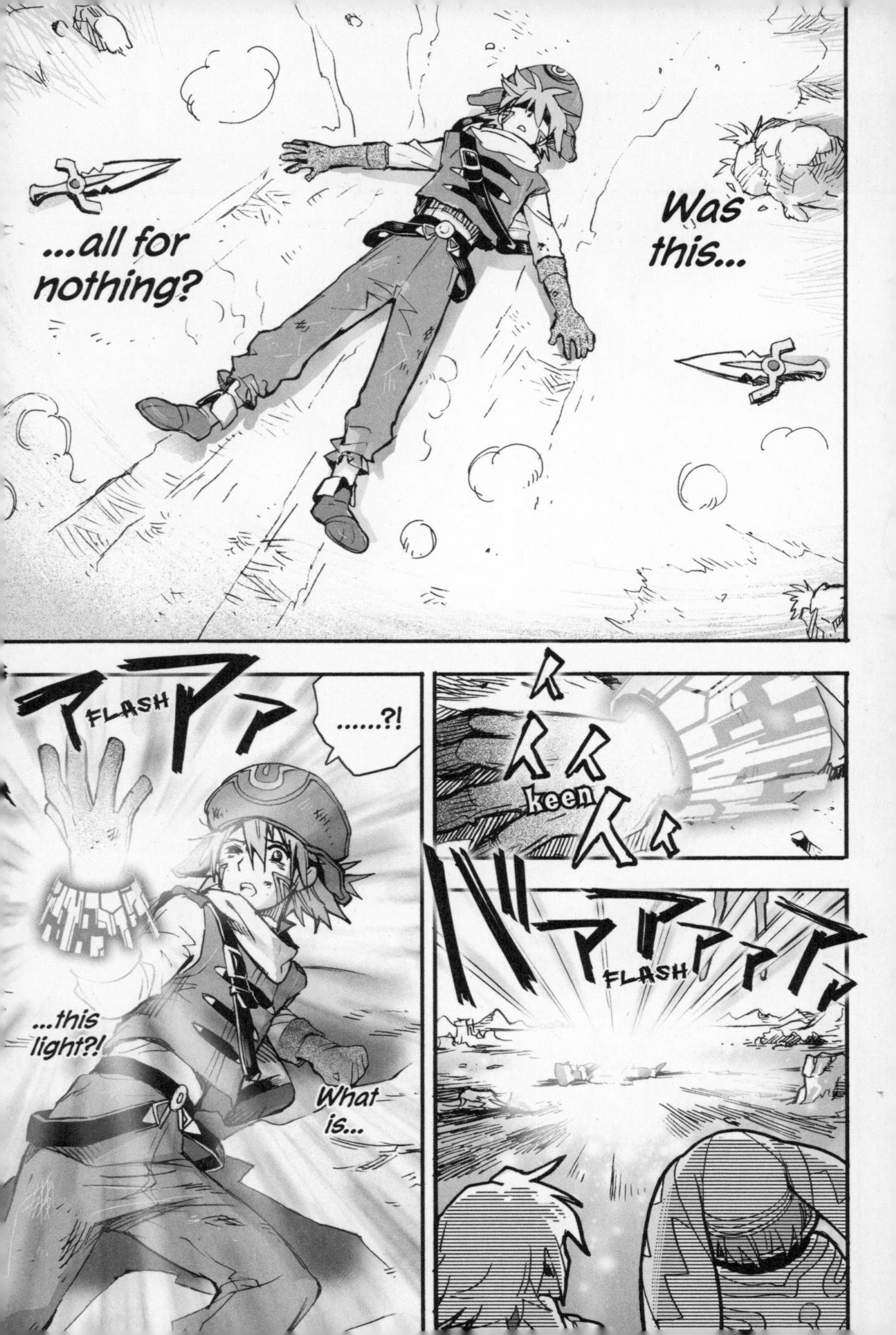

Was this...
...all for nothing?
keen
FLASH
......?!
What is...
...this light?!
FLASH

The power it holds

can bring forth

either salvation   or destruction

at the whim of the user.

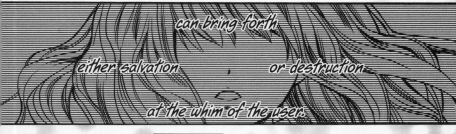

There's only one thing I want.

I want...

I want to save him...

My whim ...?

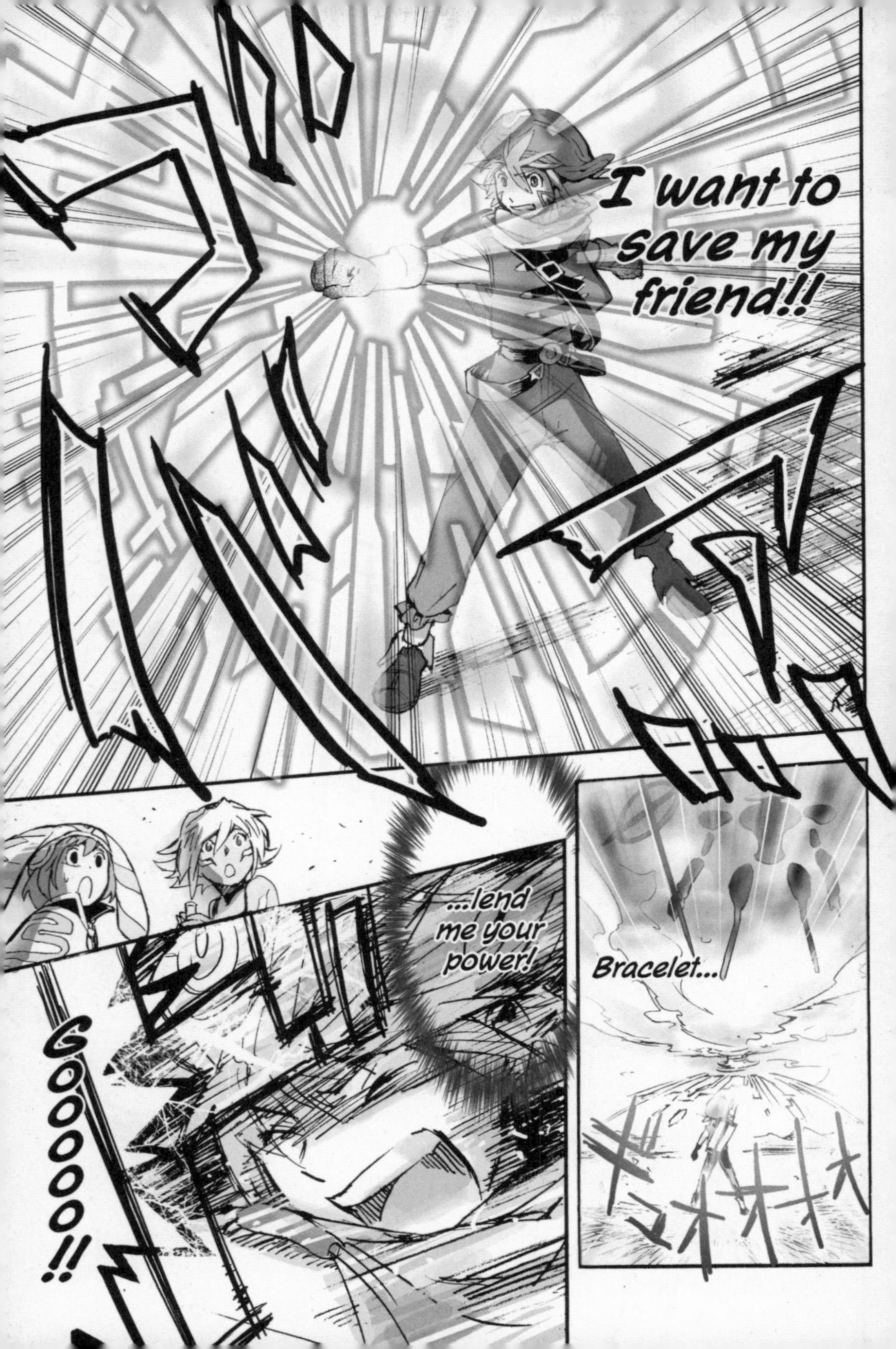
I want to save my friend!!
Bracelet...
...lend me your power!
GOOOOOO!!

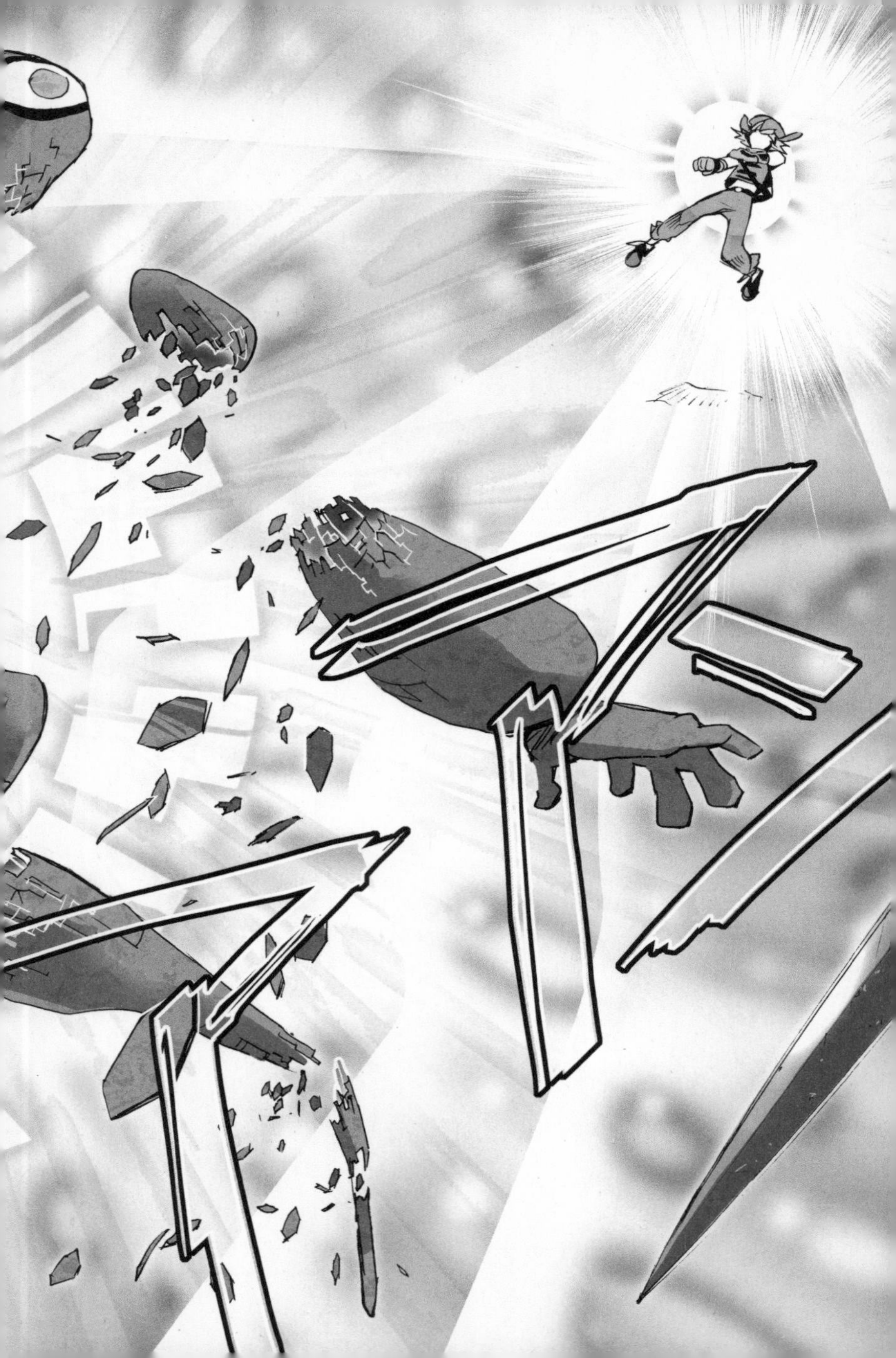

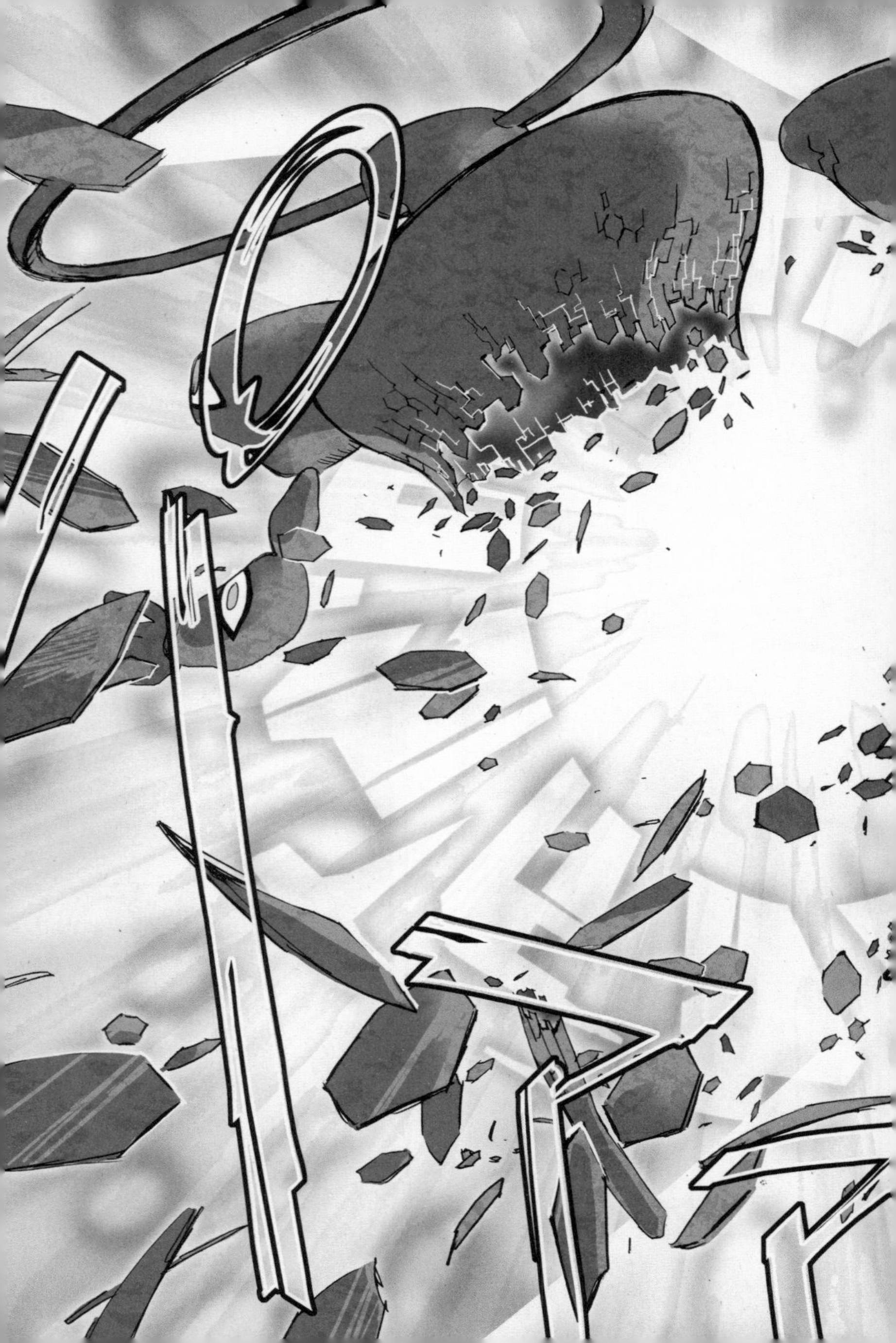

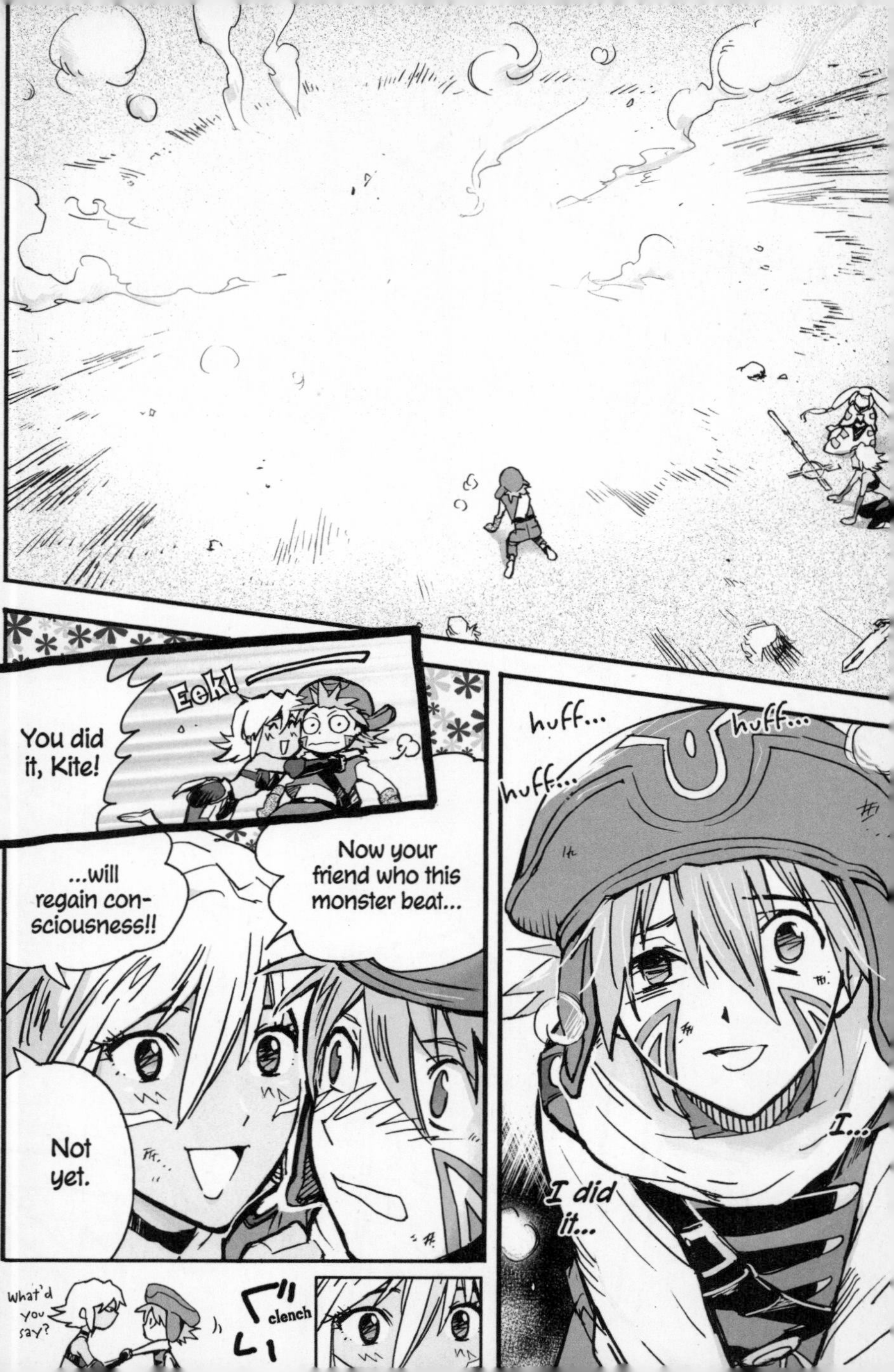

huff...
huff...
huff...
I...
I did it...
Eek!
You did it, Kite!
Now your friend who this monster beat...
...will regain consciousness!!
Not yet.
clench
What'd you say?

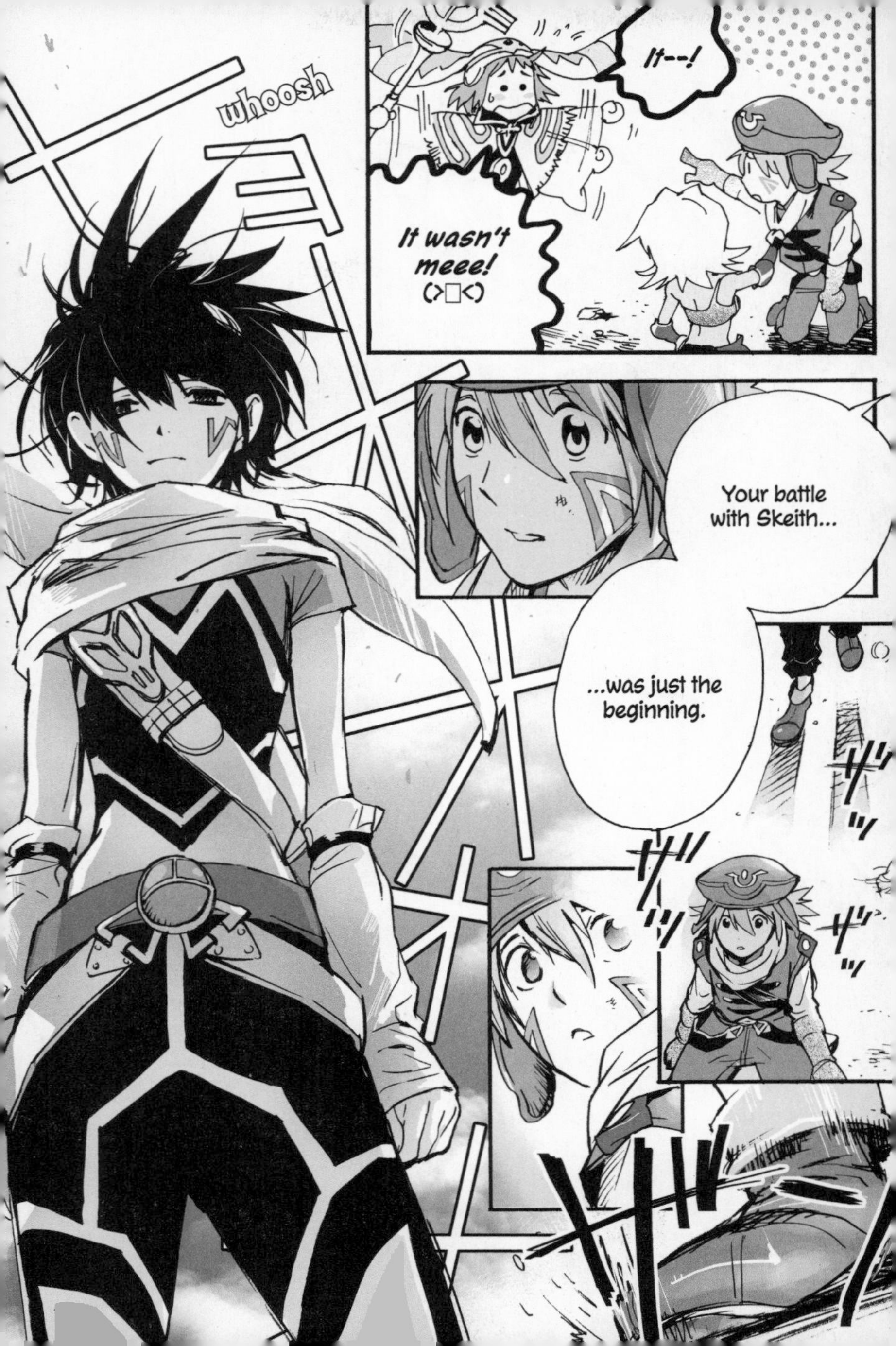
whoosh
It--!
It wasn't meee! (>□<)
Your battle with Skeith...
...was just the beginning.
ザッ
ザッ
ザッ

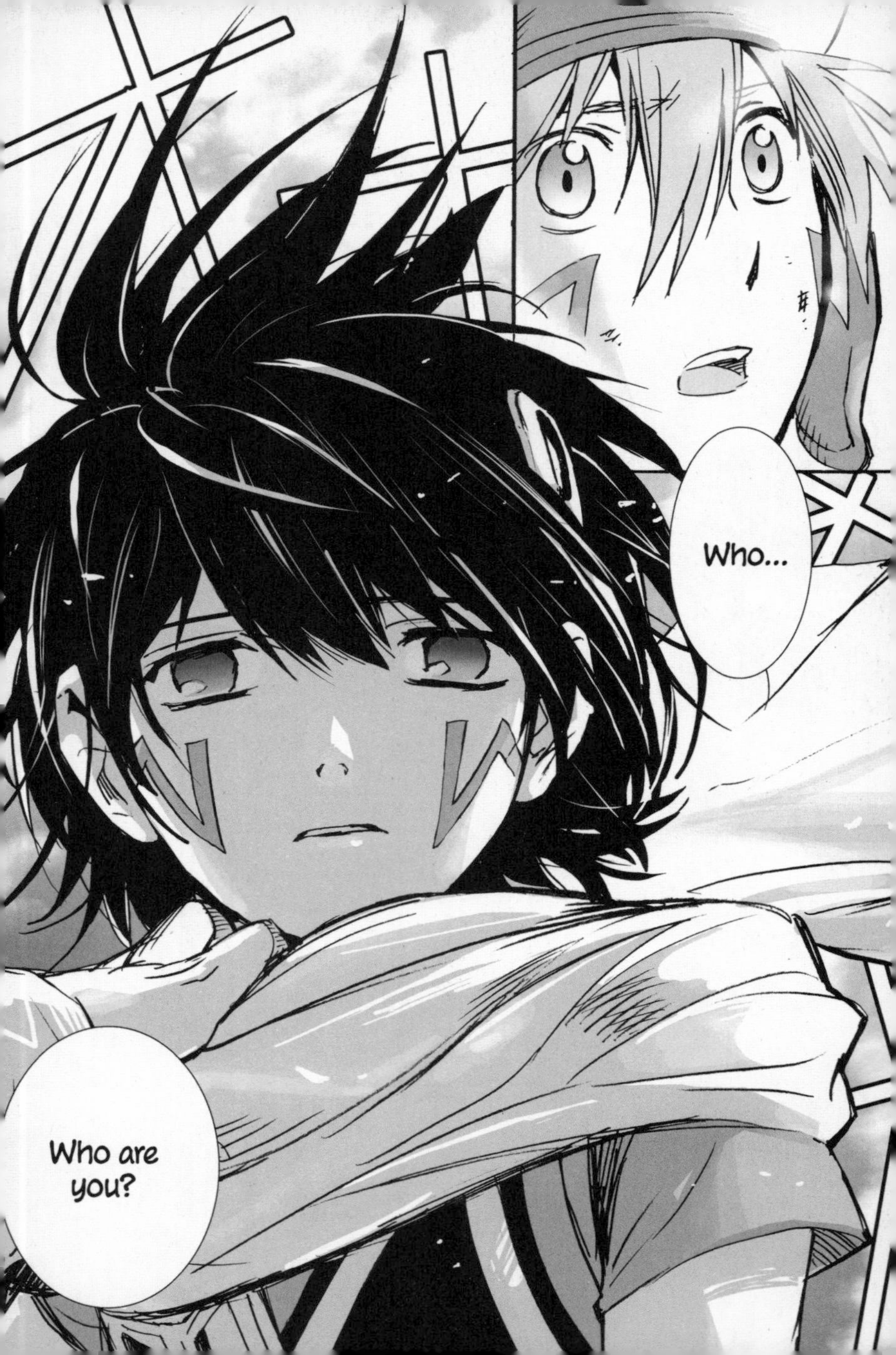
Who...
Who are you?

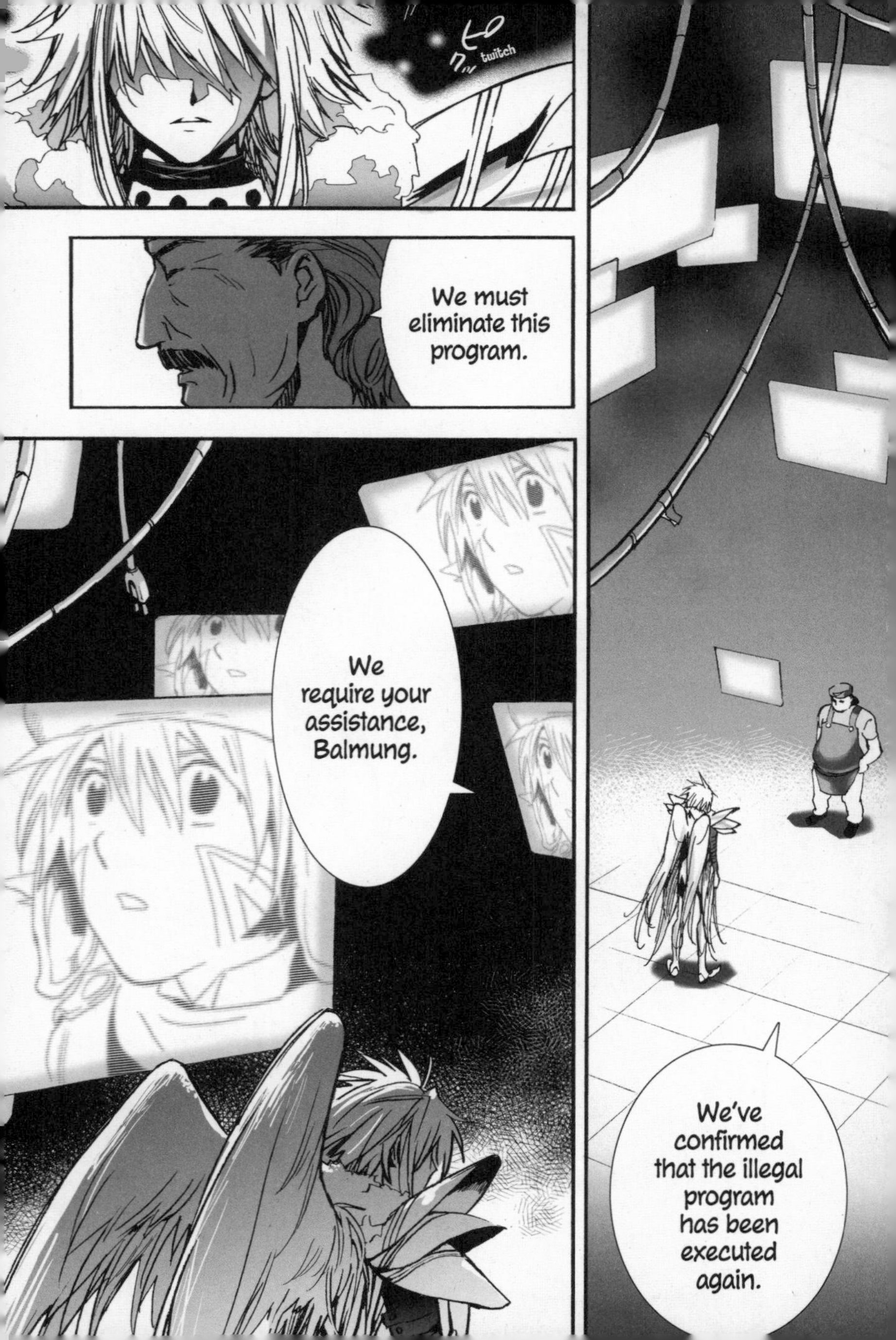
We've confirmed that the illegal program has been executed again.
twitch
We must eliminate this program.
We require your assistance, Balmung.

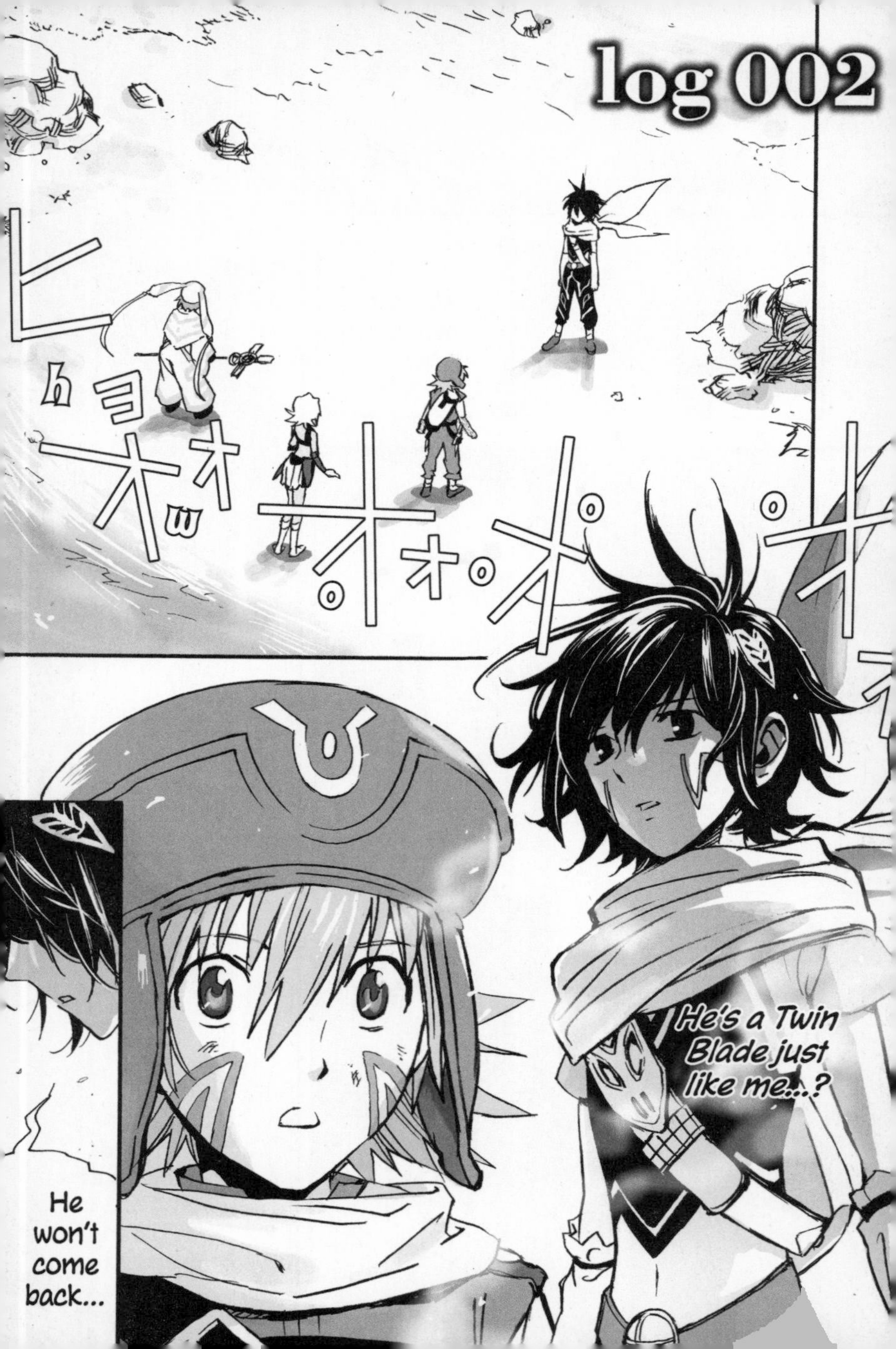
log 002
He's a Twin Blade just like me...?
He won't come back...

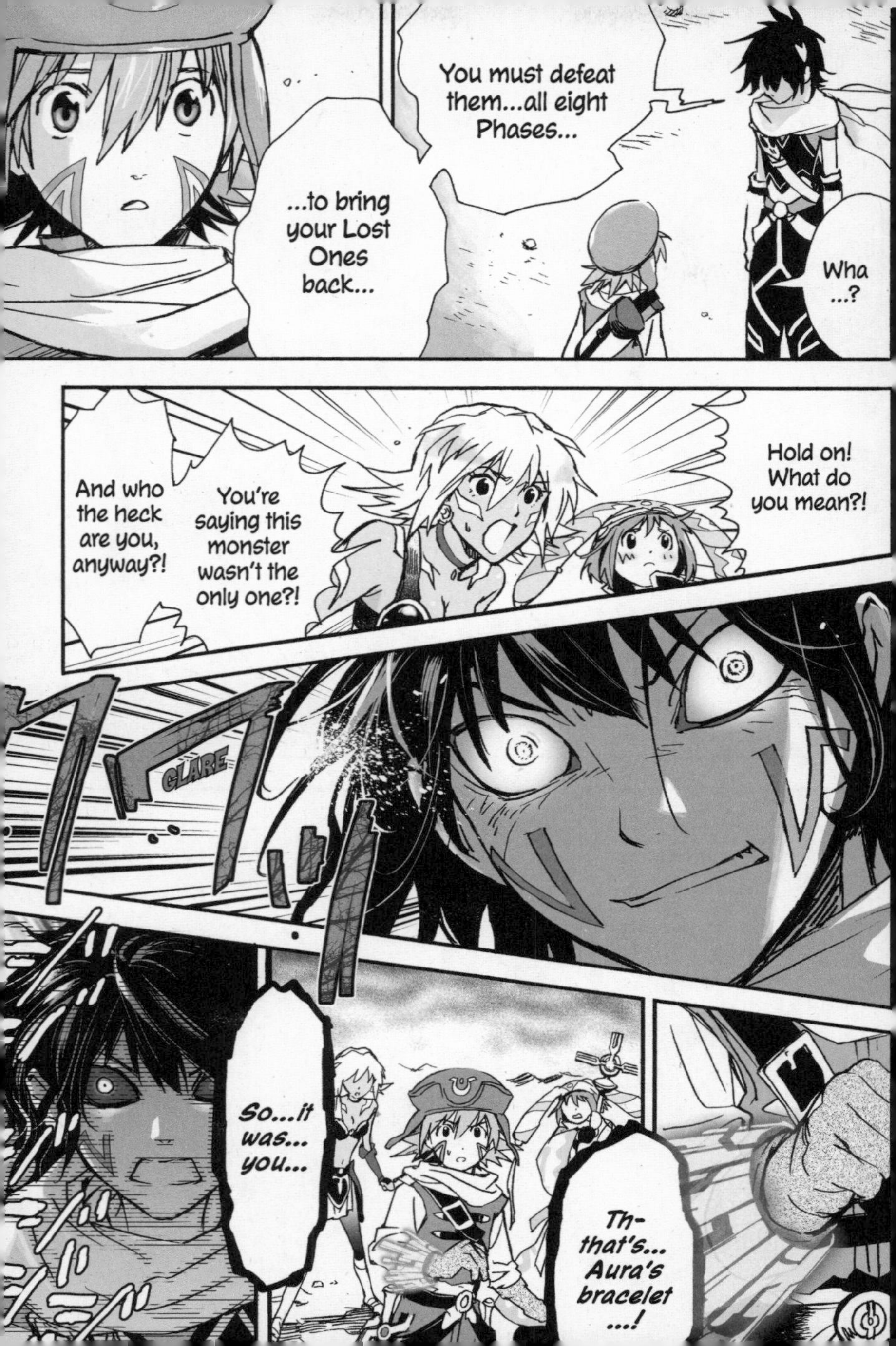
Wha ...?
You must defeat them...all eight Phases...
...to bring your Lost Ones back...
Hold on! What do you mean?!
You're saying this monster wasn't the only one?!
And who the heck are you, anyway?!
GLARE
Th-that's... Aura's bracelet ...!
So...it was... you...

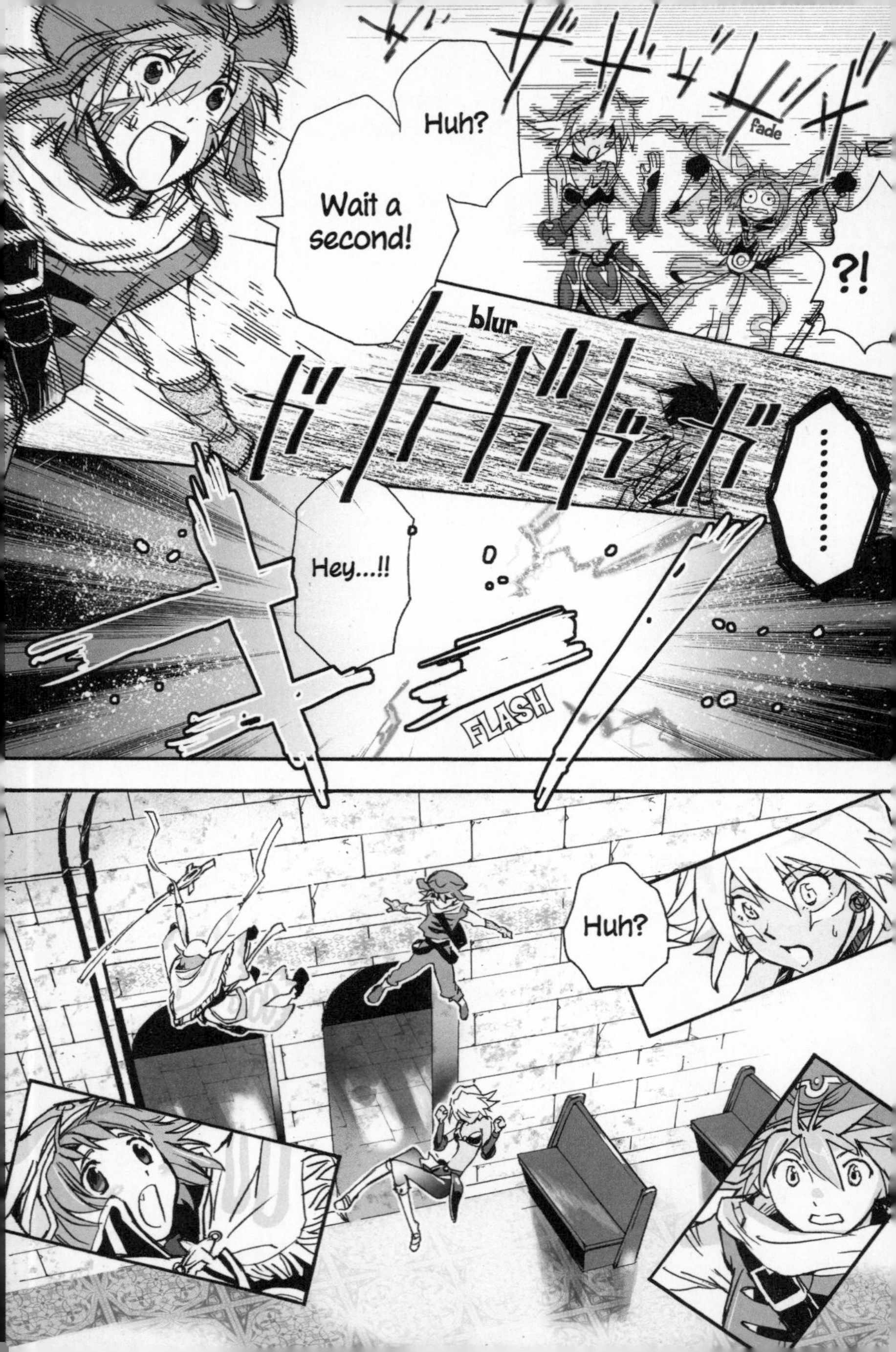

fade
Huh?
Wait a second!
?!
blur
......
Hey...!!
FLASH
Huh?

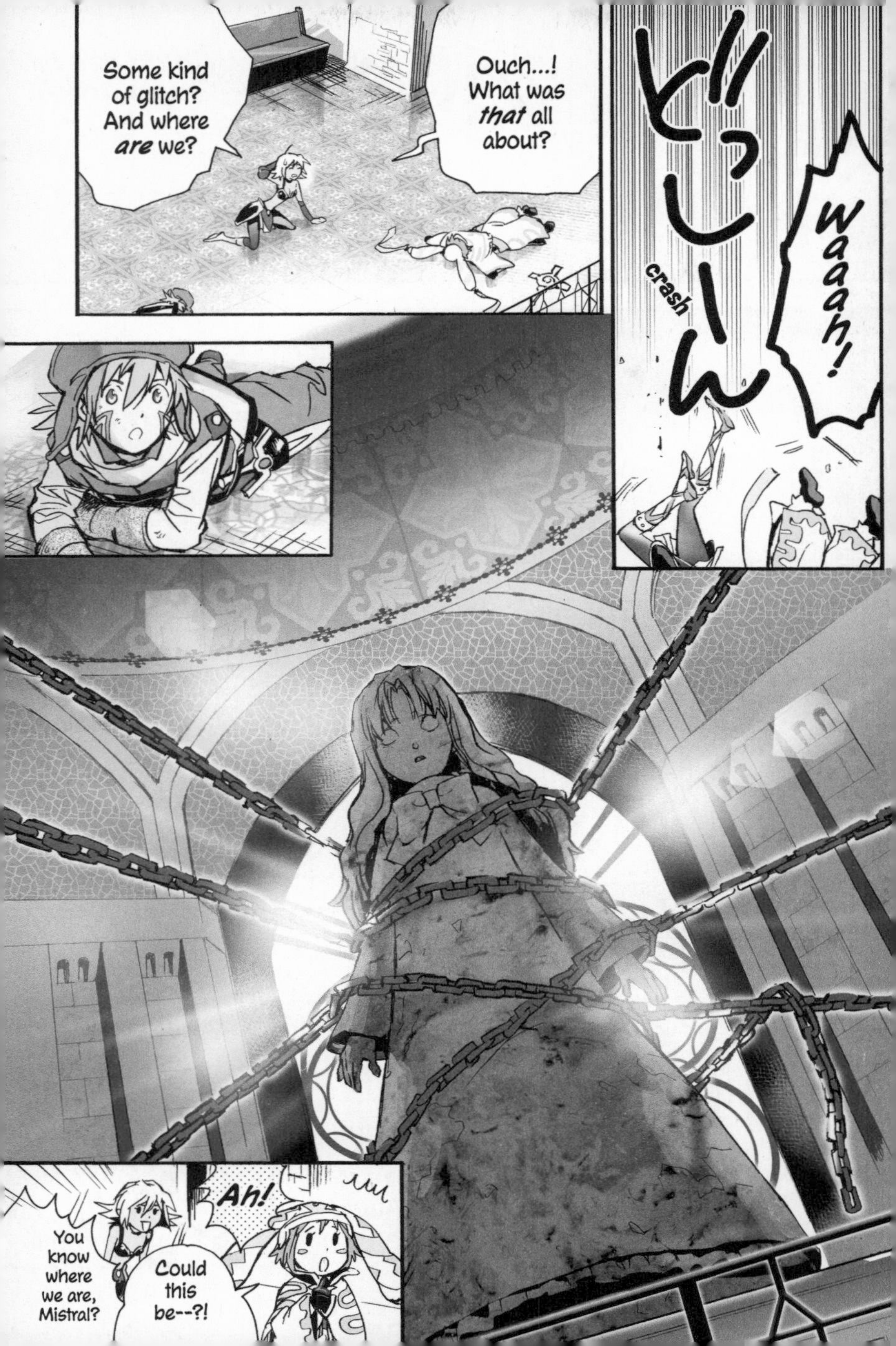

どっしーん
crash
Waaah!
Ouch...! What was *that* all about?
Some kind of glitch? And where *are* we?
Ah!
Could this be--?!
You know where we are, Mistral?

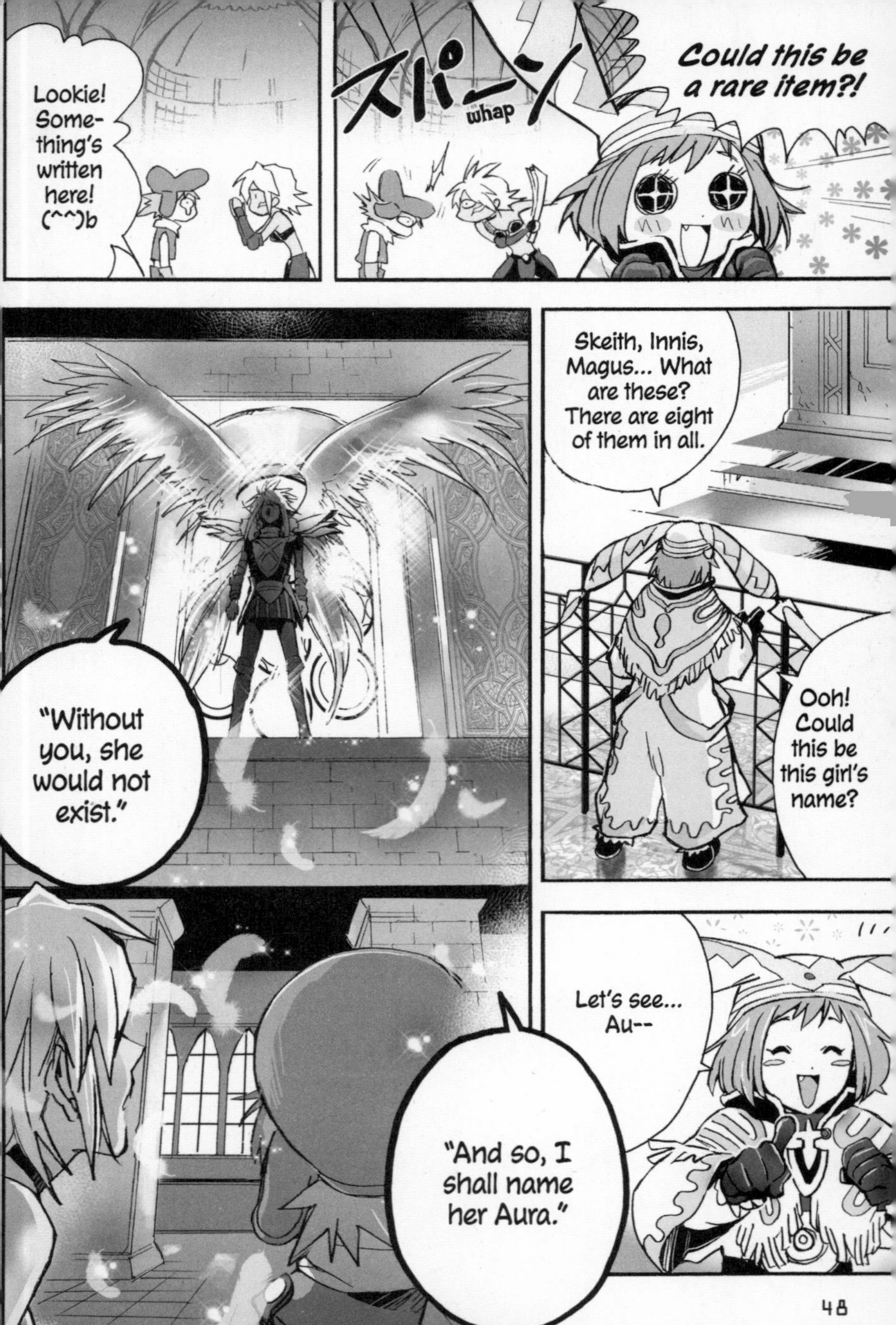

Lookie! Some-thing's written here! (^^)b
スパーン
whap
Could this be a rare item?!
Skeith, Innis, Magus... What are these? There are eight of them in all.
Ooh! Could this be this girl's name?
"Without you, she would not exist."
Let's see... Au--
"And so, I shall name her Aura."

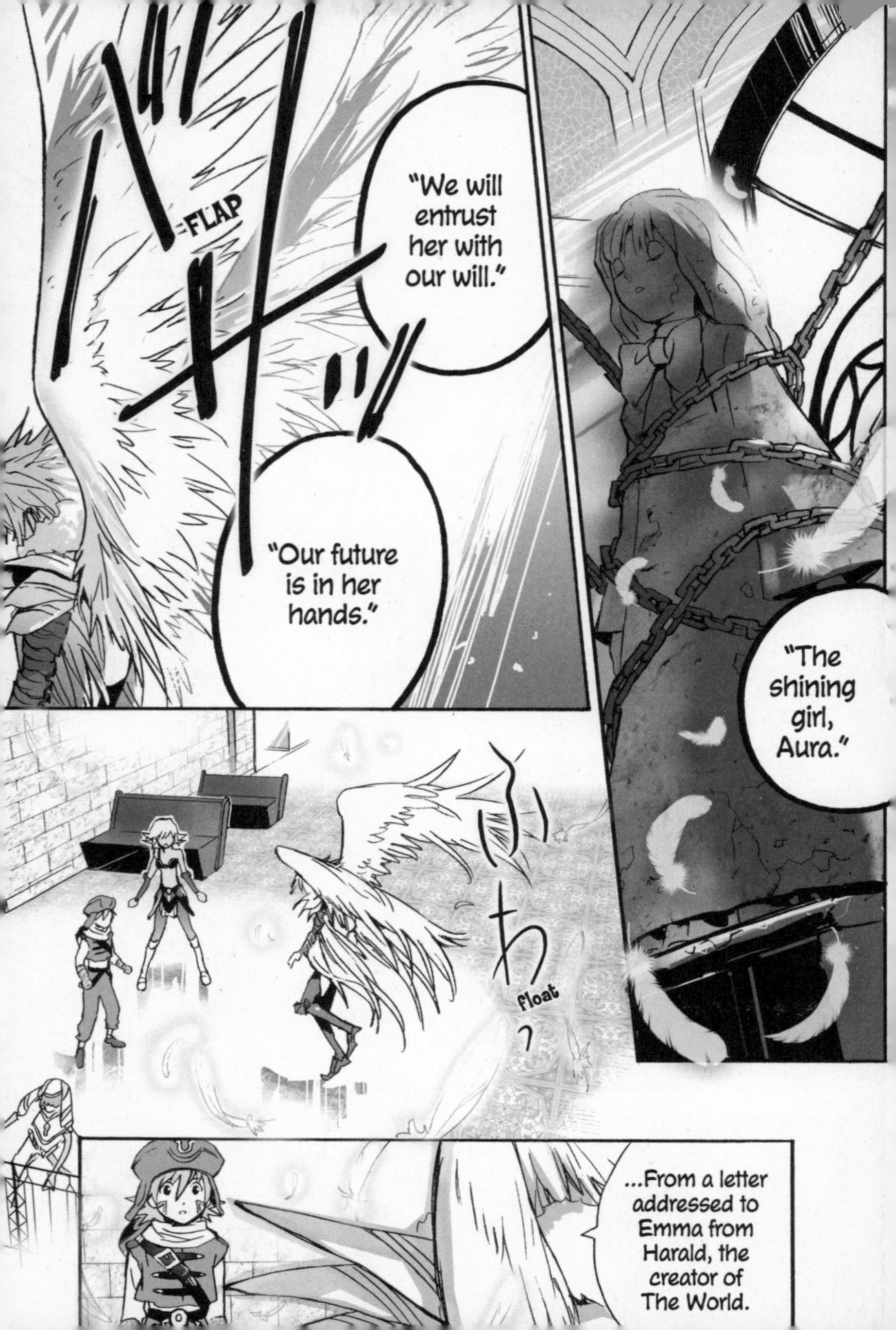

FLAP
"The shining girl, Aura."
"We will entrust her with our will."
"Our future is in her hands."
float
...From a letter addressed to Emma from Harald, the creator of The World.

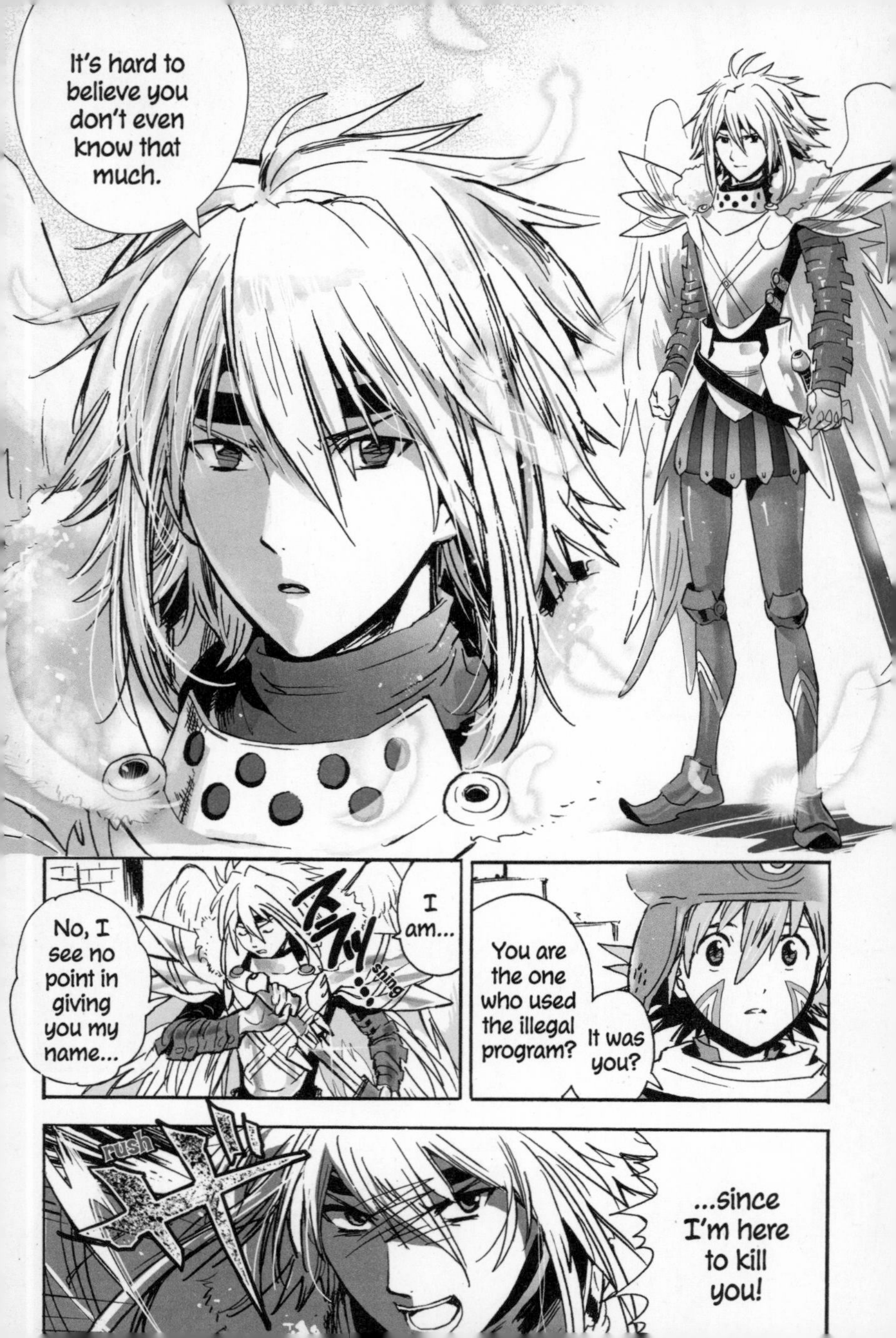
It's hard to believe you don't even know that much.
You are the one who used the illegal program?
It was you?
I am...
shing
No, I see no point in giving you my name...
rush
...since I'm here to kill you!

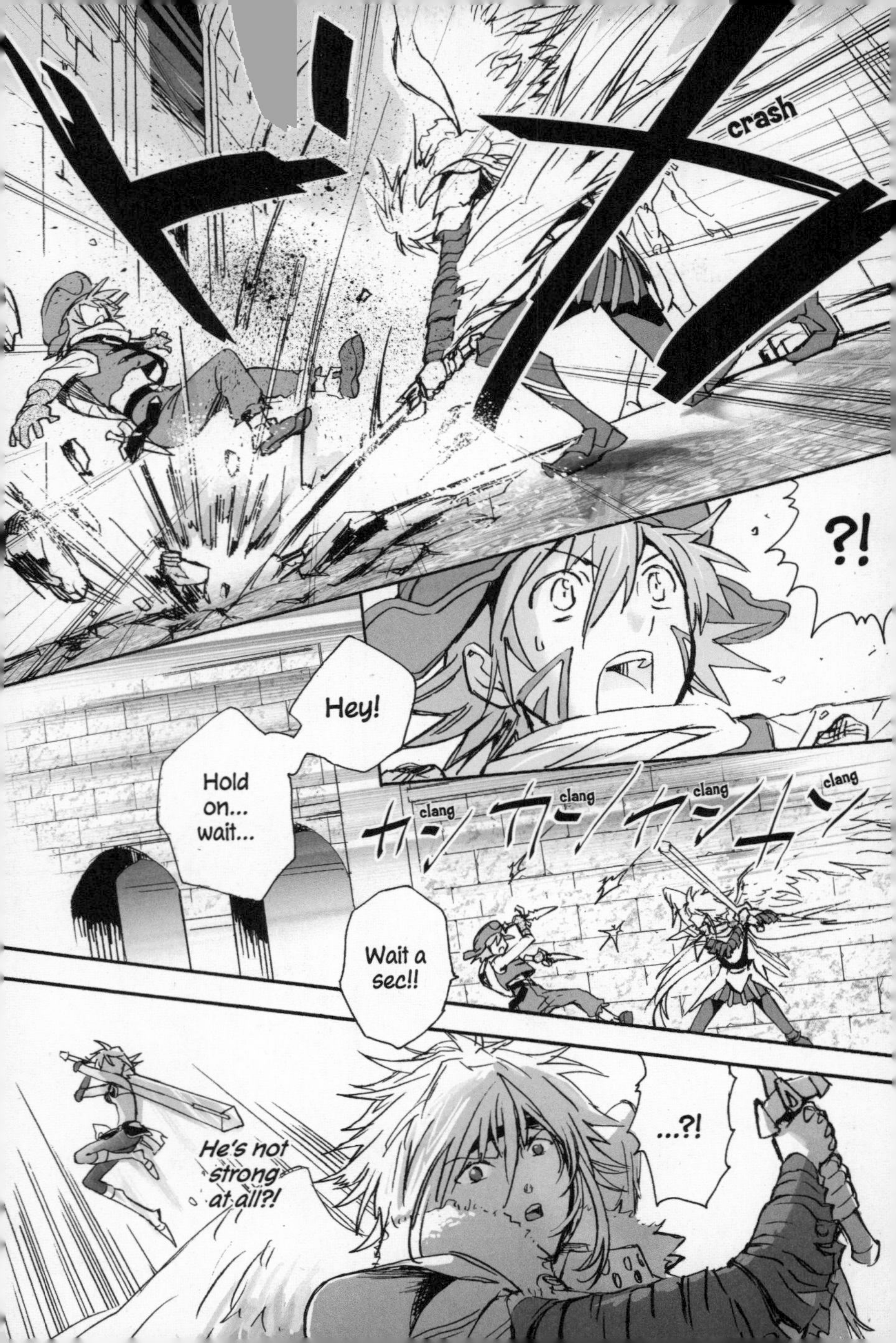
crash
?!
Hey!
Hold on... wait...
clang
clang
clang
clang
Wait a sec!!
...?!
He's not strong at all?!

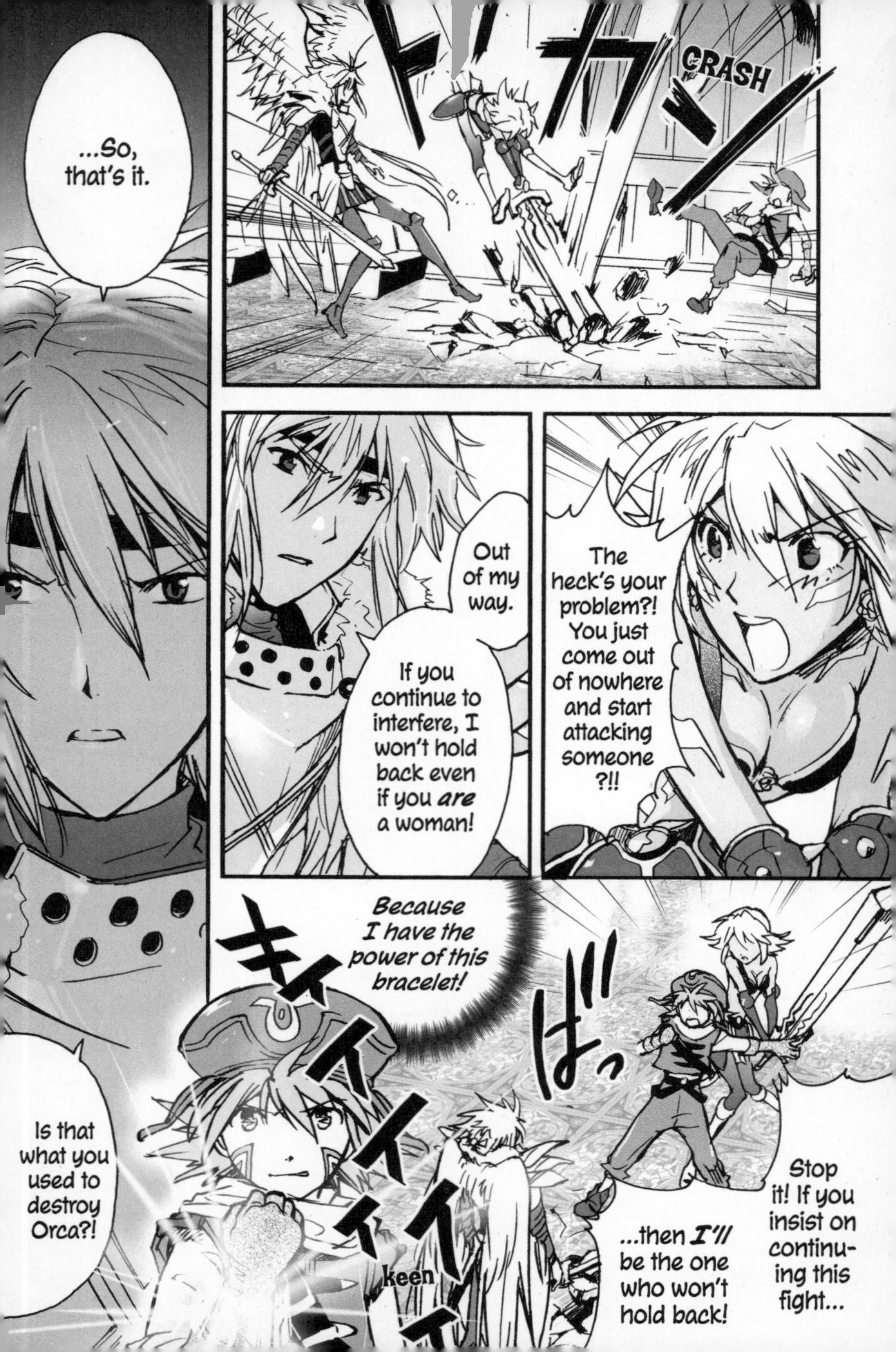

CRASH
The heck's your problem?! You just come out of nowhere and start attacking someone?!!
Out of my way.
If you continue to interfere, I won't hold back even if you *are* a woman!
Stop it! If you insist on continuing this fight...
...then *I'll* be the one who won't hold back!
Because I have the power of this bracelet!
keen
...So, that's it.
Is that what you used to destroy Orca?!

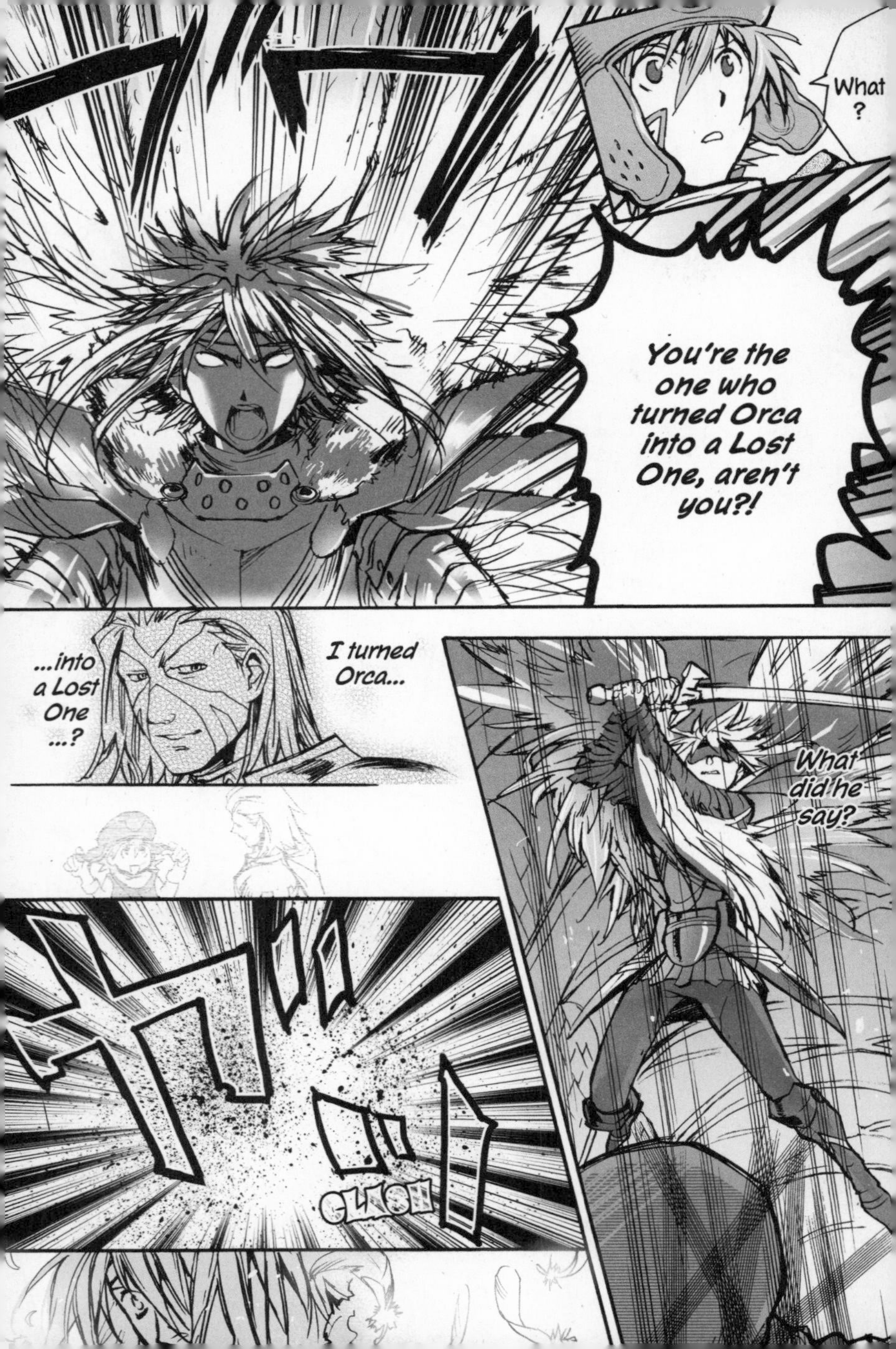
What?
You're the one who turned Orca into a Lost One, aren't you?!
What did he say?
I turned Orca...
...into a Lost One ...?
CLASH

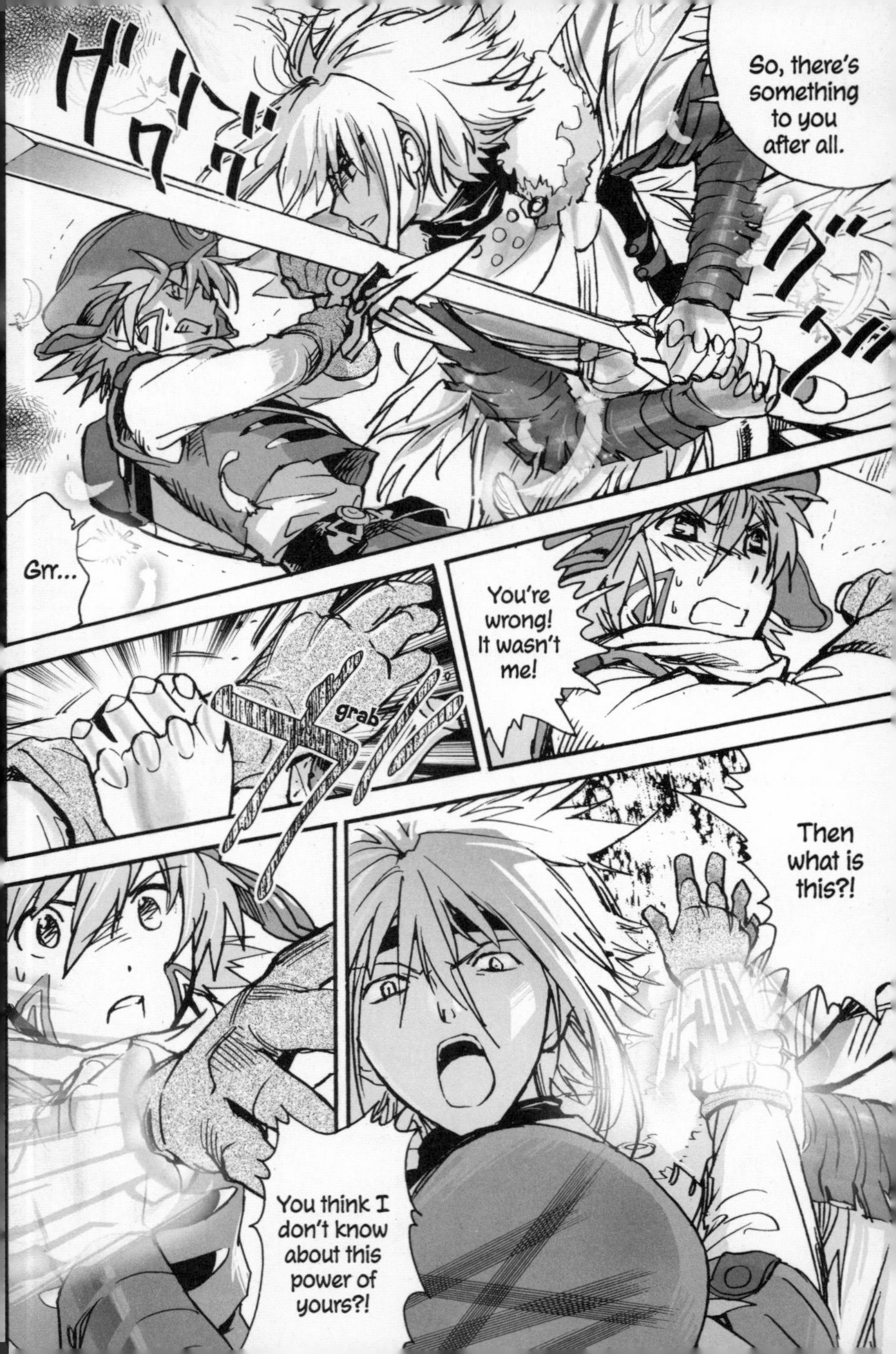
So, there's something to you after all.
Grr...
You're wrong! It wasn't me!
grab
Then what is this?!
You think I don't know about this power of yours?!

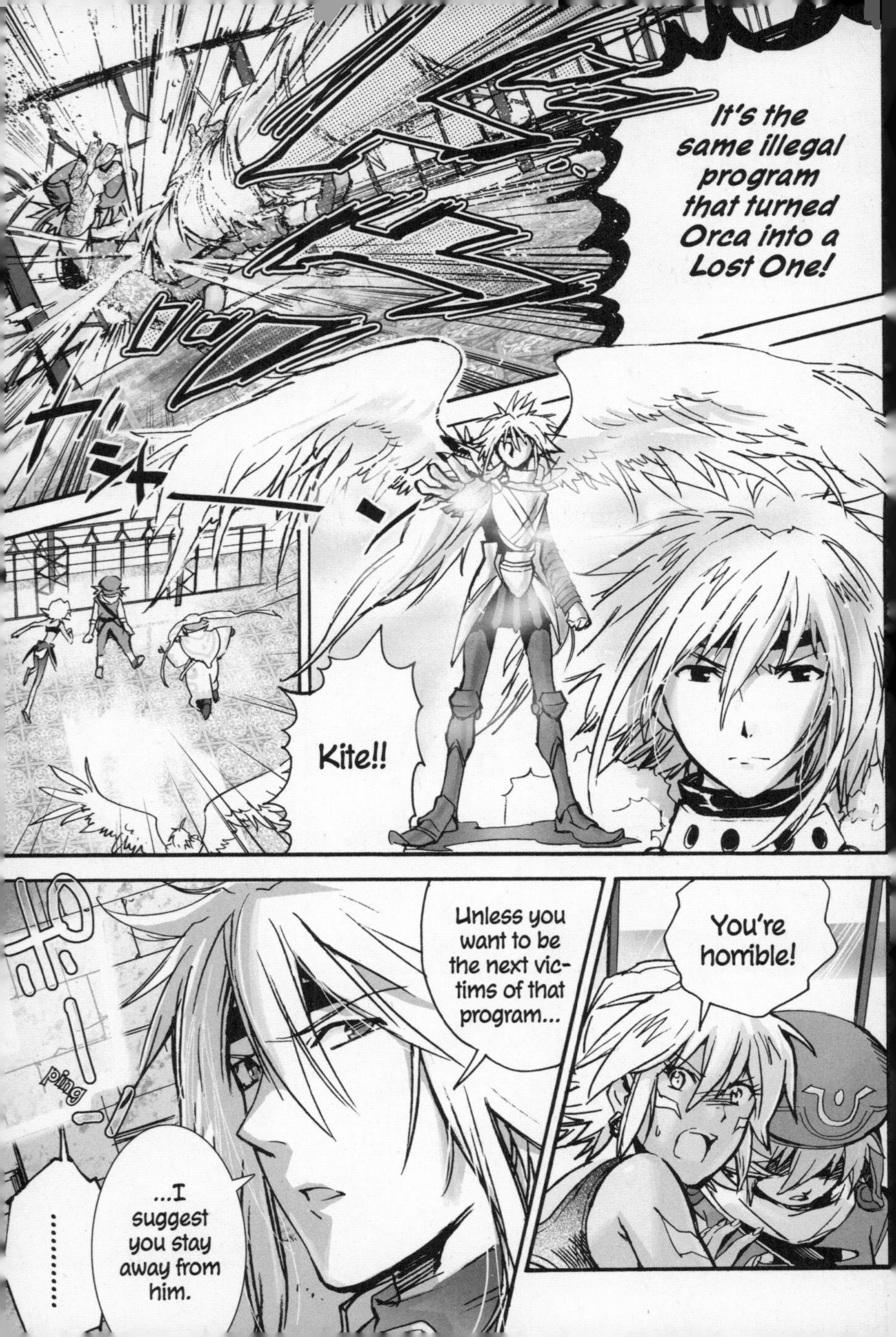
It's the same illegal program that turned Orca into a Lost One!
Kite!!
You're horrible!
Unless you want to be the next vic-tims of that program...
ping
...I suggest you stay away from him.
......

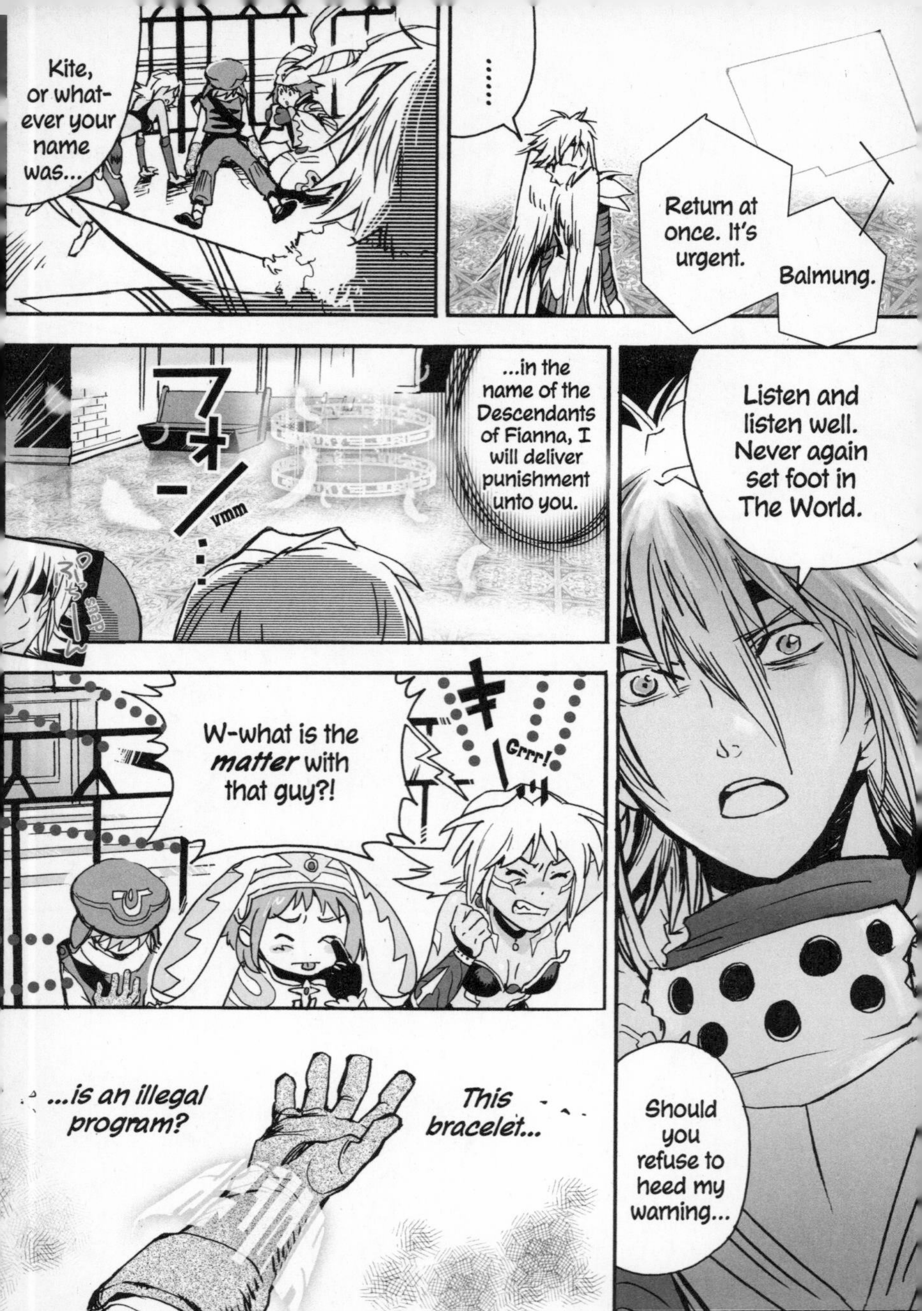
Balmung.
Return at once. It's urgent.
......
Kite, or whatever your name was...
Listen and listen well. Never again set foot in The World.
Should you refuse to heed my warning...
...in the name of the Descendants of Fianna, I will deliver punishment unto you.
vmm
snap
W-what is the *matter* with that guy?!
Grrr!
This bracelet...
...is an illegal program?

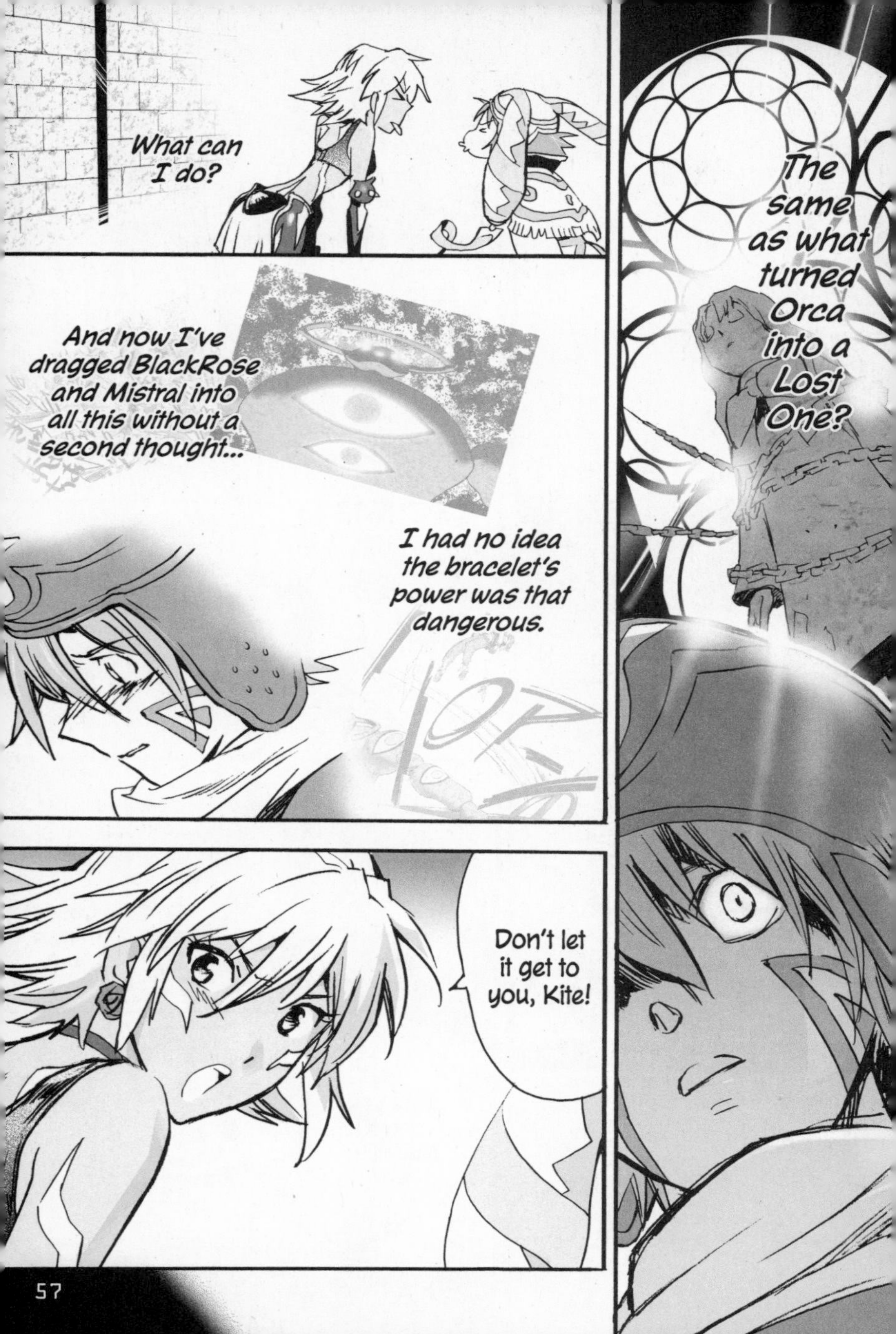
The same as what turned Orca into a Lost One?
What can I do?
And now I've dragged BlackRose and Mistral into all this without a second thought...
I had no idea the bracelet's power was that dangerous.
Don't let it get to you, Kite!

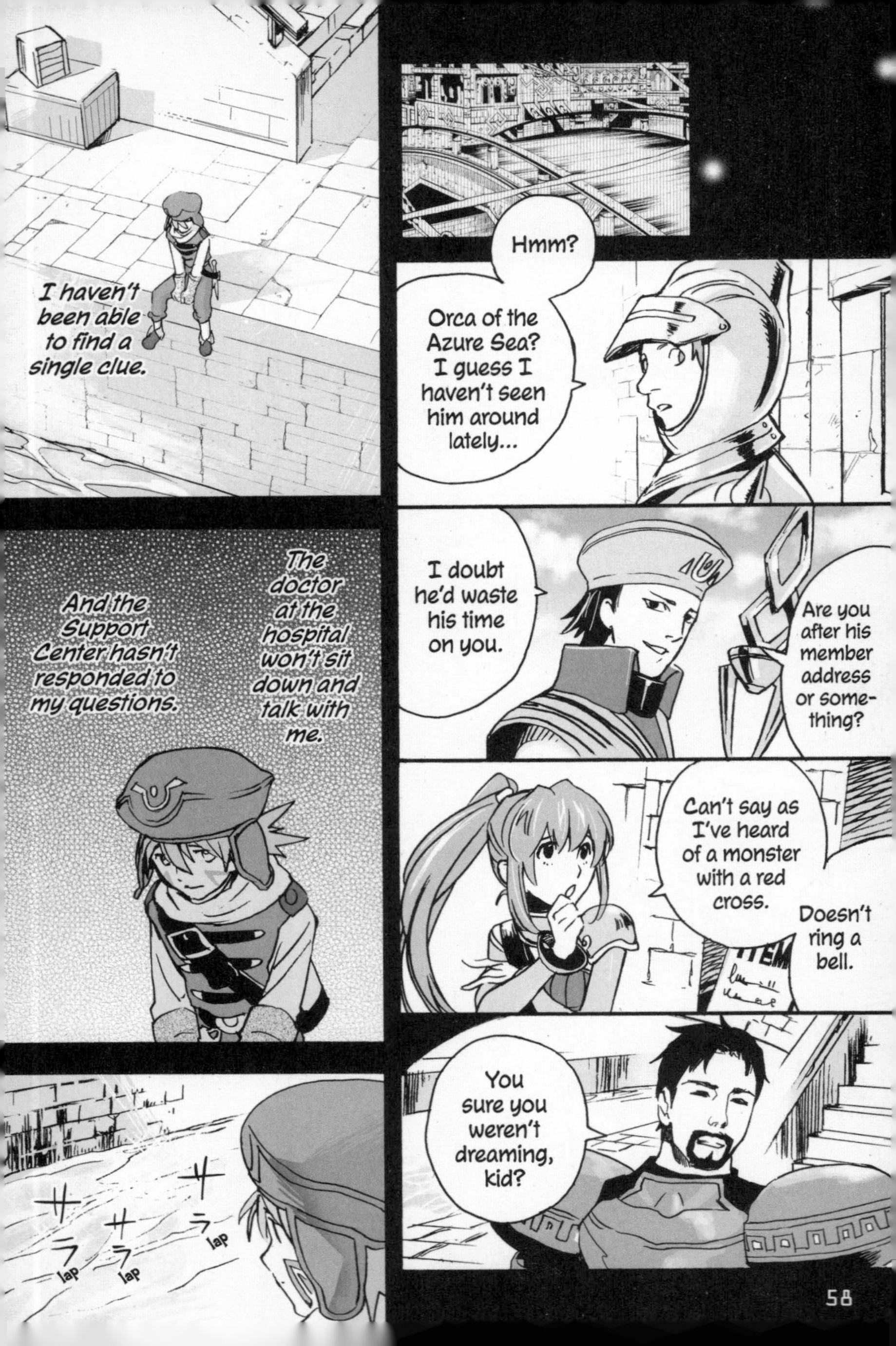
Hmm?
Orca of the Azure Sea? I guess I haven't seen him around lately...
Are you after his member address or some-thing?
I doubt he'd waste his time on you.
Can't say as I've heard of a monster with a red cross.
Doesn't ring a bell.
You sure you weren't dreaming, kid?
I haven't been able to find a single clue.
The doctor at the hospital won't sit down and talk with me.
And the Support Center hasn't responded to my questions.
サラ lap
サラ lap
サラ lap

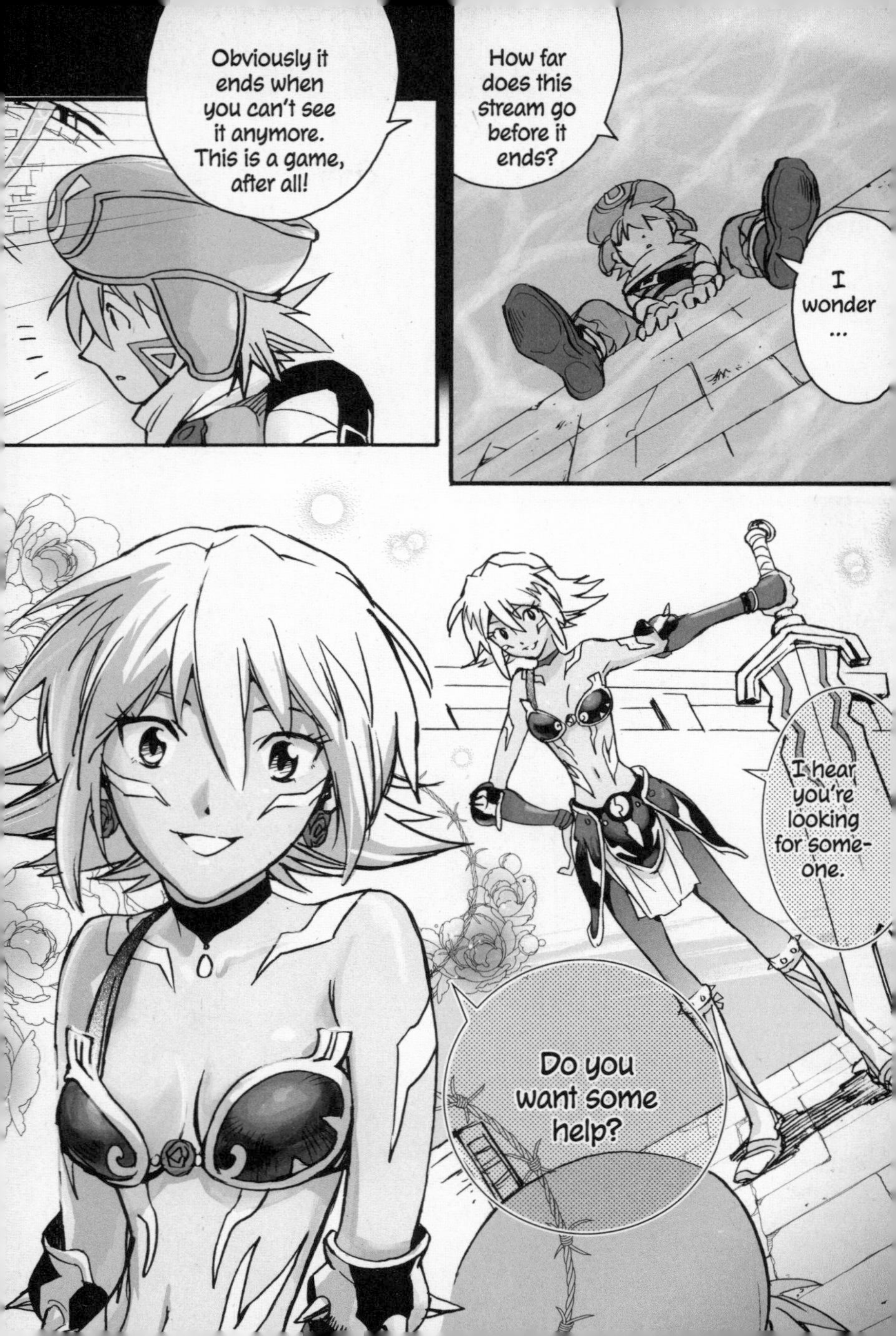
Obviously it ends when you can't see it anymore. This is a game, after all!
How far does this stream go before it ends?
I wonder ...
I hear you're looking for some-one.
Do you want some help?

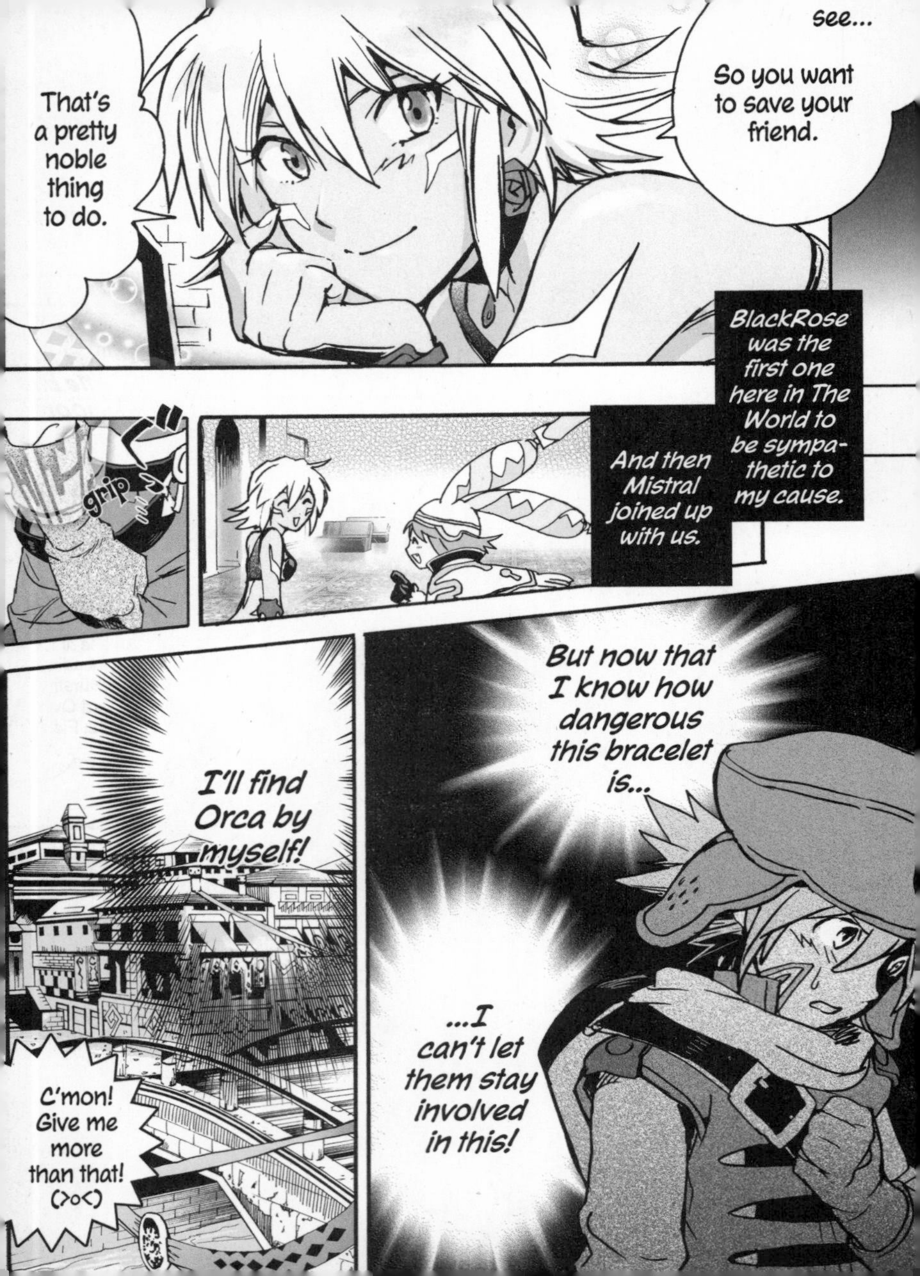
see...
So you want to save your friend.
That's a pretty noble thing to do.
BlackRose was the first one here in The World to be sympathetic to my cause.
And then Mistral joined up with us.
grip
But now that I know how dangerous this bracelet is...
...I can't let them stay involved in this!
I'll find Orca by myself!
C'mon! Give me more than that! (>o<)

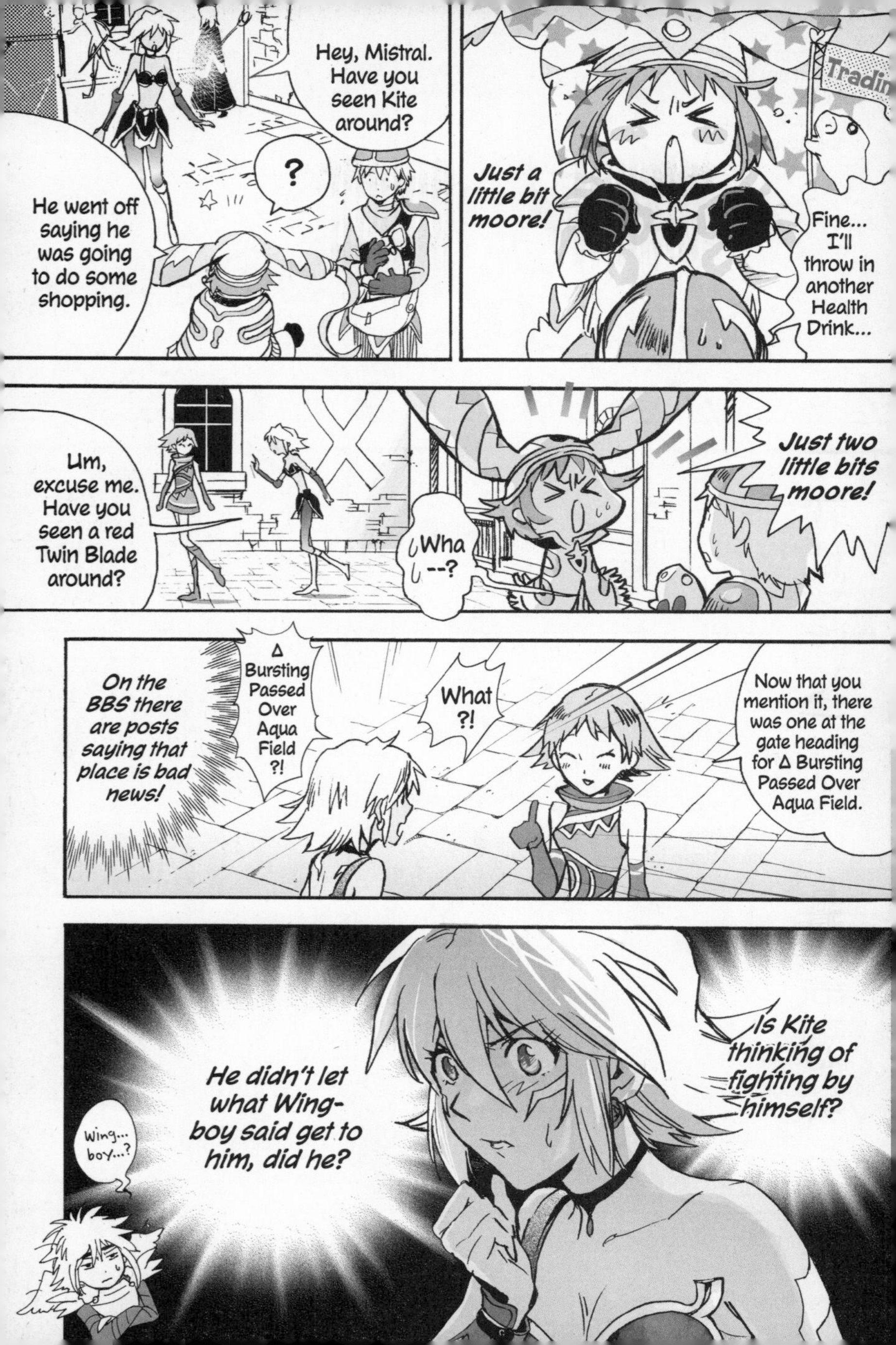
Hey, Mistral. Have you seen Kite around?
?
He went off saying he was going to do some shopping.
Tradin
Just a little bit moore!
Fine... I'll throw in another Health Drink...
Um, excuse me. Have you seen a red Twin Blade around?
Wha --?
Just two little bits moore!
Now that you mention it, there was one at the gate heading for Δ Bursting Passed Over Aqua Field.
What ?!
Δ Bursting Passed Over Aqua Field ?!
On the BBS there are posts saying that place is bad news!
Is Kite thinking of fighting by himself?
He didn't let what Wing-boy said get to him, did he?
Wing... boy...?

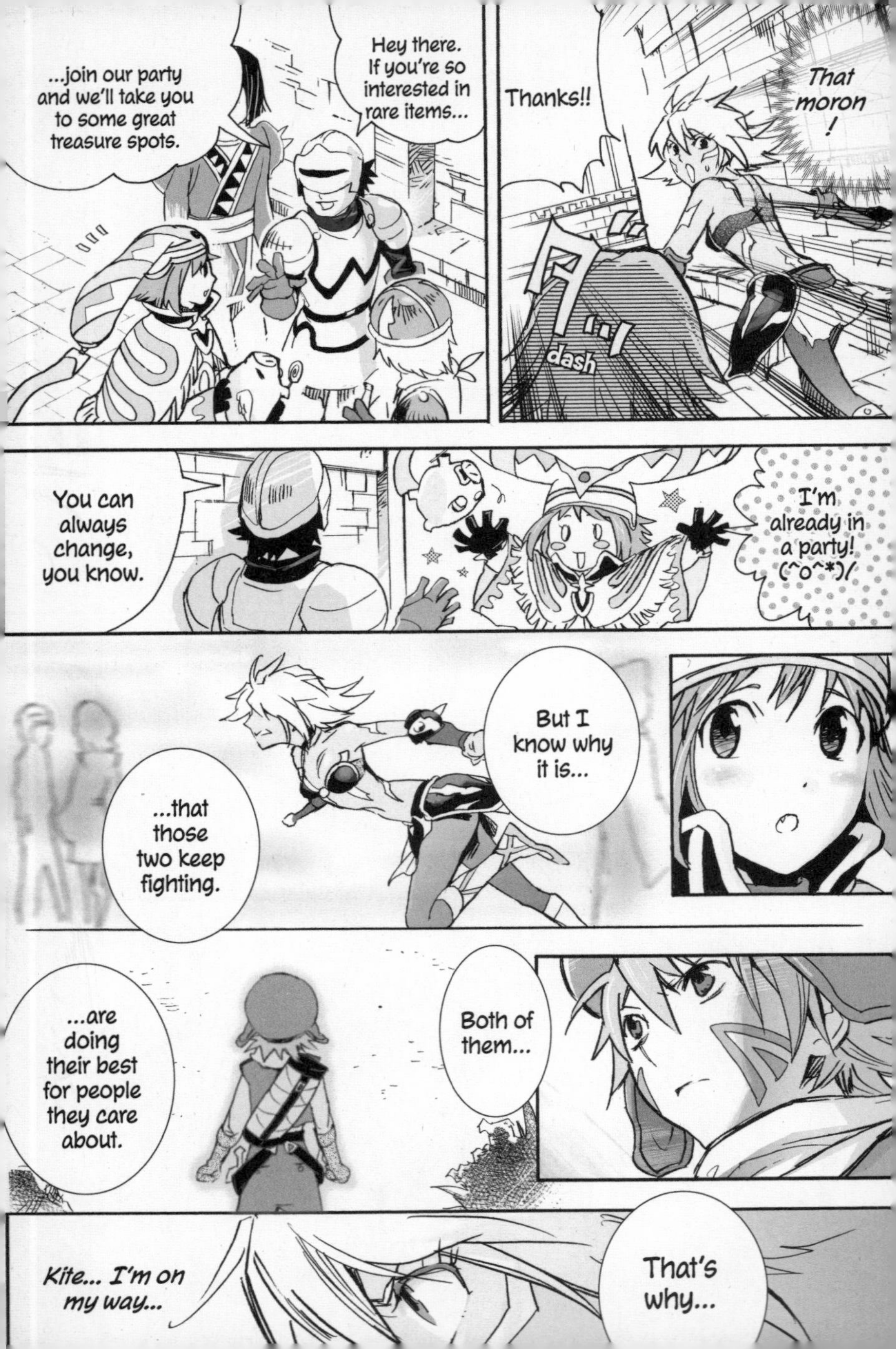
That moron!
Thanks!!
dash
Hey there. If you're so interested in rare items...
...join our party and we'll take you to some great treasure spots.
I'm already in a party! (^o^*)/
You can always change, you know.
But I know why it is...
...that those two keep fighting.
Both of them...
...are doing their best for people they care about.
That's why...
Kite... I'm on my way...

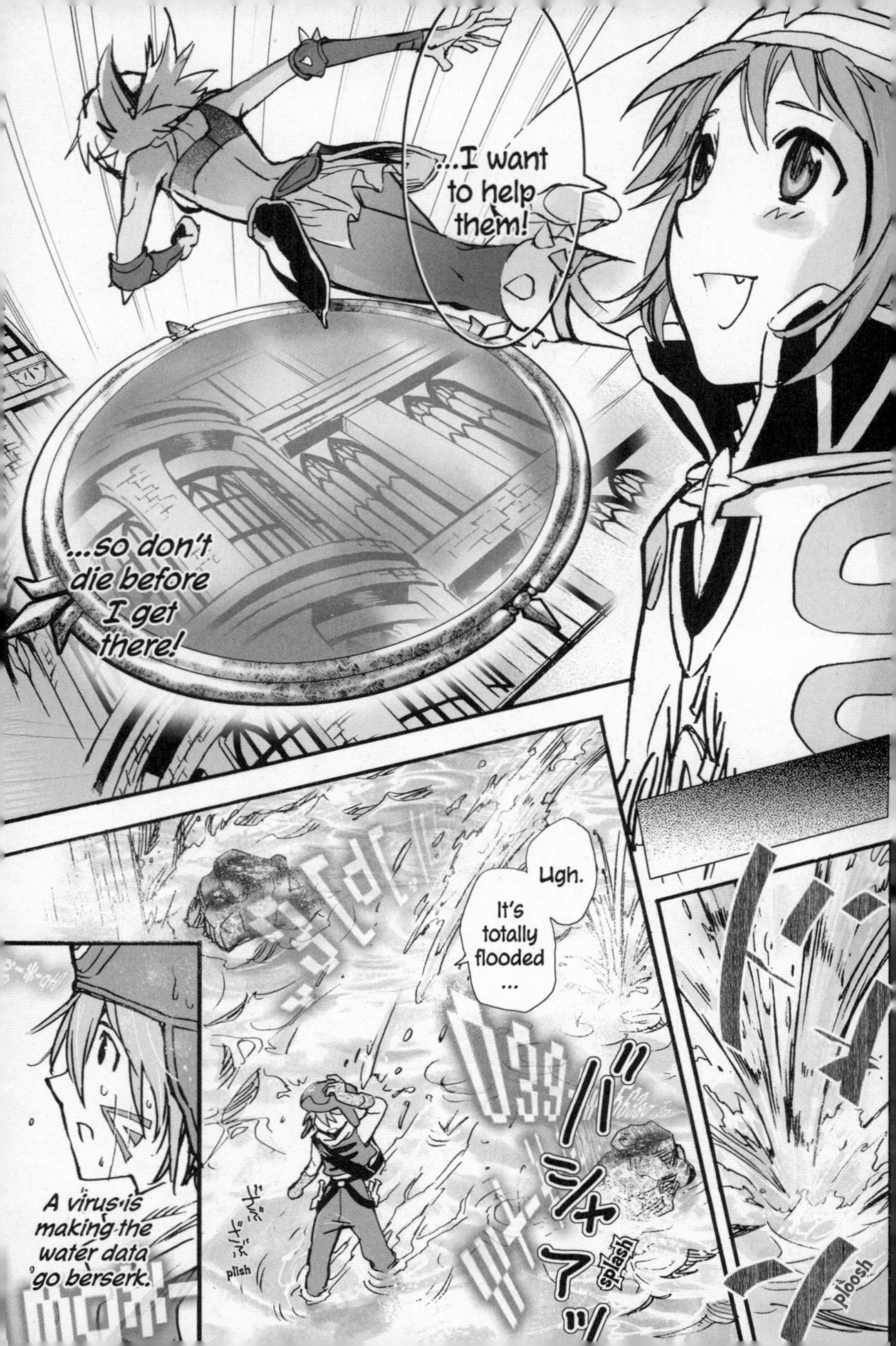

...I want to help them!
...so don't die before I get there!
Ugh.
It's totally flooded ...
splash
ploosh
plish
A virus is making the water data go berserk.

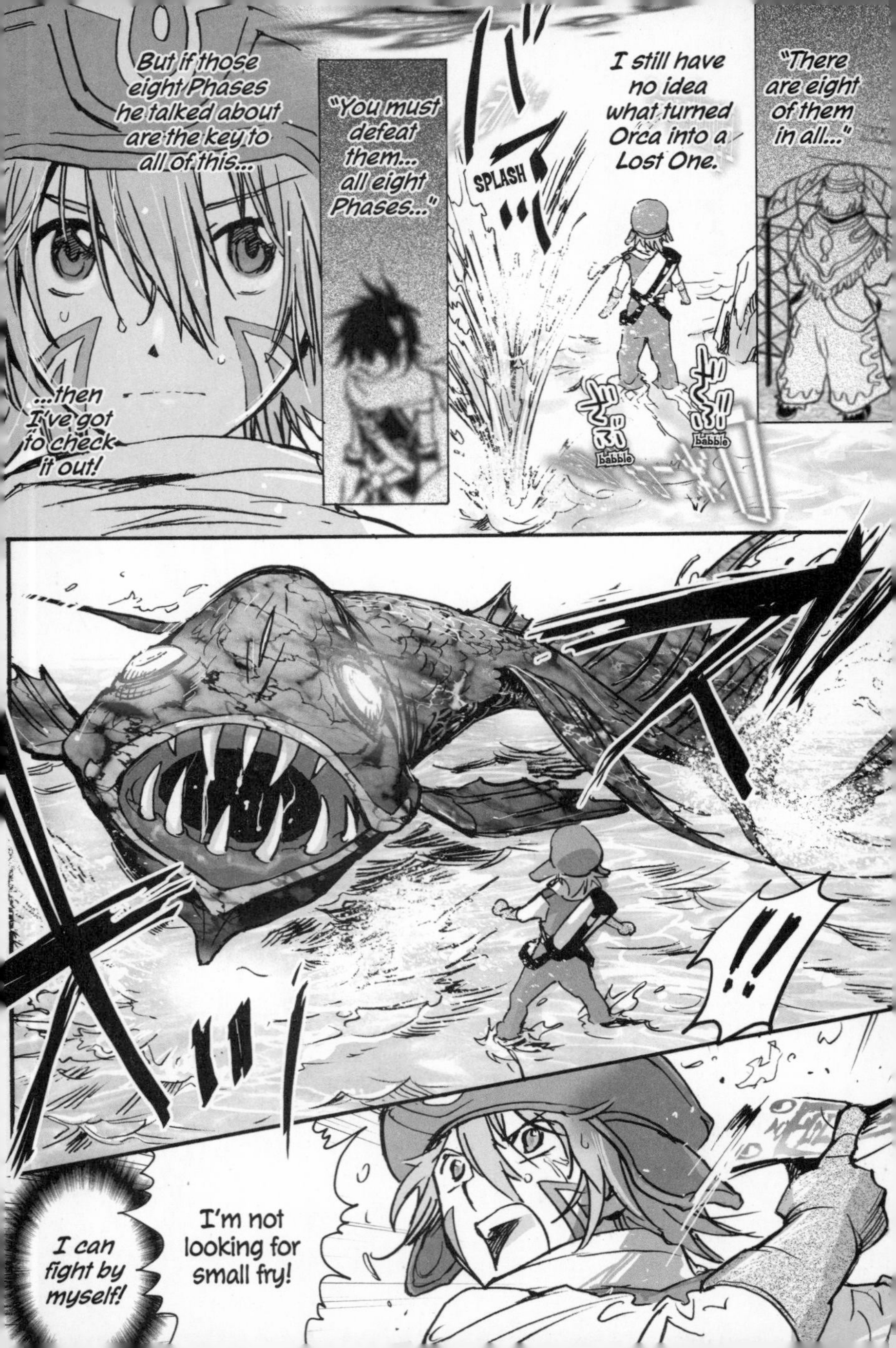
"There are eight of them in all..."
I still have no idea what turned Orca into a Lost One.
SPLASH
babble
babble
"You must defeat them... all eight Phases..."
But if those eight Phases he talked about are the key to all of this...
...then I've got to check it out!
!!
I'm not looking for small fry!
I can fight by myself!

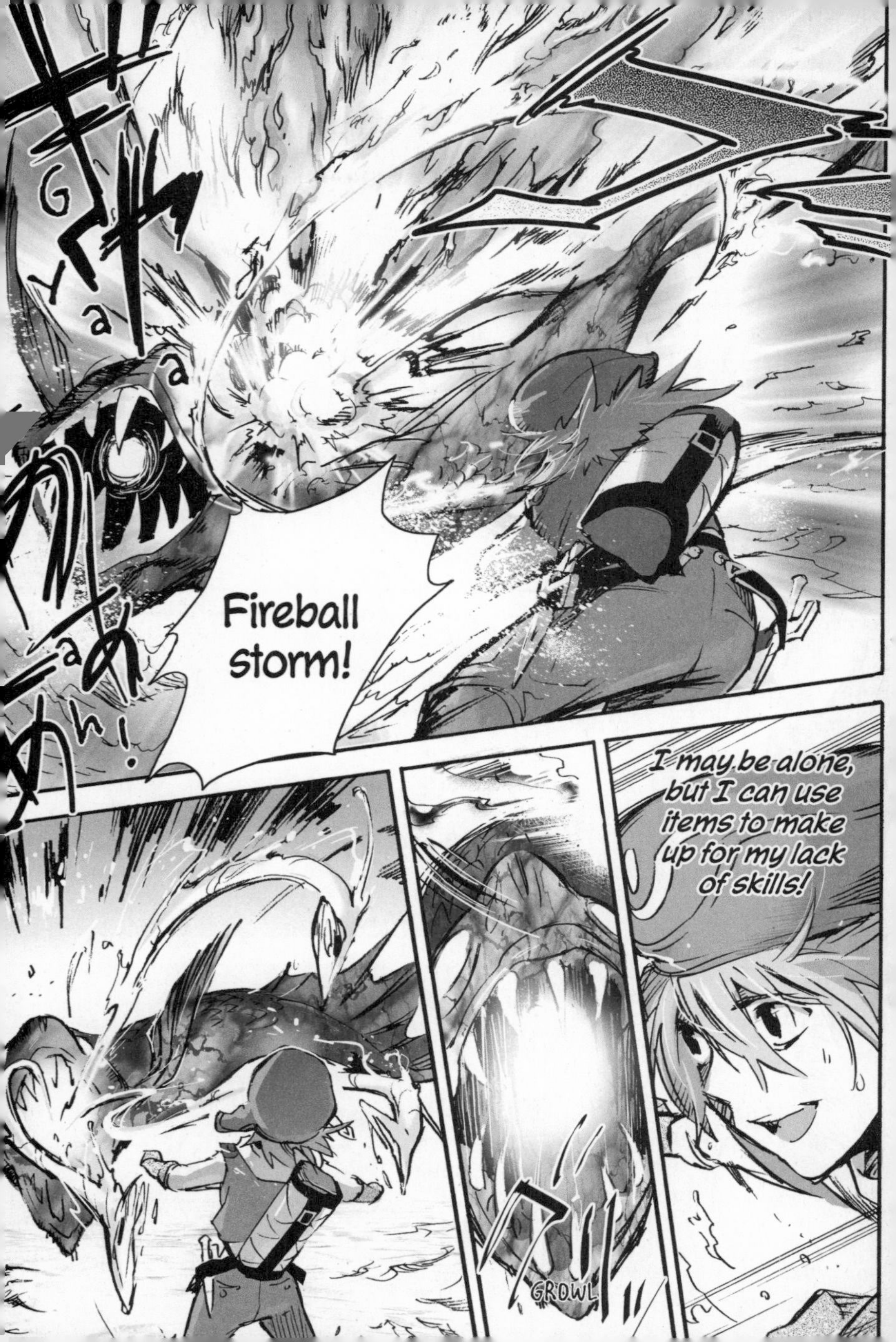
Gyaaah!
Fireball storm!
I may be alone, but I can use items to make up for my lack of skills!
GROWL

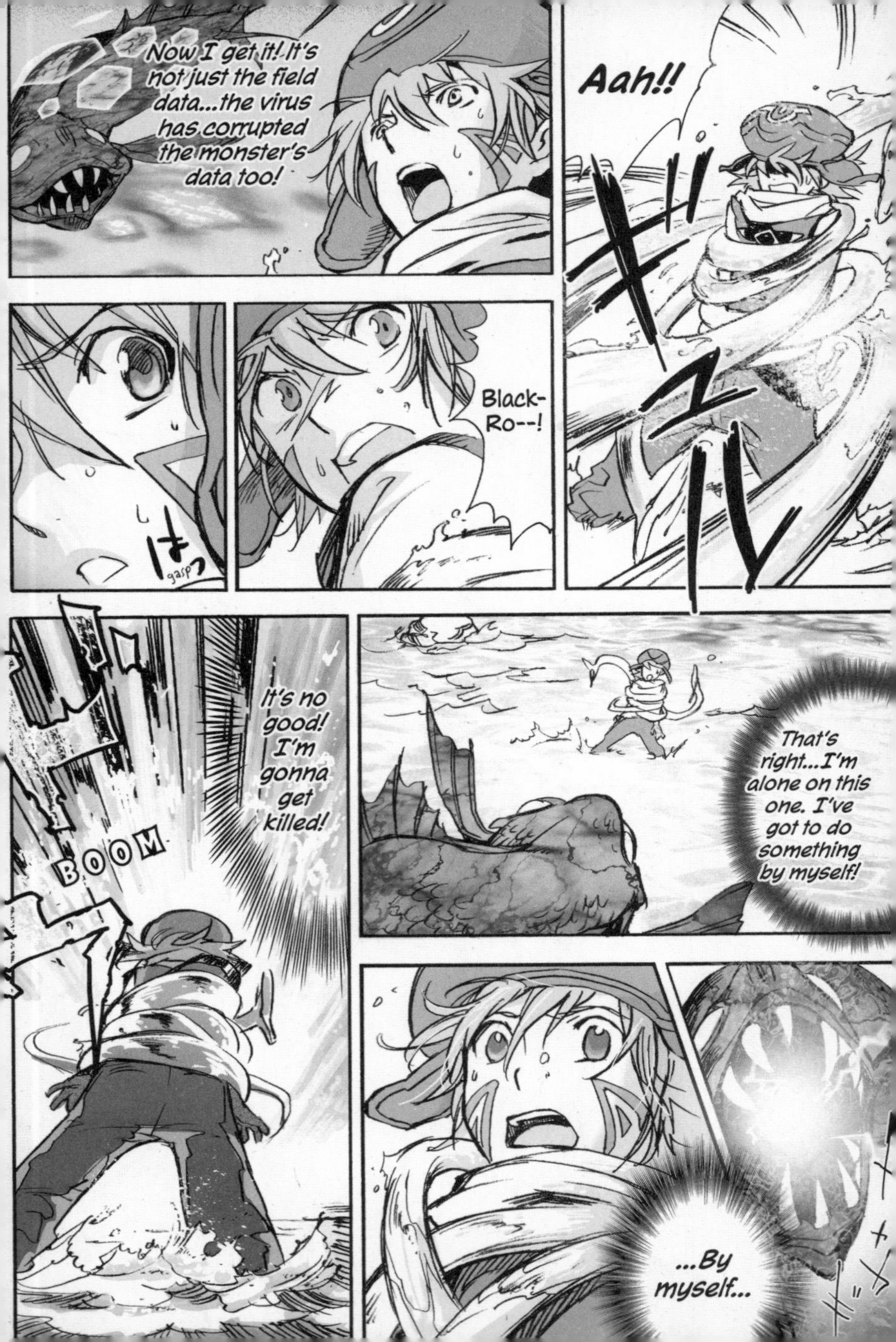

Aah!!
Now I get it! It's not just the field data...the virus has corrupted the monster's data too!
Black-Ro--!
gasp
That's right...I'm alone on this one. I've got to do something by myself!
It's no good! I'm gonna get killed!
BOOM
...By myself...

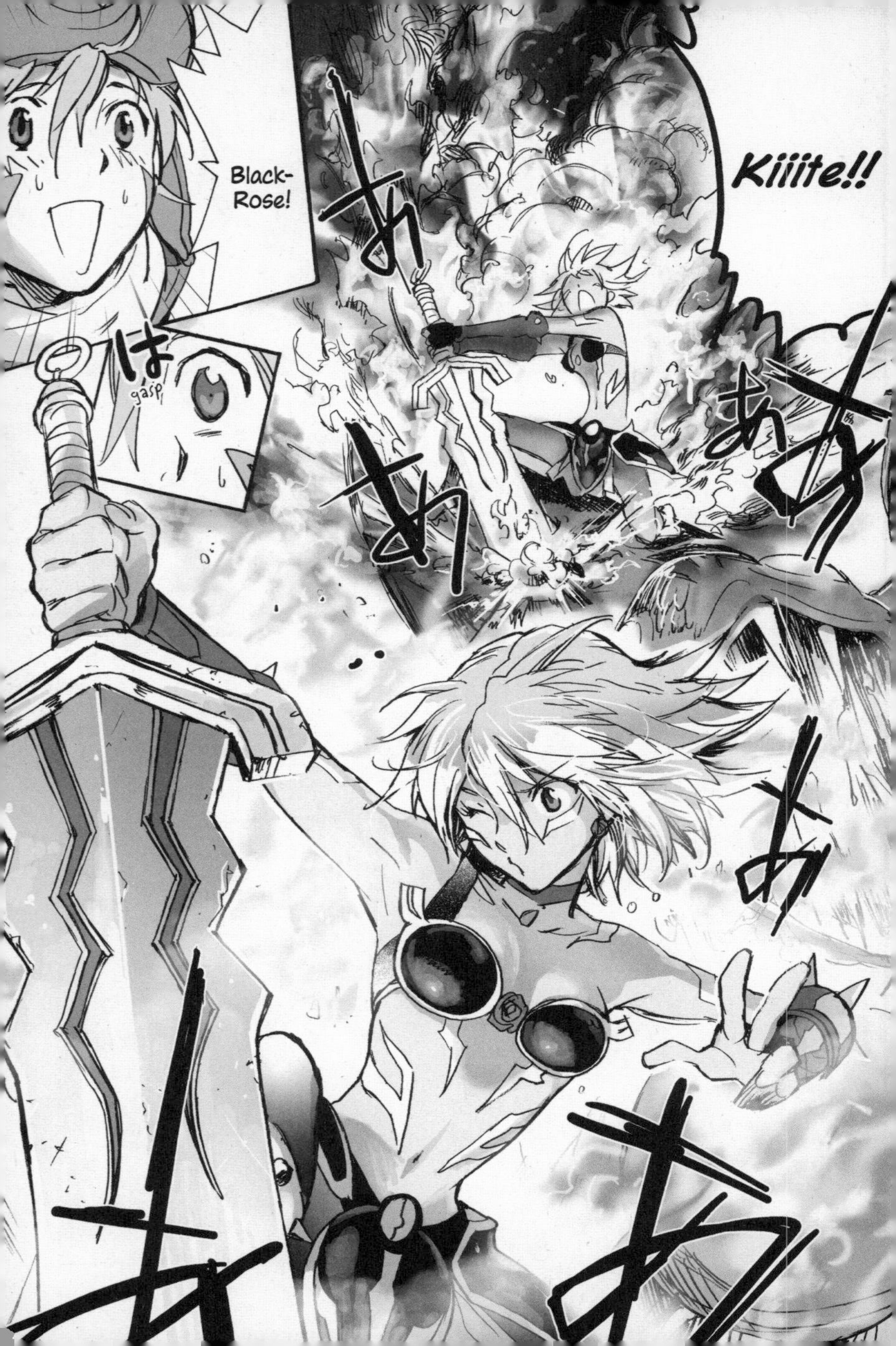

Kiiite!!
Black-Rose!
は
gasp

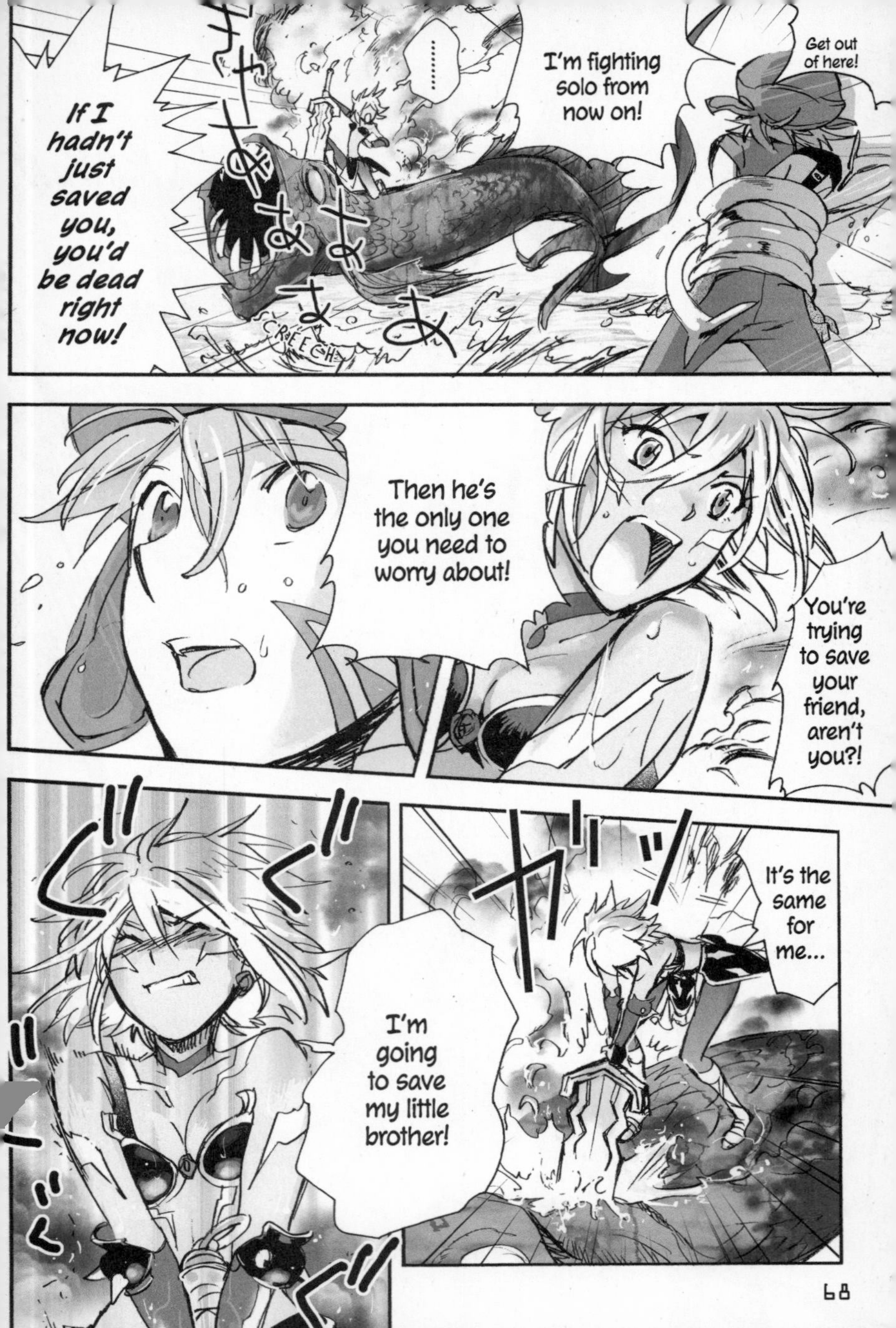
Get out of here!
I'm fighting solo from now on!
……
CREEECH
If I hadn't just saved you, you'd be dead right now!
You're trying to save your friend, aren't you?!
Then he's the only one you need to worry about!
It's the same for me...
I'm going to save my little brother!

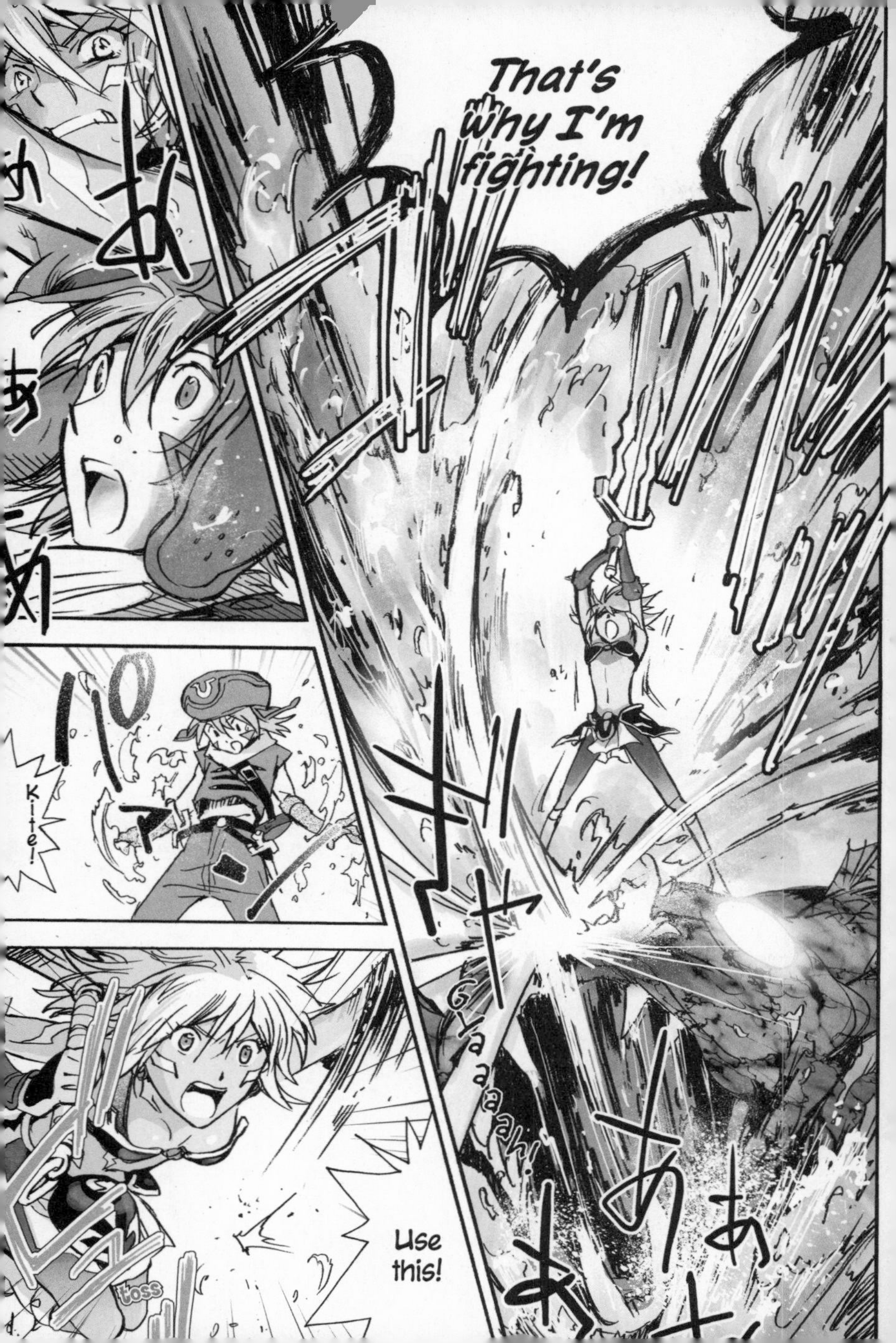
That's why I'm fighting!
Gyaaaaah!
Kite!
Use this!
toss

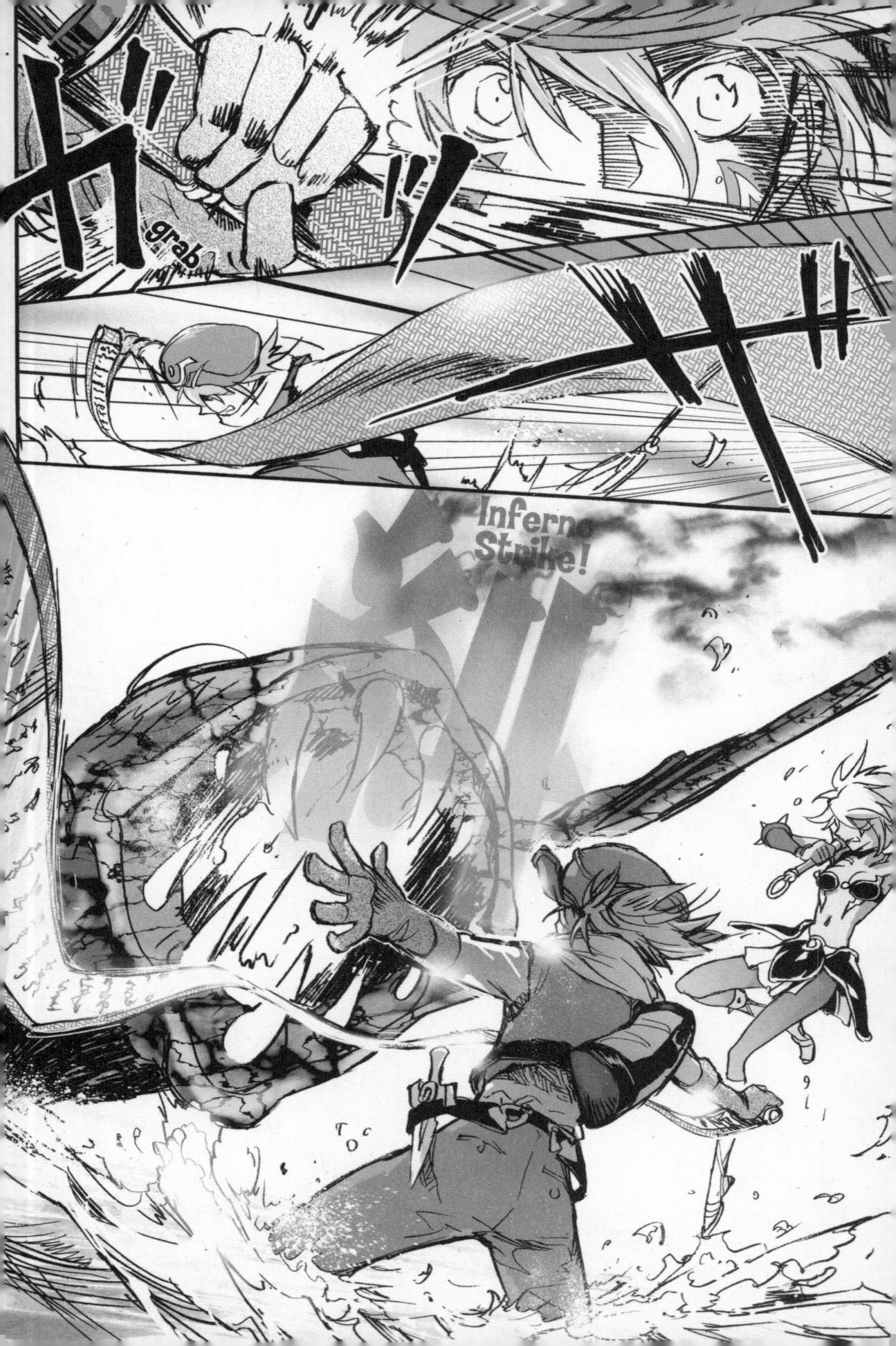
grab
Inferno Strike!

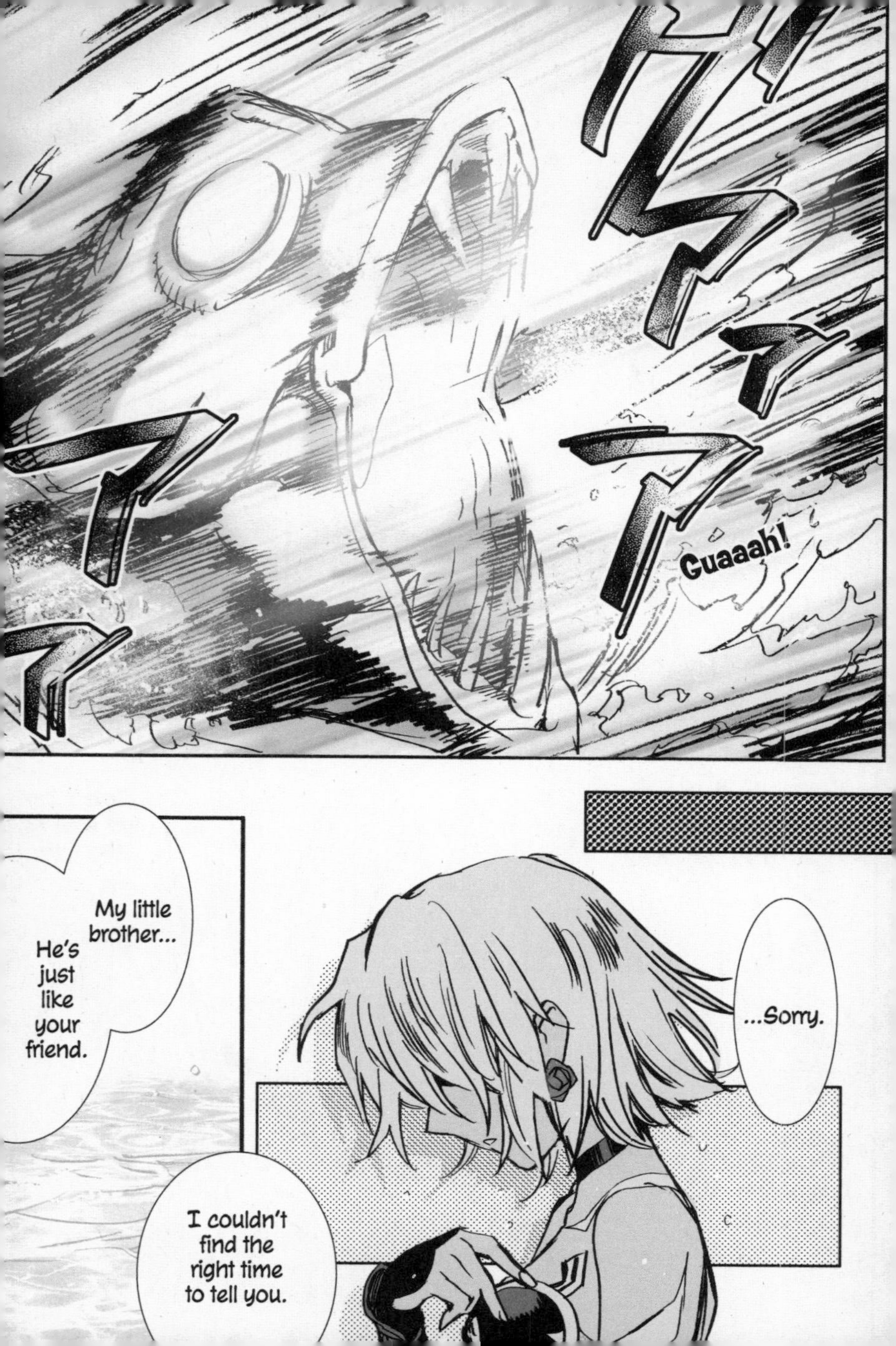
Guaaah!
...Sorry.
I couldn't find the right time to tell you.
My little brother...
He's just like your friend.

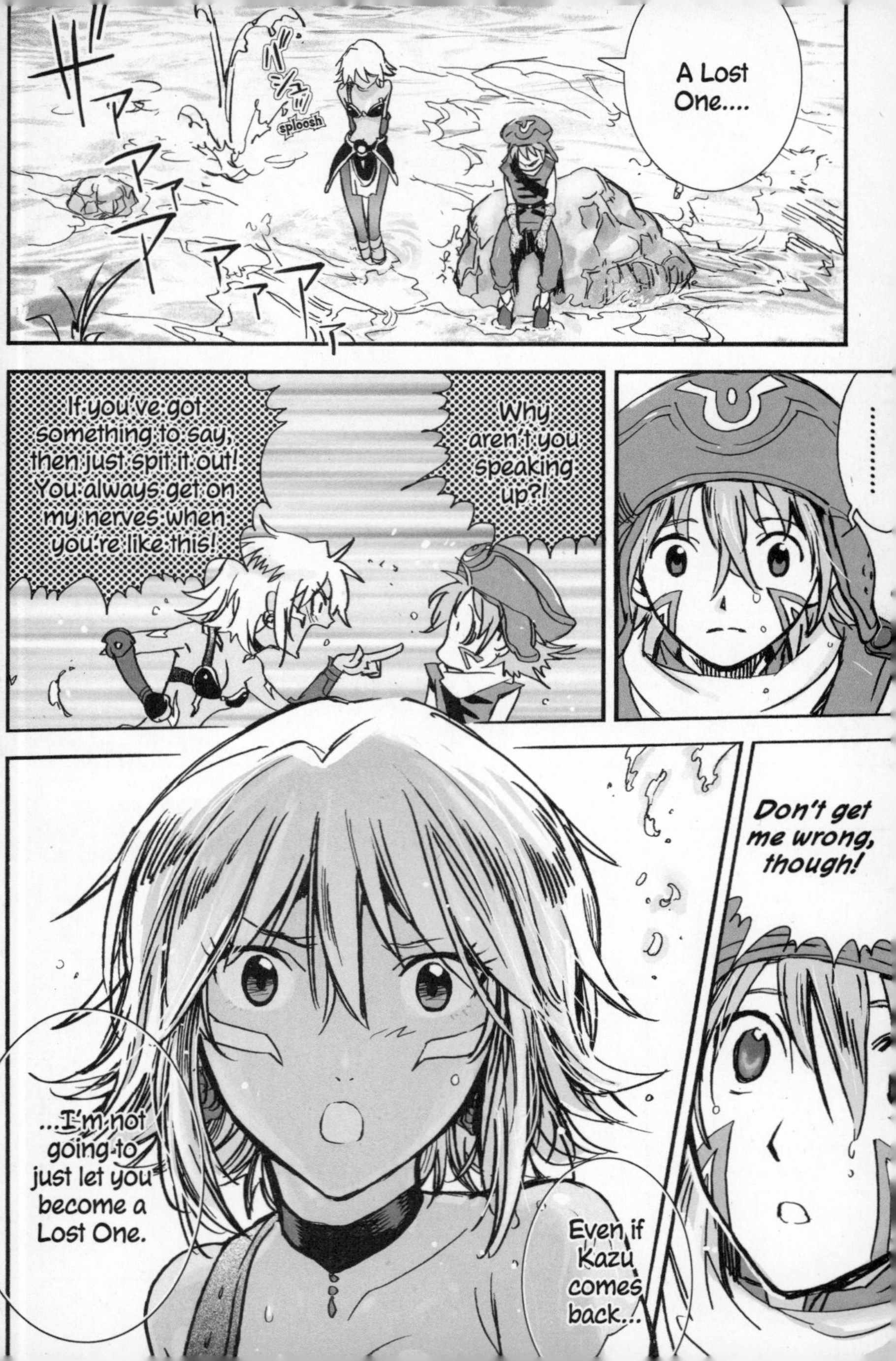
A Lost One....
sploosh
......
Why aren't you speaking up?!
If you've got something to say, then just spit it out! You always get on my nerves when you're like this!
Don't get me wrong, though!
Even if Kazu comes back...
...I'm not going to just let you become a Lost One.

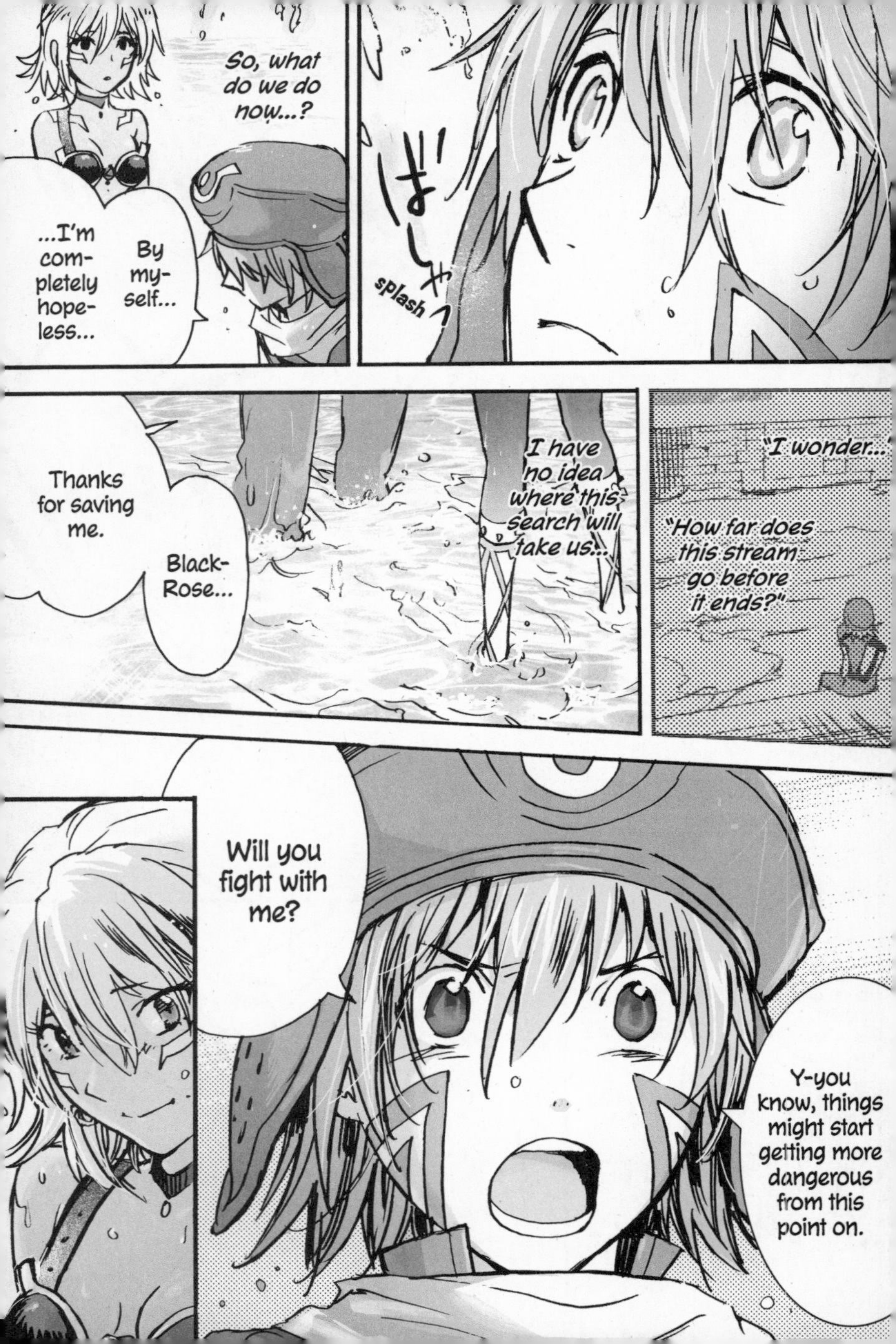
So, what do we do now...?
By myself...
...I'm completely hopeless...
splash
Thanks for saving me.
Black-Rose...
I have no idea where this search will take us...
"I wonder...
"How far does this stream go before it ends?"
Will you fight with me?
Y-you know, things might start getting more dangerous from this point on.

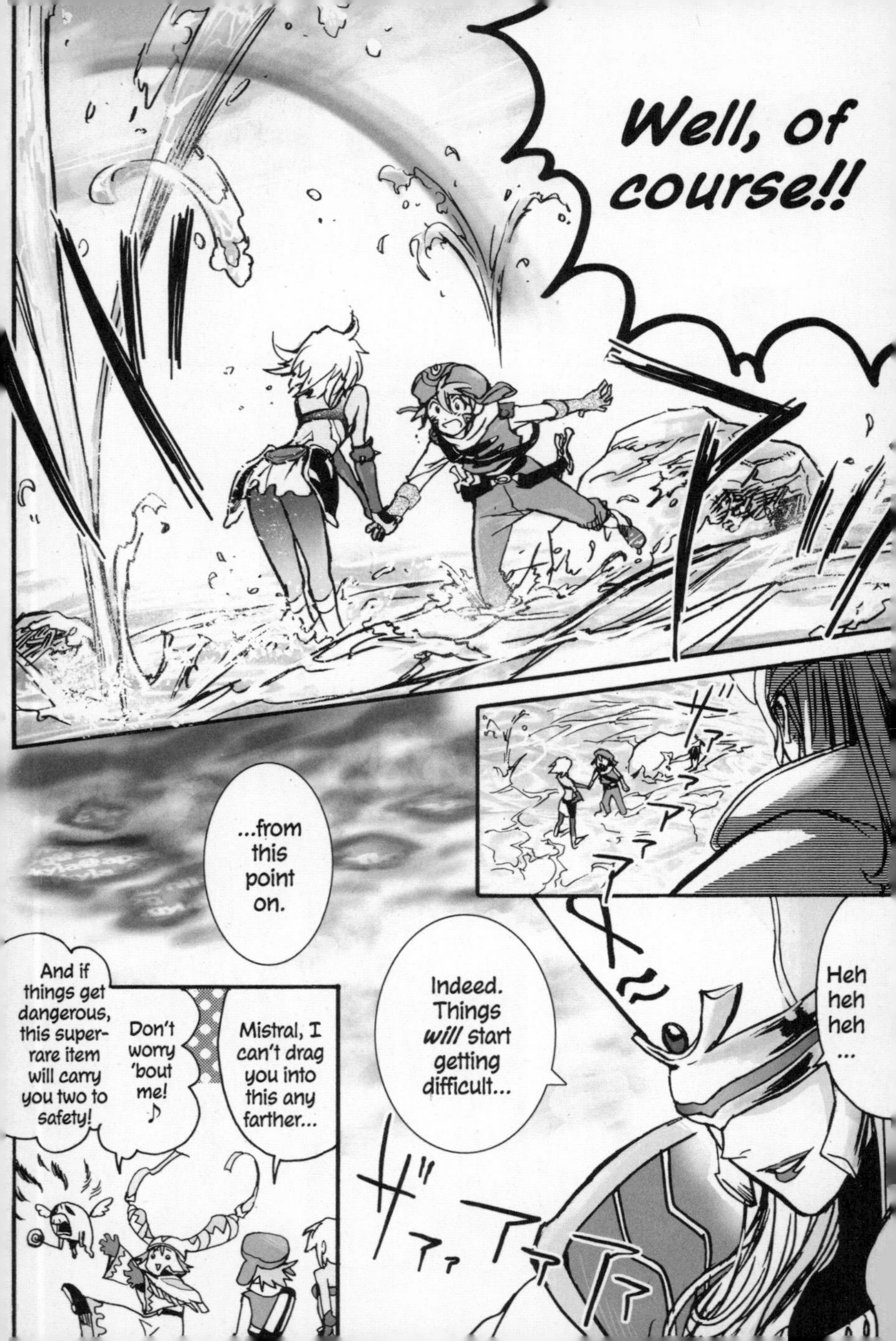
Well, of course!!
Heh heh heh...
Indeed. Things *will* start getting difficult...
...from this point on.
Mistral, I can't drag you into this any farther...
Don't worry 'bout me! ♪
And if things get dangerous, this super-rare item will carry you two to safety!

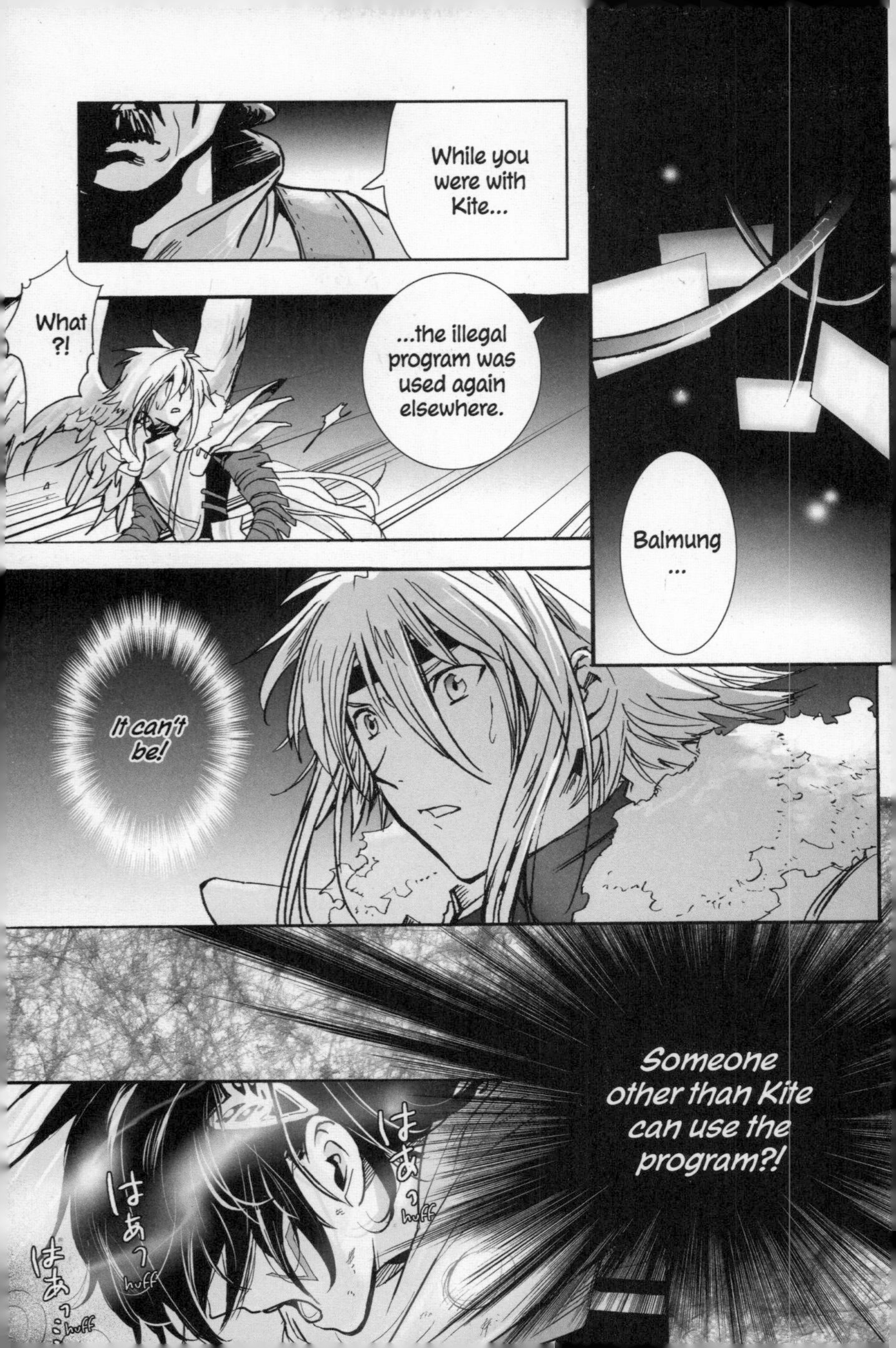
Balmung
...
While you were with Kite...
...the illegal program was used again elsewhere.
What ?!
It can't be!
Someone other than Kite can use the program?!
はあっ
huff
はあっ
huff
はあっ
huff

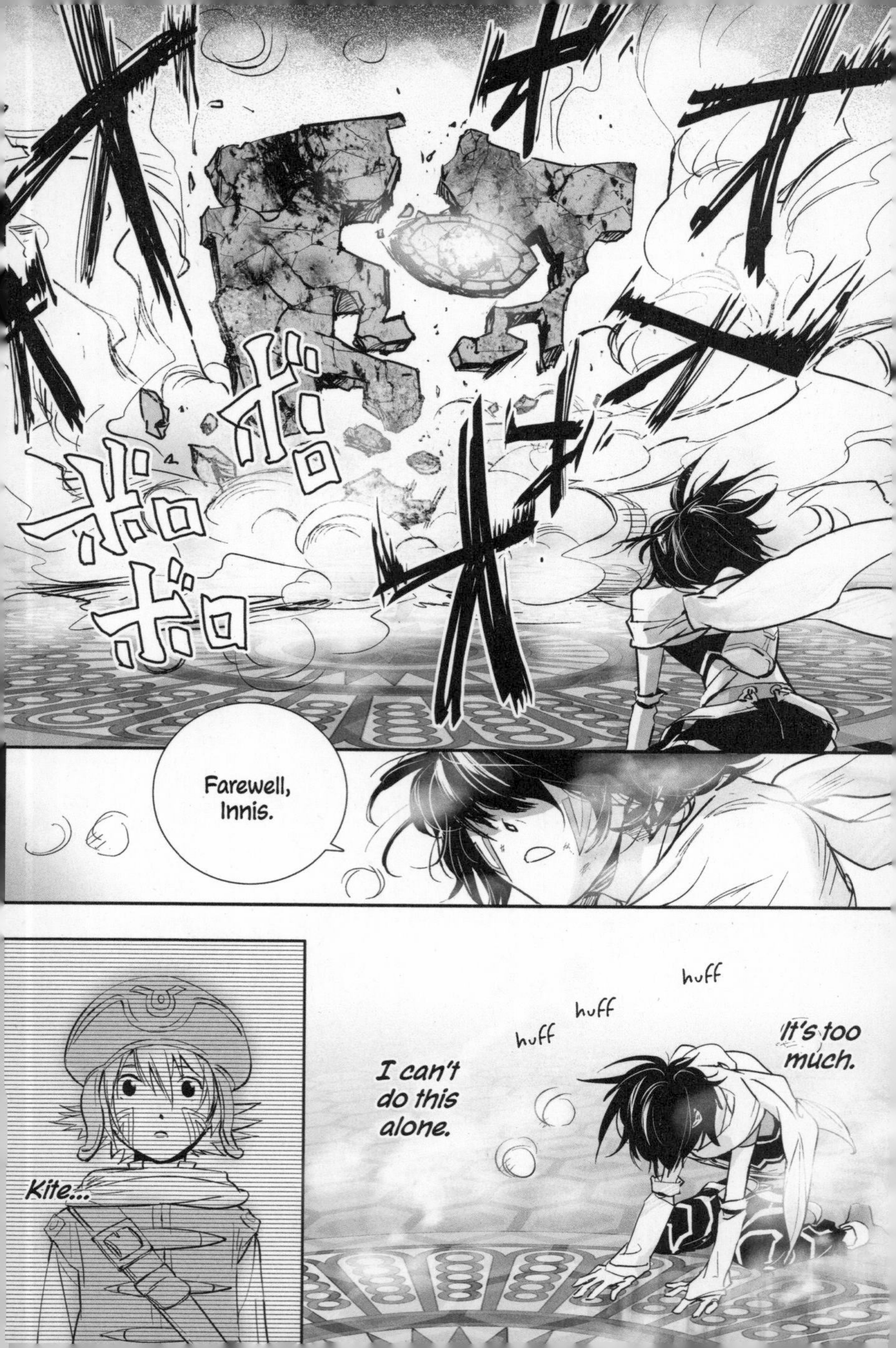
Farewell, Innis.
It's too much.
huff
huff
huff
I can't do this alone.
Kite...

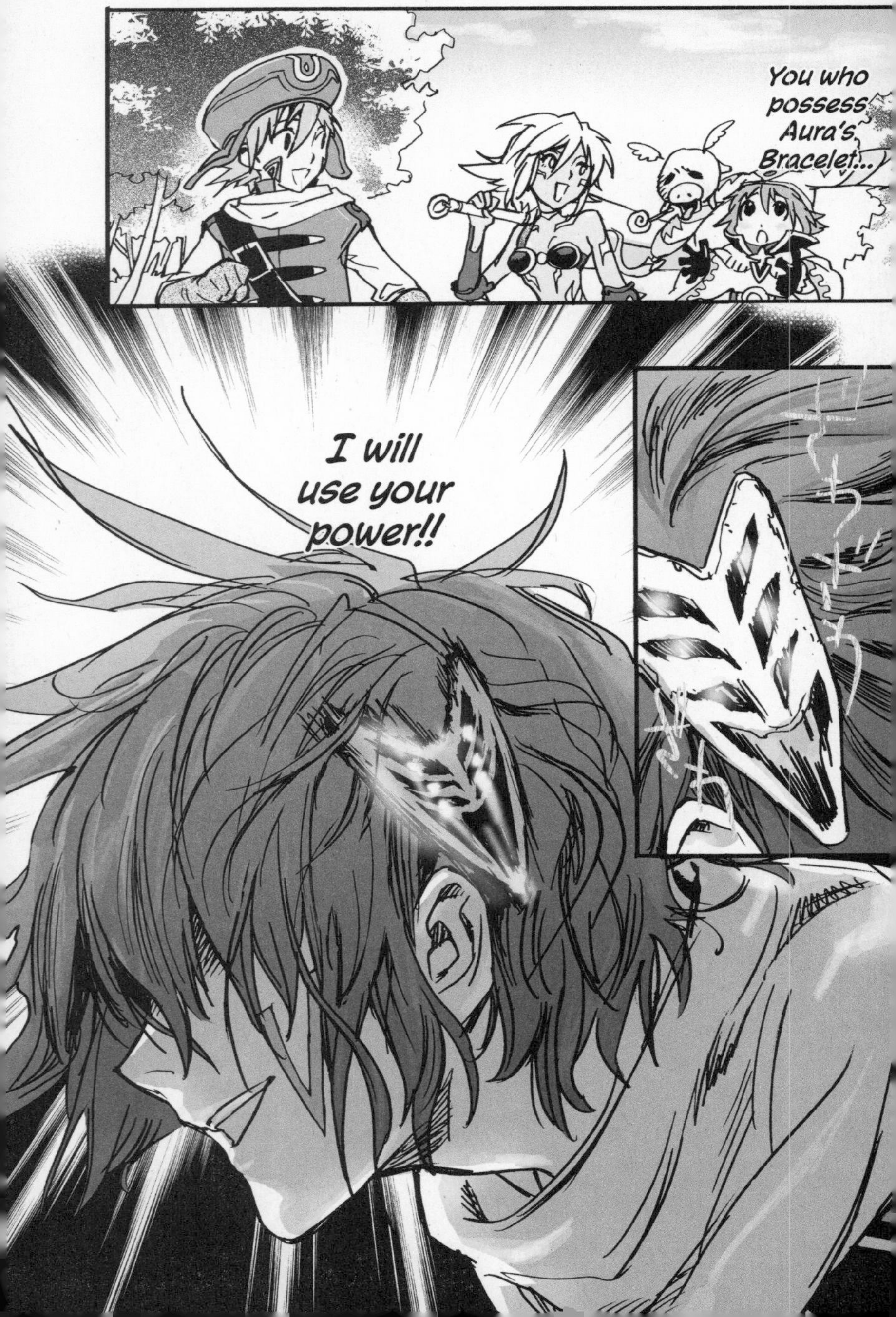
You who possess Aura's Bracelet...
I will use your power!!

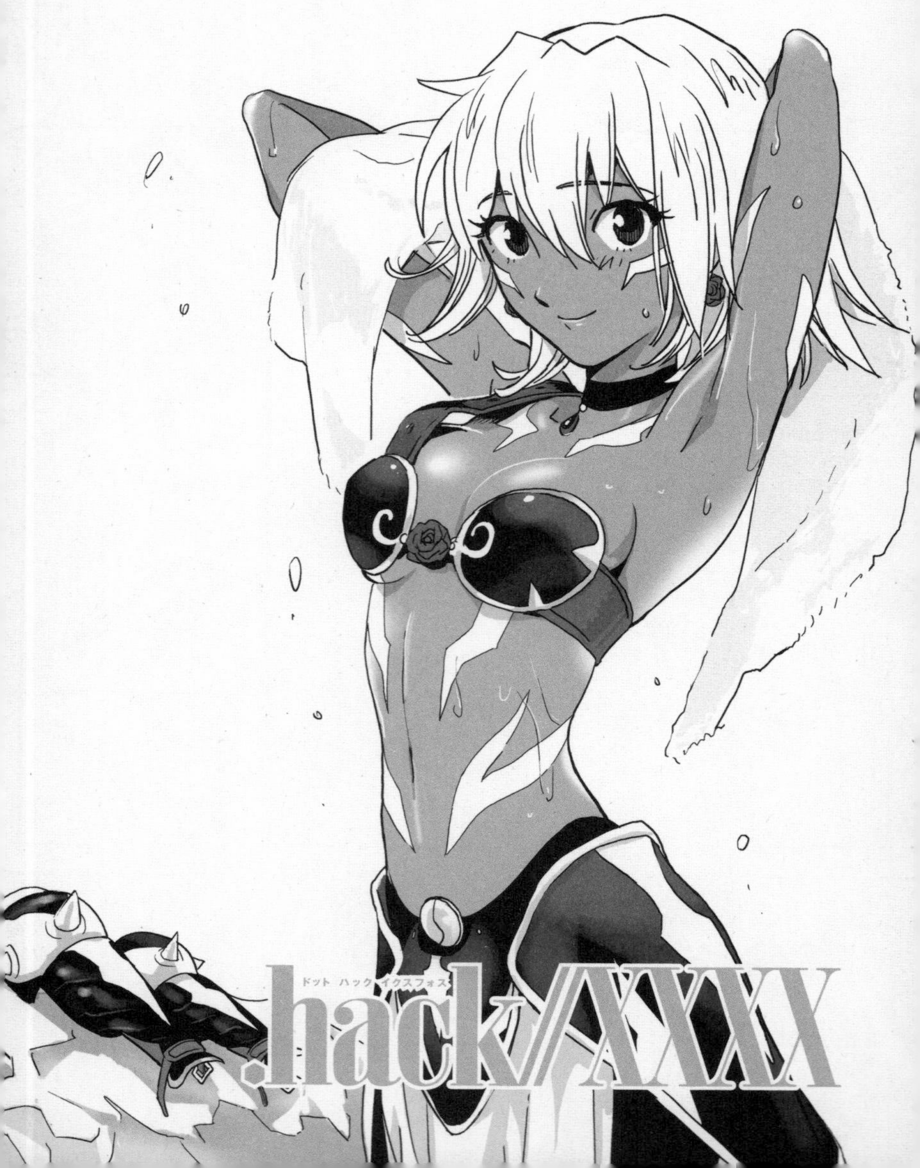
ドット ハック イクスフォス
.hack//XXXX

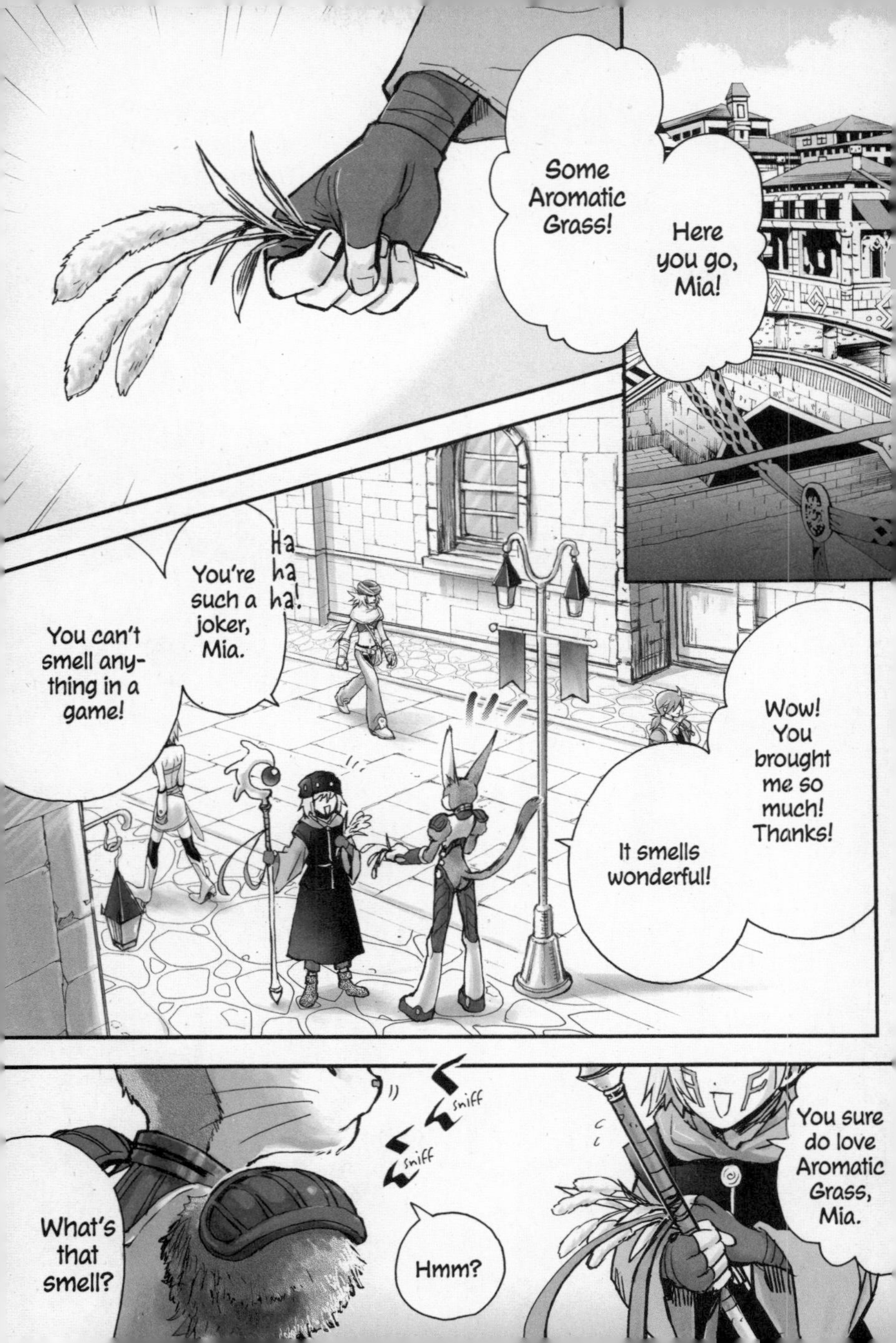
Some Aromatic Grass!
Here you go, Mia!
Wow! You brought me so much! Thanks!
It smells wonderful!
Ha ha ha!
You're such a joker, Mia.
You can't smell anything in a game!
You sure do love Aromatic Grass, Mia.
sniff
sniff
Hmm?
What's that smell?

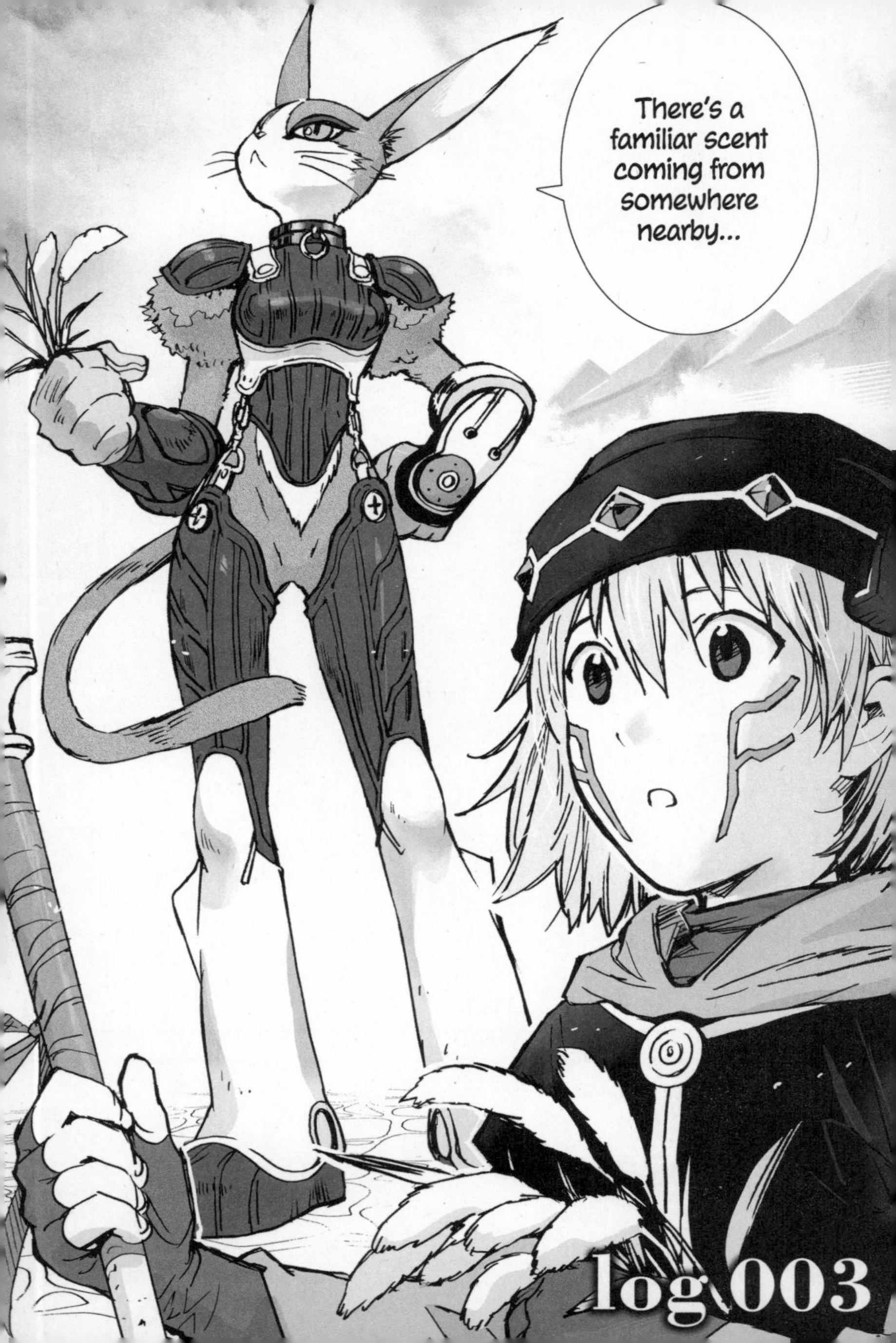
There's a familiar scent coming from somewhere nearby...
log 003

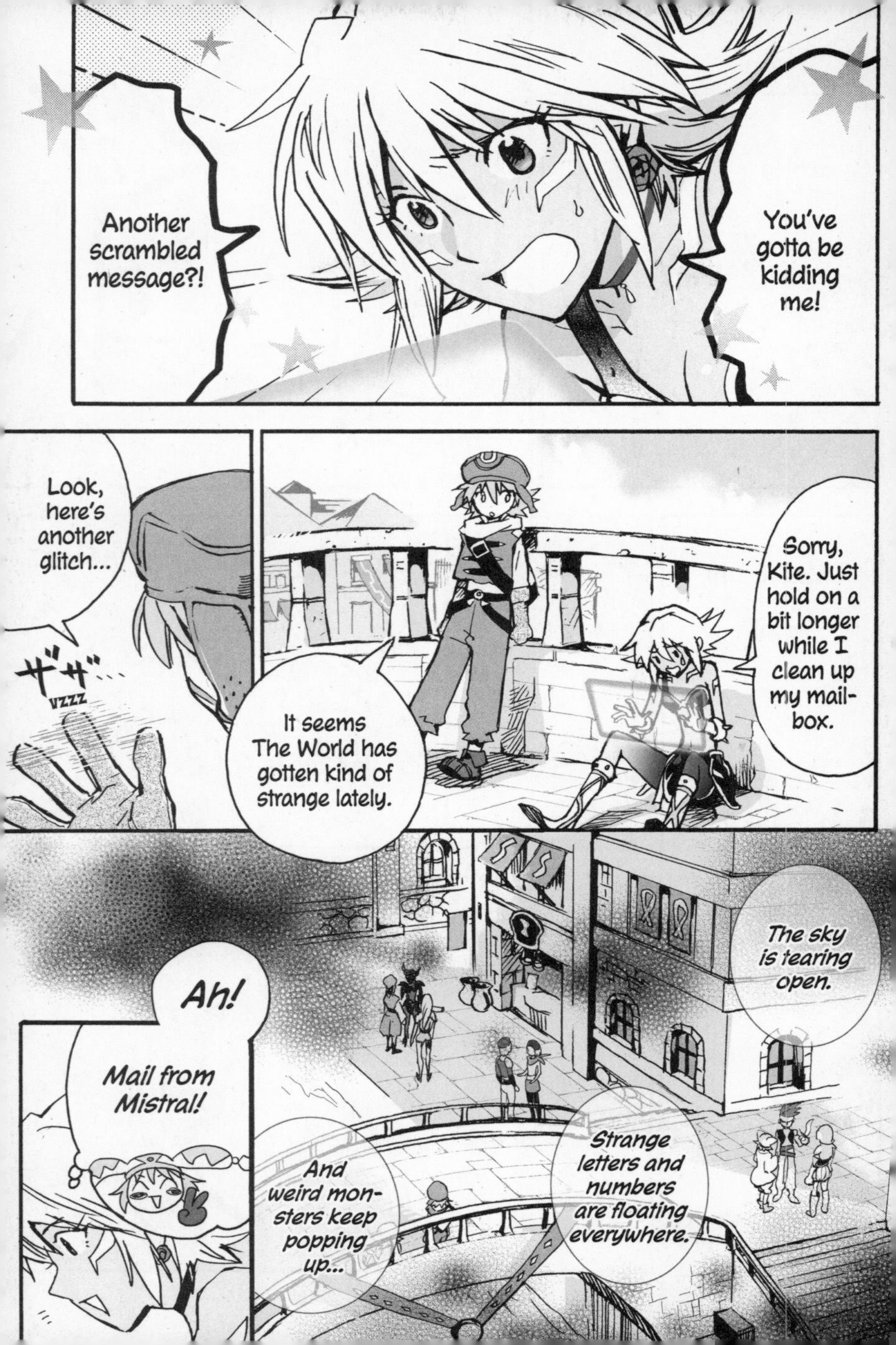

You've gotta be kidding me!
Another scrambled message?!
Sorry, Kite. Just hold on a bit longer while I clean up my mail-box.
It seems The World has gotten kind of strange lately.
Look, here's another glitch...
ザザ…
VZZZ
The sky is tearing open.
Strange letters and numbers are floating everywhere.
And weird mon-sters keep popping up...
Ah!
Mail from Mistral!

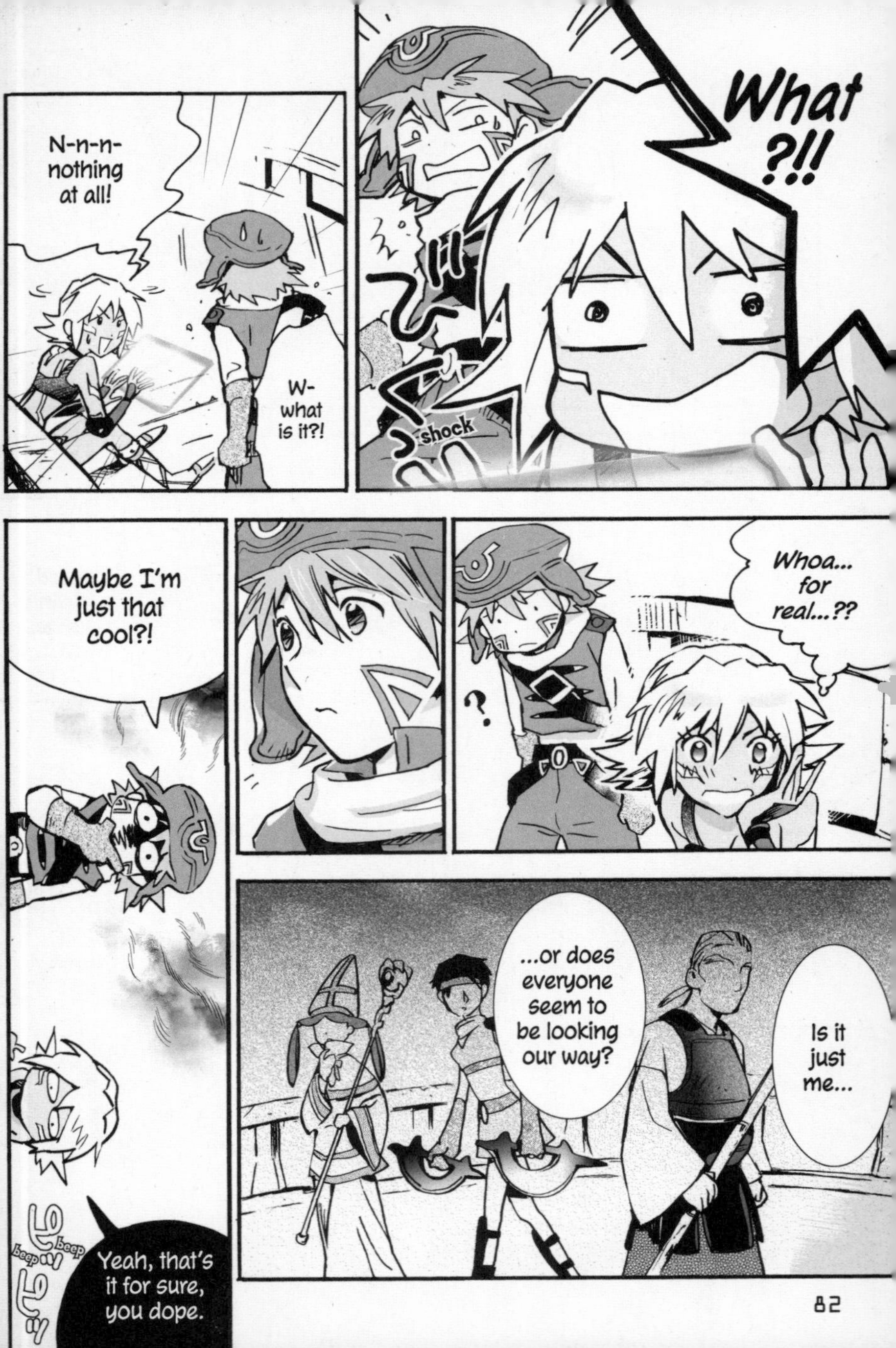
N-n-n-nothing at all!
W-what is it?!
shock
What?!!
Maybe I'm just that cool?!
Whoa... for real...??
Is it just me...
...or does everyone seem to be looking our way?
beep beep
Yeah, that's it for sure, you dope.

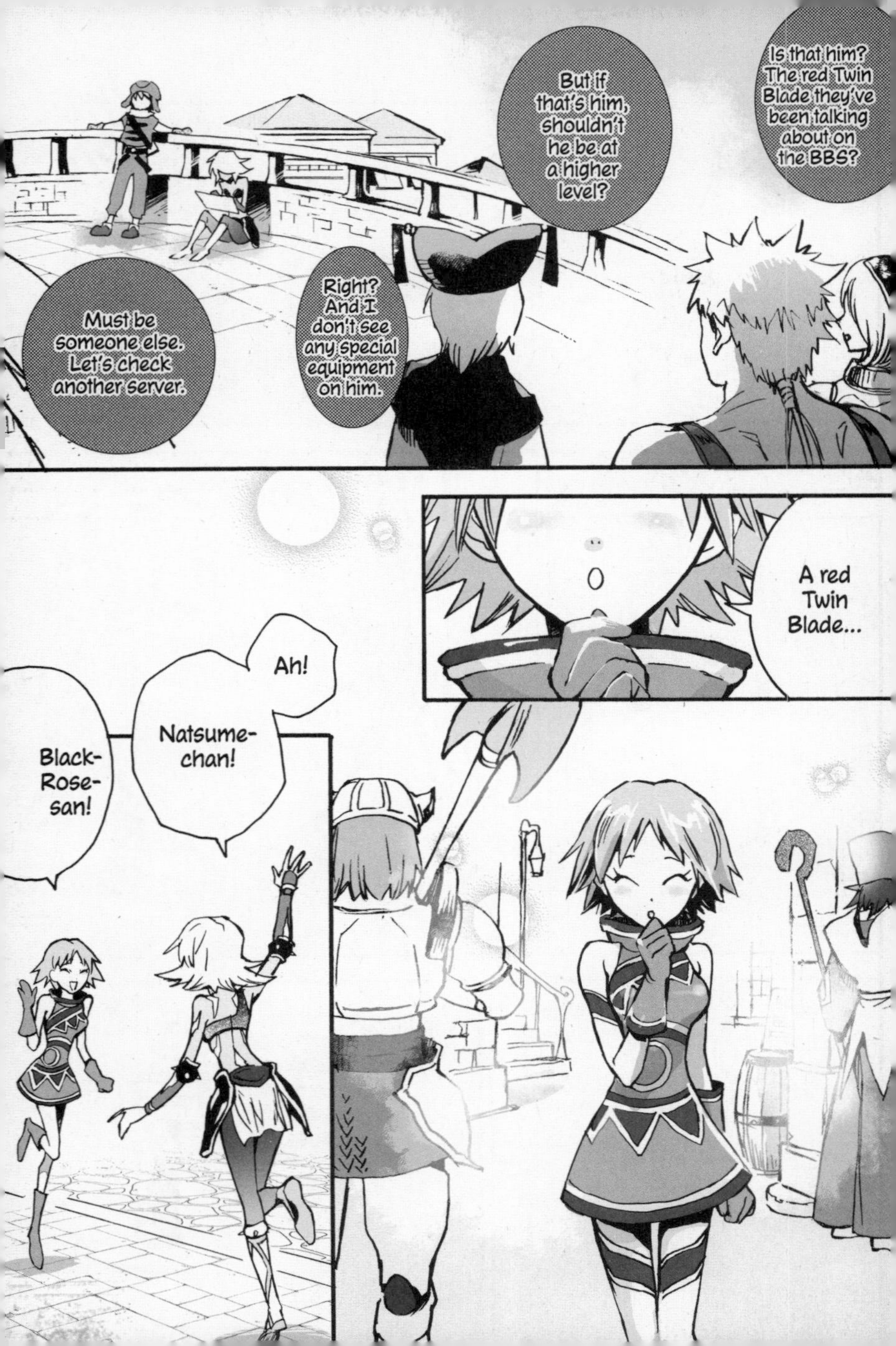
Is that him? The red Twin Blade they've been talking about on the BBS?
But if that's him, shouldn't he be at a higher level?
Right? And I don't see any special equipment on him.
Must be someone else. Let's check another server.
A red Twin Blade...
Ah!
Natsume-chan!
Black-Rose-san!

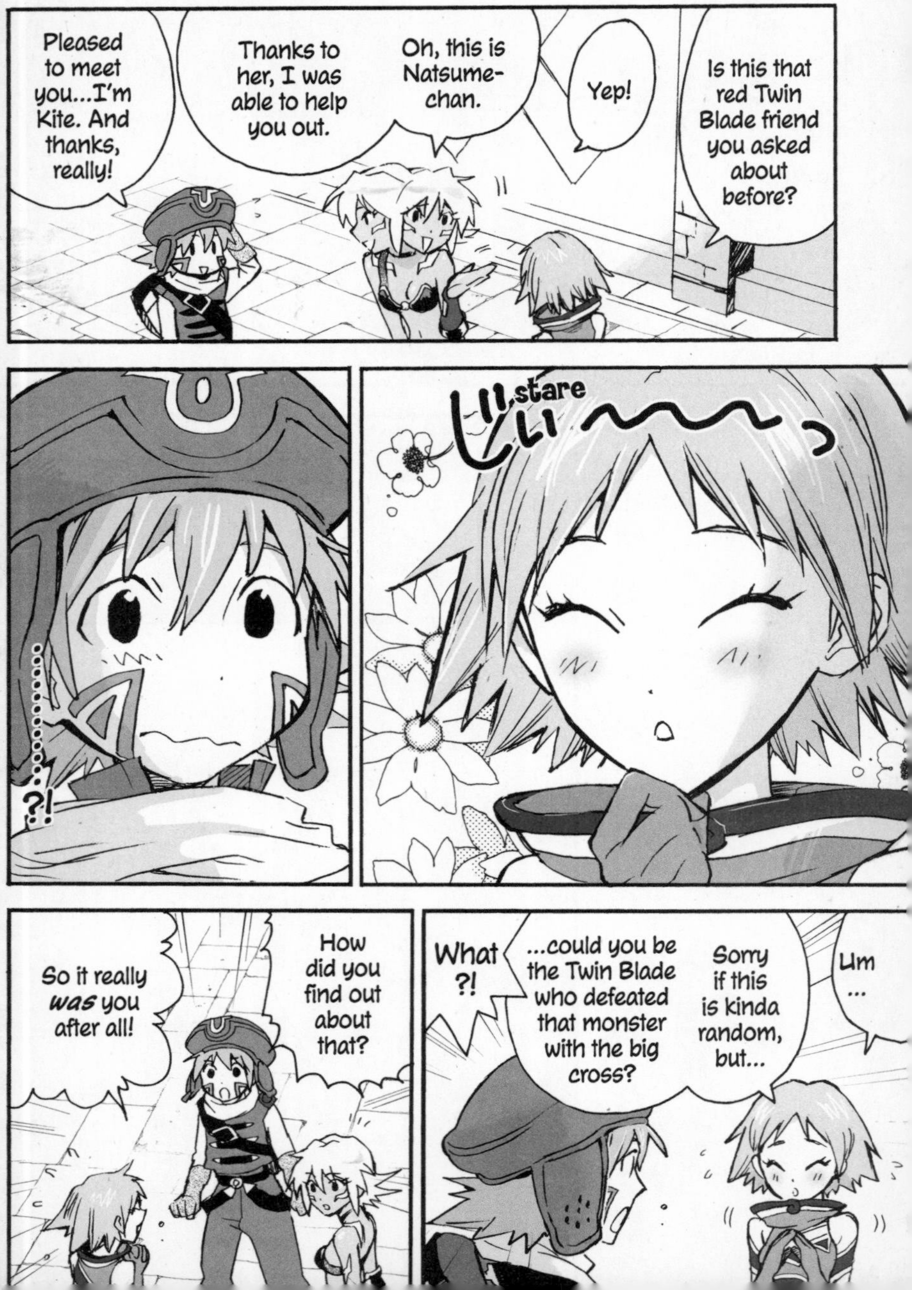
Is this that red Twin Blade friend you asked about before?
Yep!
Oh, this is Natsume-chan.
Thanks to her, I was able to help you out.
Pleased to meet you...I'm Kite. And thanks, really!
stare
..............?!
Um...
Sorry if this is kinda random, but...
...could you be the Twin Blade who defeated that monster with the big cross?
What?!
How did you find out about that?
So it really *was* you after all!

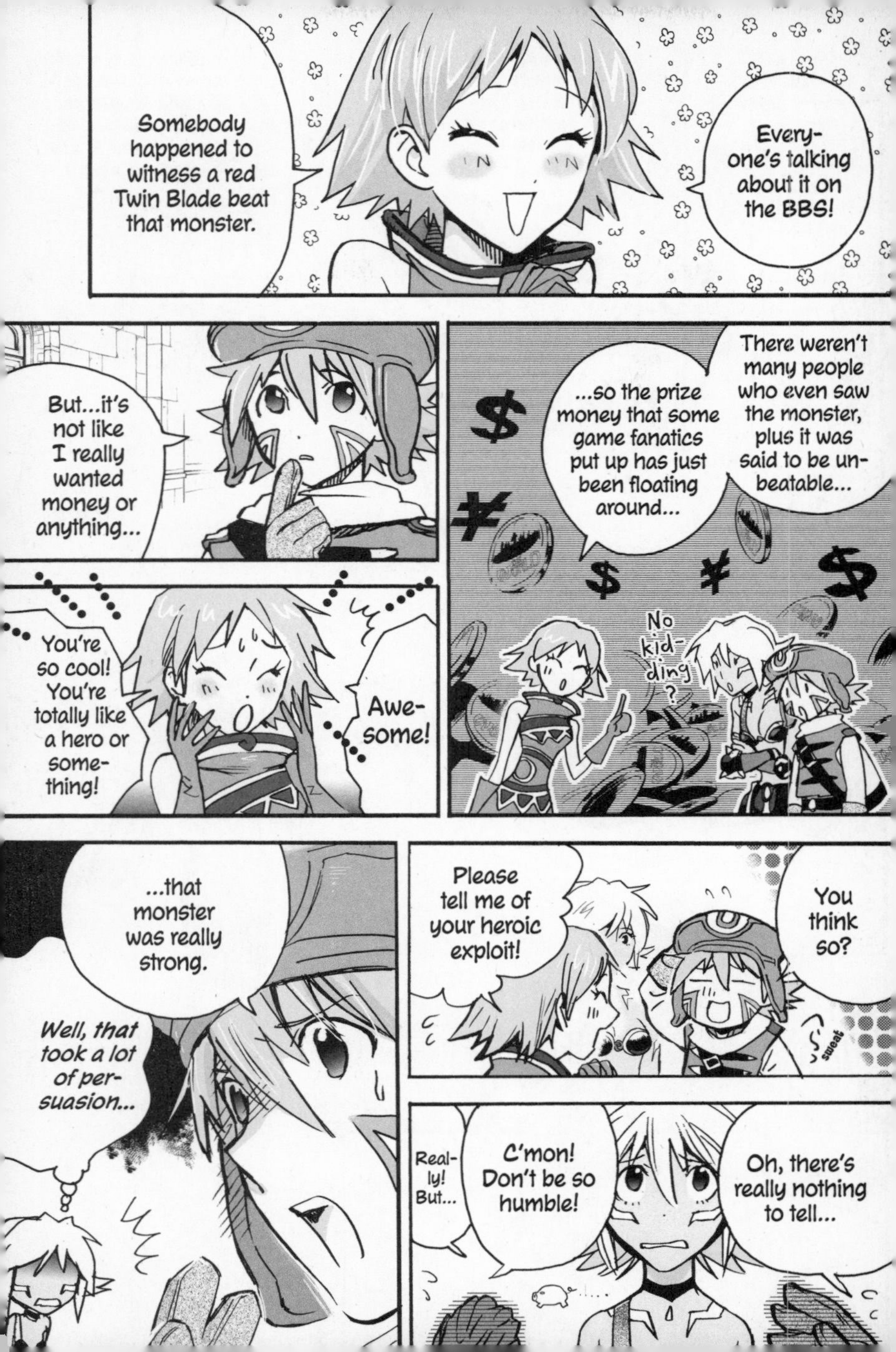

Every-one's talking about it on the BBS!
Somebody happened to witness a red Twin Blade beat that monster.
There weren't many people who even saw the monster, plus it was said to be un-beatable...
...so the prize money that some game fanatics put up has just been floating around...
No kid-ding?
But...it's not like I really wanted money or anything...
Awe-some!
You're so cool! You're totally like a hero or some-thing!
You think so?
Please tell me of your heroic exploit!
Oh, there's really nothing to tell...
C'mon! Don't be so humble!
Real-ly! But...
...that monster was really strong.
Well, that took a lot of per-suasion...
sweat

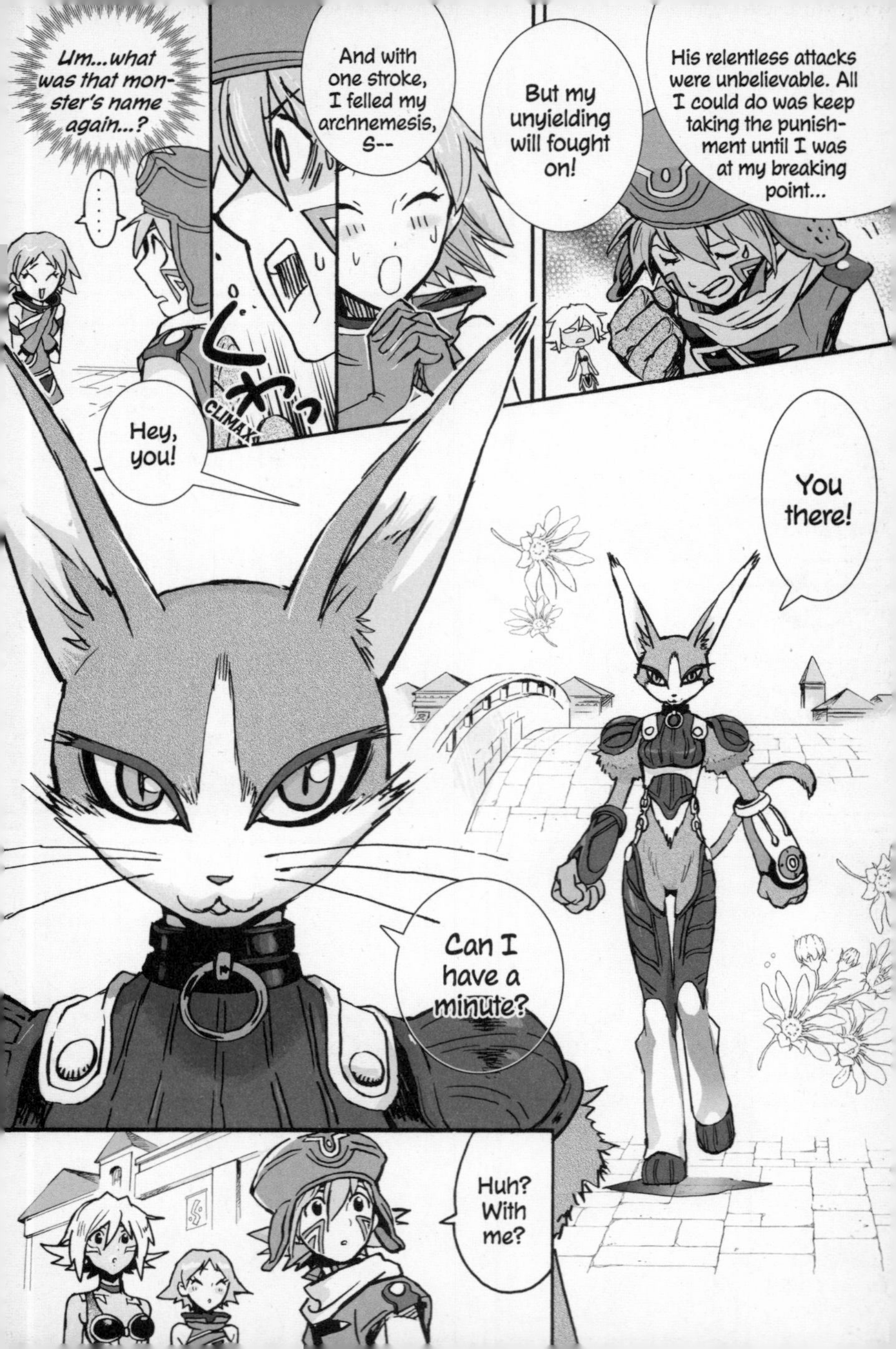

His relentless attacks were unbelievable. All I could do was keep taking the punishment until I was at my breaking point...
But my unyielding will fought on!
And with one stroke, I felled my archnemesis, S--
Um...what was that monster's name again...?
...
CLIMAX!!
Hey, you!
You there!
Can I have a minute?
Huh? With me?

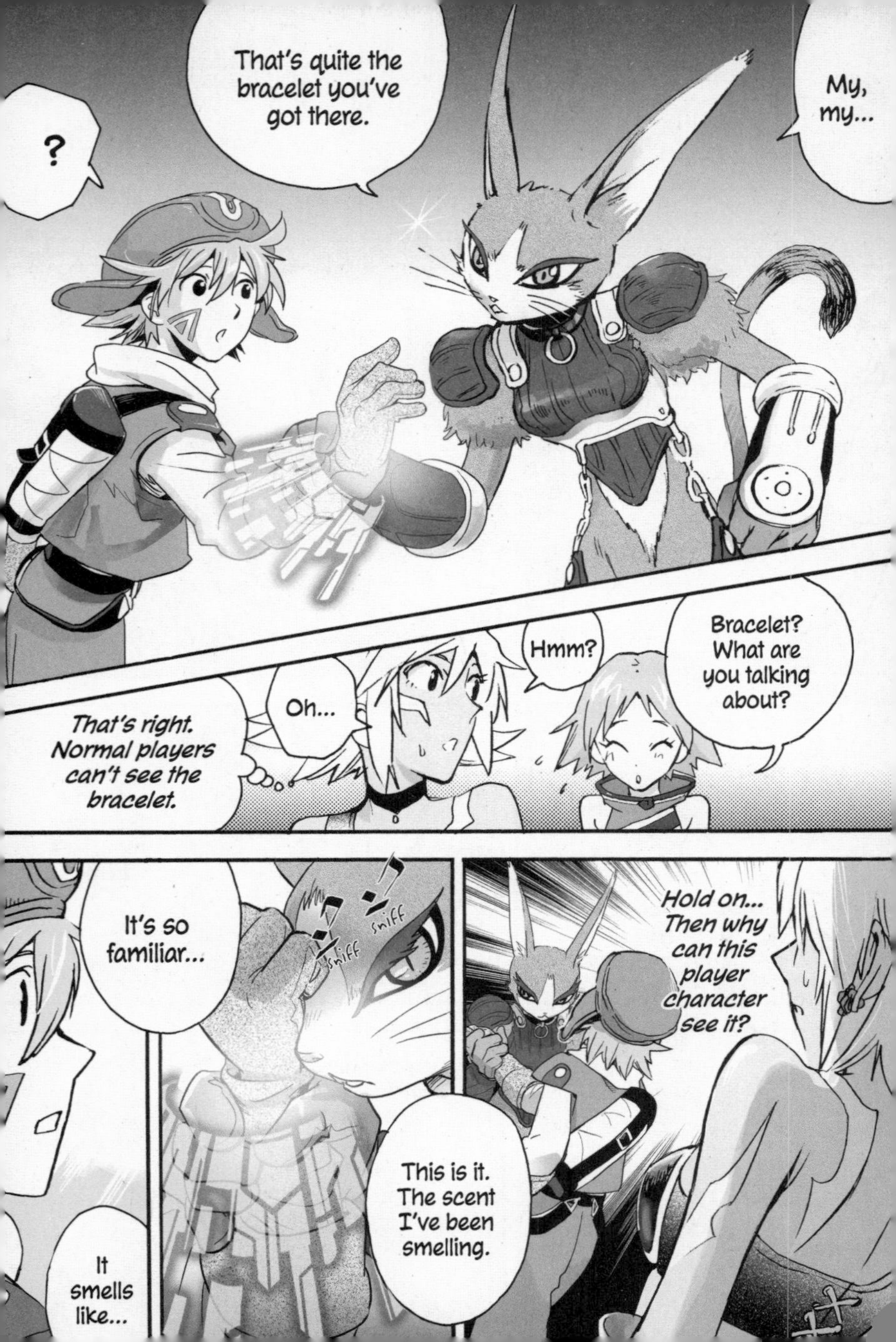
My, my...
That's quite the bracelet you've got there.
?
Bracelet? What are you talking about?
Hmm?
Oh...
That's right. Normal players can't see the bracelet.
Hold on... Then why can this player character see it?
This is it. The scent I've been smelling.
sniff
sniff
It's so familiar...
It smells like...

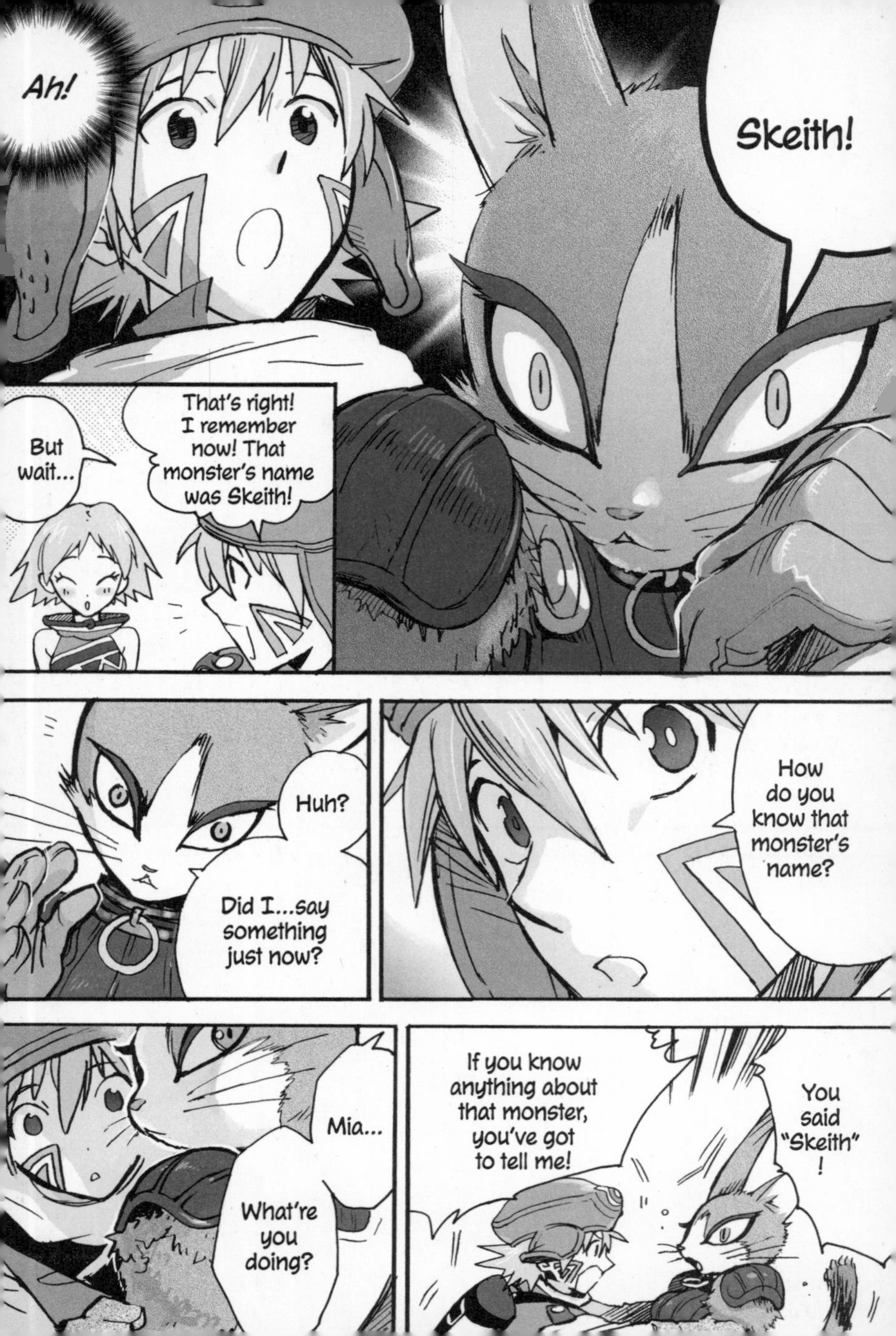
Ah!
Skeith!
That's right! I remember now! That monster's name was Skeith!
But wait...
Huh?
Did I...say something just now?
How do you know that monster's name?
You said "Skeith"!
If you know anything about that monster, you've got to tell me!
Mia...
What're you doing?

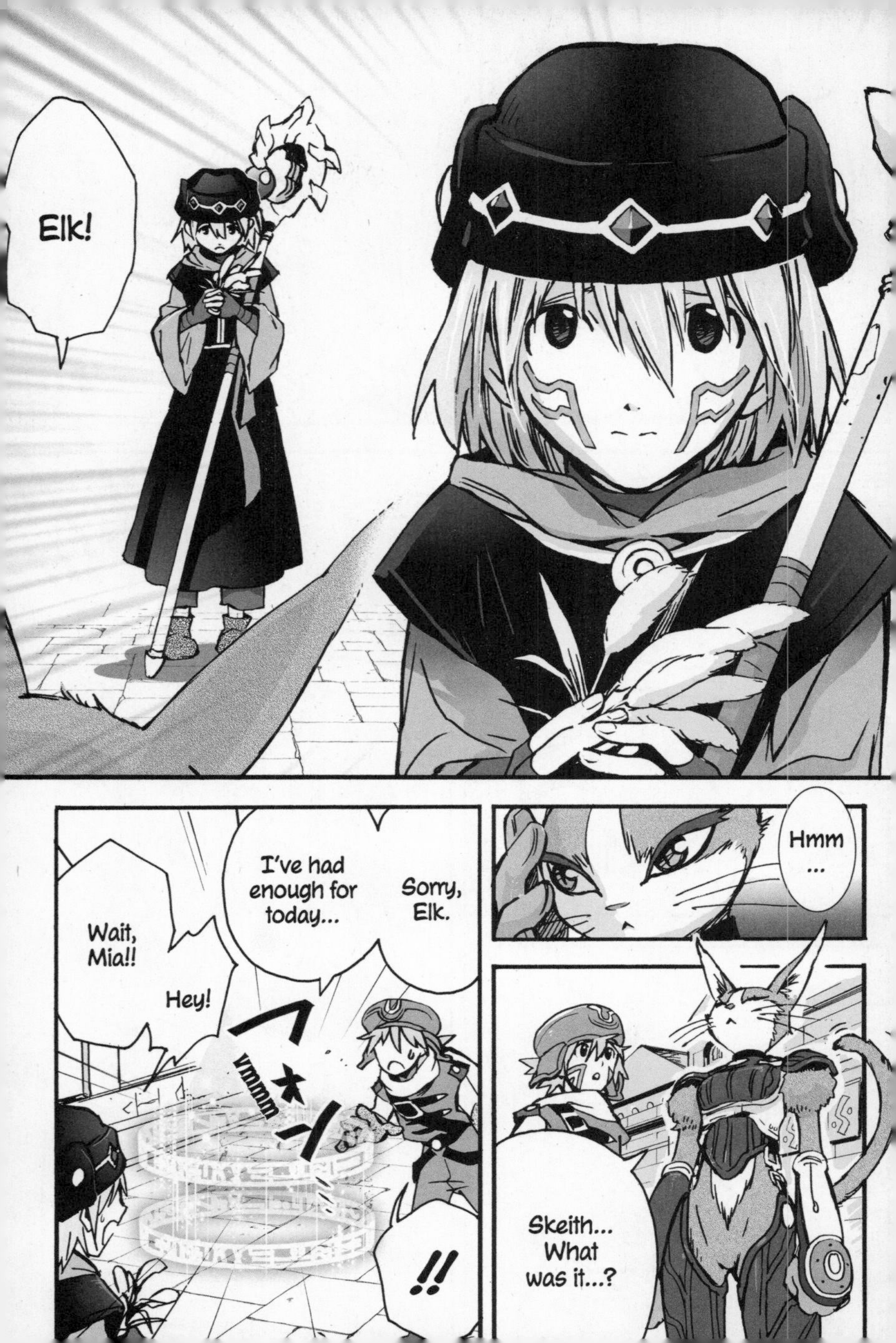
Elk!
Hmm ...
Skeith... What was it...?
Sorry, Elk.
I've had enough for today...
Hey!
Wait, Mia!!
vmmm
!!

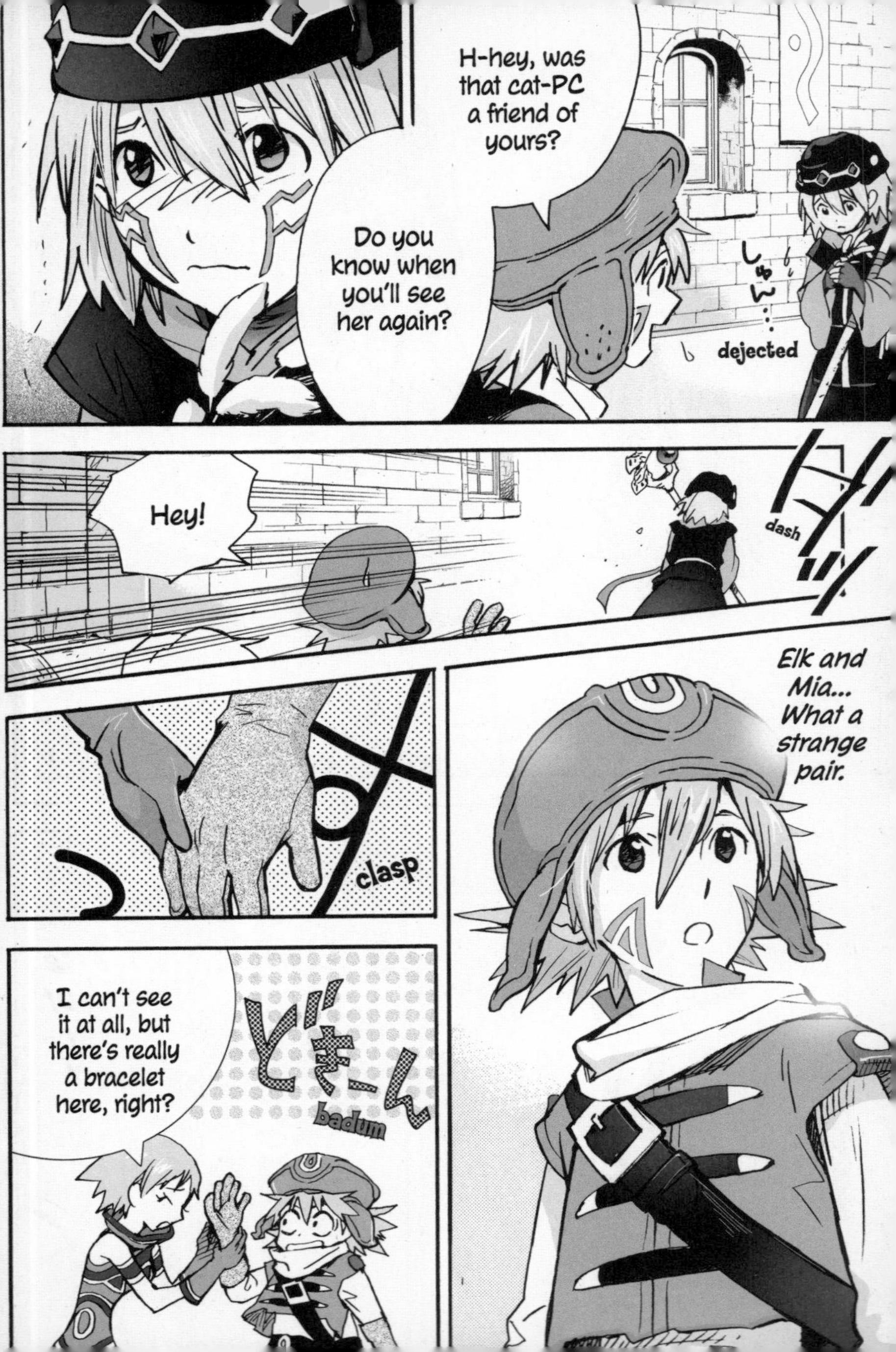
H-hey, was that cat-PC a friend of yours?
Do you know when you'll see her again?
しゅん…
dejected
ダッ
dash
Hey!
clasp
I can't see it at all, but there's really a bracelet here, right?
どきーん
badum
Elk and Mia... What a strange pair.

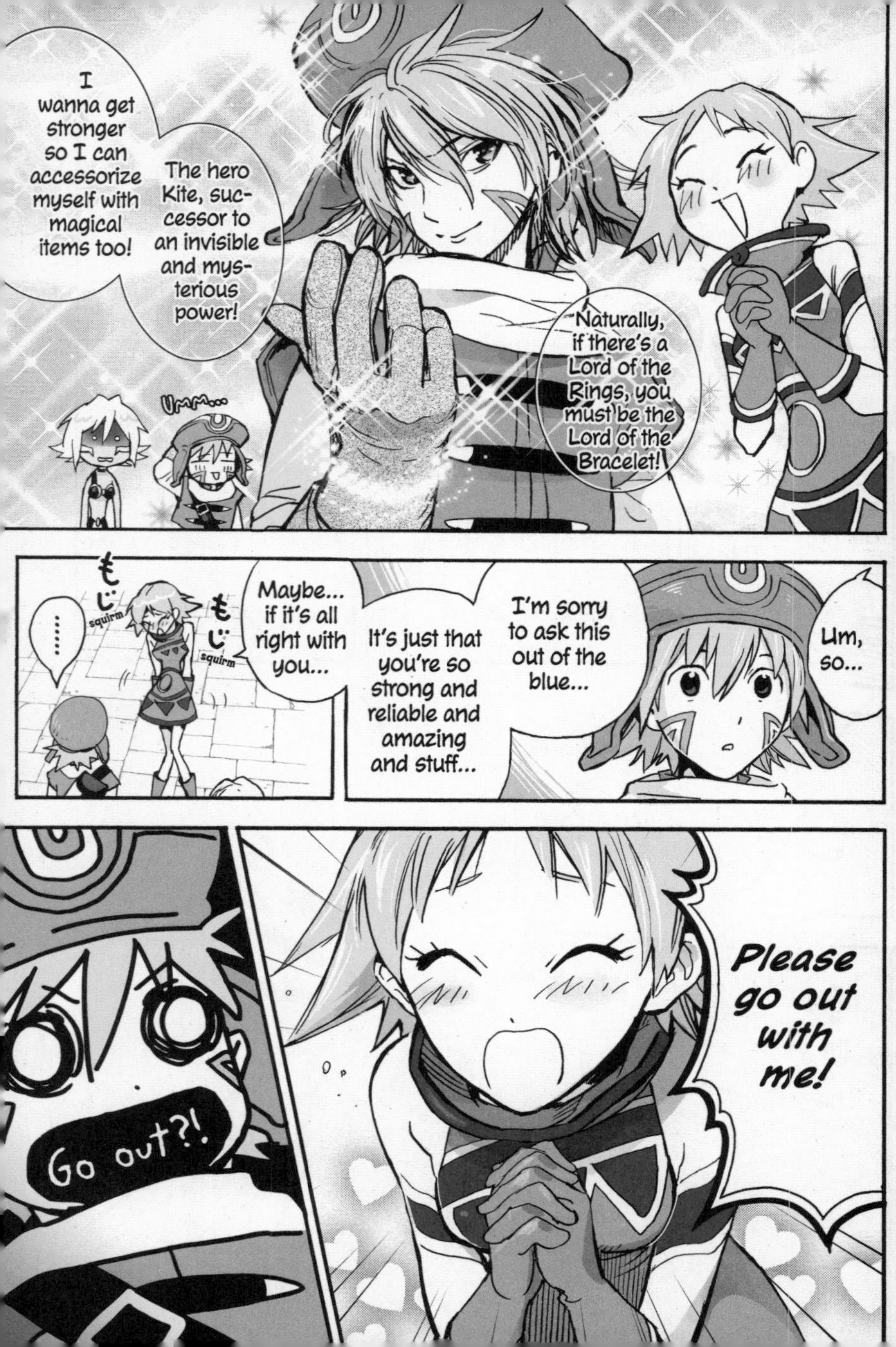
Naturally, if there's a Lord of the Rings, you must be the Lord of the Bracelet!
The hero Kite, successor to an invisible and mysterious power!
I wanna get stronger so I can accessorize myself with magical items too!
Umm...
Um, so...
I'm sorry to ask this out of the blue...
It's just that you're so strong and reliable and amazing and stuff...
Maybe... if it's all right with you...
もじ squirm
もじ squirm
......
Please go out with me!
Go out?!

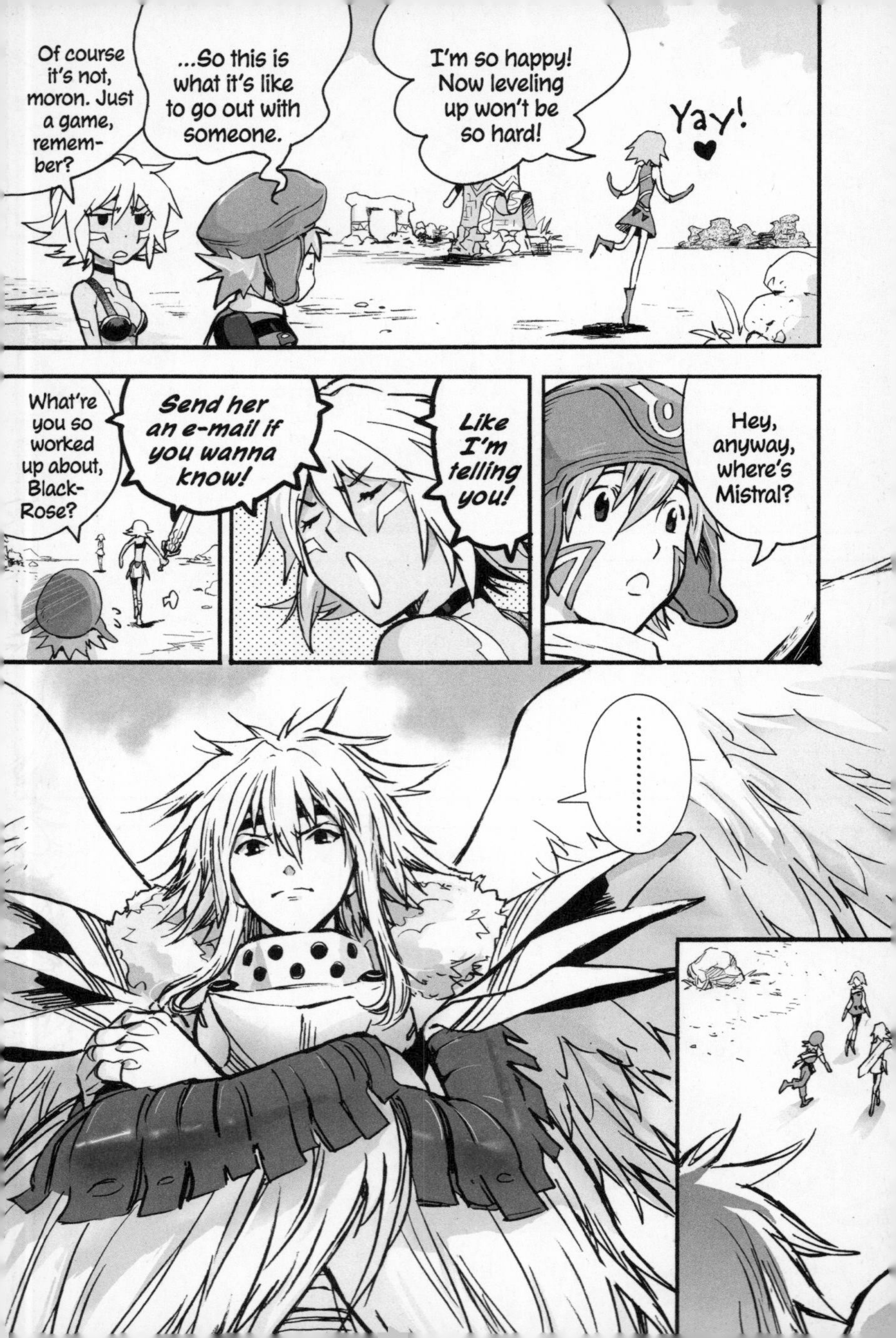
Of course it's not, moron. Just a game, remem-ber?
...So this is what it's like to go out with someone.
I'm so happy! Now leveling up won't be so hard!
Yay!
What're you so worked up about, Black-Rose?
Send her an e-mail if you wanna know!
Like I'm telling you!
Hey, anyway, where's Mistral?
....

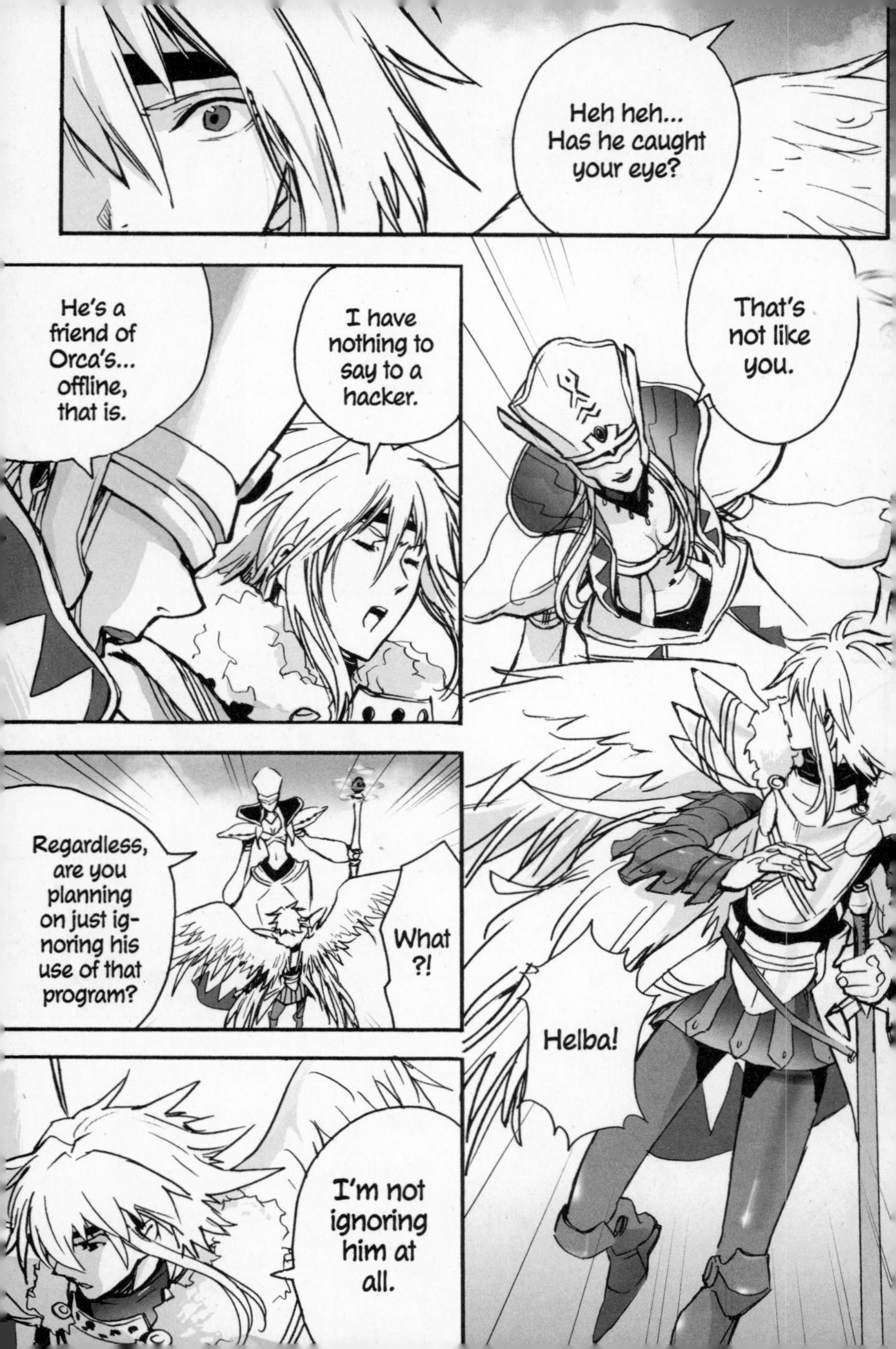
Heh heh... Has he caught your eye?
He's a friend of Orca's... offline, that is.
I have nothing to say to a hacker.
That's not like you.
Regardless, are you planning on just ignoring his use of that program?
What ?!
Helba!
I'm not ignoring him at all.

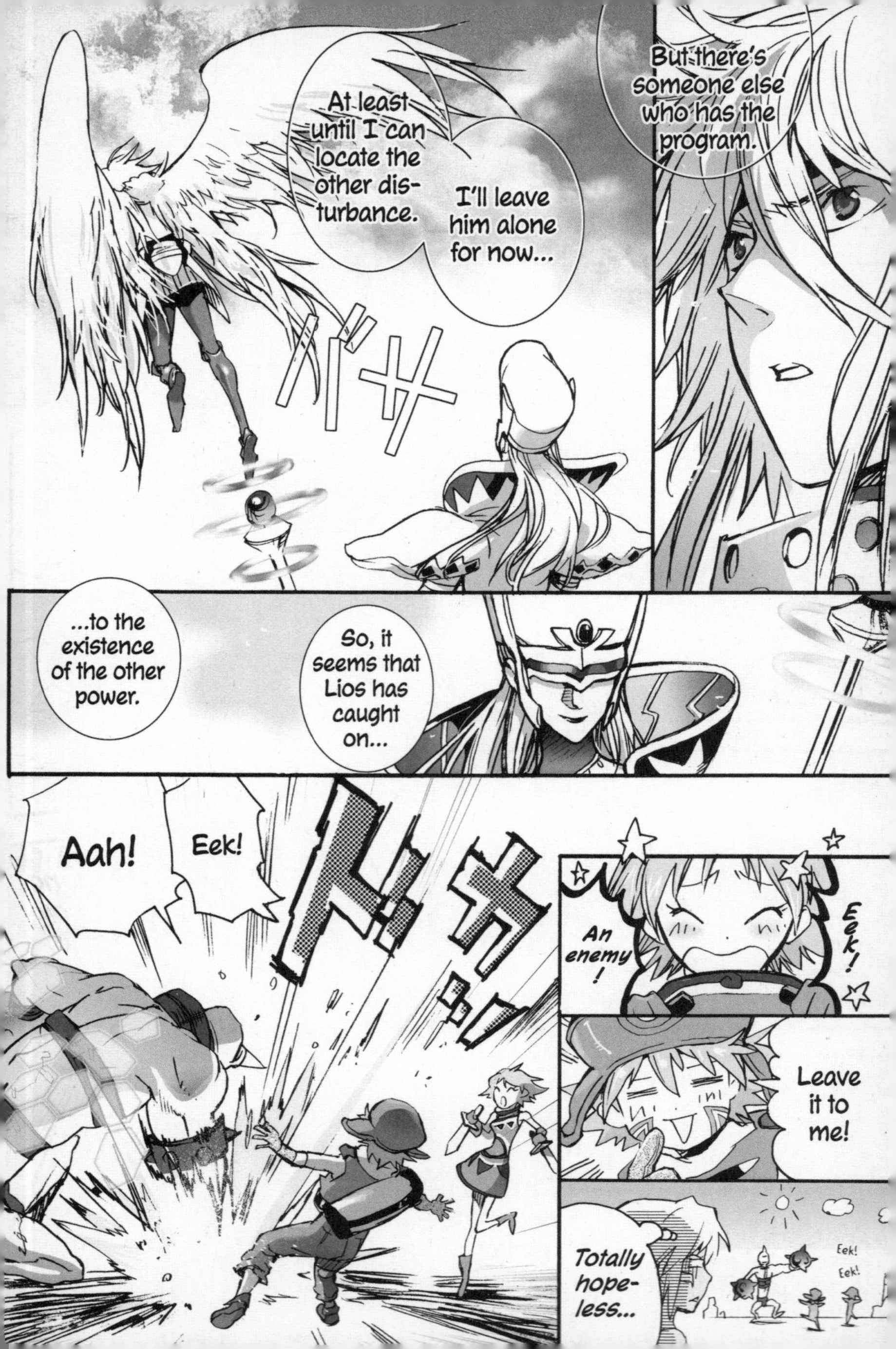

But there's someone else who has the program.
I'll leave him alone for now...
At least until I can locate the other disturbance.
So, it seems that Lios has caught on...
...to the existence of the other power.
Eek!
An enemy!
Leave it to me!
Totally hopeless...
Eek!
Eek!
Eek!
Aah!

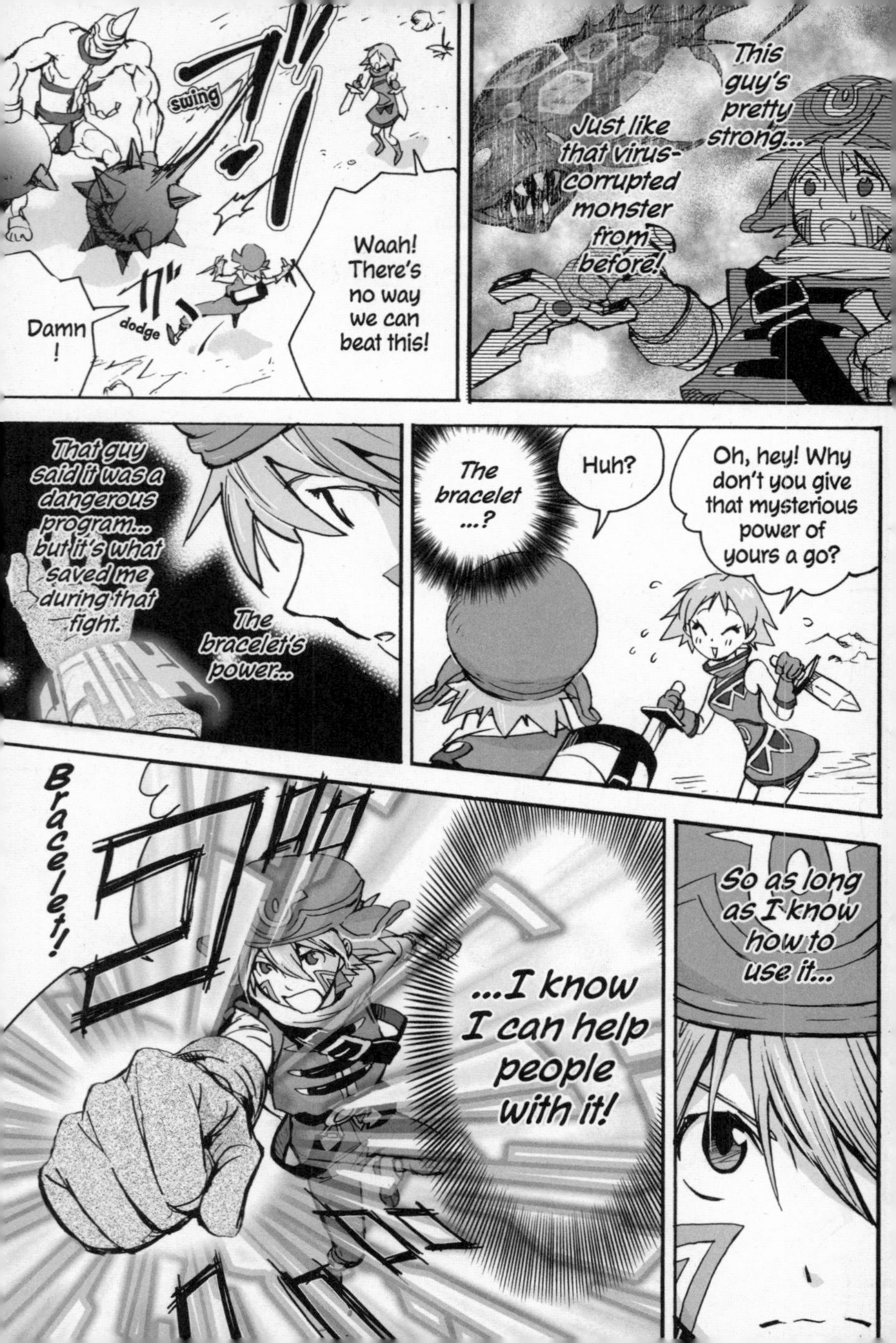
swing
Waah! There's no way we can beat this!
dodge
Damn!
This guy's pretty strong...
Just like that virus-corrupted monster from before!
That guy said it was a dangerous program... but it's what saved me during that fight.
The bracelet's power...
The bracelet ...?
Huh?
Oh, hey! Why don't you give that mysterious power of yours a go?
So as long as I know how to use it...
...I know I can help people with it!
Bracelet!

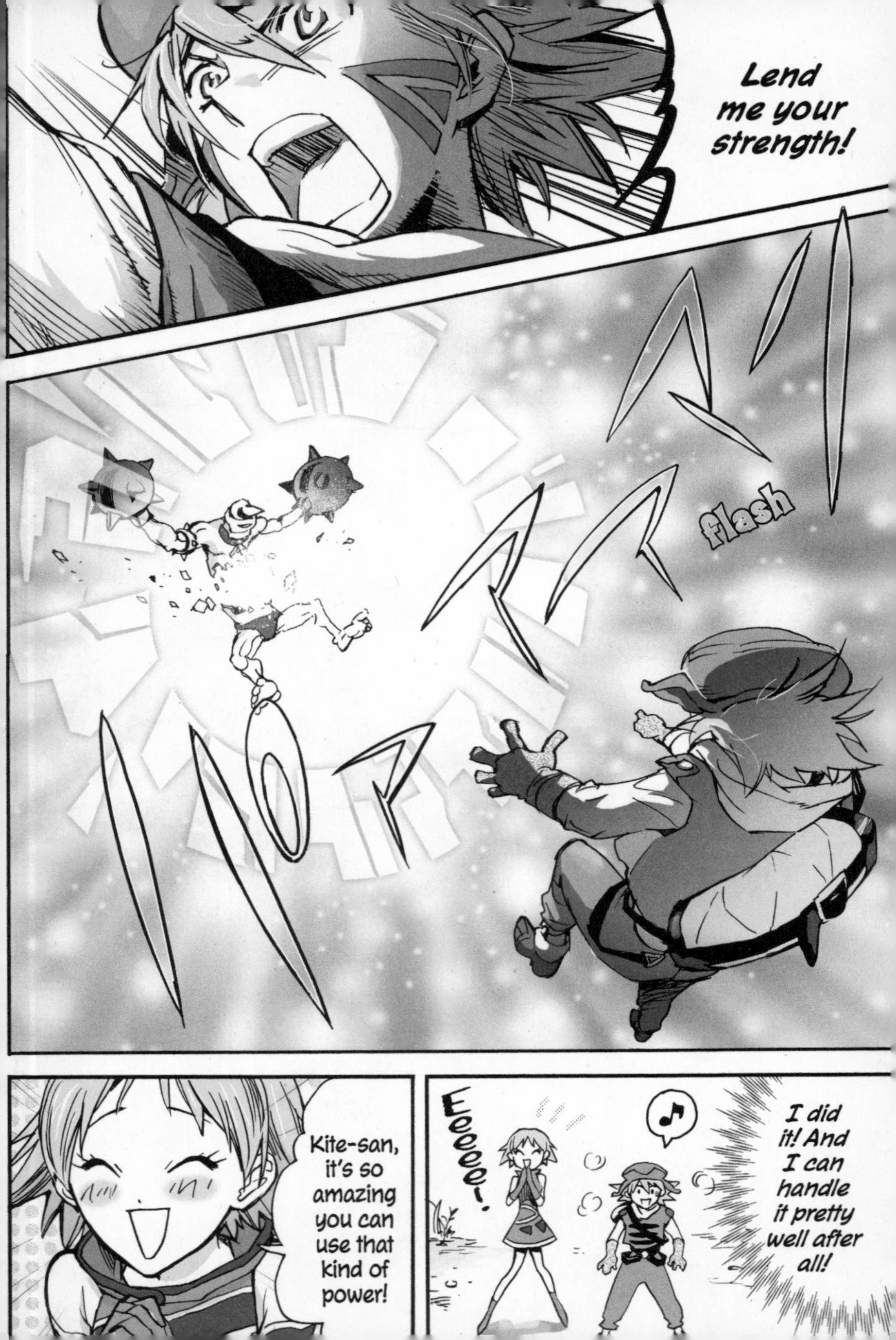

Lend me your strength!
flash
Kite-san, it's so amazing you can use that kind of power!
Eeeee!
I did it! And I can handle it pretty well after all!

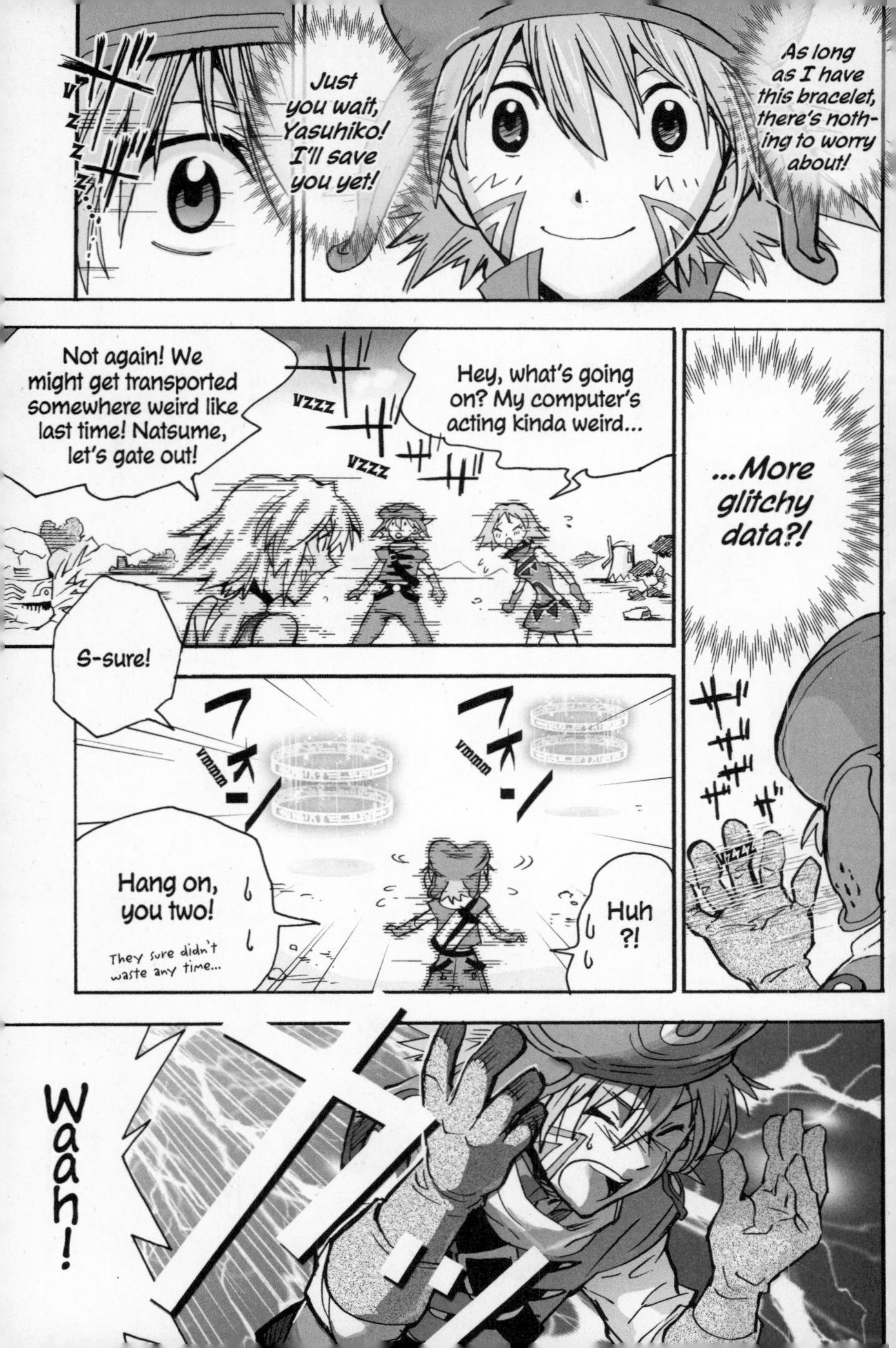

As long as I have this bracelet, there's nothing to worry about!
Just you wait, Yasuhiko! I'll save you yet!
vzzz
...More glitchy data?!
vzzz
Hey, what's going on? My computer's acting kinda weird...
vzzz
vzzz
Not again! We might get transported somewhere weird like last time! Natsume, let's gate out!
S-sure!
vmmm
vmmm
Huh?!
Hang on, you two!
They sure didn't waste any time...
Waaah!

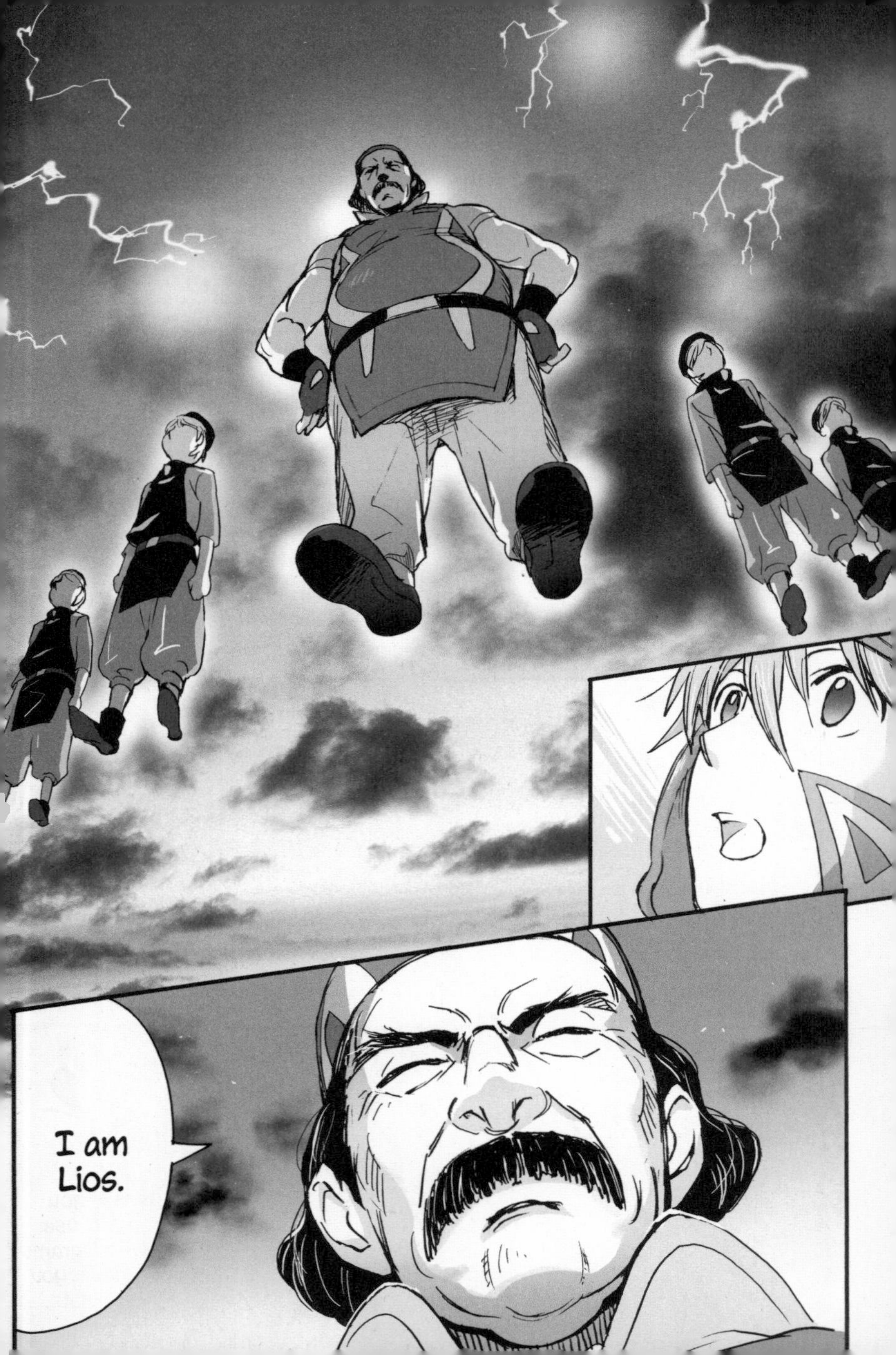
I am Lios.

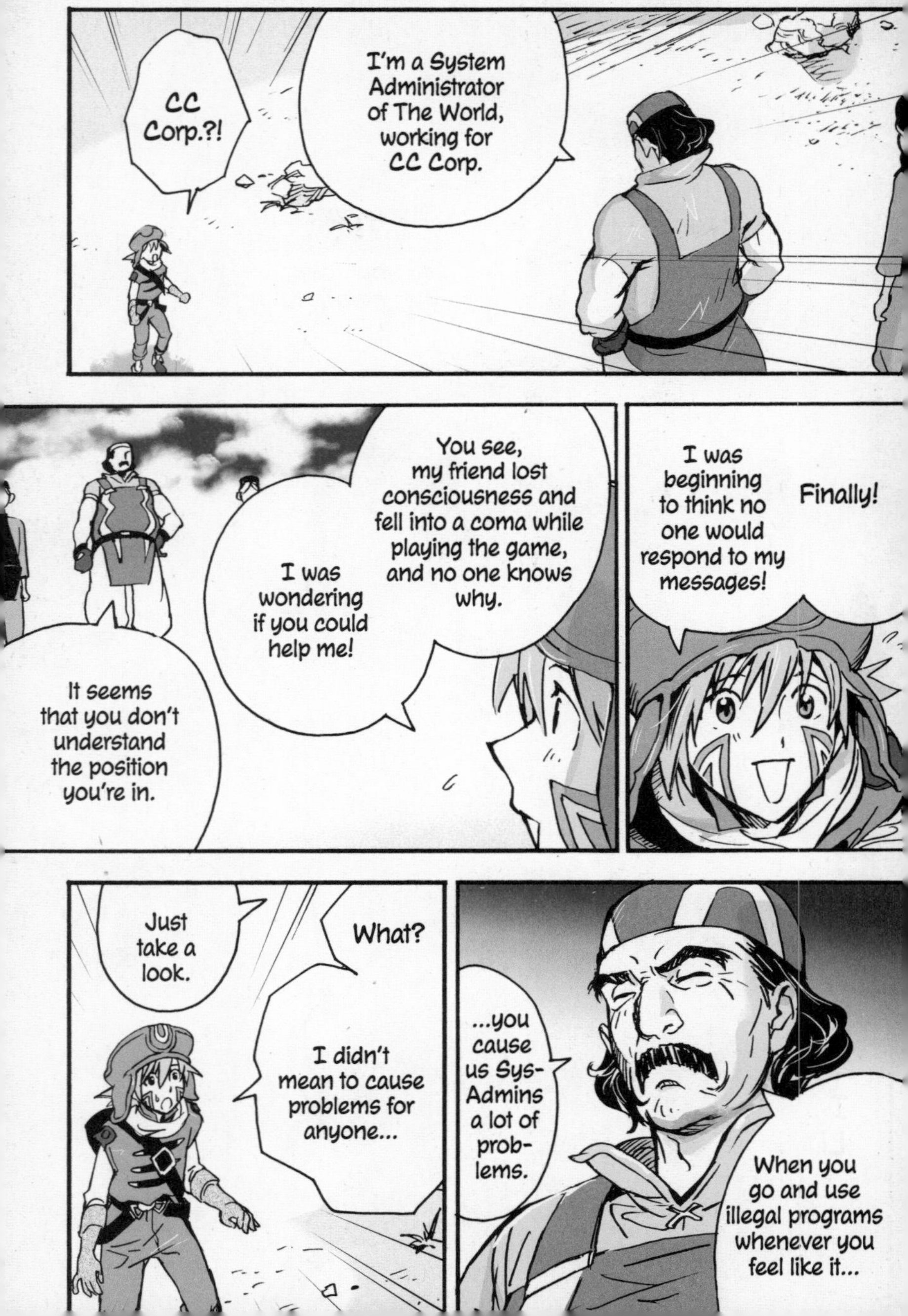

I'm a System Administrator of The World, working for CC Corp.
CC Corp.?!
Finally!
I was beginning to think no one would respond to my messages!
You see, my friend lost consciousness and fell into a coma while playing the game, and no one knows why.
I was wondering if you could help me!
It seems that you don't understand the position you're in.
When you go and use illegal programs whenever you feel like it...
...you cause us Sys-Admins a lot of prob-lems.
What?
Just take a look.
I didn't mean to cause problems for anyone...

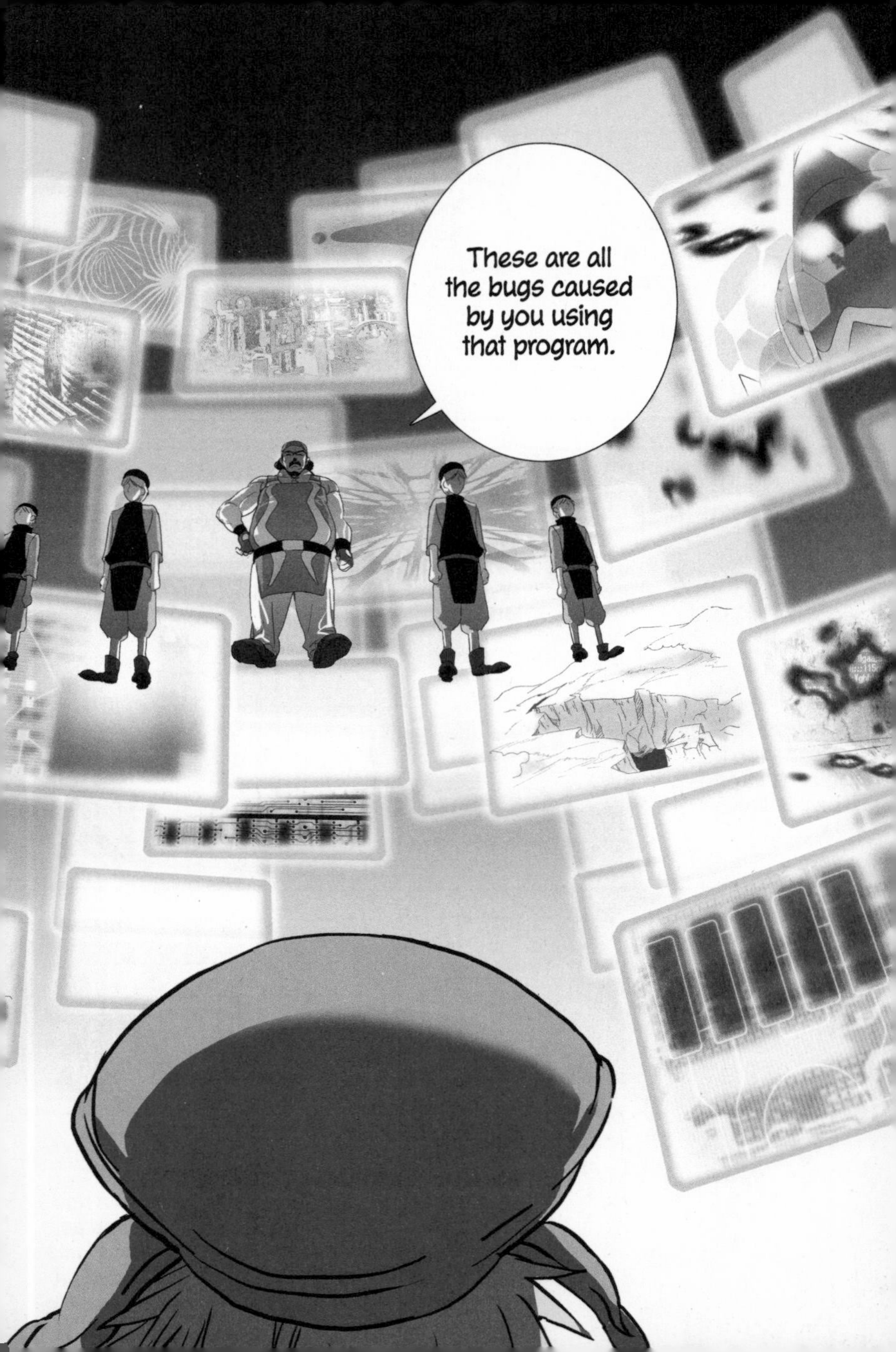
These are all the bugs caused by you using that program.

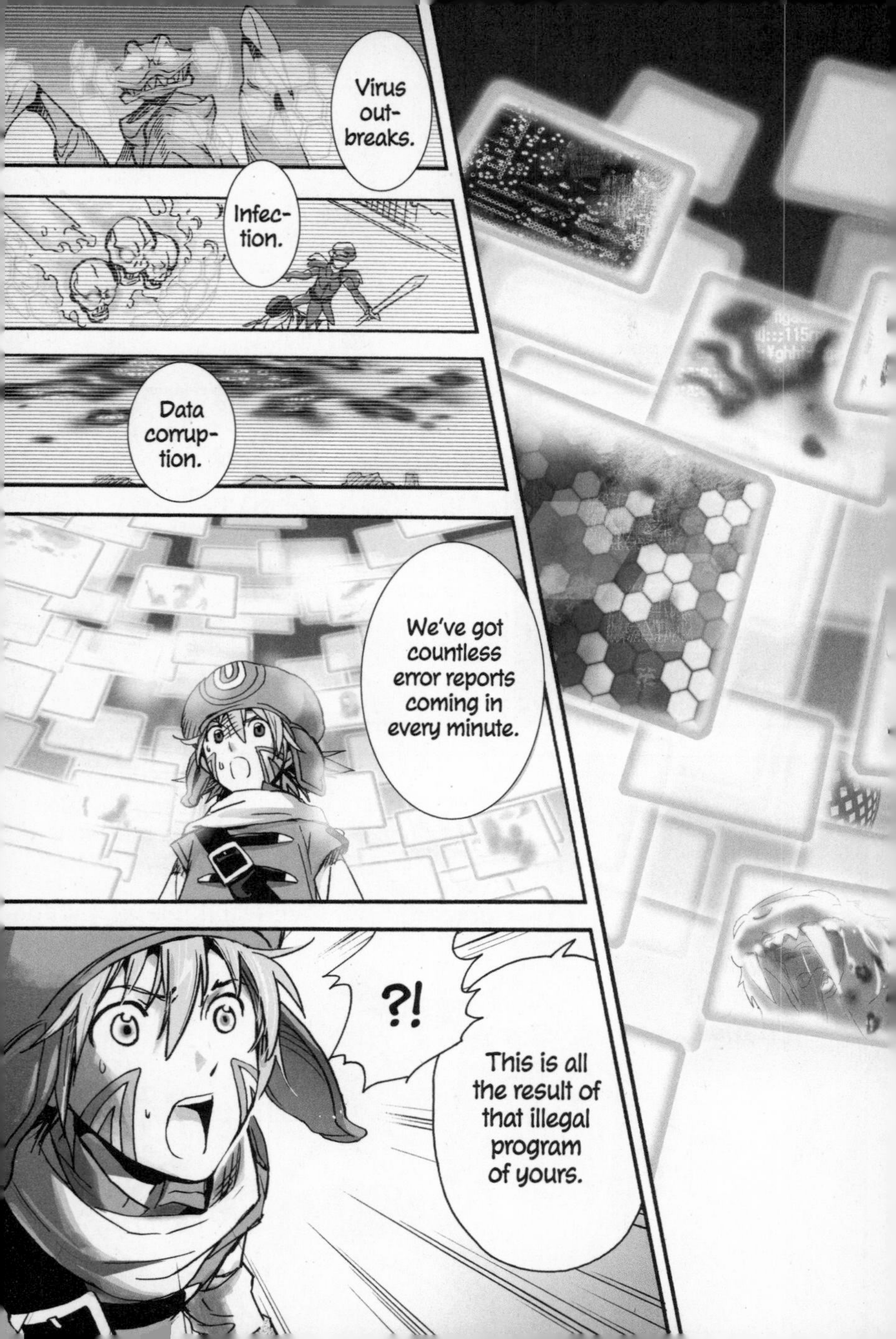
Virus out-breaks.
Infec-tion.
Data corrup-tion.
We've got countless error reports coming in every minute.
?!
This is all the result of that illegal program of yours.

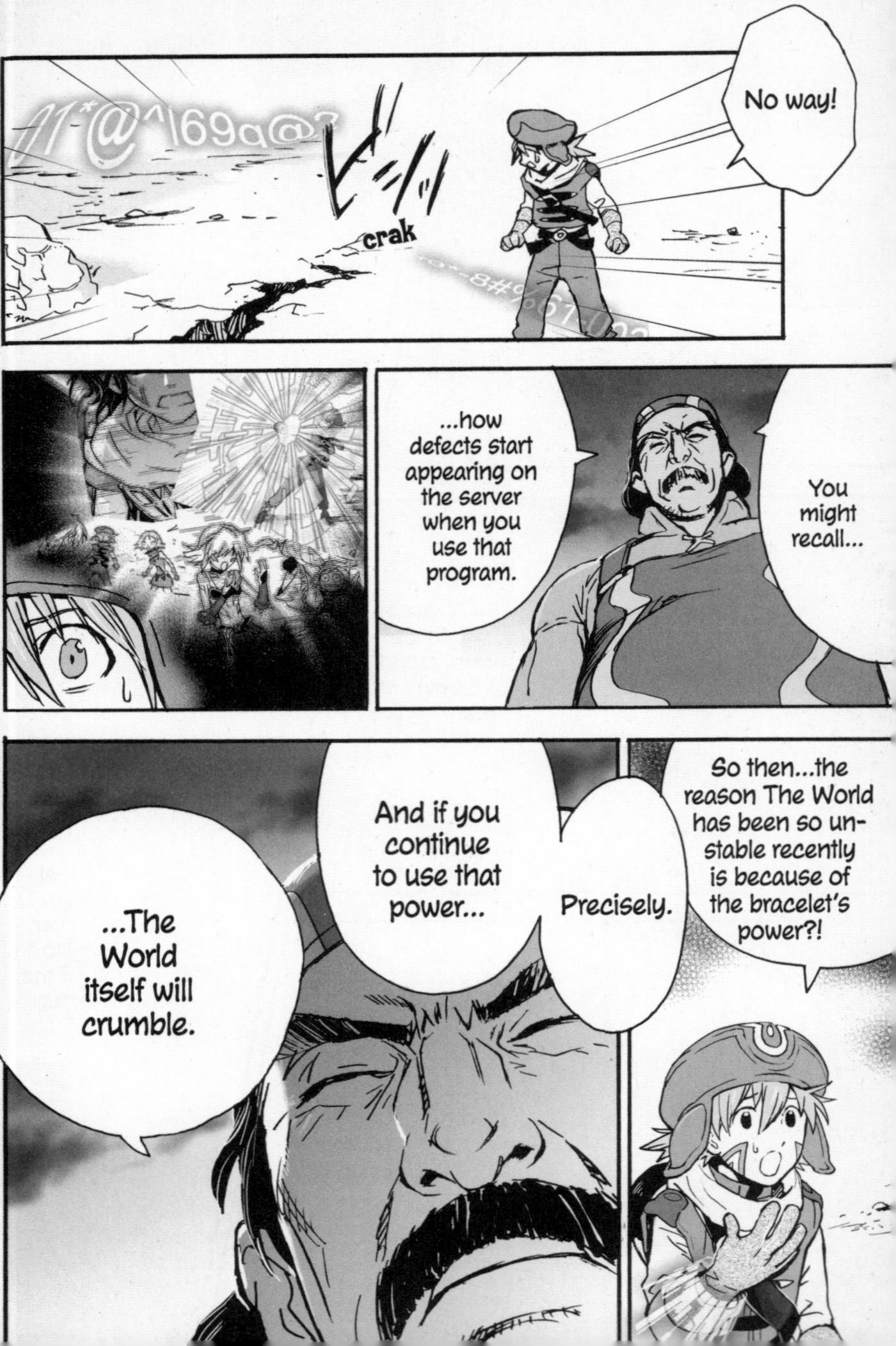
No way!
crak
You might recall...
...how defects start appearing on the server when you use that program.
So then...the reason The World has been so unstable recently is because of the bracelet's power?!
Precisely.
And if you continue to use that power...
...The World itself will crumble.

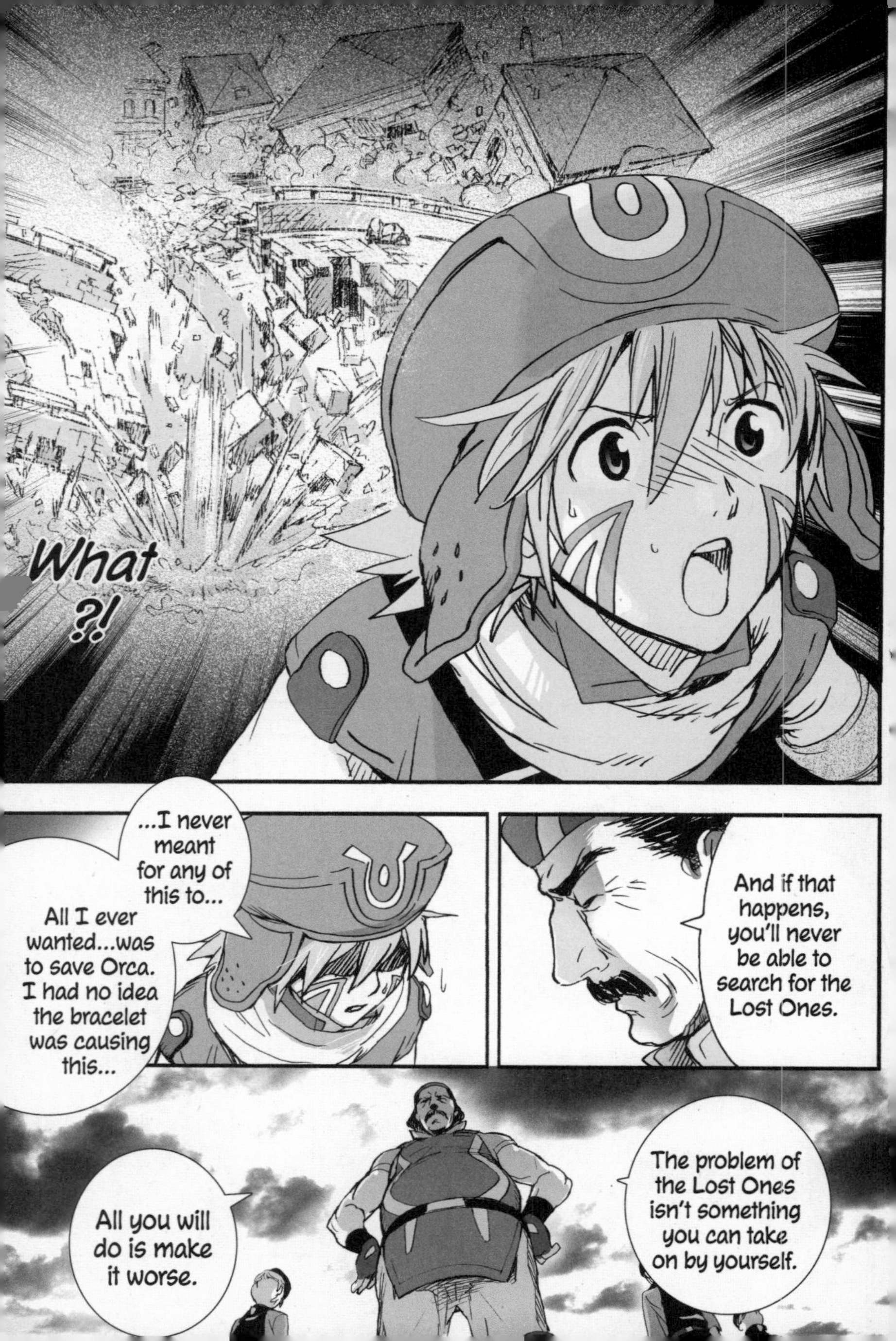
What?!
...I never meant for any of this to...
All I ever wanted...was to save Orca. I had no idea the bracelet was causing this...
And if that happens, you'll never be able to search for the Lost Ones.
The problem of the Lost Ones isn't something you can take on by yourself.
All you will do is make it worse.

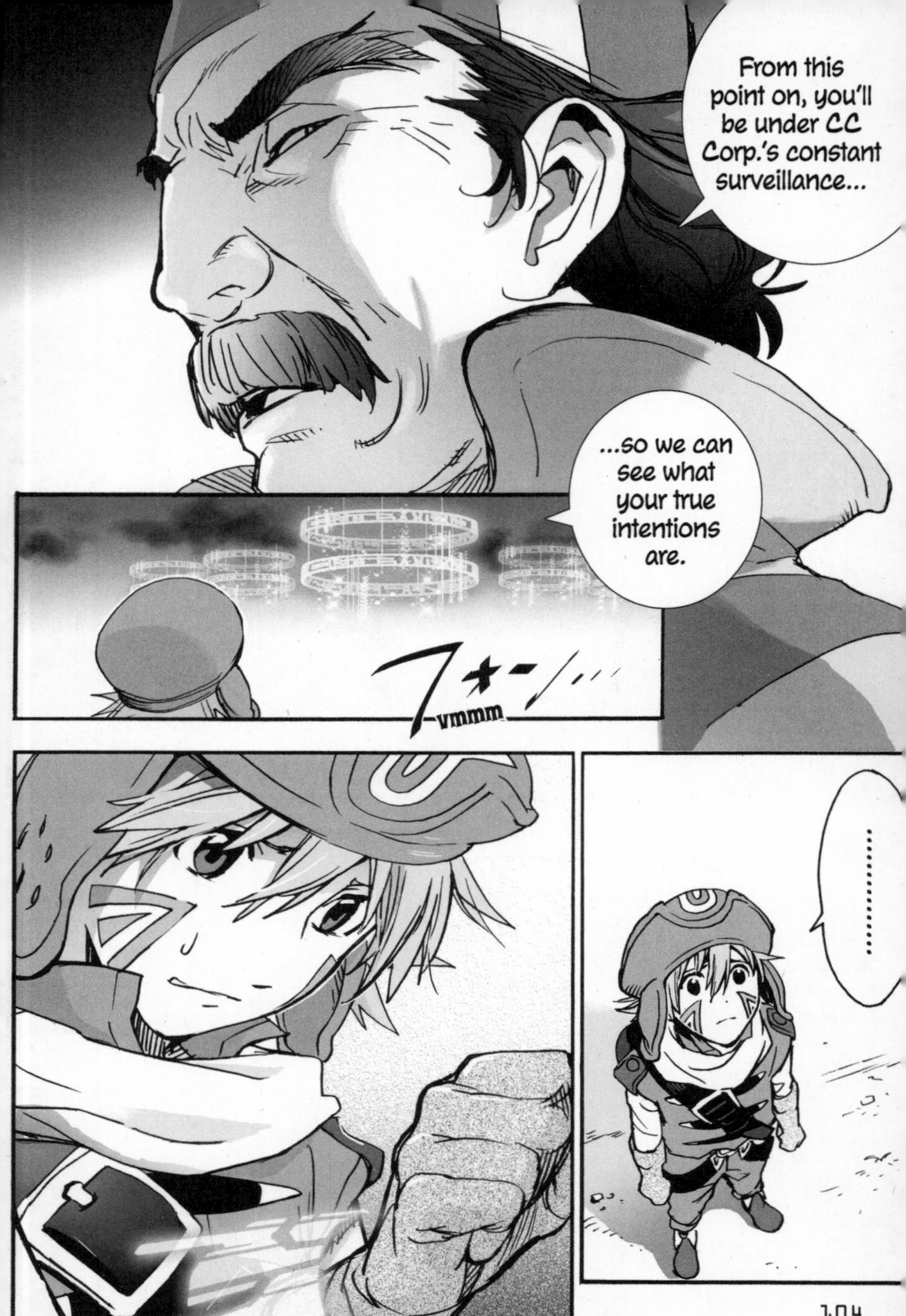
From this point on, you'll be under CC Corp.'s constant surveillance...
...so we can see what your true intentions are.
フォーン…
vmmm
......

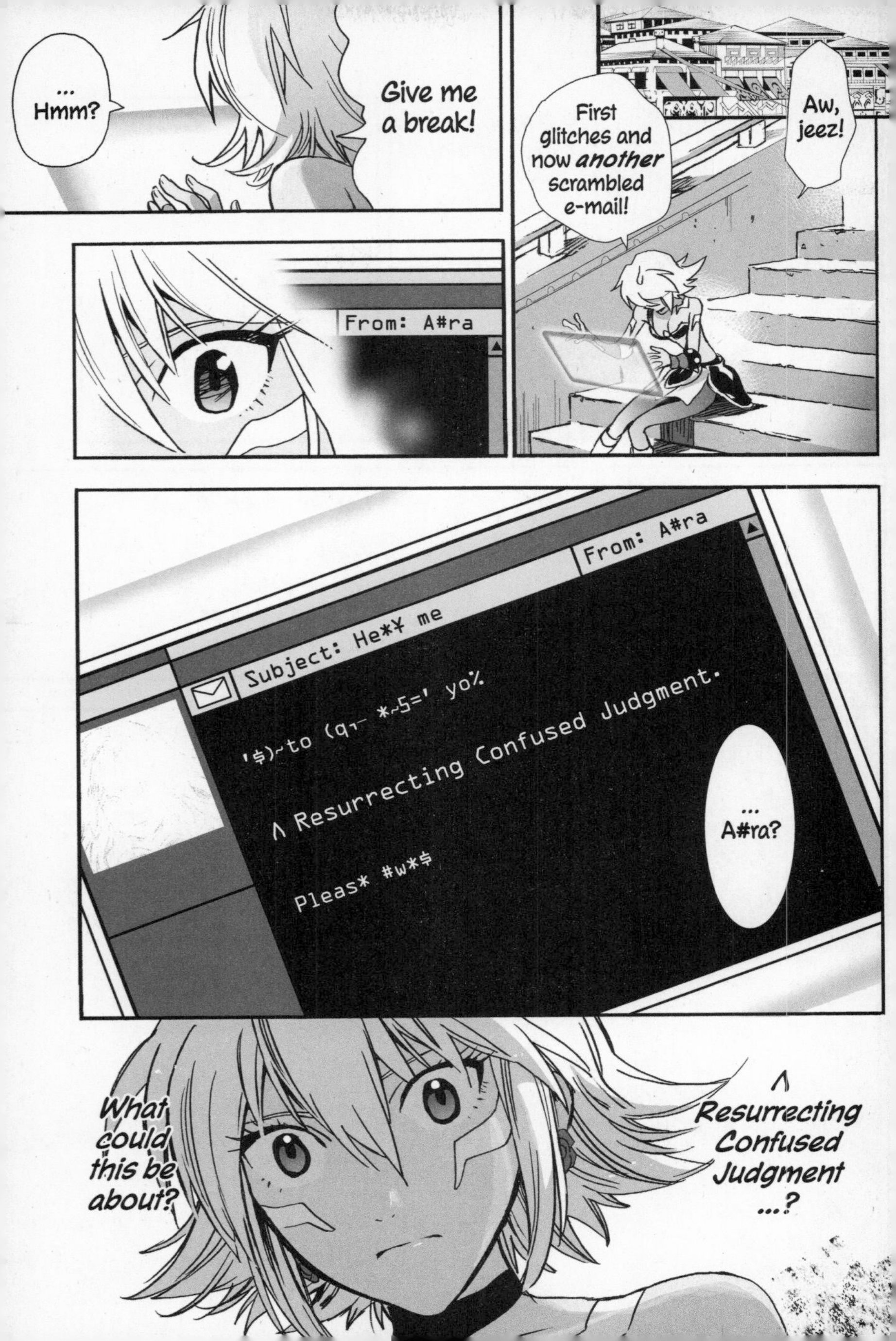
Aw, jeez!
First glitches and now another scrambled e-mail!
Give me a break!
... Hmm?
From: A#ra
From: A#ra
Subject: He*¥ me
'$)~to (q¬ *~5=' yo%
^ Resurrecting Confused Judgment.
Pleas* #w*$
... A#ra?
^ Resurrecting Confused Judgment ...?
What could this be about?

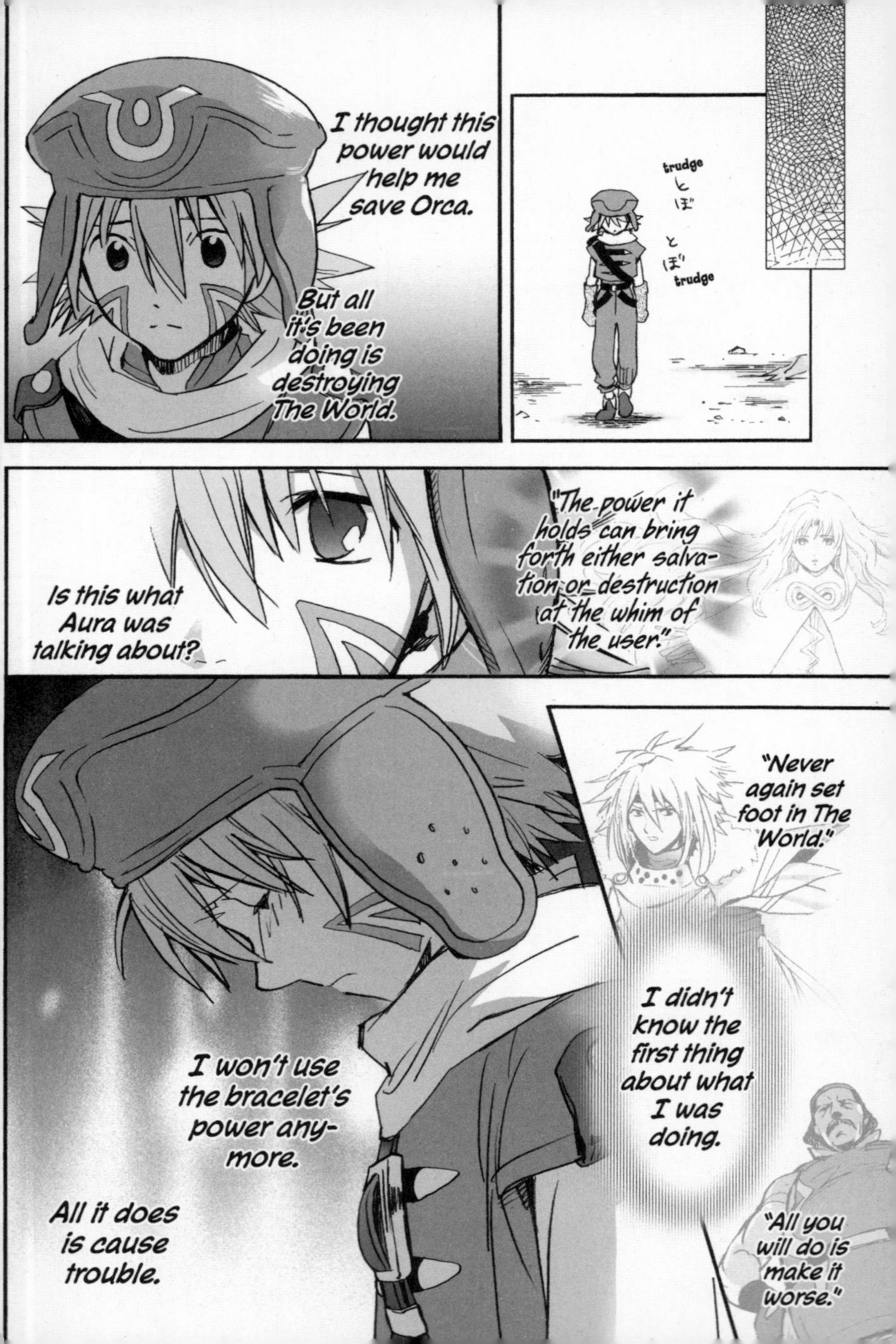
trudge
とぼ
とぼ
trudge
I thought this power would help me save Orca.
But all it's been doing is destroying The World.
"The power it holds can bring forth either salvation or destruction at the whim of the user."
Is this what Aura was talking about?
"Never again set foot in The World."
I didn't know the first thing about what I was doing.
"All you will do is make it worse."
I won't use the bracelet's power anymore.
All it does is cause trouble.

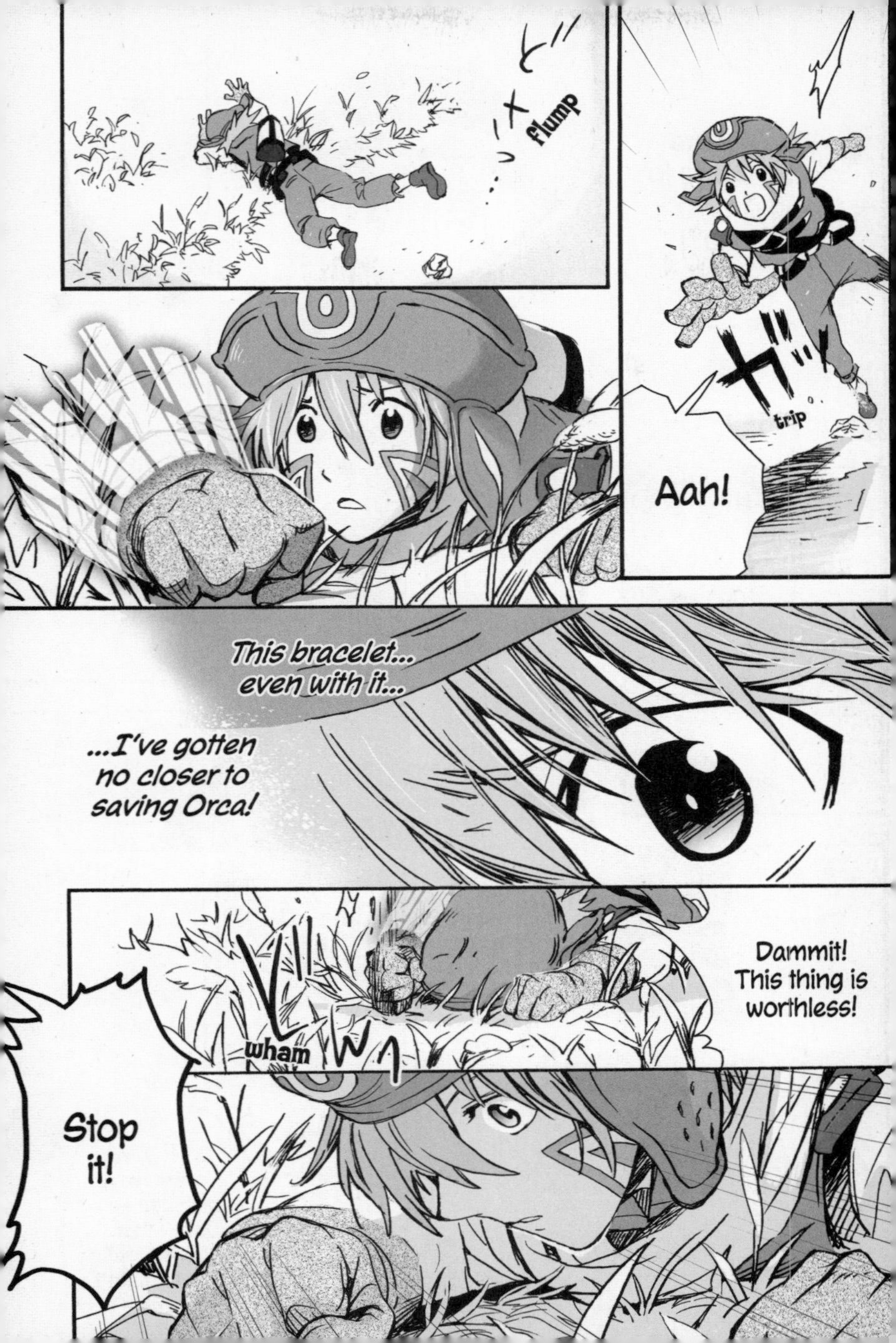
trip
Aah!
flump
This bracelet... even with it...
...I've gotten no closer to saving Orca!
Dammit! This thing is worthless!
wham
Stop it!

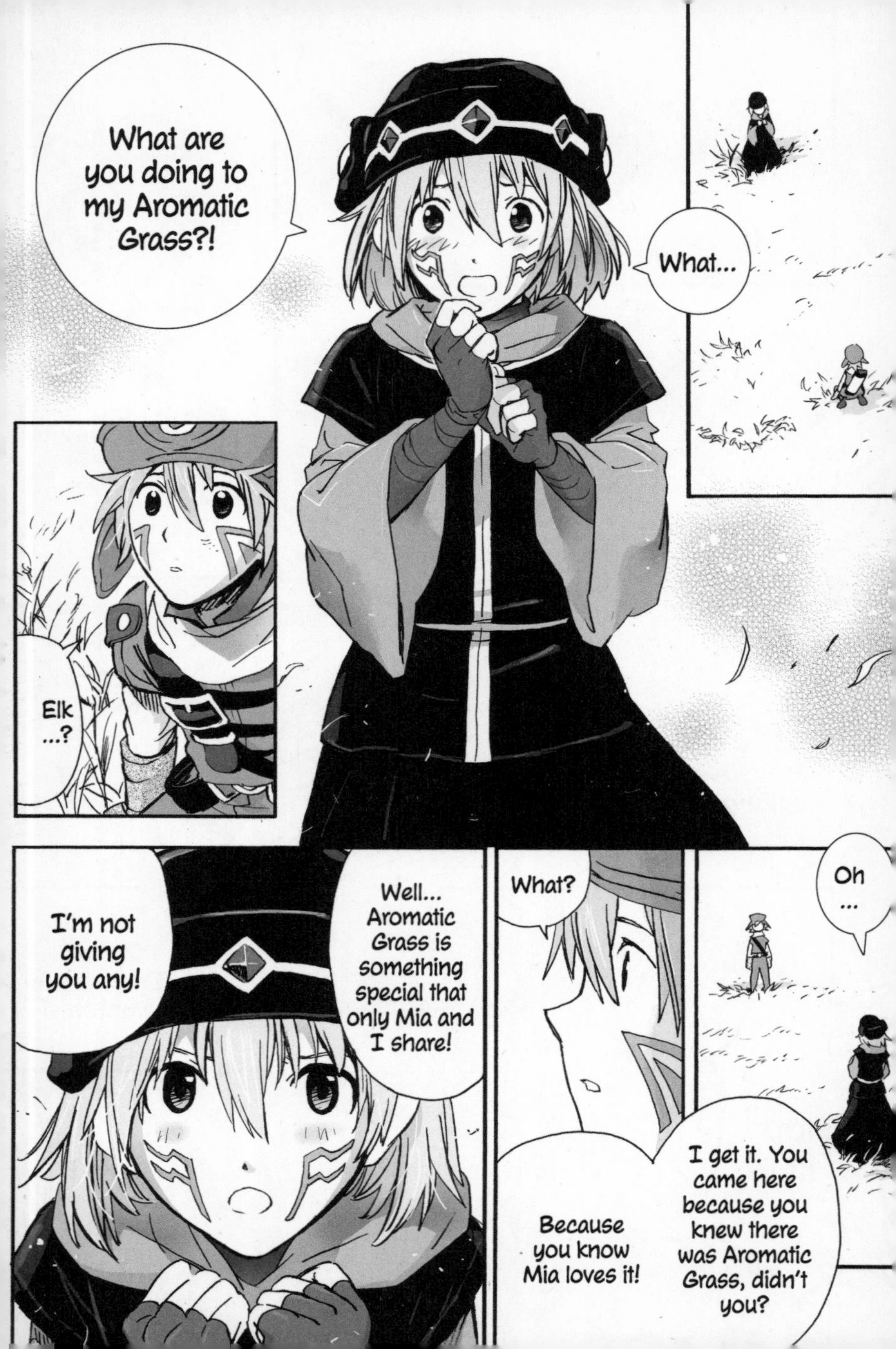
What...
What are you doing to my Aromatic Grass?!
Elk ...?
Oh ...
I get it. You came here because you knew there was Aromatic Grass, didn't you?
Because you know Mia loves it!
What?
Well... Aromatic Grass is something special that only Mia and I share!
I'm not giving you any!

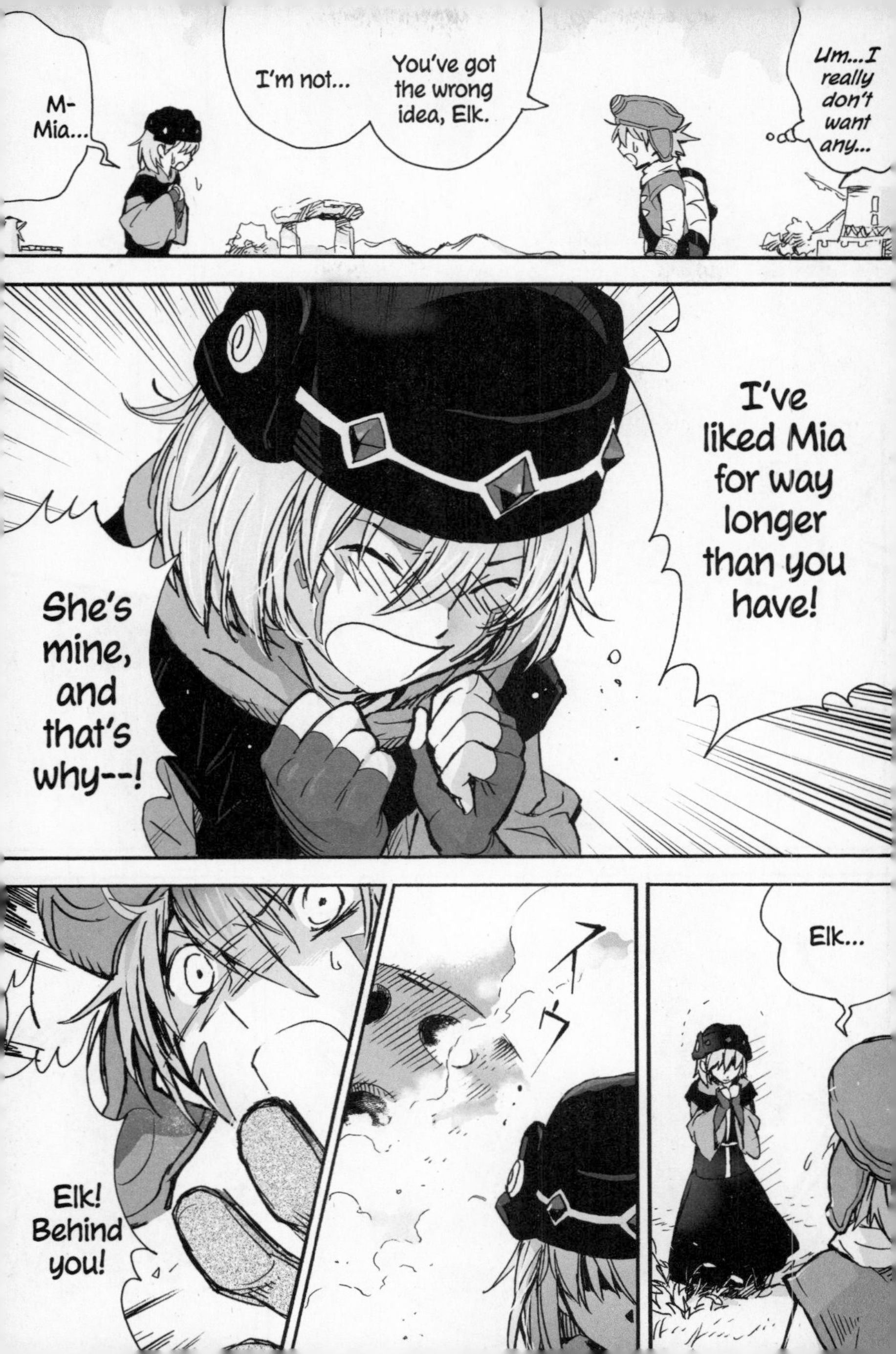

Um...I really don't want any...
You've got the wrong idea, Elk.
I'm not...
M-Mia...
I've liked Mia for way longer than you have!
She's mine, and that's why--!
Elk...
Elk! Behind you!

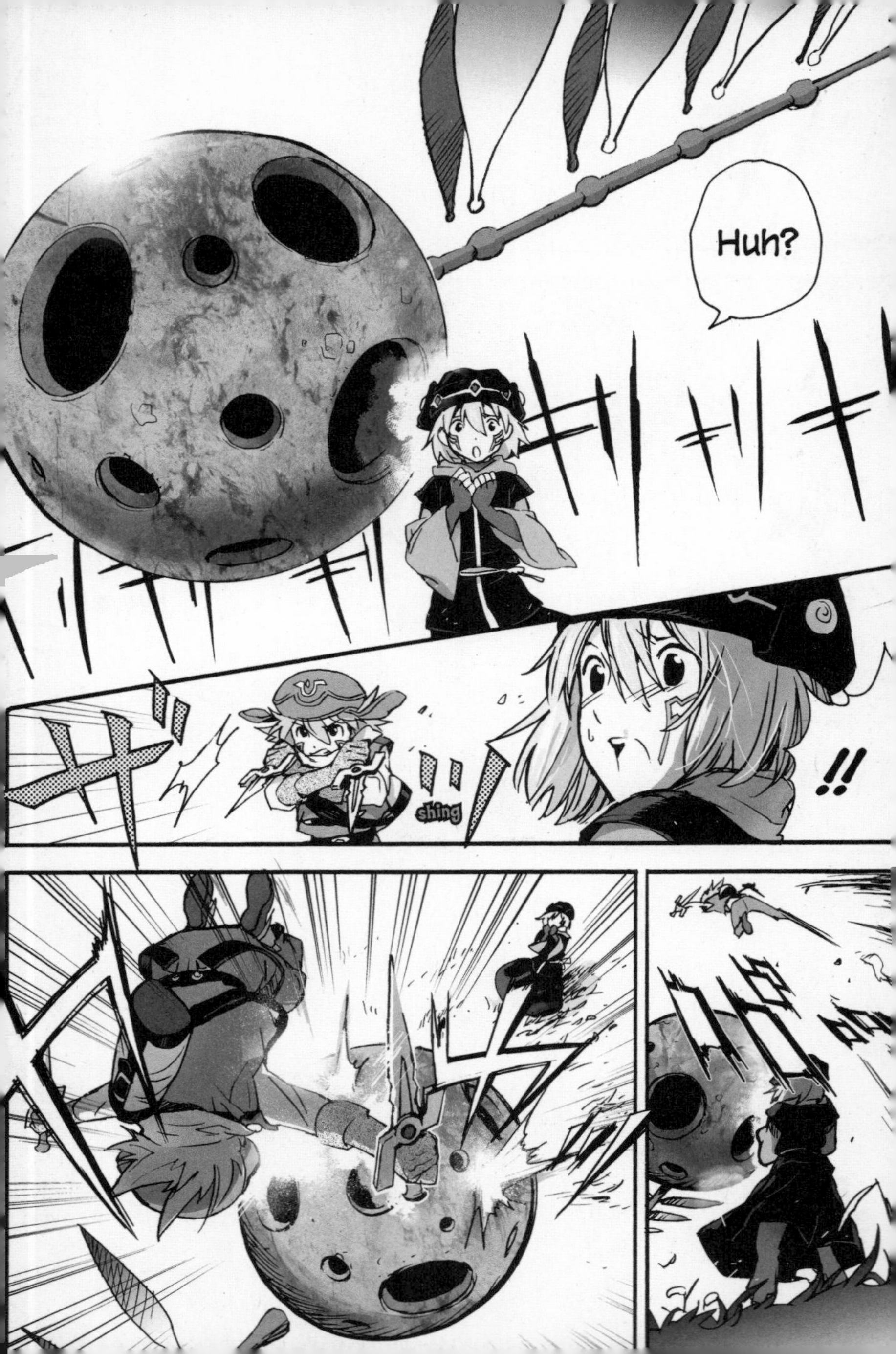
Huh?
!!
shing

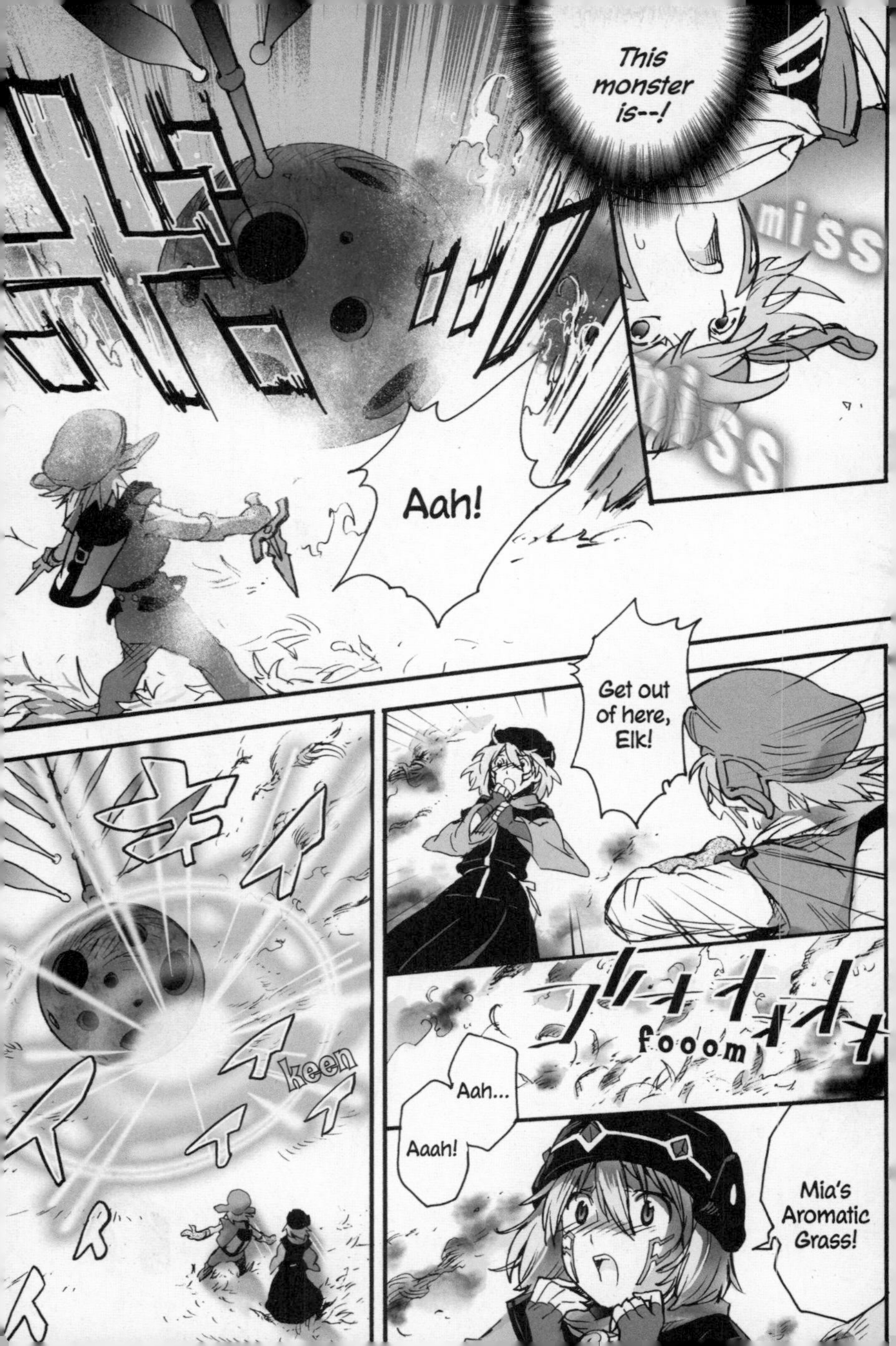
This monster is--!
miss
Aah!
Get out of here, Elk!
fooom
Aah...
Aaah!
Mia's Aromatic Grass!
keen

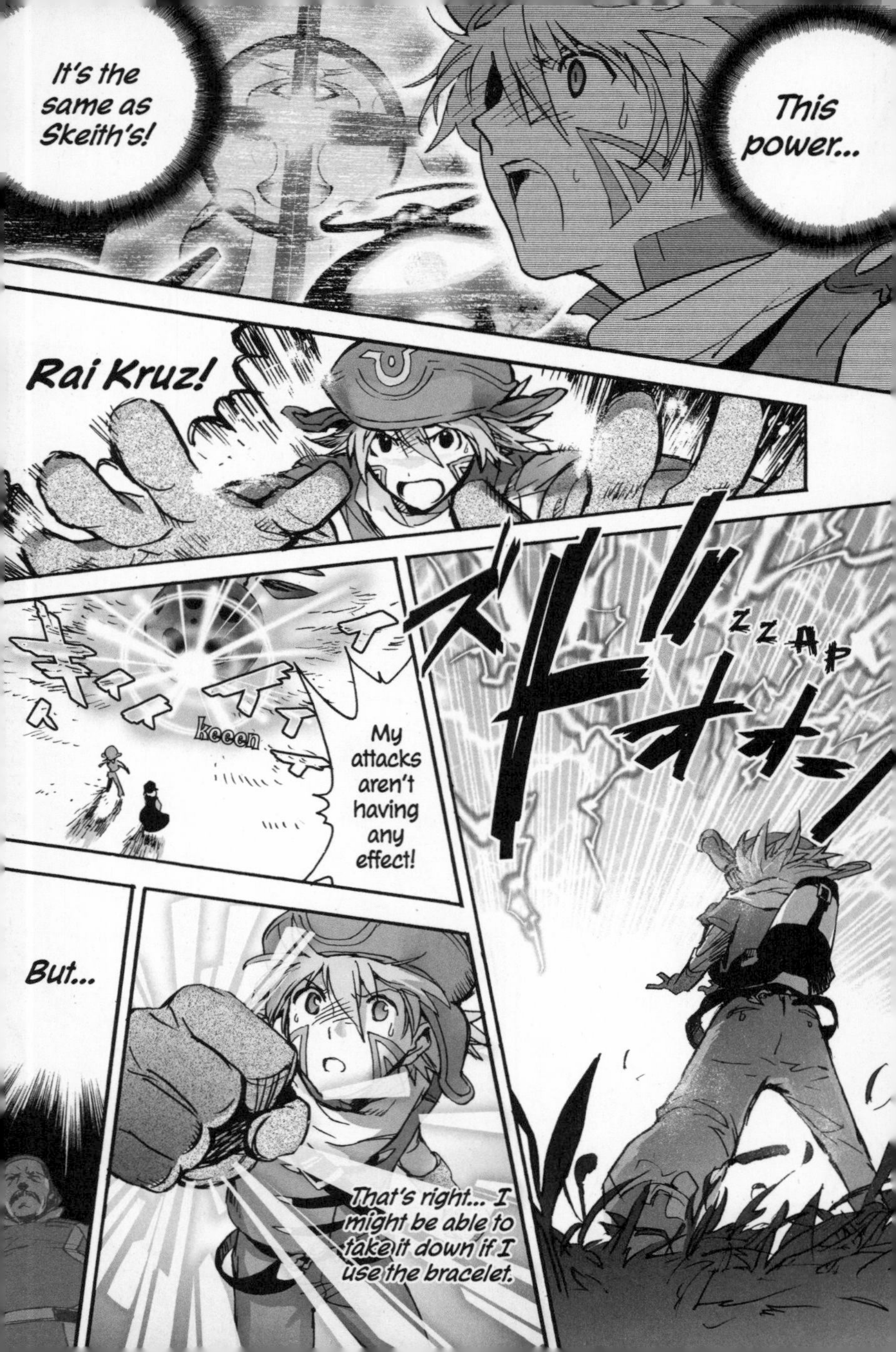
This power...
It's the same as Skeith's!
Rai Kruz!
ZZAP
keeen
My attacks aren't having any effect!
But...
That's right... I might be able to take it down if I use the bracelet.

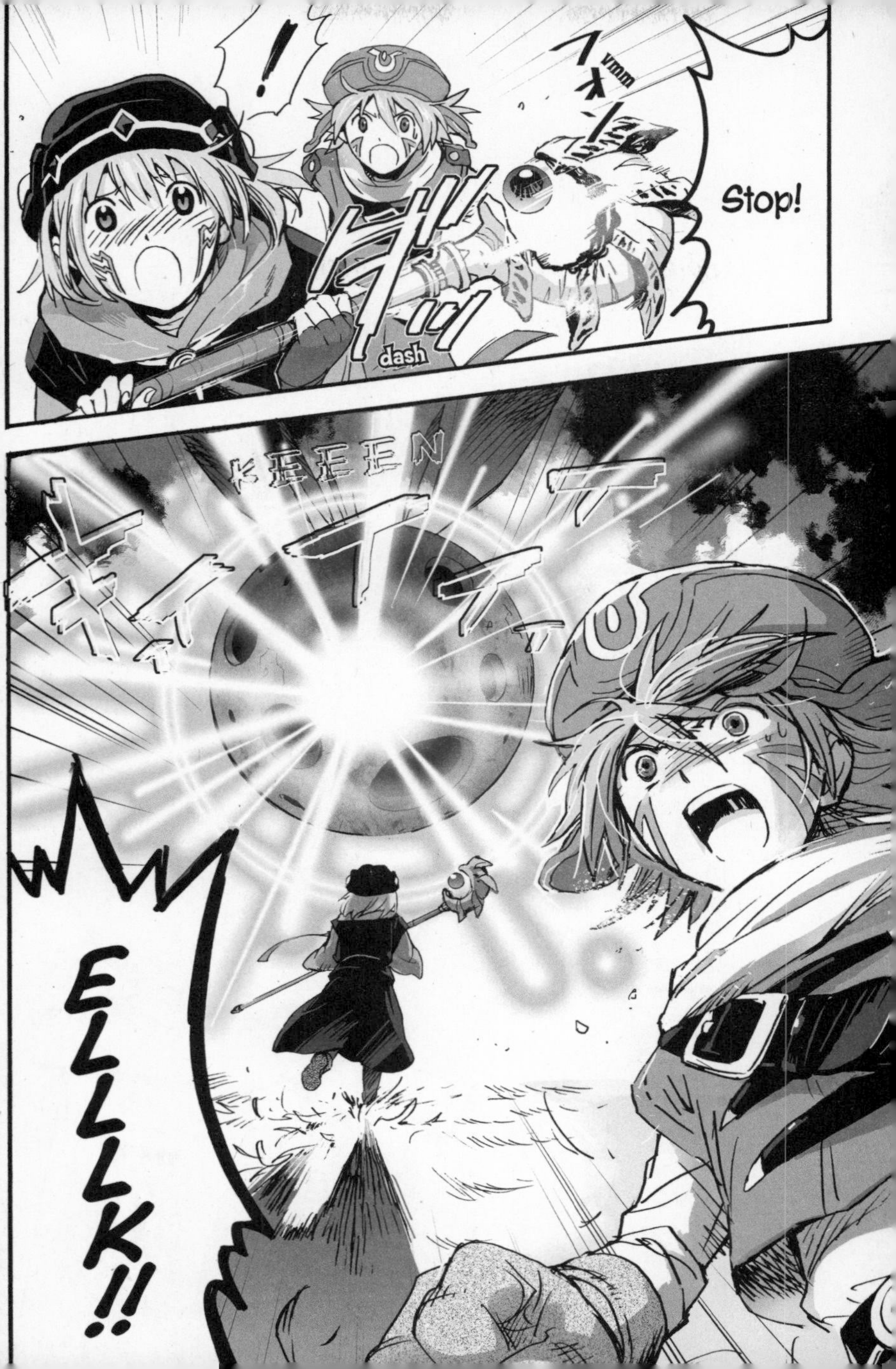

Stop!
vmm
!
dash
KEEEN
ELLLK!!

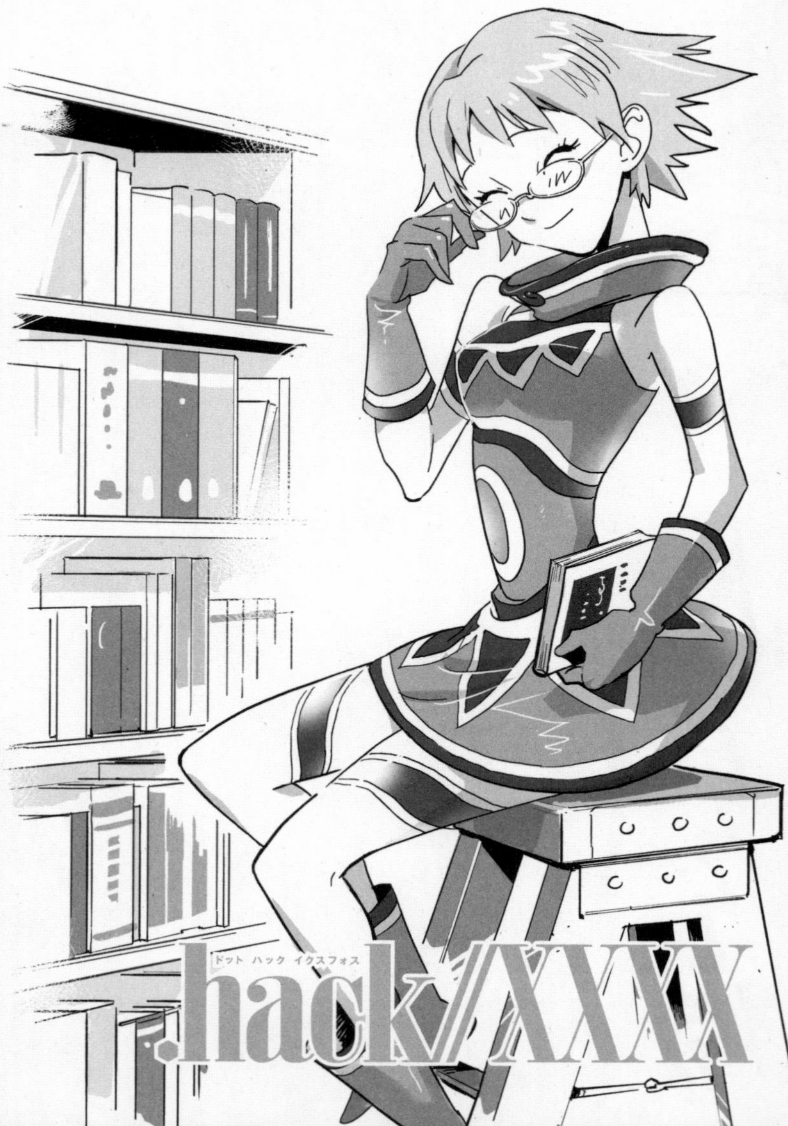
ドット ハック イクスフォス
.hack//XXXX

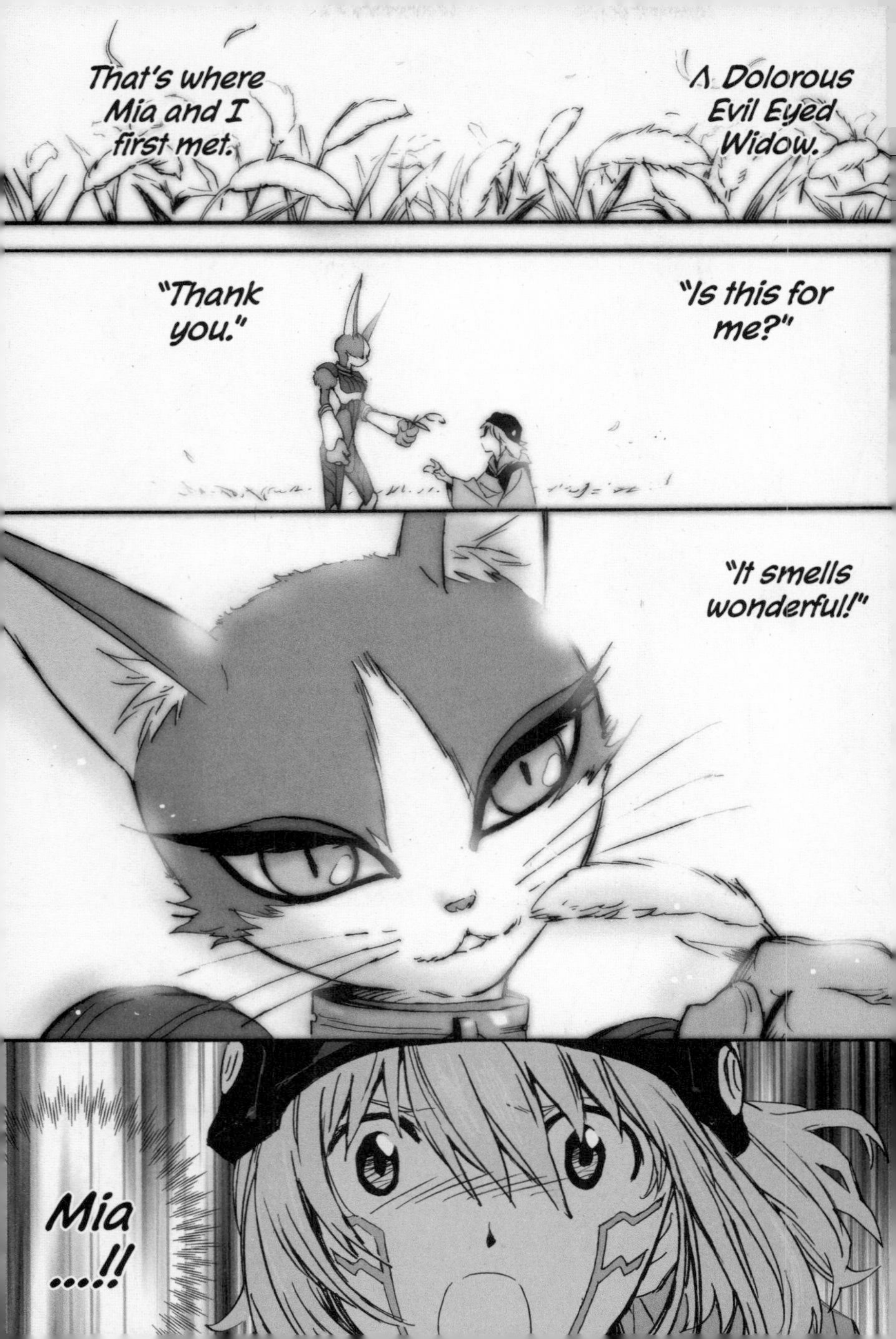
A Dolorous Evil Eyed Widow.
That's where Mia and I first met.
"Is this for me?"
"Thank you."
"It smells wonderful!"
Mia ...!!

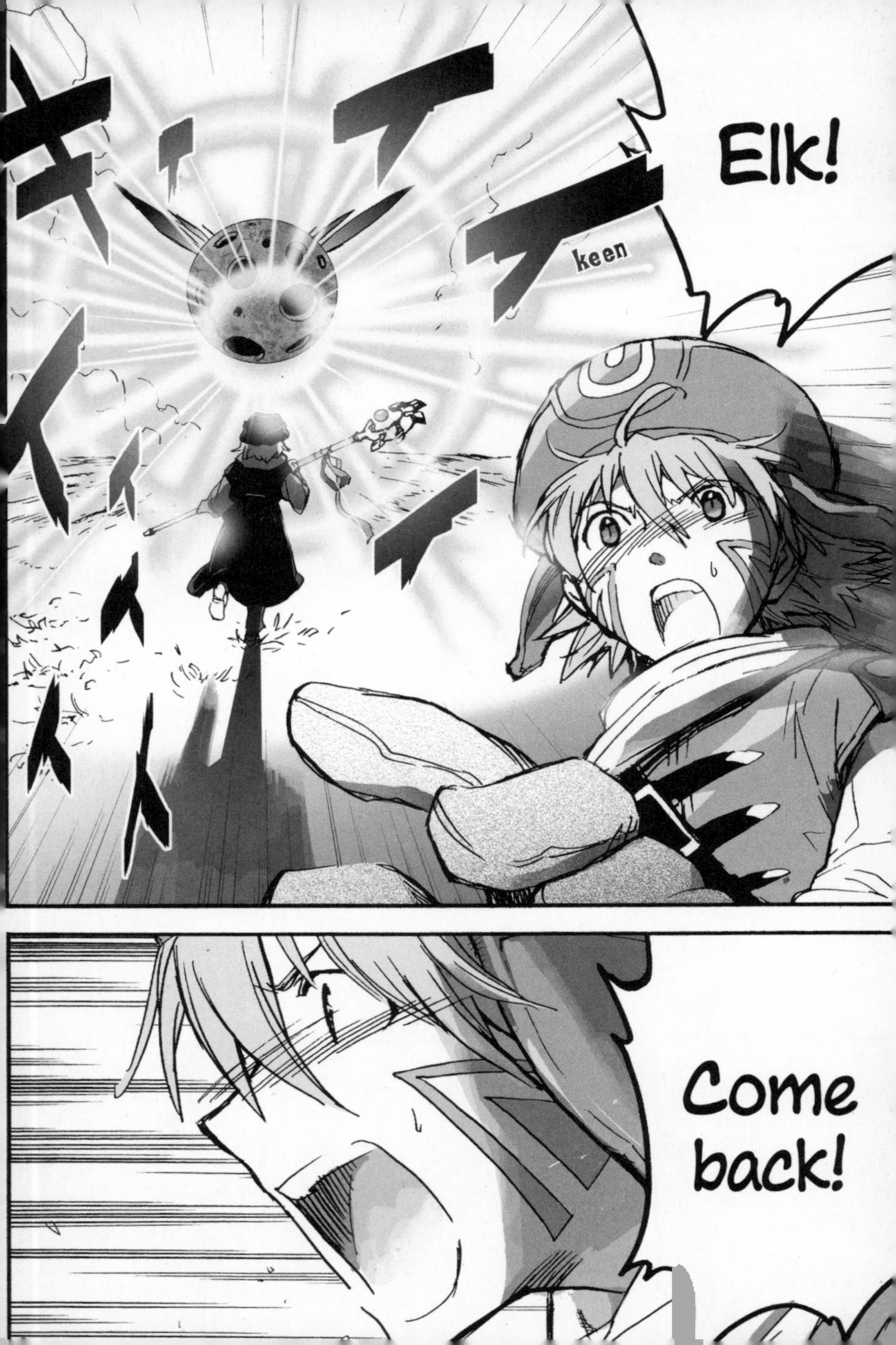

キィイイイイン
keen
Elk!
Come back!

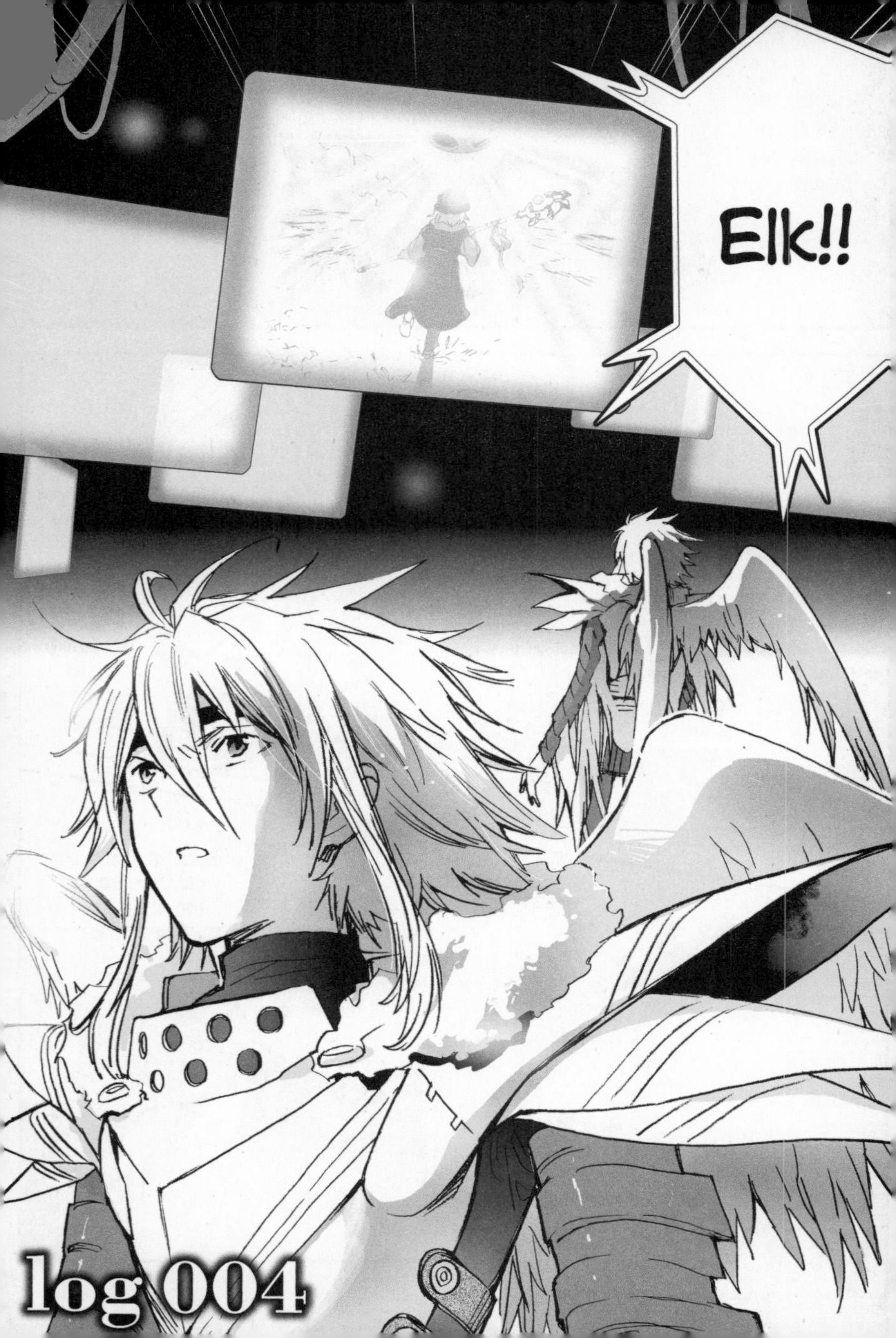
Elk!!
log 004

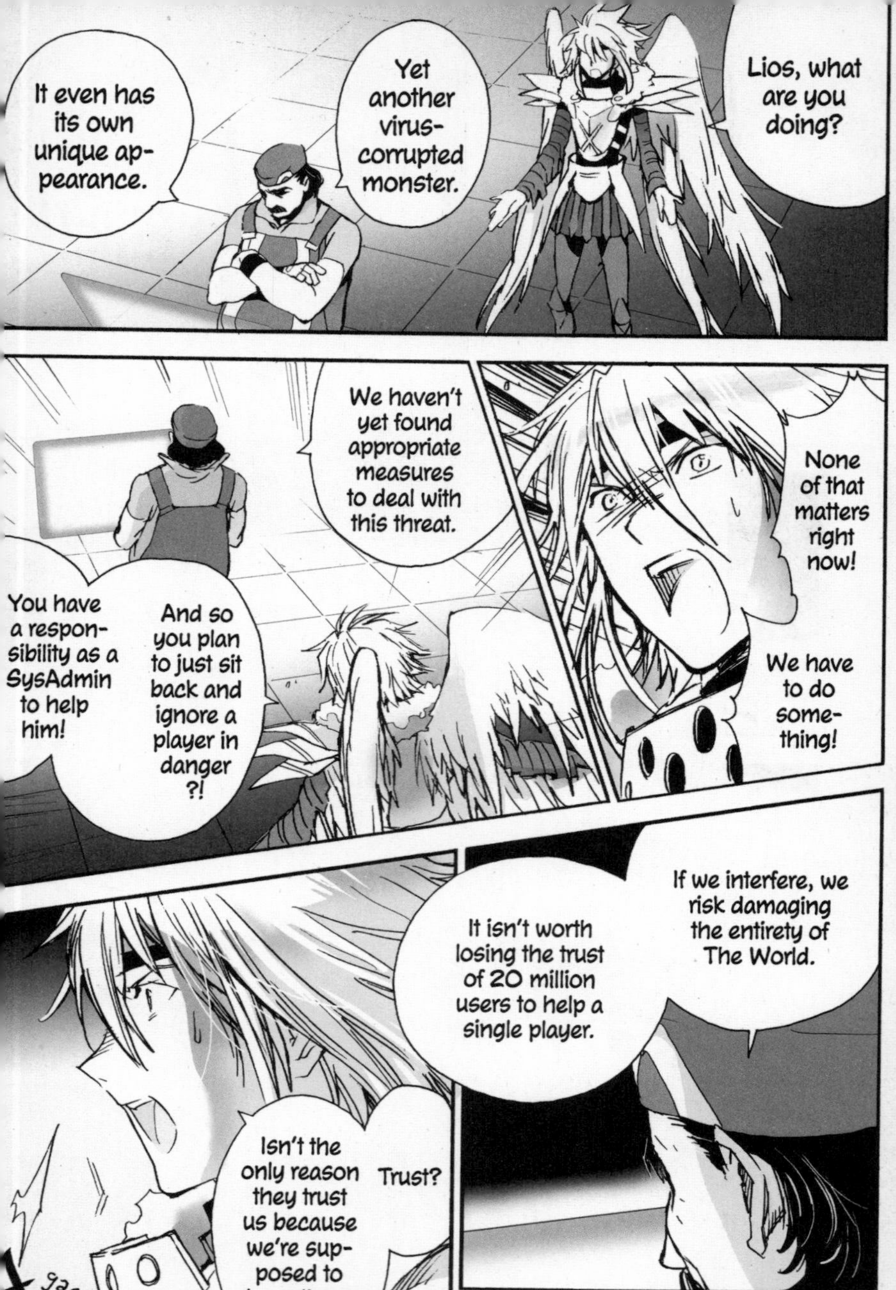

Lios, what are you doing?
Yet another virus-corrupted monster.
It even has its own unique appearance.
None of that matters right now!
We have to do something!
We haven't yet found appropriate measures to deal with this threat.
And so you plan to just sit back and ignore a player in danger?!
You have a responsibility as a SysAdmin to help him!
If we interfere, we risk damaging the entirety of The World.
It isn't worth losing the trust of 20 million users to help a single player.
Trust?
Isn't the only reason they trust us because we're supposed to keep them safe?!
gasp

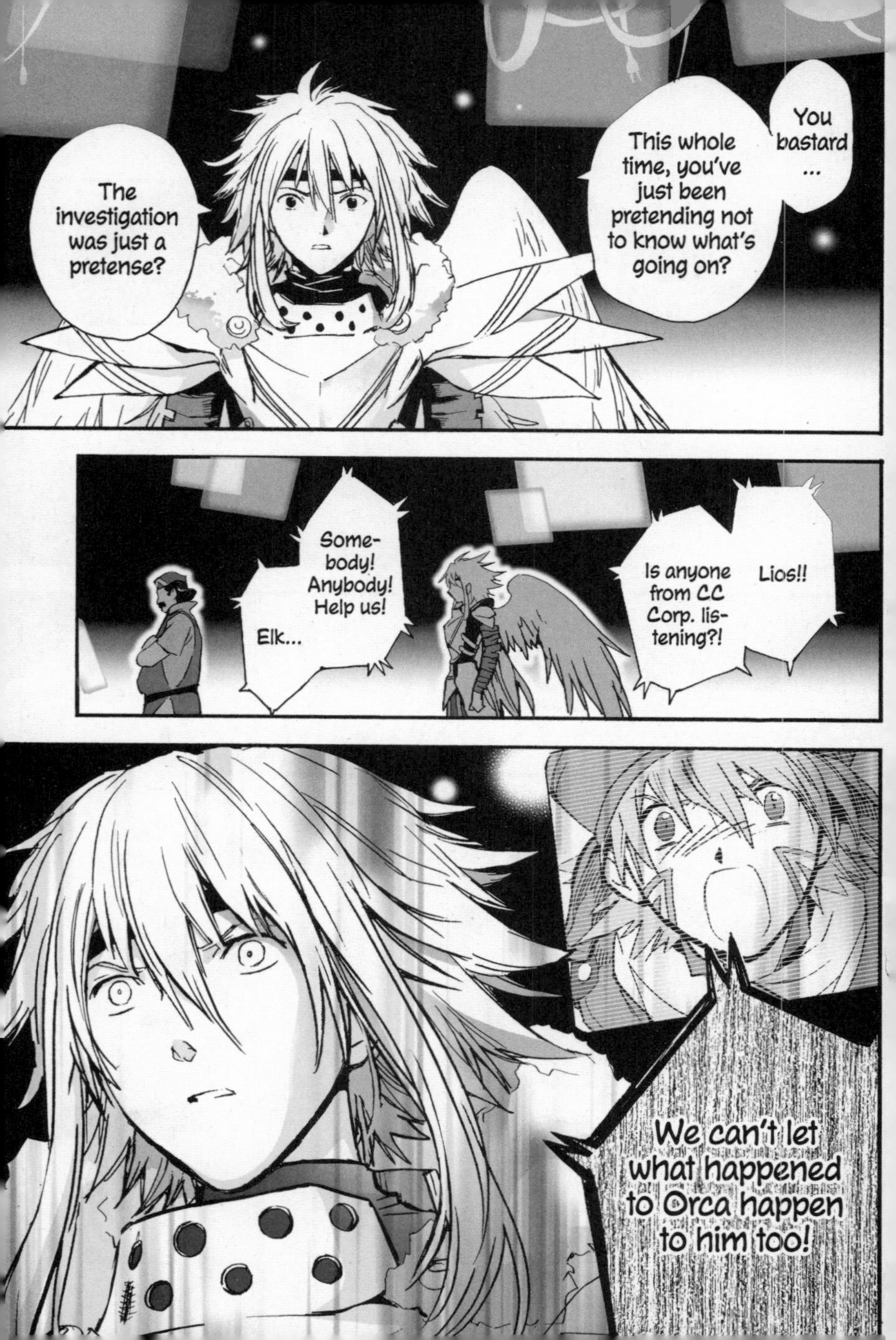
You bastard ...
This whole time, you've just been pretending not to know what's going on?
The investigation was just a pretense?
Lios!!
Is anyone from CC Corp. lis-tening?!
Some-body! Anybody! Help us!
Elk...
We can't let what happened to Orca happen to him too!

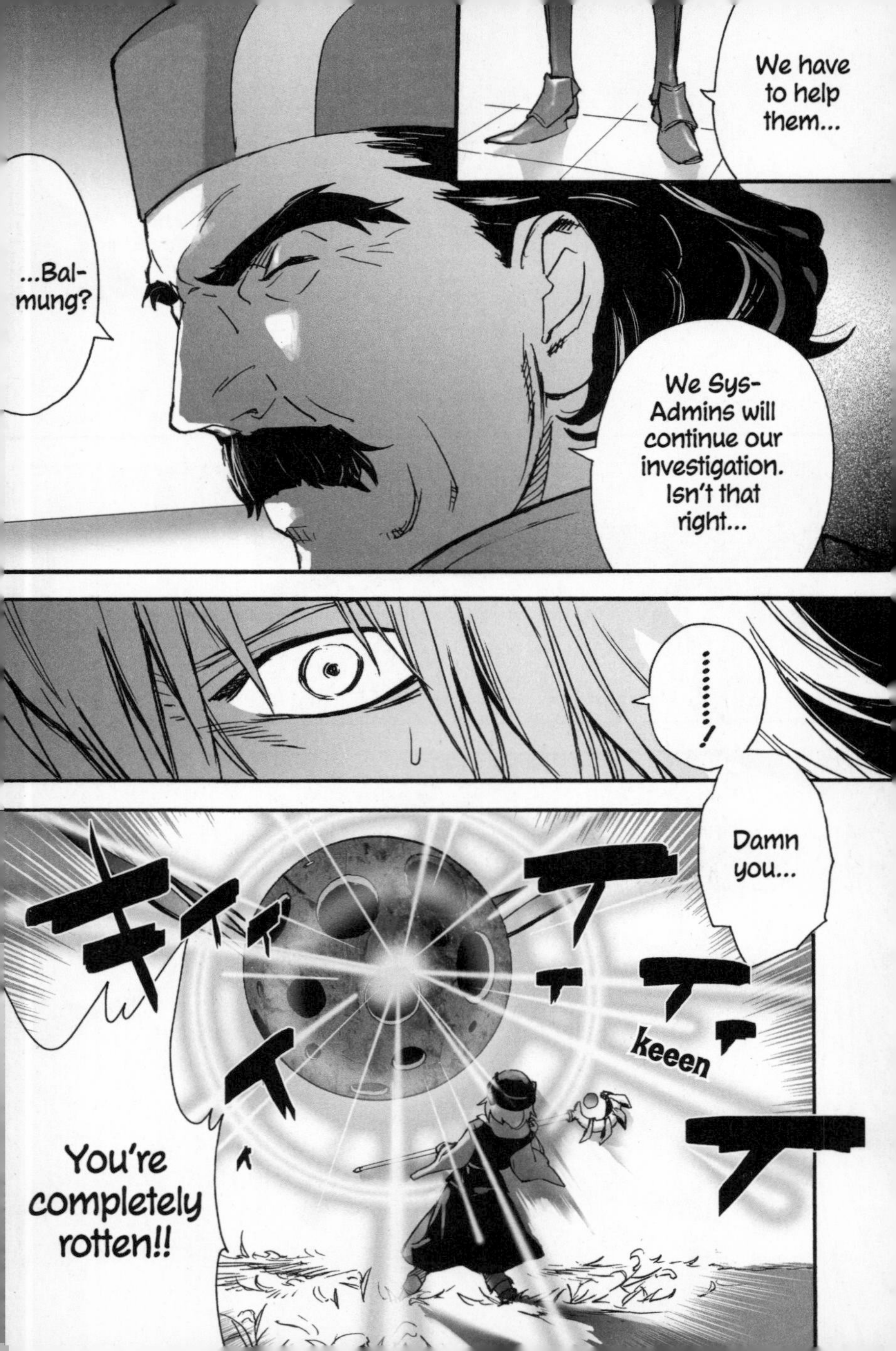
We have to help them...
We Sys-Admins will continue our investigation. Isn't that right...
...Bal-mung?
......!
Damn you...
keeeen
You're completely rotten!!

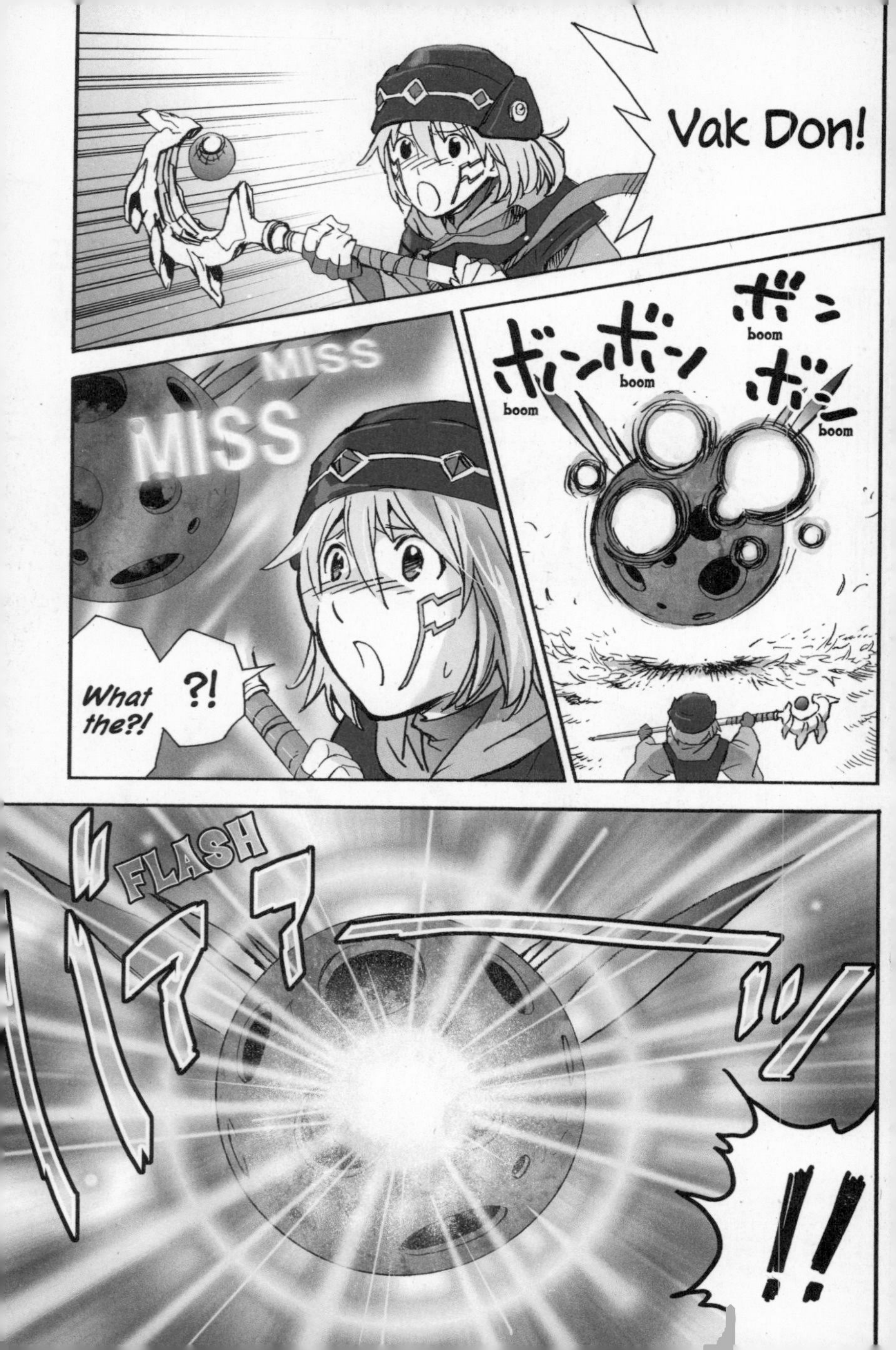

Vak Don!
ボンボンボンボン
boom
boom
boom
boom
MISS
MISS
?!
What the?!
FLASH
パァァーーッ
!!

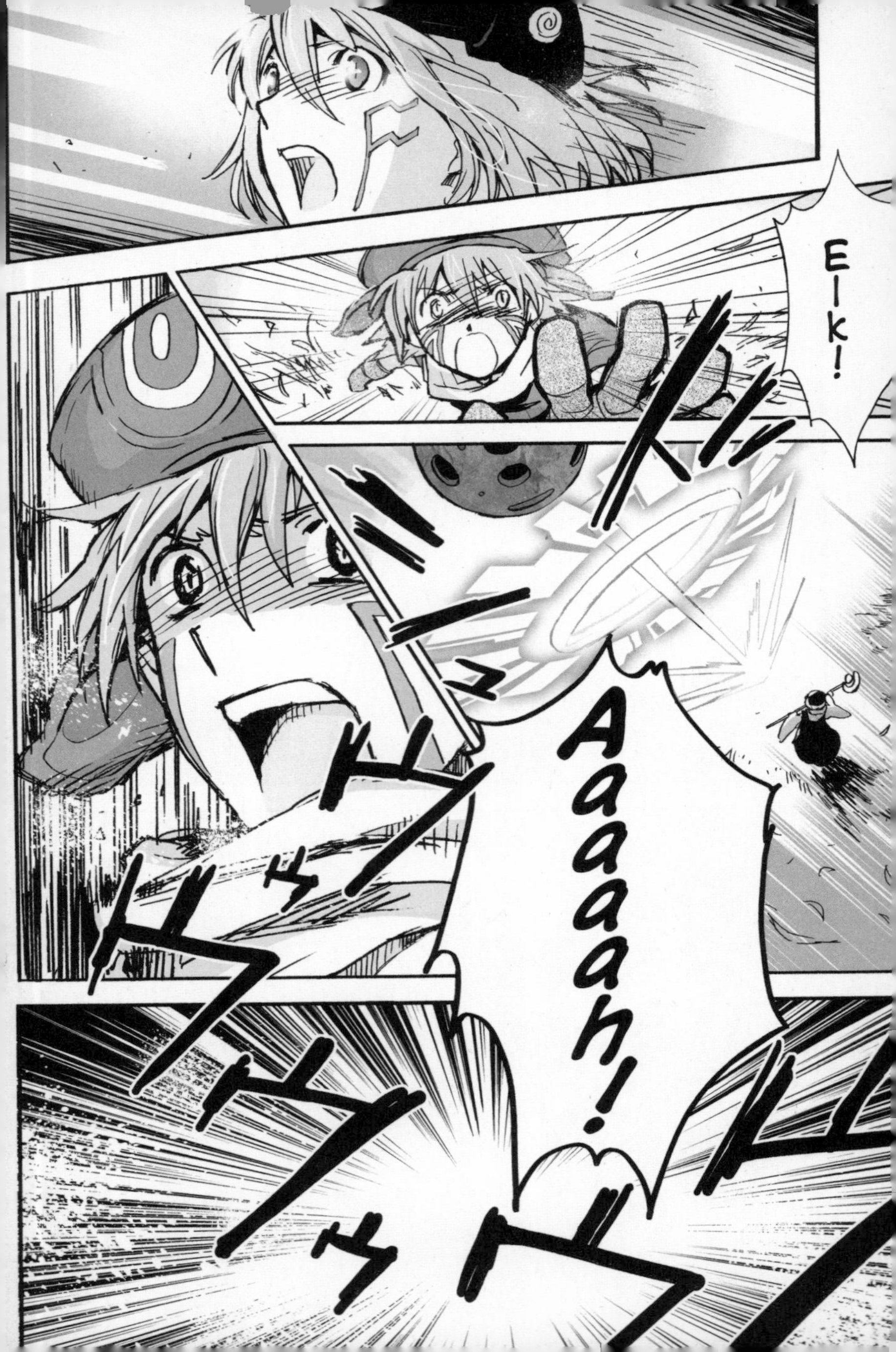
Eik!
Aaaaah!!

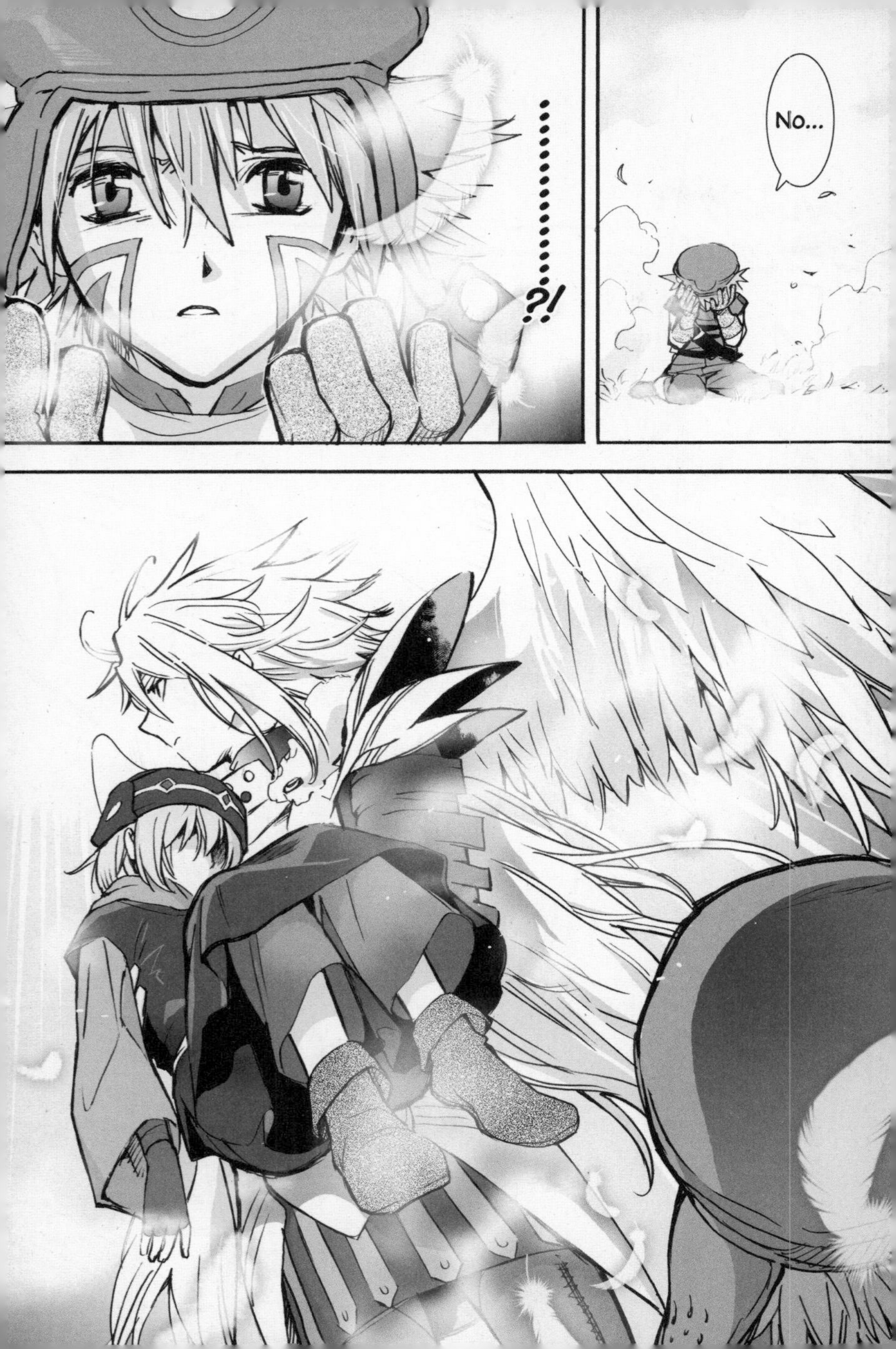
No...
......?!

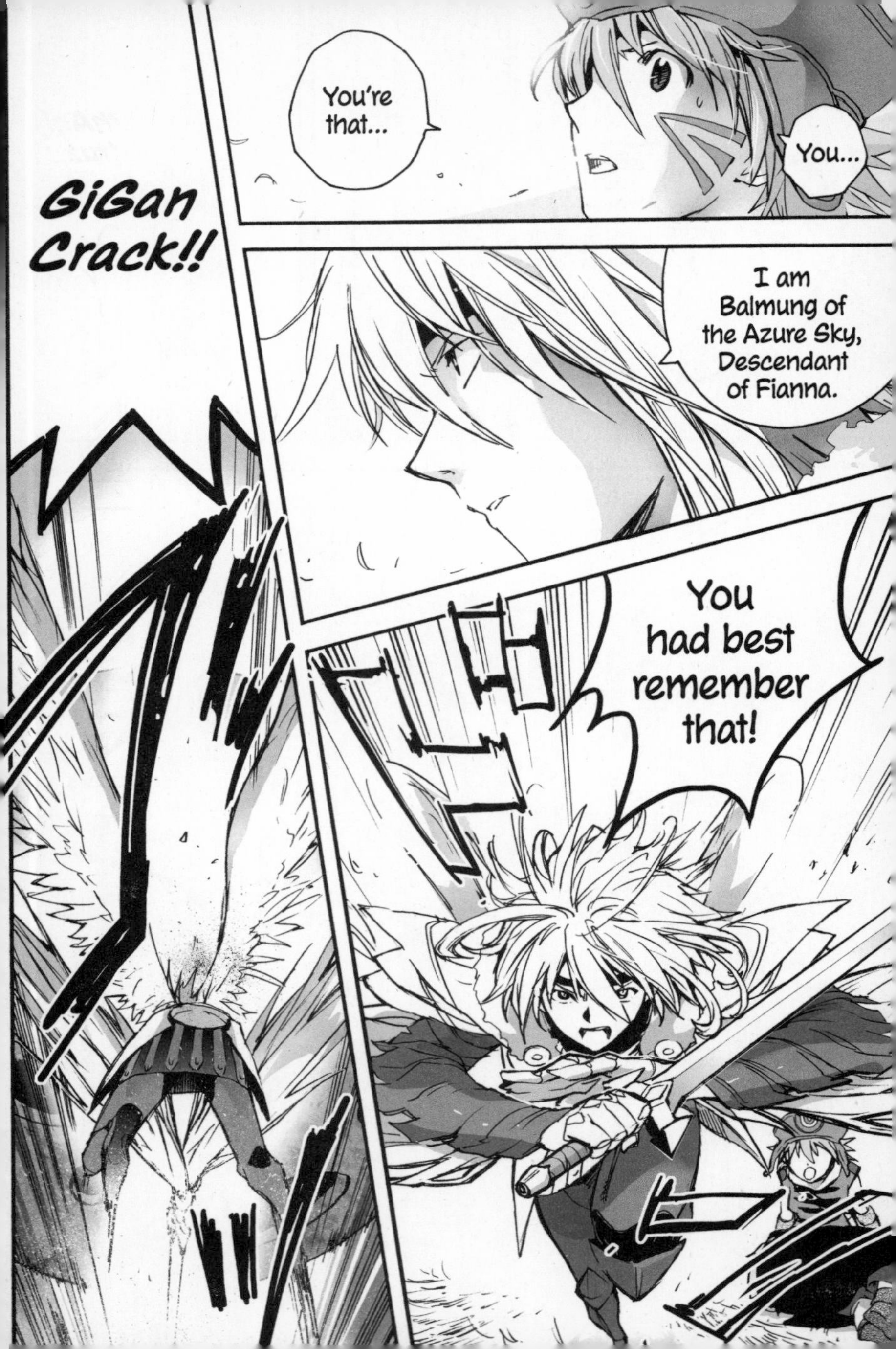
You...
You're that...
GiGan Crack!!
I am Balmung of the Azure Sky, Descendant of Fianna.
You had best remember that!

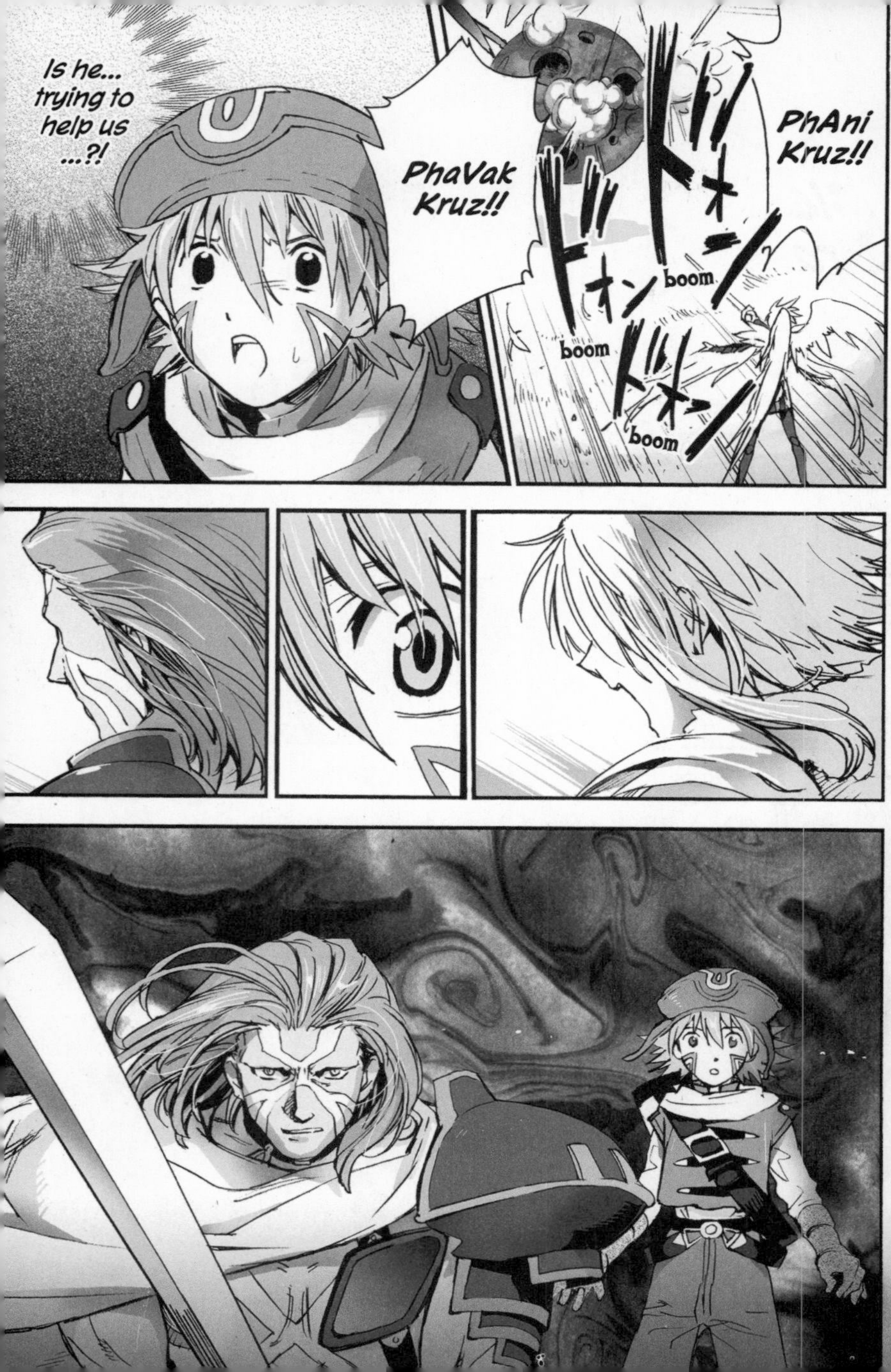

PhAni Kruz!!
PhaVak Kruz!!
boom
boom
boom
Is he... trying to help us ...?!

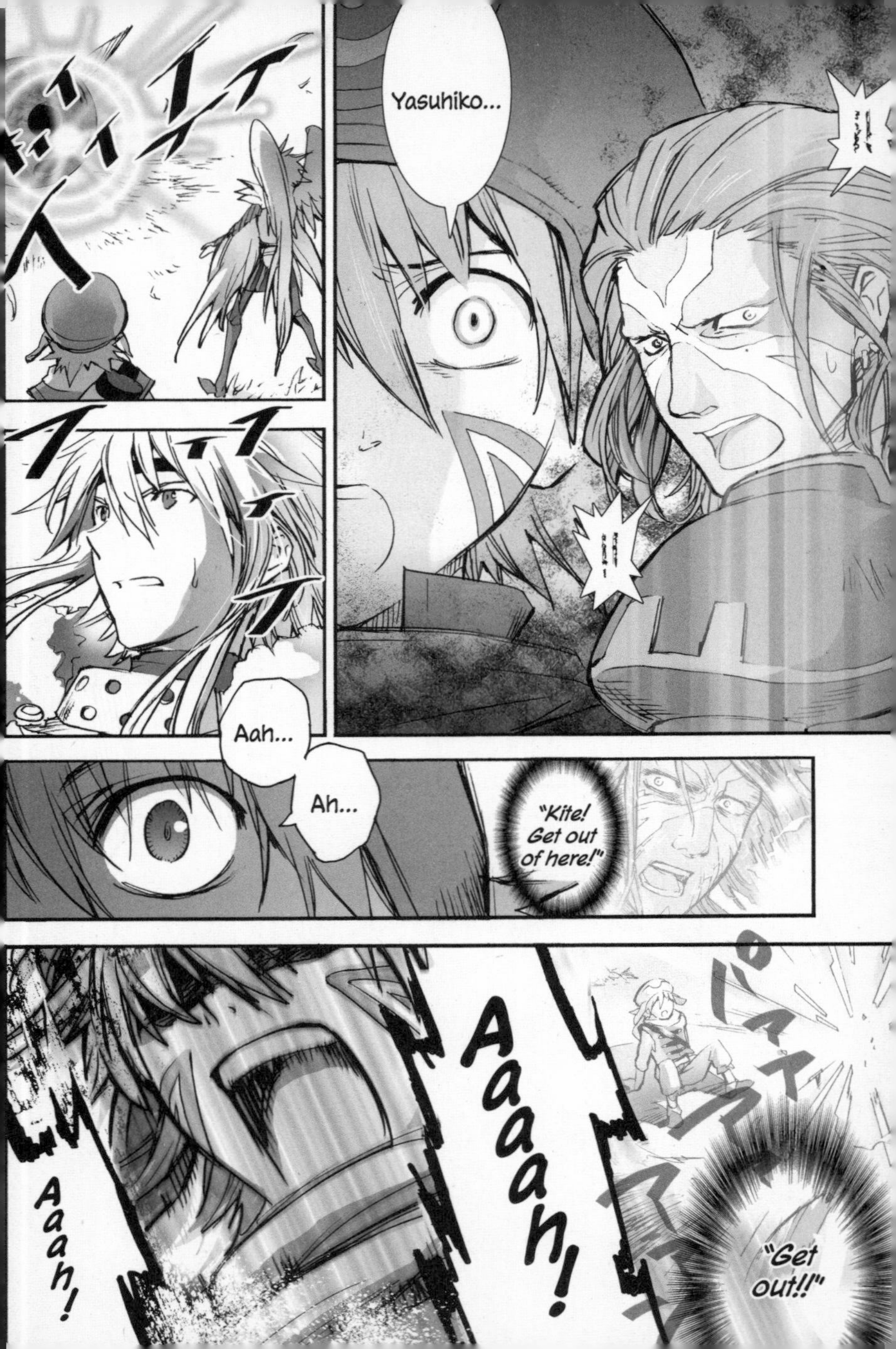

Yasuhiko...
Aah...
Ah...
"Kite! Get out of here!"
"Get out!!"
Aaaaah!
Aaaah!

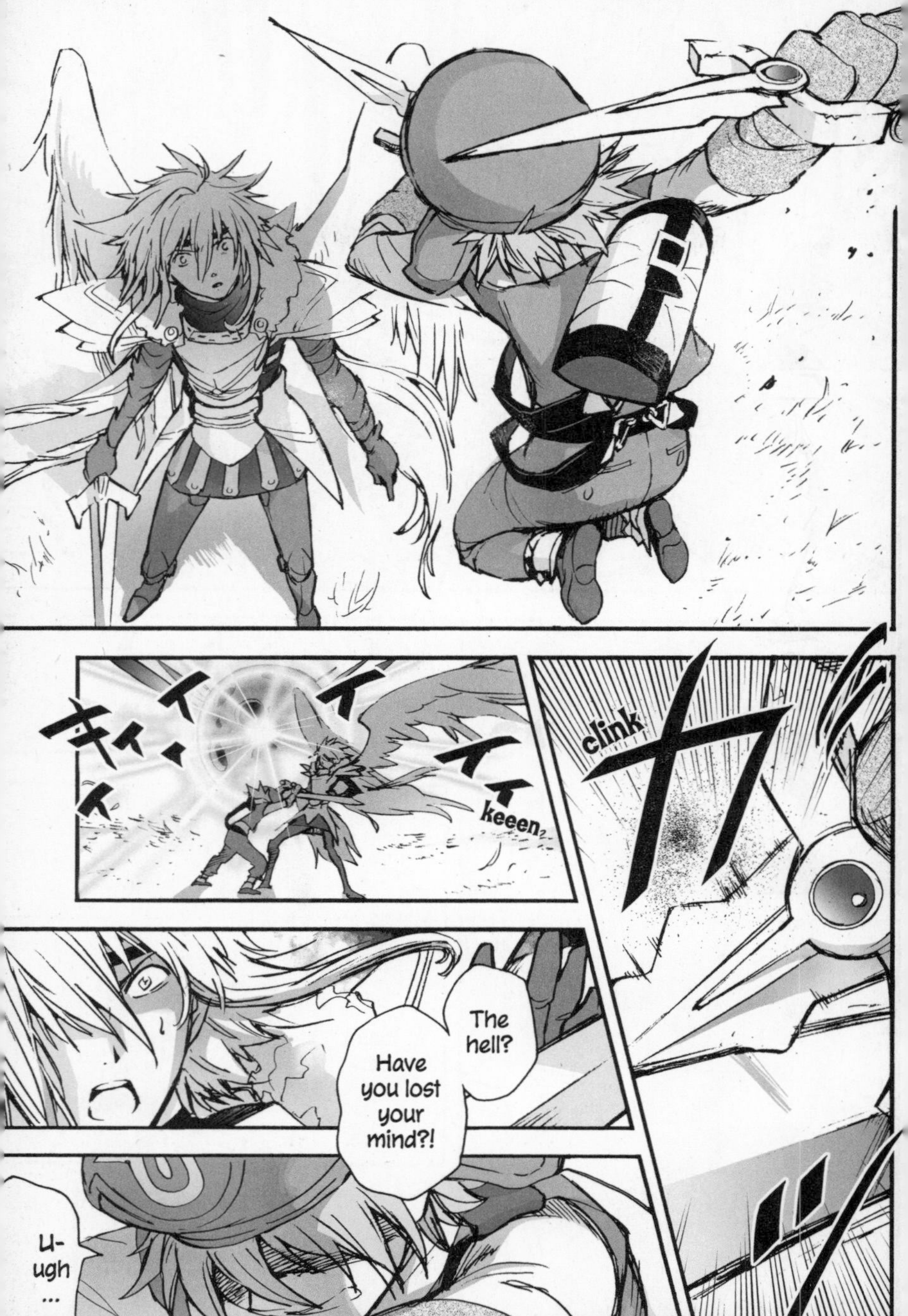
clink
keeen
The hell?
Have you lost your mind?!
U-ugh ...

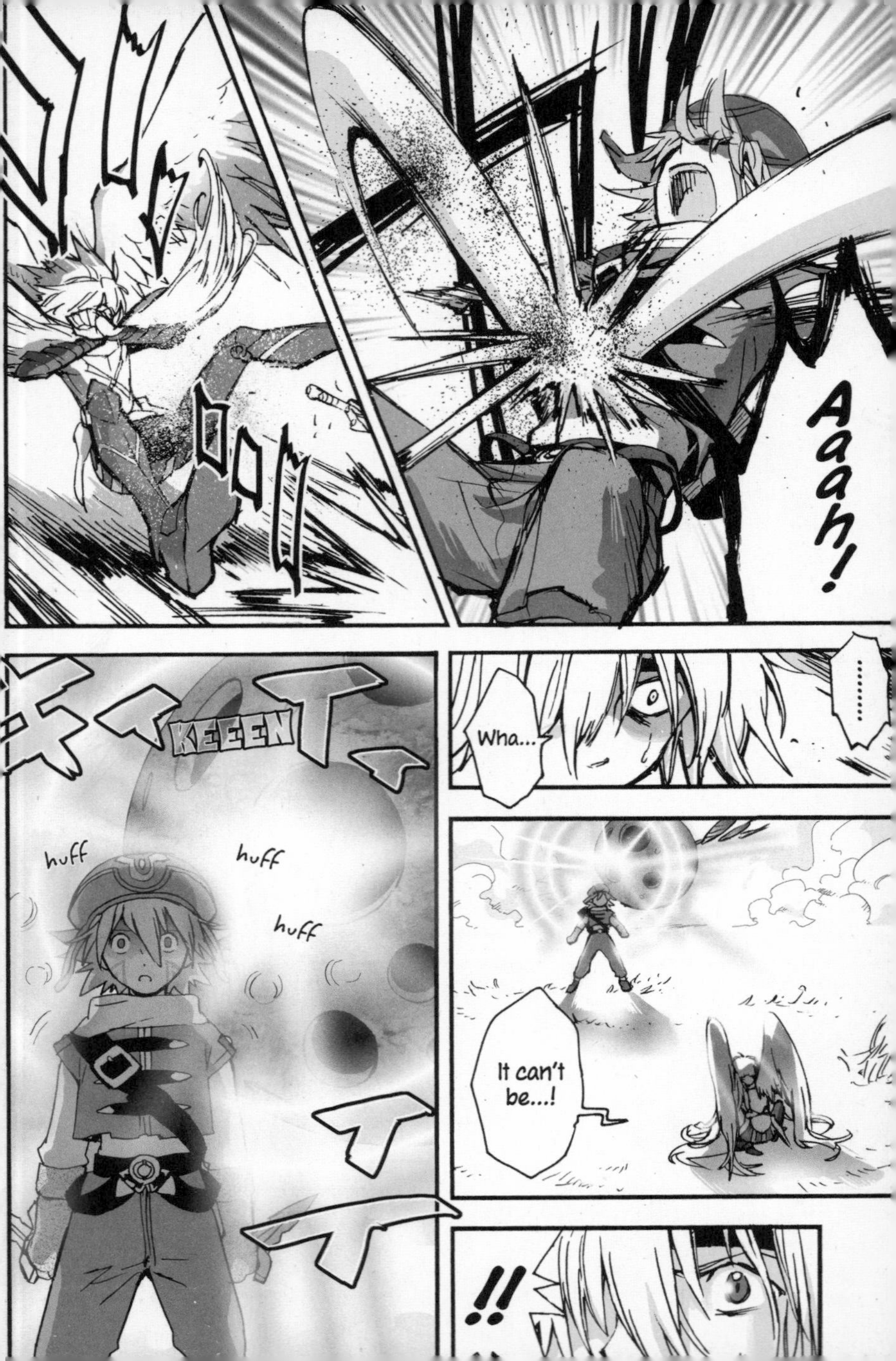
Aaaah!
KEEEN
huff
huff
huff
......
Wha...
It can't be...!
!!

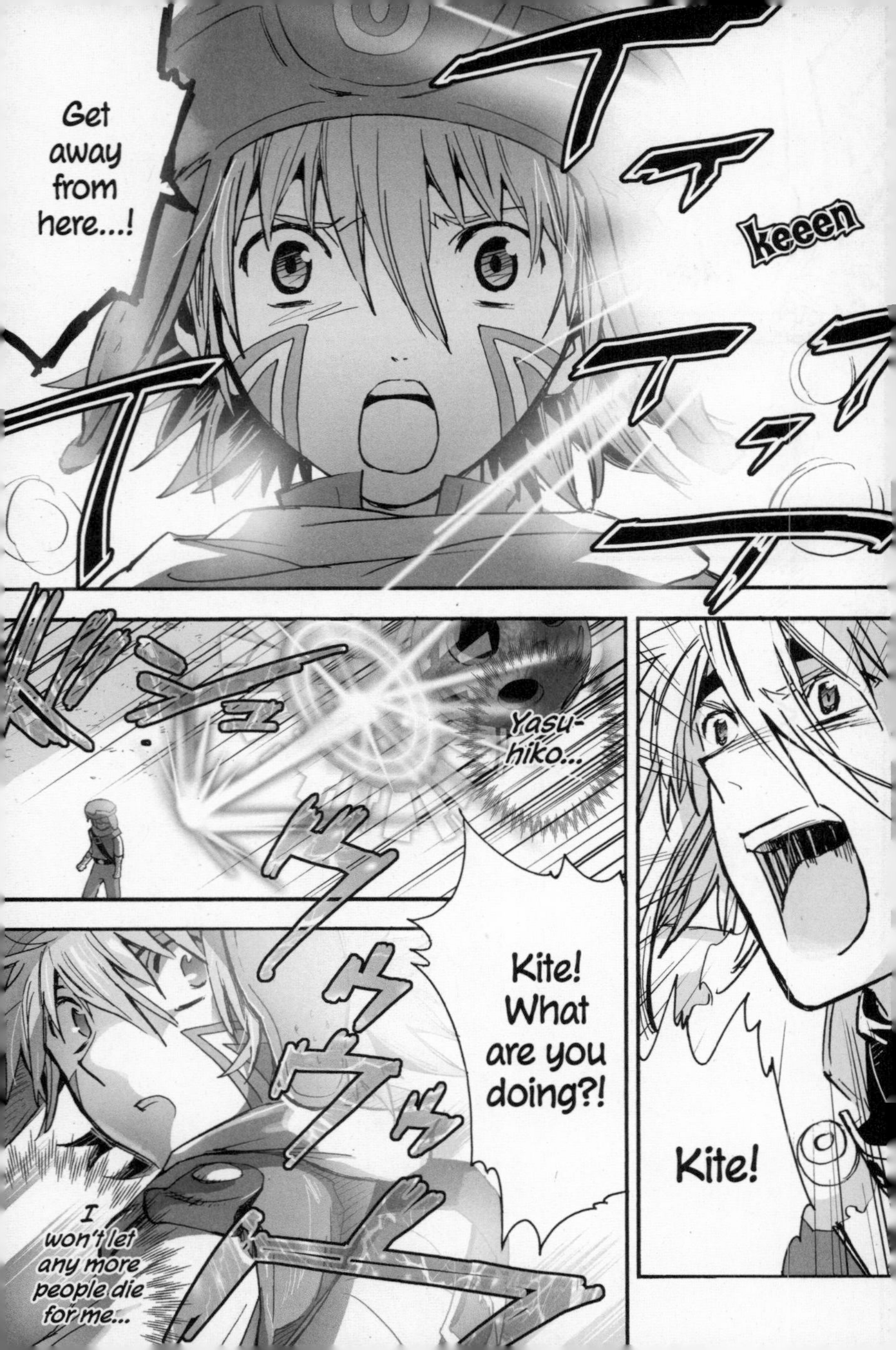
keeen
Get away from here...!
Yasu-hiko...
Kite!
Kite! What are you doing?!
I won't let any more people die for me...

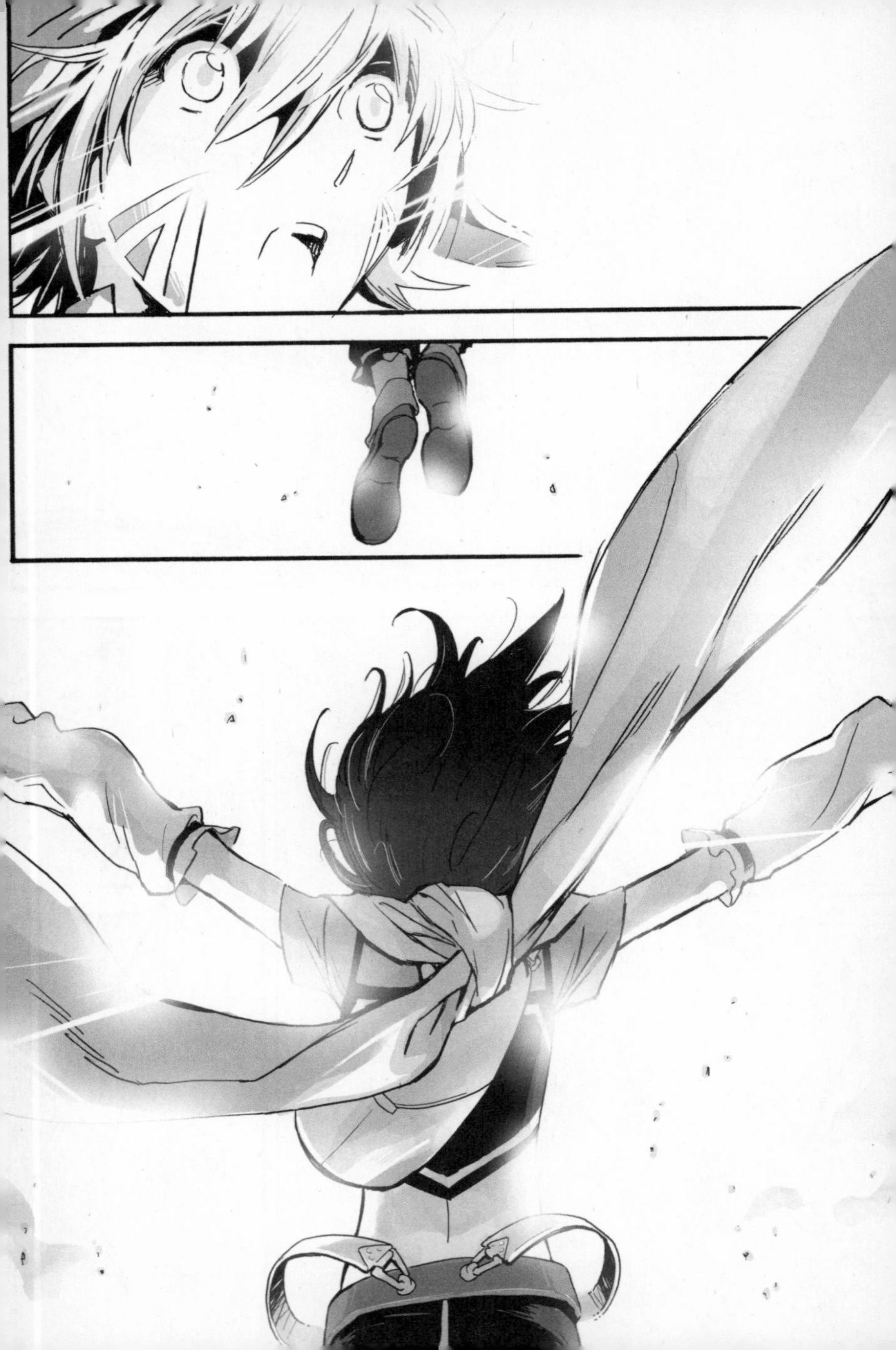

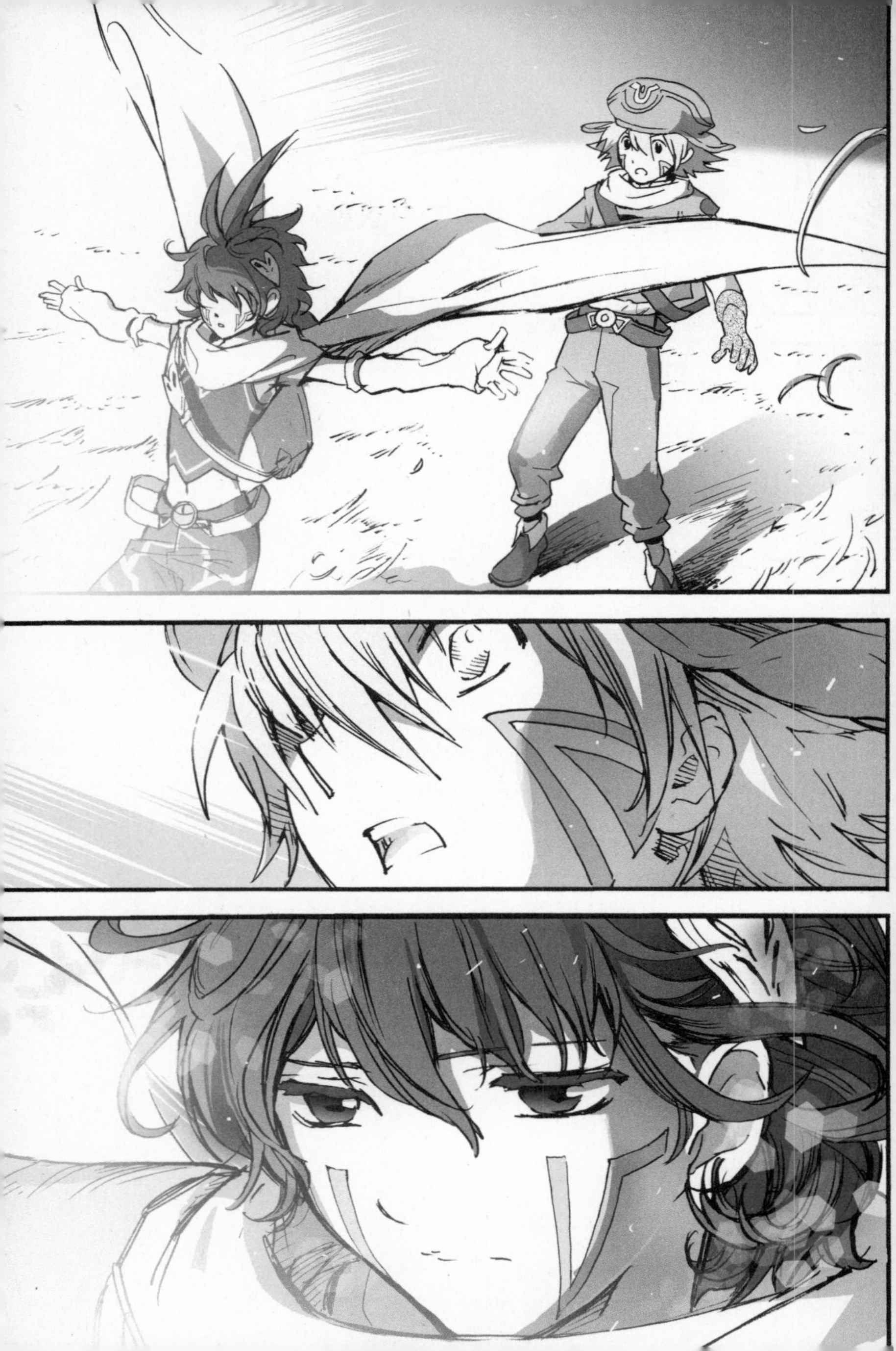

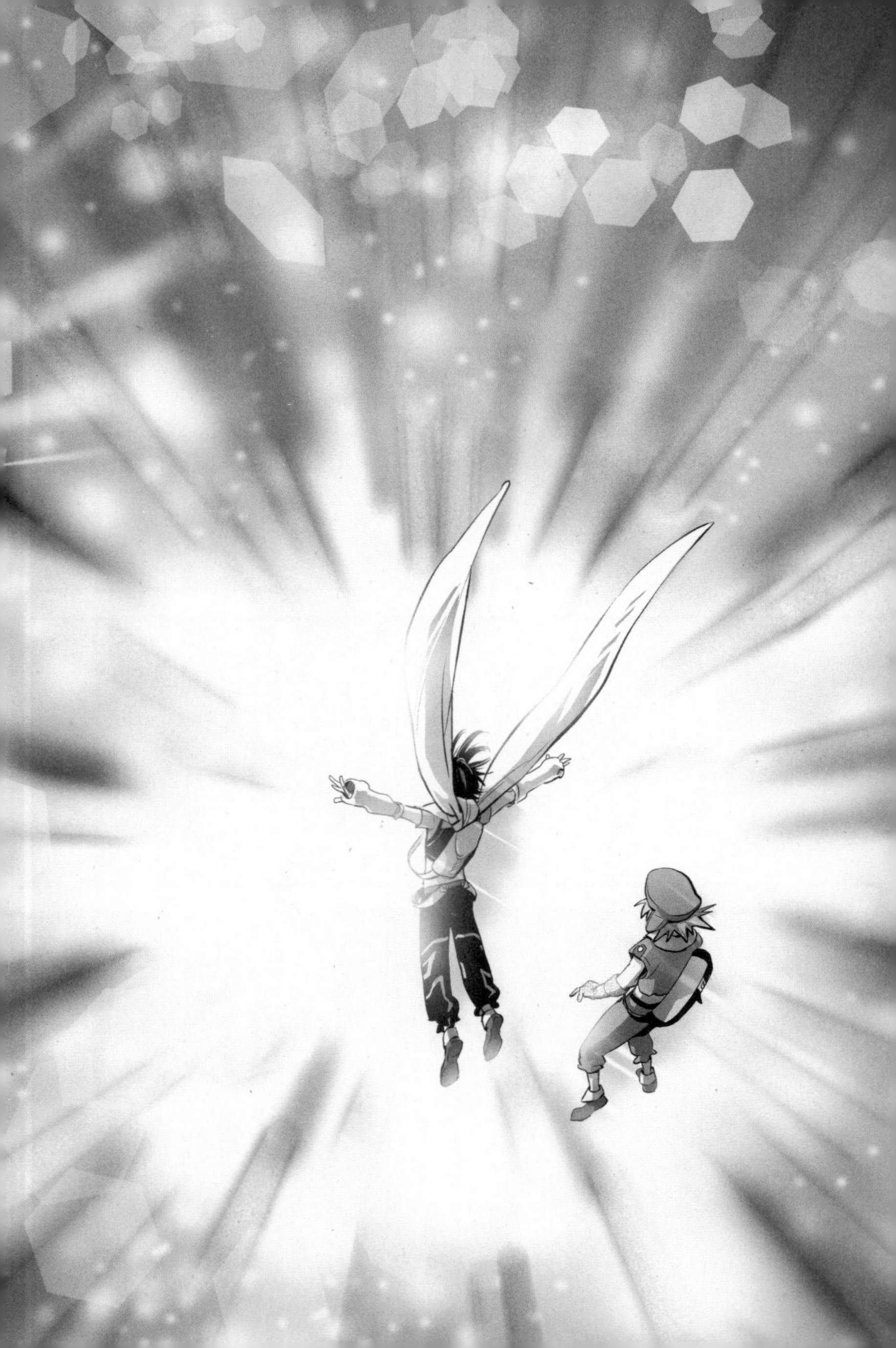

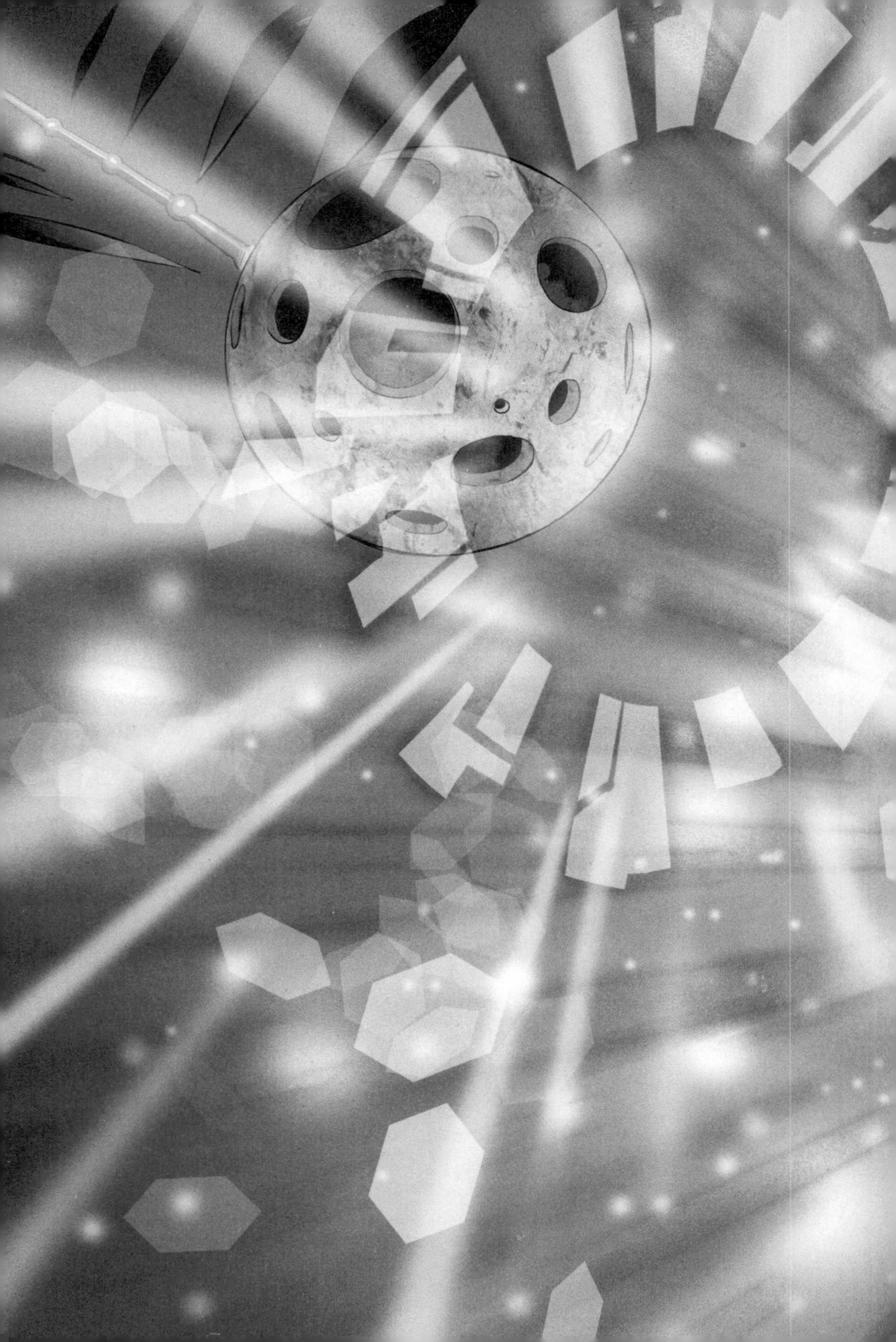

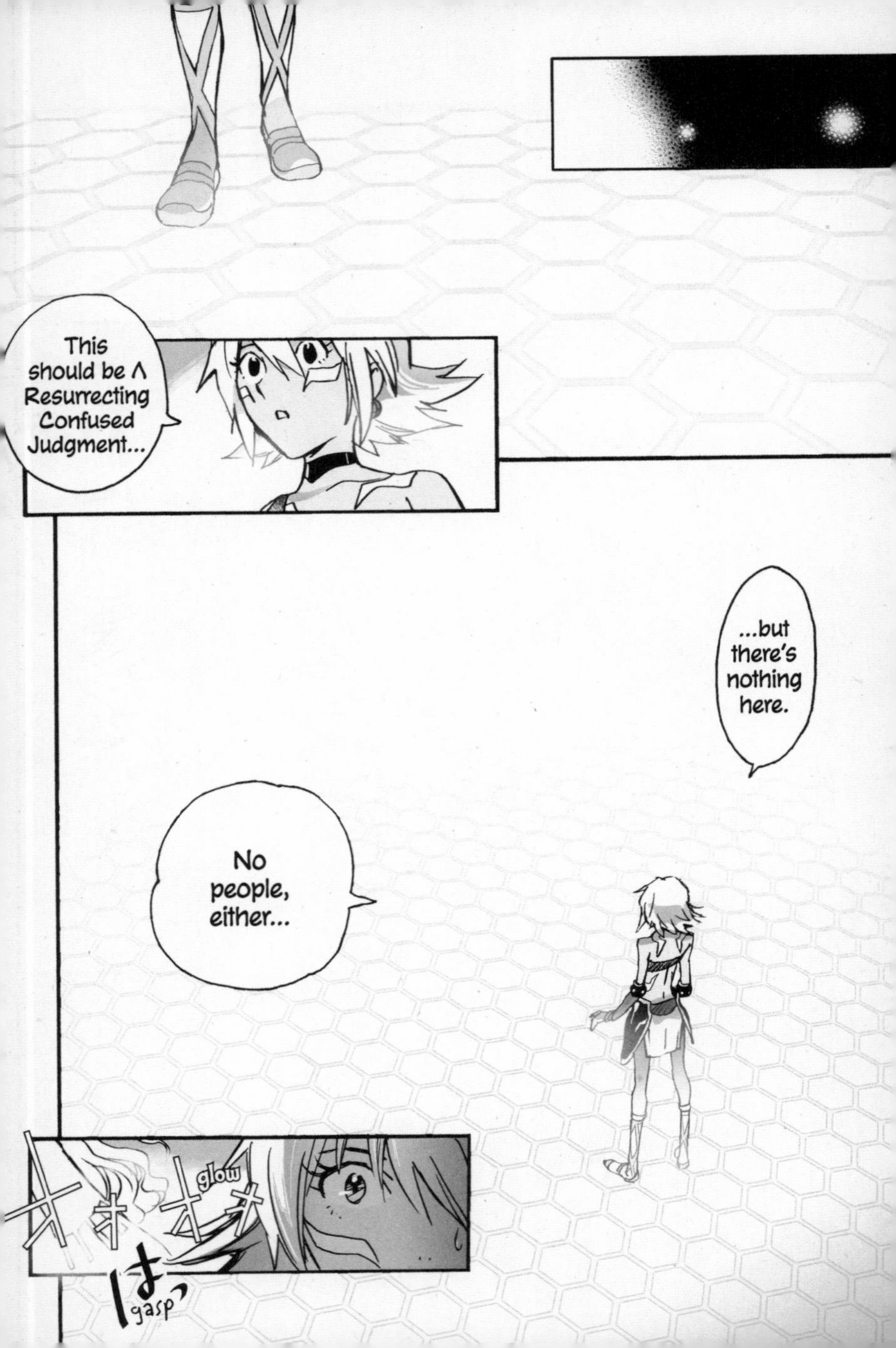
This should be Λ Resurrecting Confused Judgment...
...but there's nothing here.
No people, either...
glow
gasp

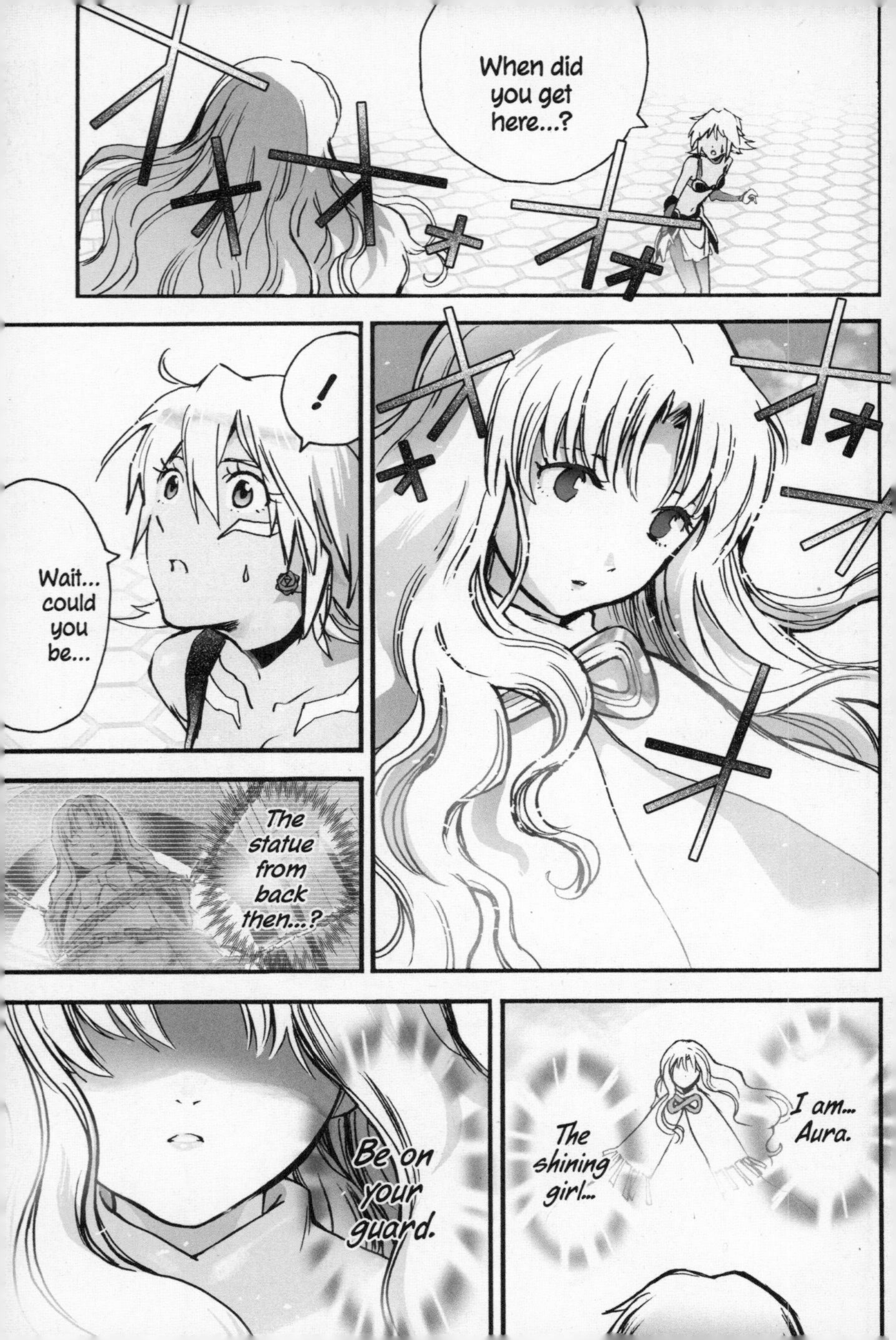
When did you get here...?
!
Wait... could you be...
The statue from back then...?
I am... Aura.
The shining girl...
Be on your guard.

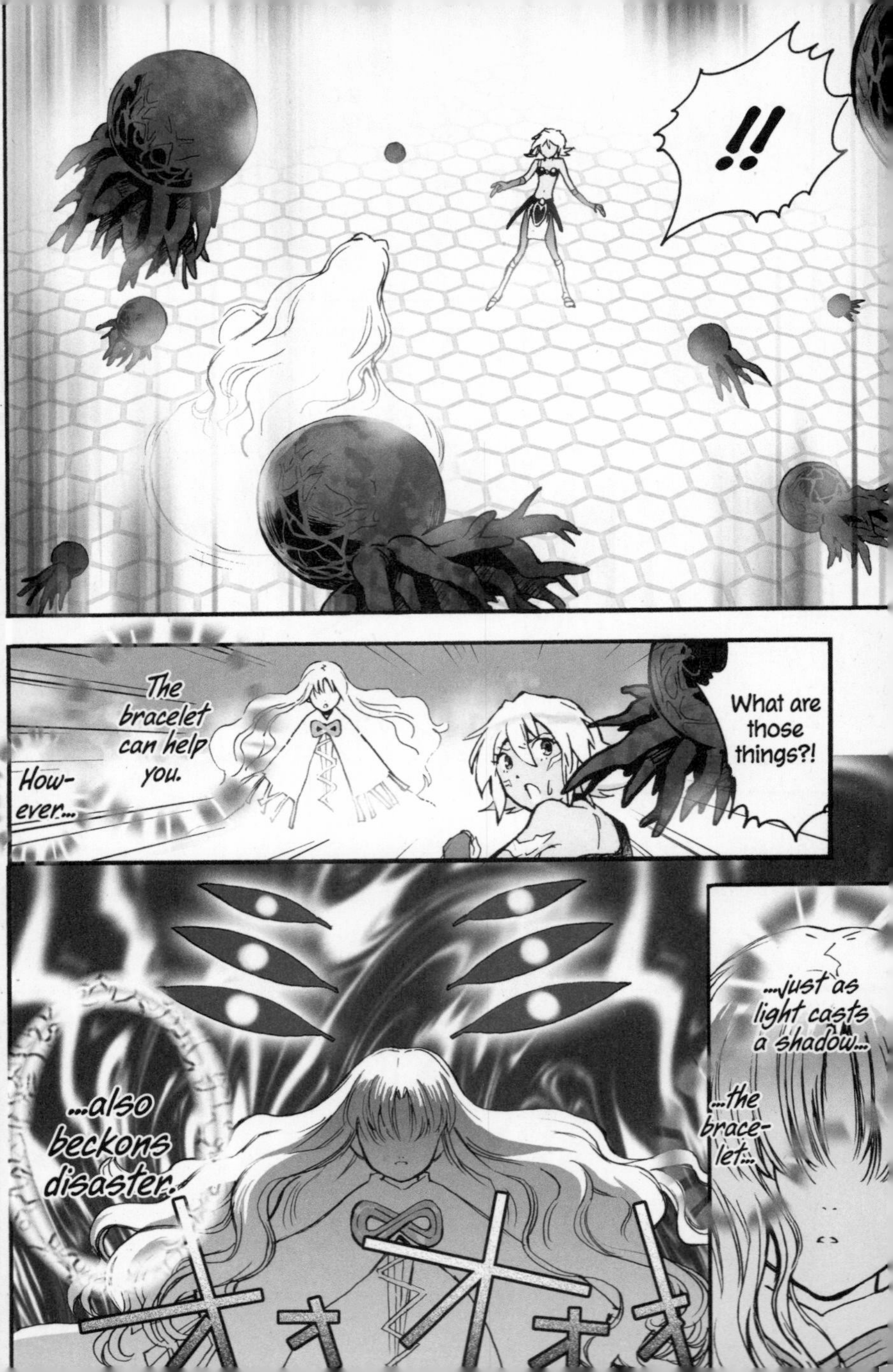
!!
What are those things?!
The bracelet can help you.
However...
...just as light casts a shadow...
...the bracelet...
...also beckons disaster.

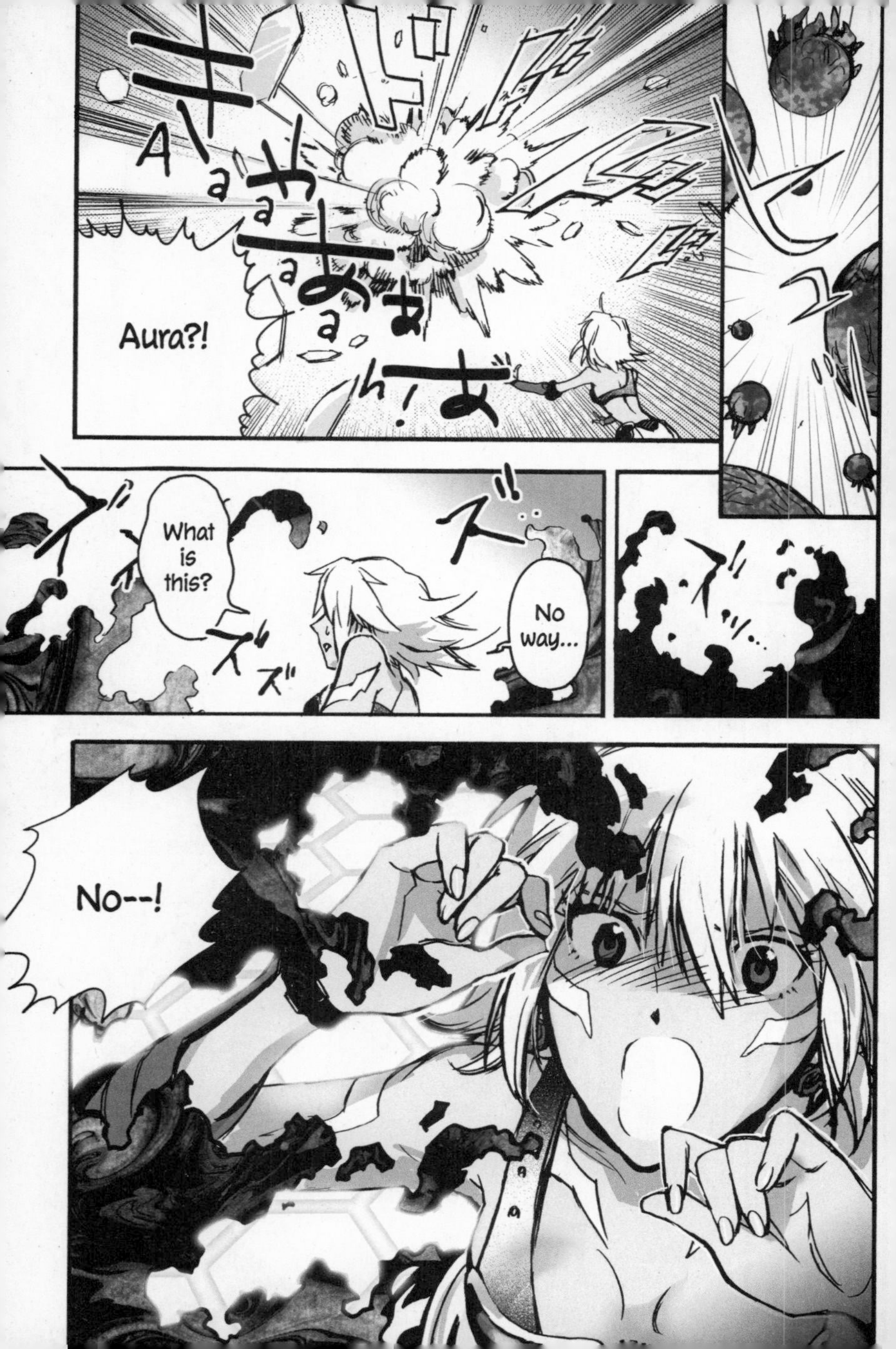

Aaaaaa!
Aura?!
What is this?
No way...
No--!

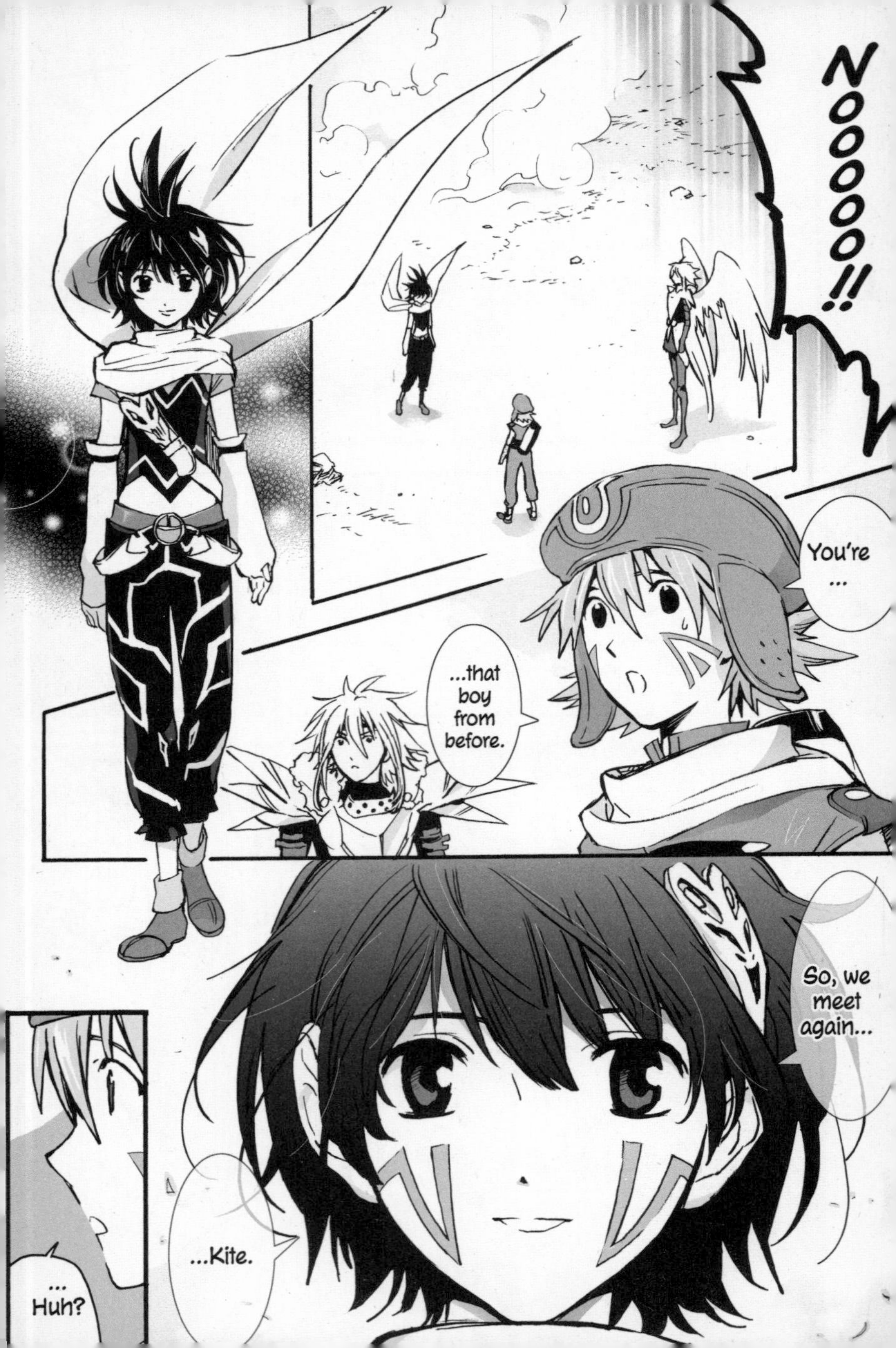
NOOOOOO!!
You're ...
...that boy from before.
So, we meet again...
...Kite.
... Huh?

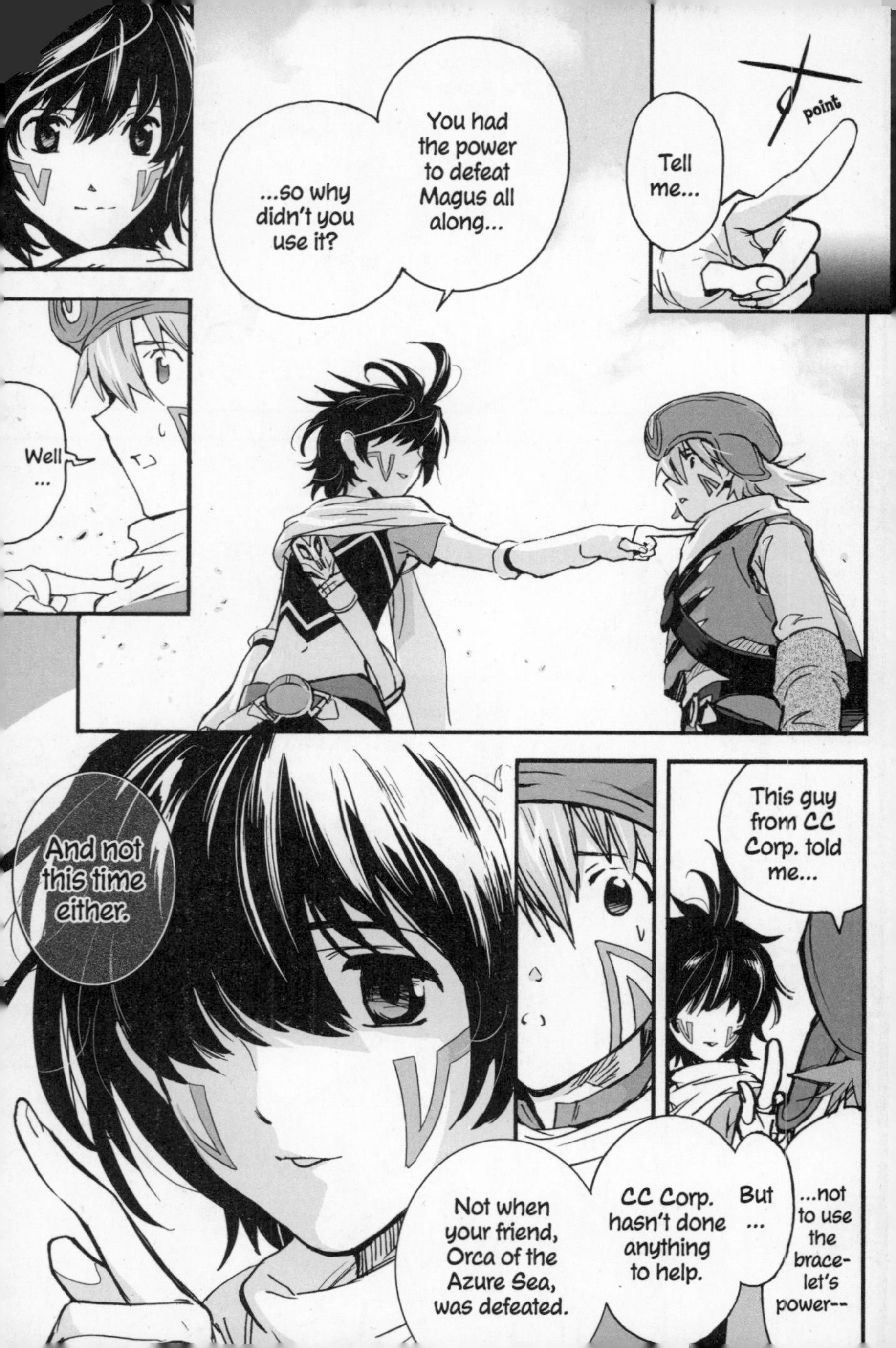
point
Tell me...
You had the power to defeat Magus all along...
...so why didn't you use it?
Well...
This guy from CC Corp. told me...
...not to use the bracelet's power--
But...
CC Corp. hasn't done anything to help.
Not when your friend, Orca of the Azure Sea, was defeated.
And not this time either.

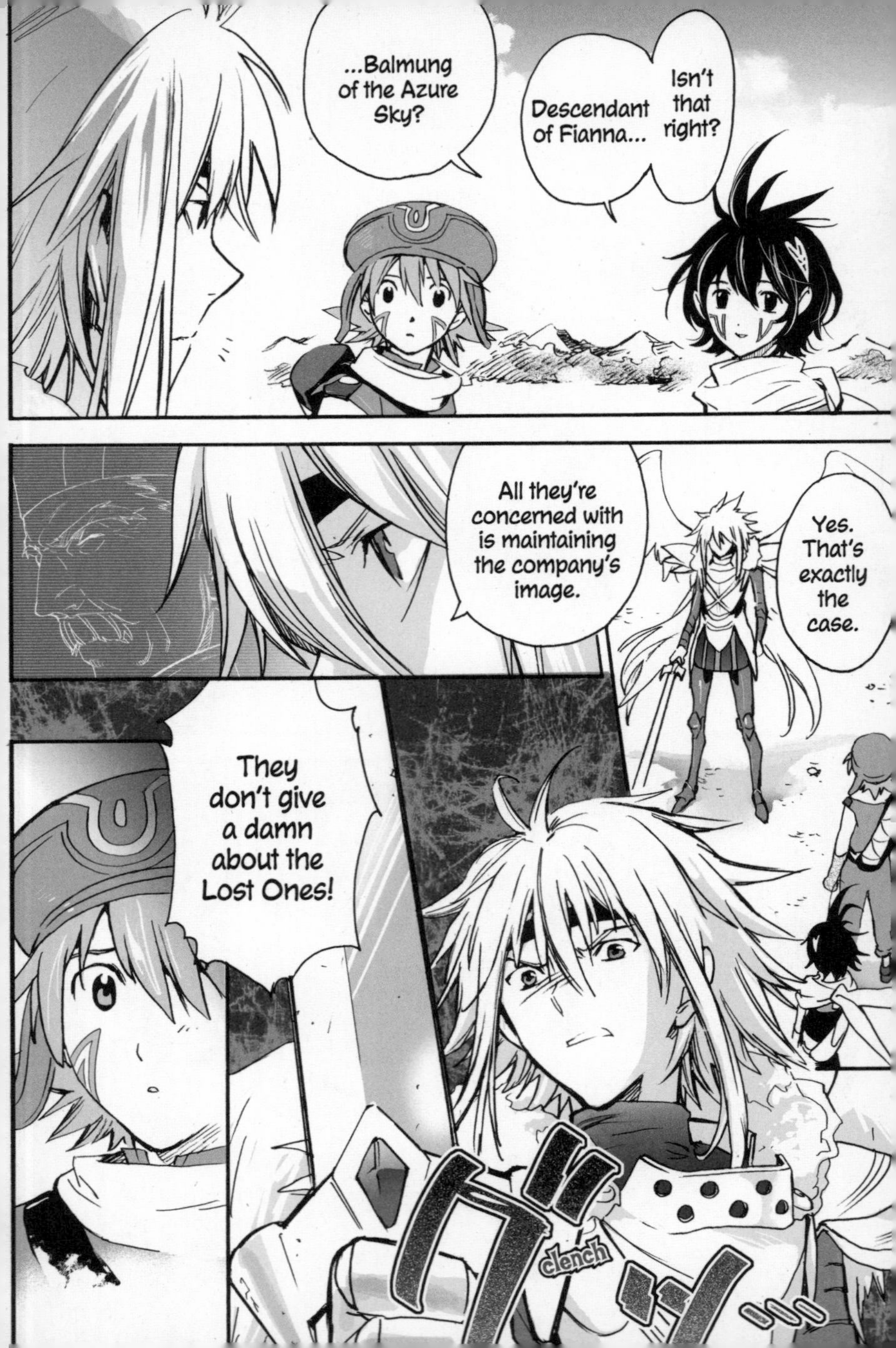
Descendant of Fianna... Isn't that right?
...Balmung of the Azure Sky?
Yes. That's exactly the case.
All they're concerned with is maintaining the company's image.
They don't give a damn about the Lost Ones!
clench

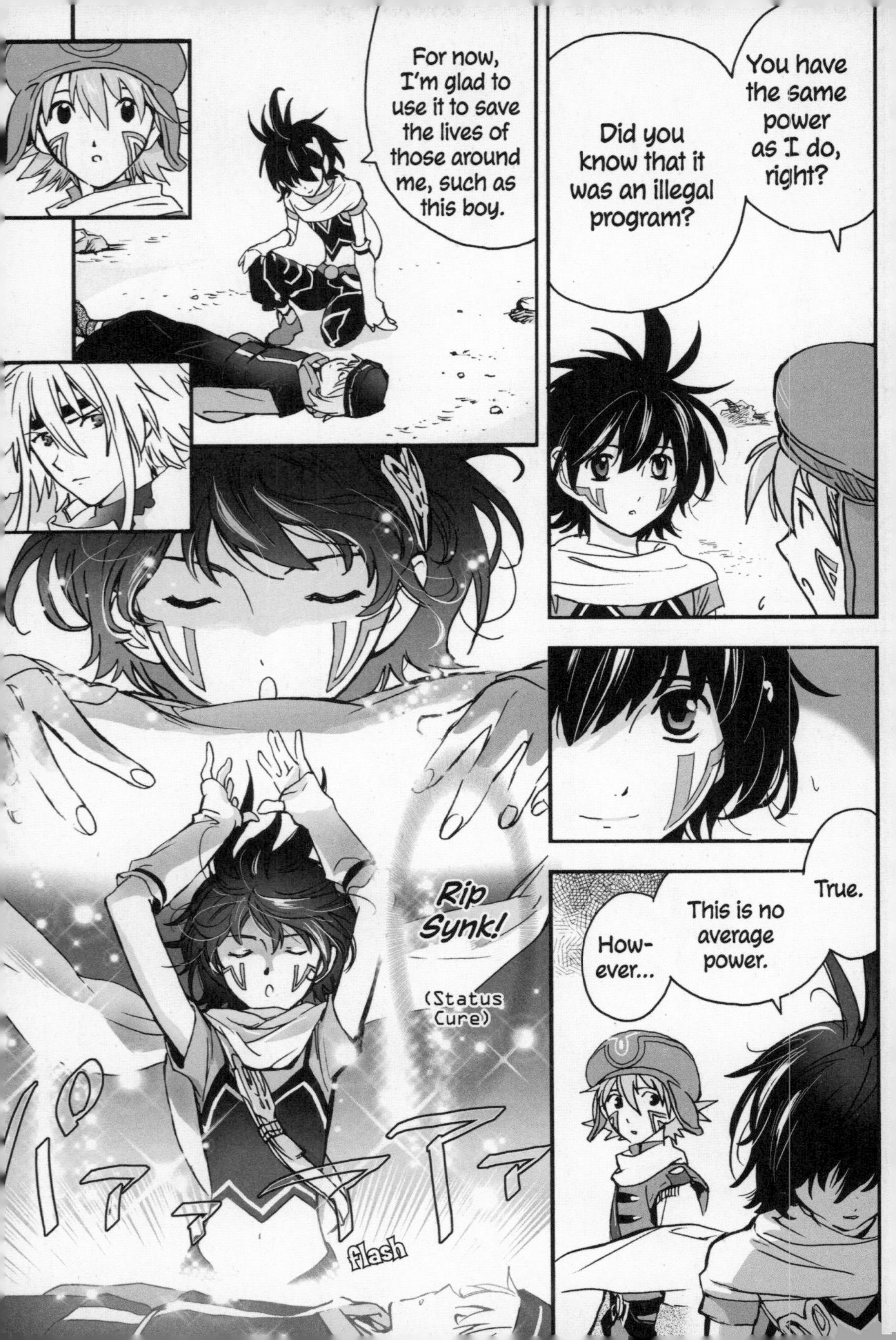

For now, I'm glad to use it to save the lives of those around me, such as this boy.
You have the same power as I do, right?
Did you know that it was an illegal program?
Rip Synk!
(Status Cure)
flash
True.
This is no average power.
How-ever...

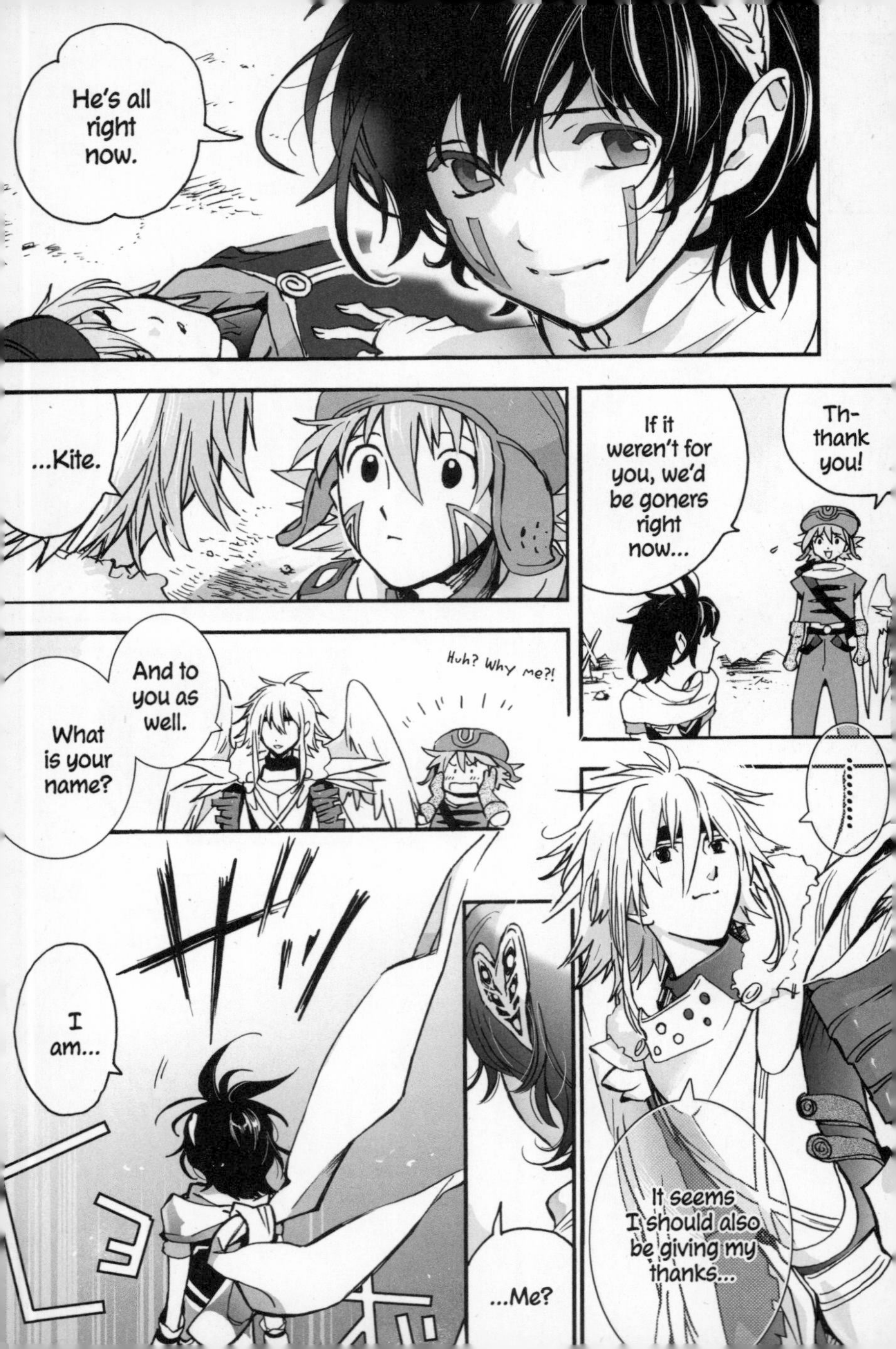
He's all right now.
Th-thank you!
If it weren't for you, we'd be goners right now...
...Kite.
And to you as well.
What is your name?
Huh? Why me?!
......
It seems I should also be giving my thanks...
...Me?
I am...

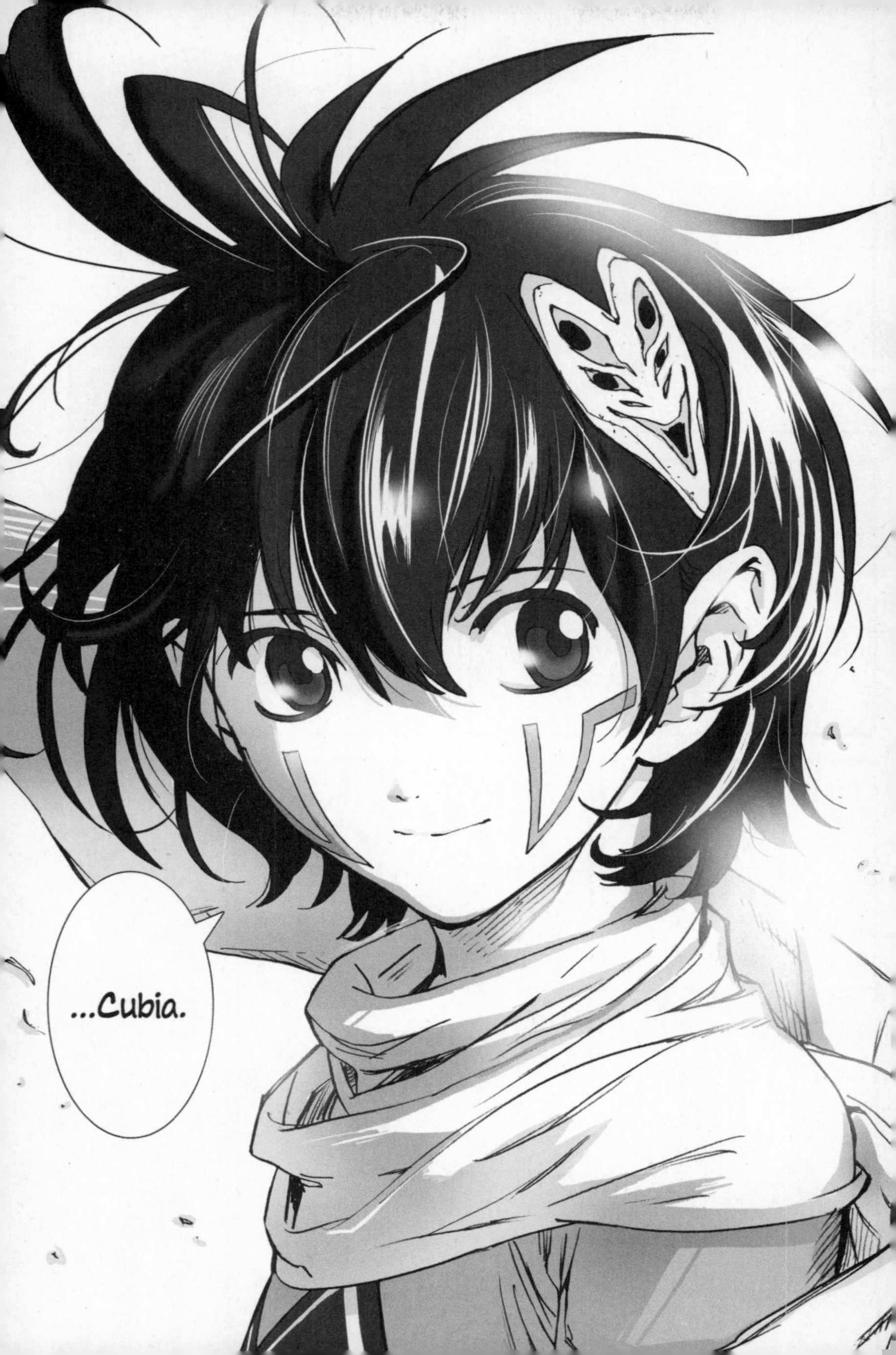
...Cubia.

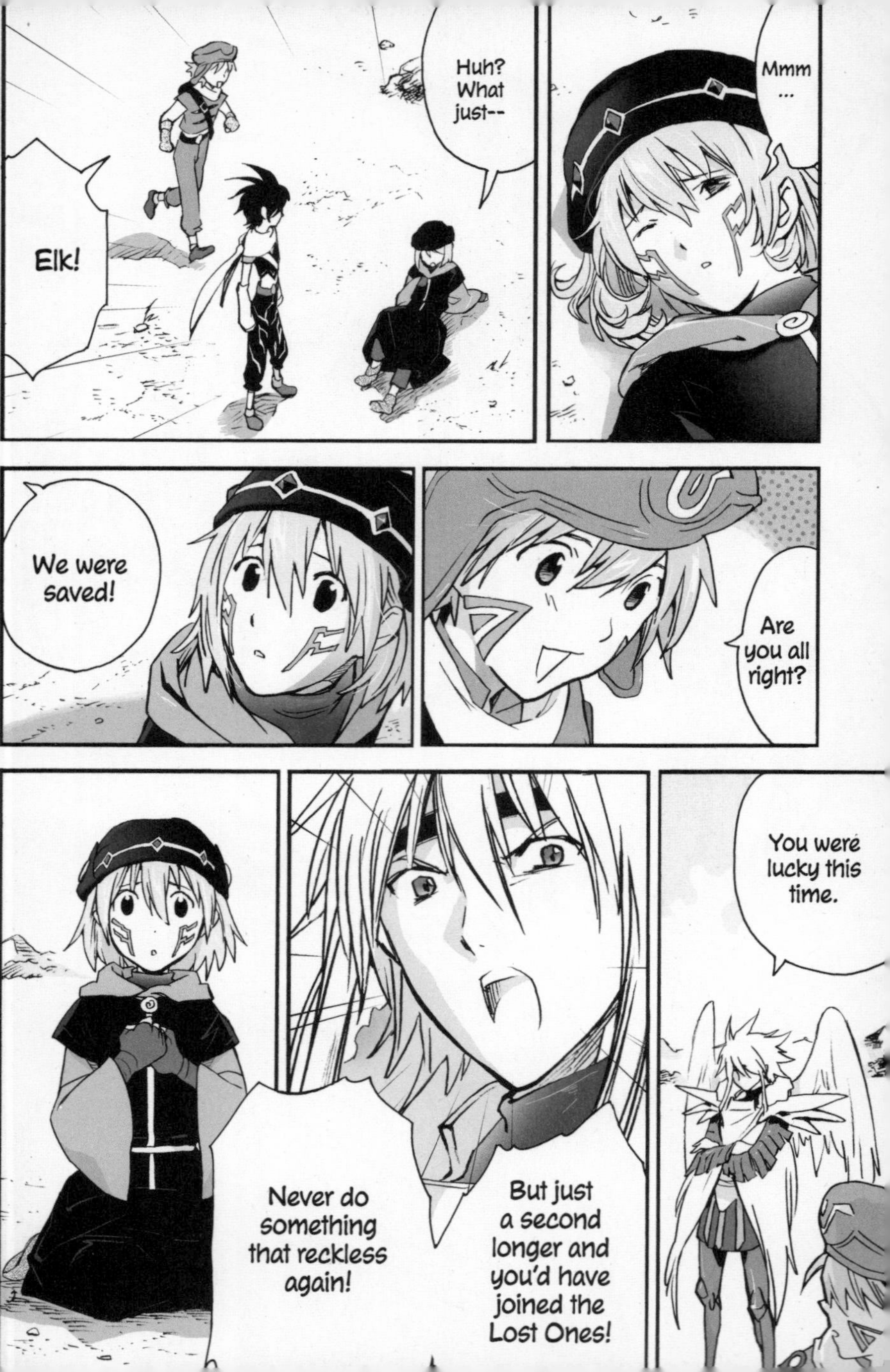
Mmm ...
Huh? What just--
Elk!
Are you all right?
We were saved!
You were lucky this time.
But just a second longer and you'd have joined the Lost Ones!
Never do something that reckless again!

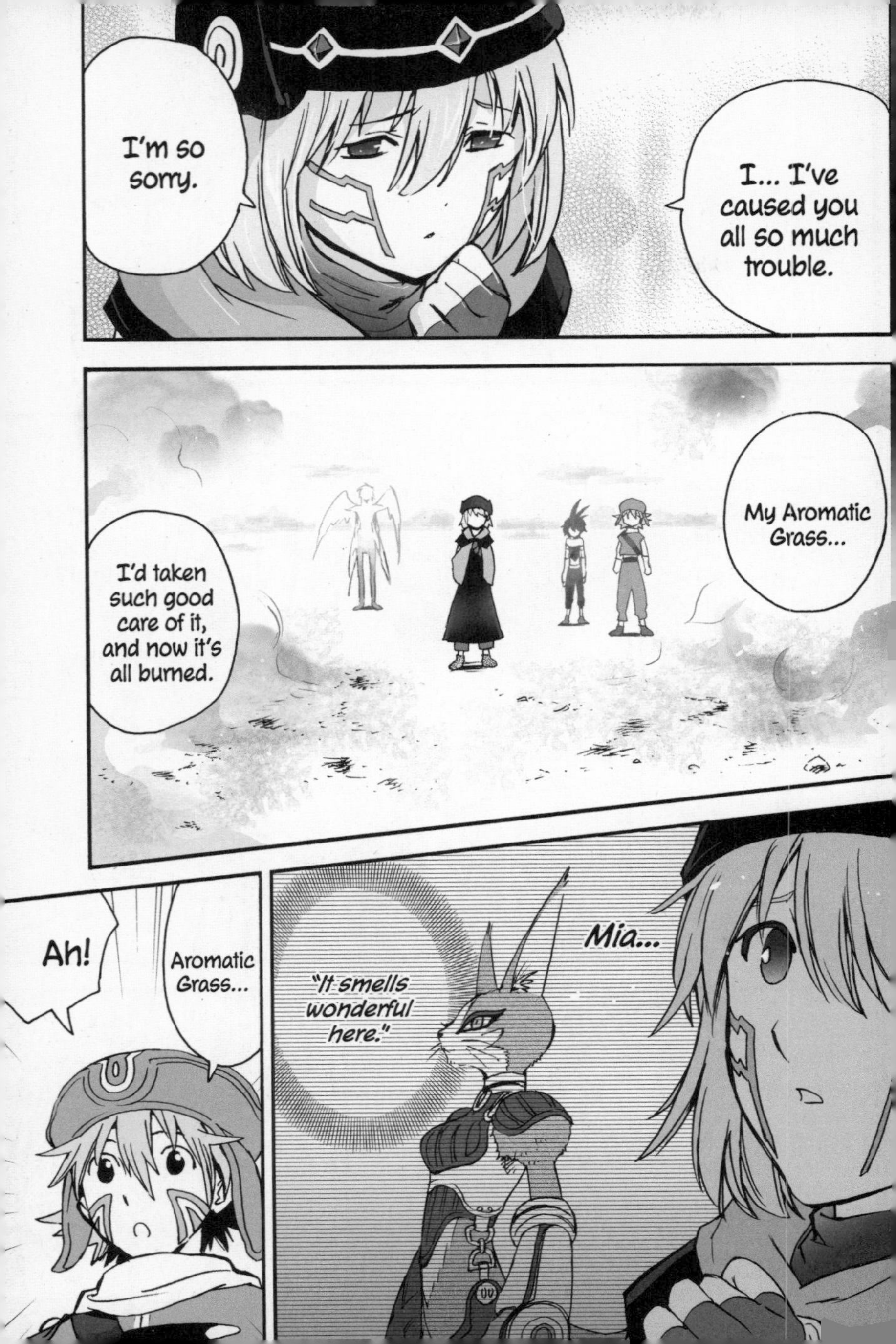

I... I've caused you all so much trouble.
I'm so sorry.
My Aromatic Grass...
I'd taken such good care of it, and now it's all burned.
Mia...
"It smells wonderful here."
Aromatic Grass...
Ah!

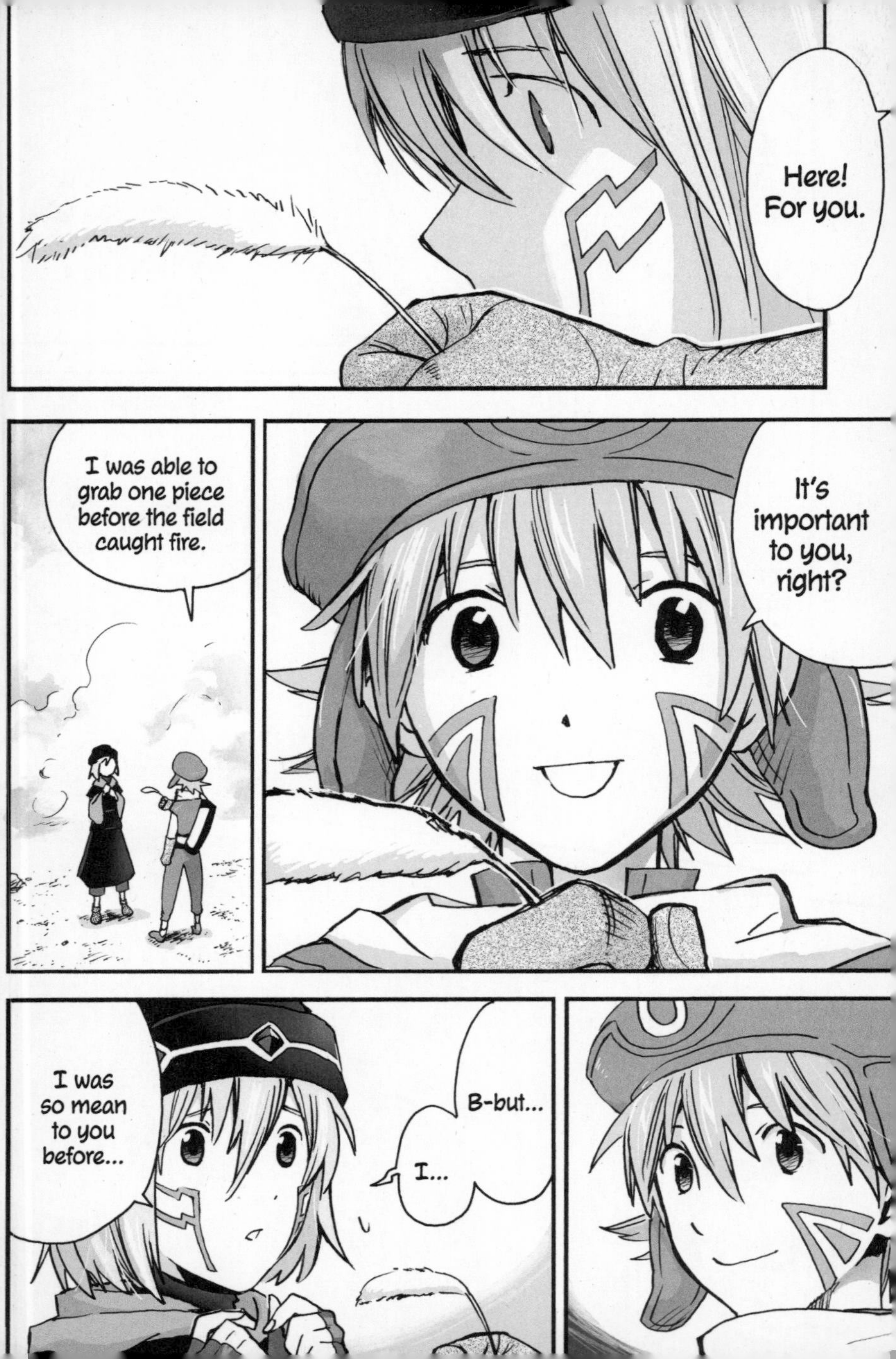
Here! For you.
It's important to you, right?
I was able to grab one piece before the field caught fire.
I was so mean to you before...
B-but...
I...

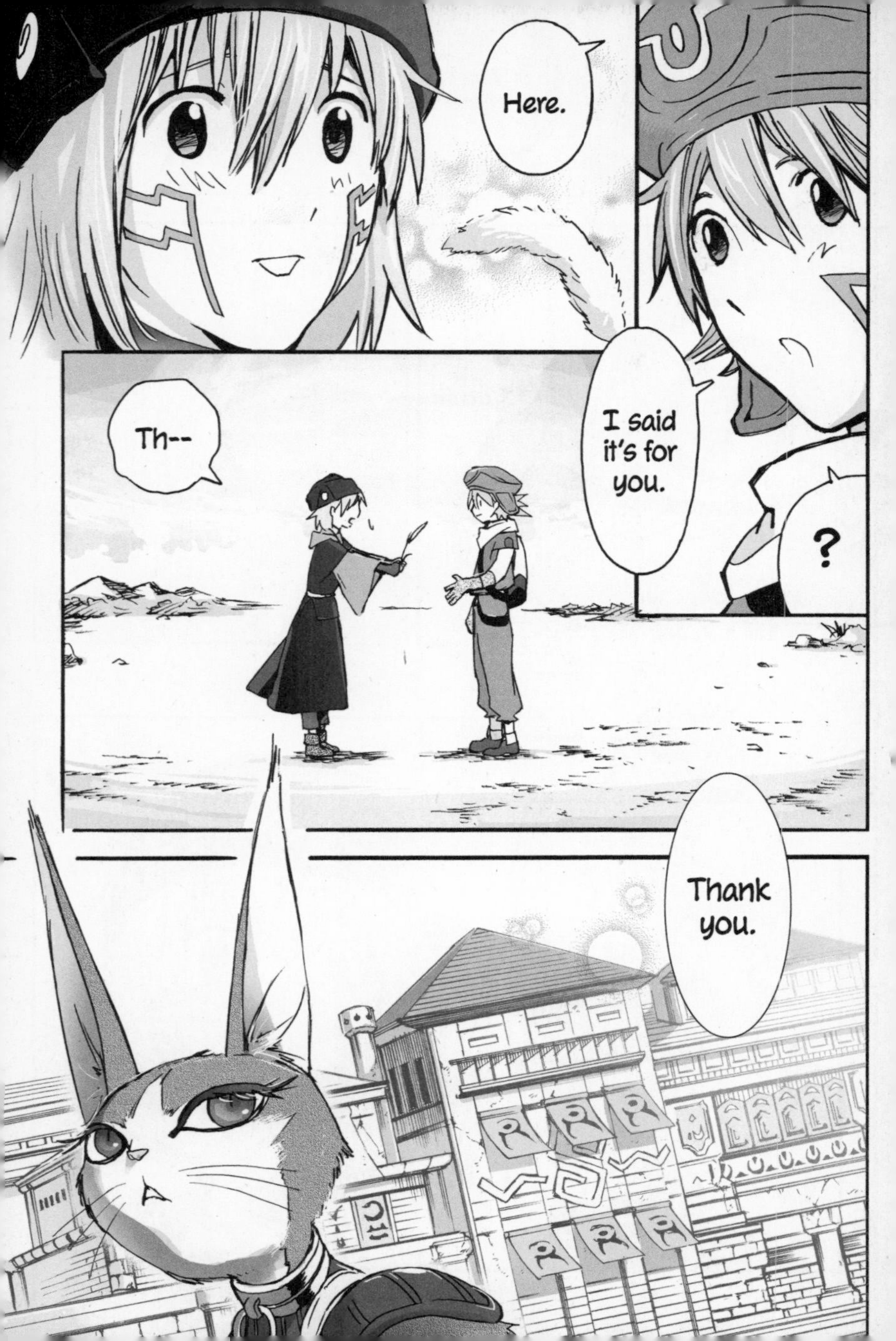
Here.
I said it's for you.
?
Th--
Thank you.

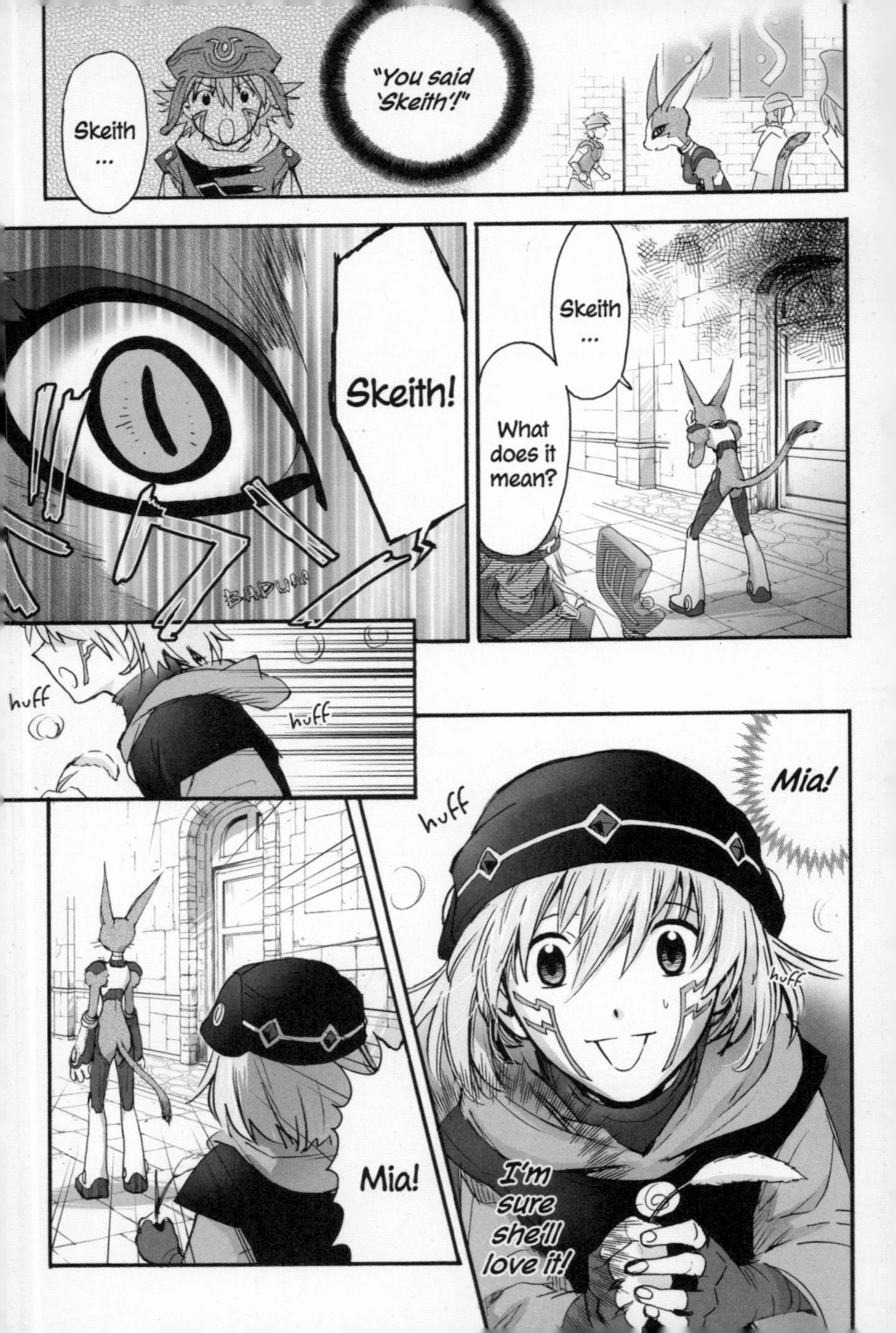
"You said 'Skeith'!"
Skeith ...
Skeith ...
What does it mean?
Skeith!
BADUM
huff
huff
Mia!
huff
huff
I'm sure she'll love it!
Mia!

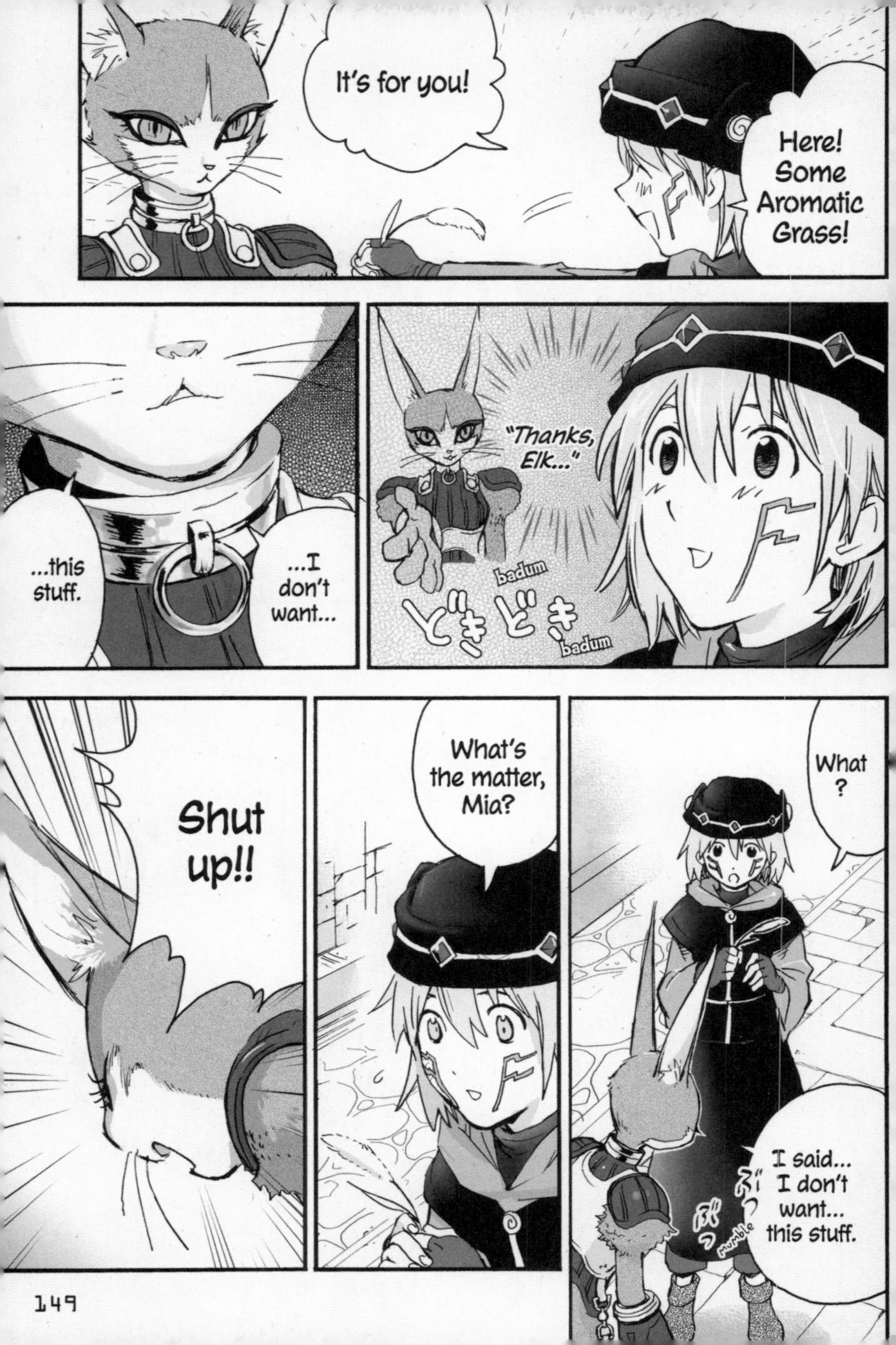
Here! Some Aromatic Grass!
It's for you!
"Thanks, Elk..."
badum
ドキドキ
badum
...I don't want...
...this stuff.
What?
I said... I don't want... this stuff.
ぶつぶつ
mumble
What's the matter, Mia?
Shut up!!

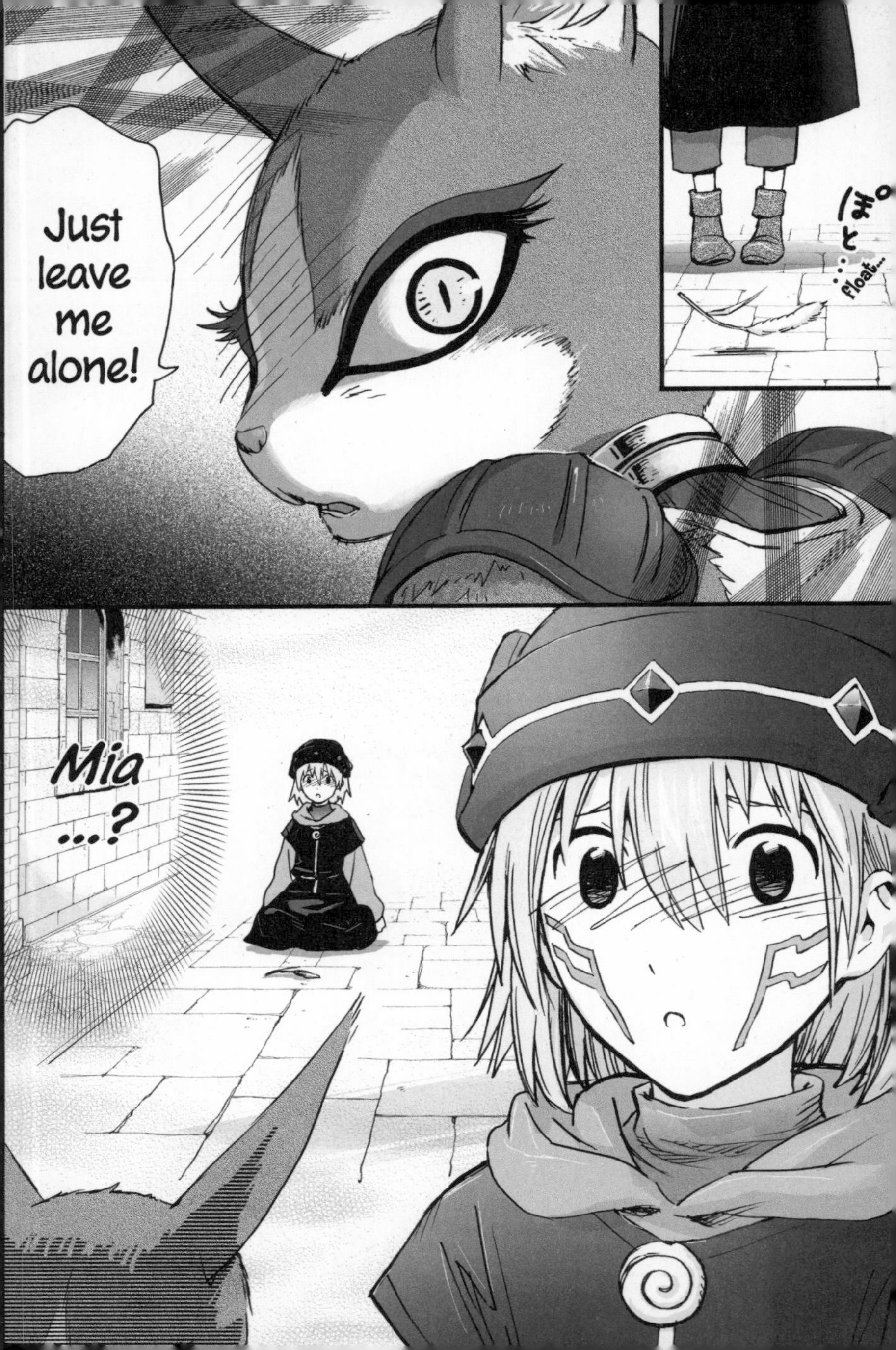
ぽと…
float...
Just leave me alone!
Mia ...?

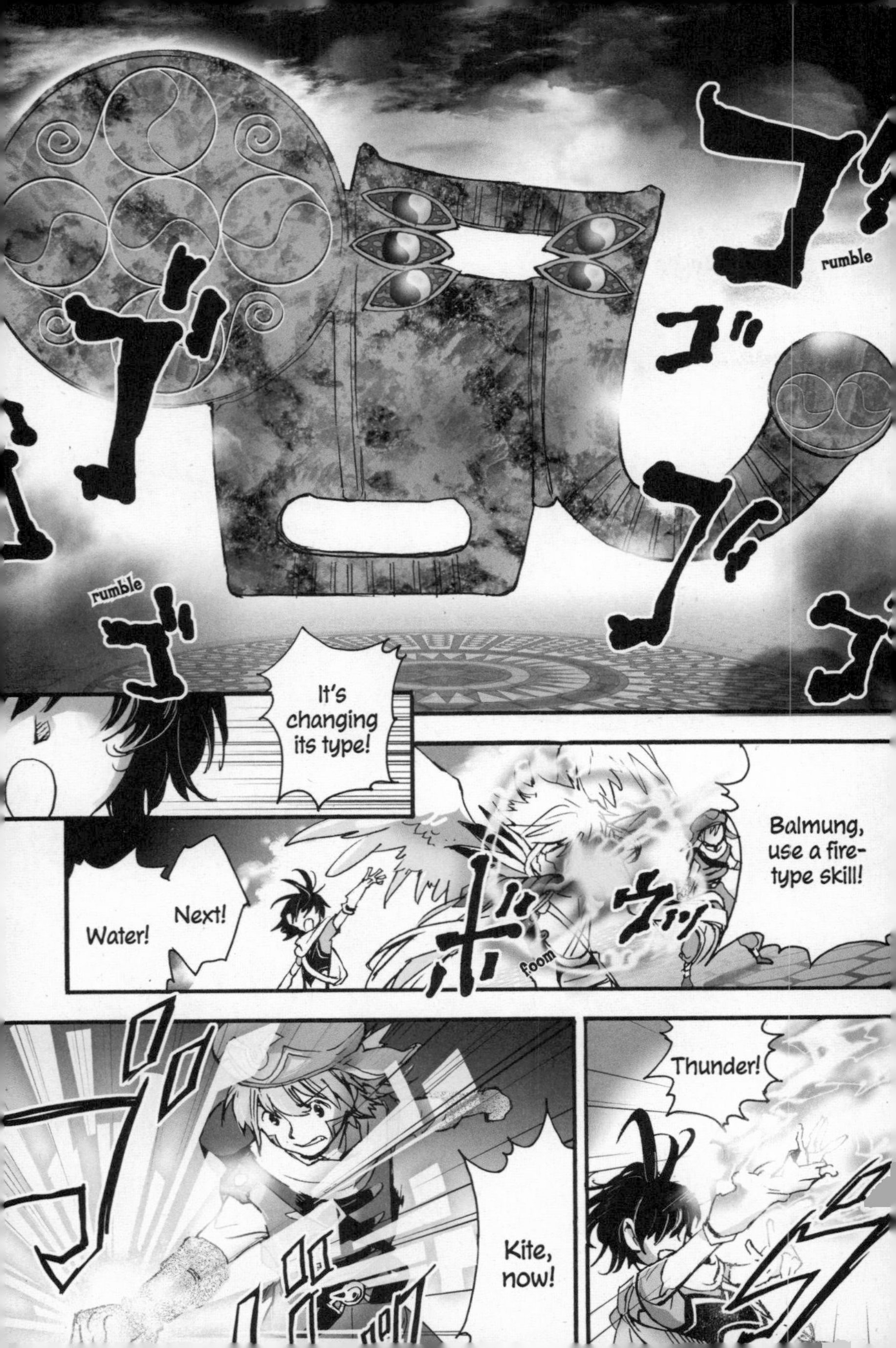
rumble
rumble
It's changing its type!
Balmung, use a fire-type skill!
foom
Next!
Water!
Thunder!
Kite, now!

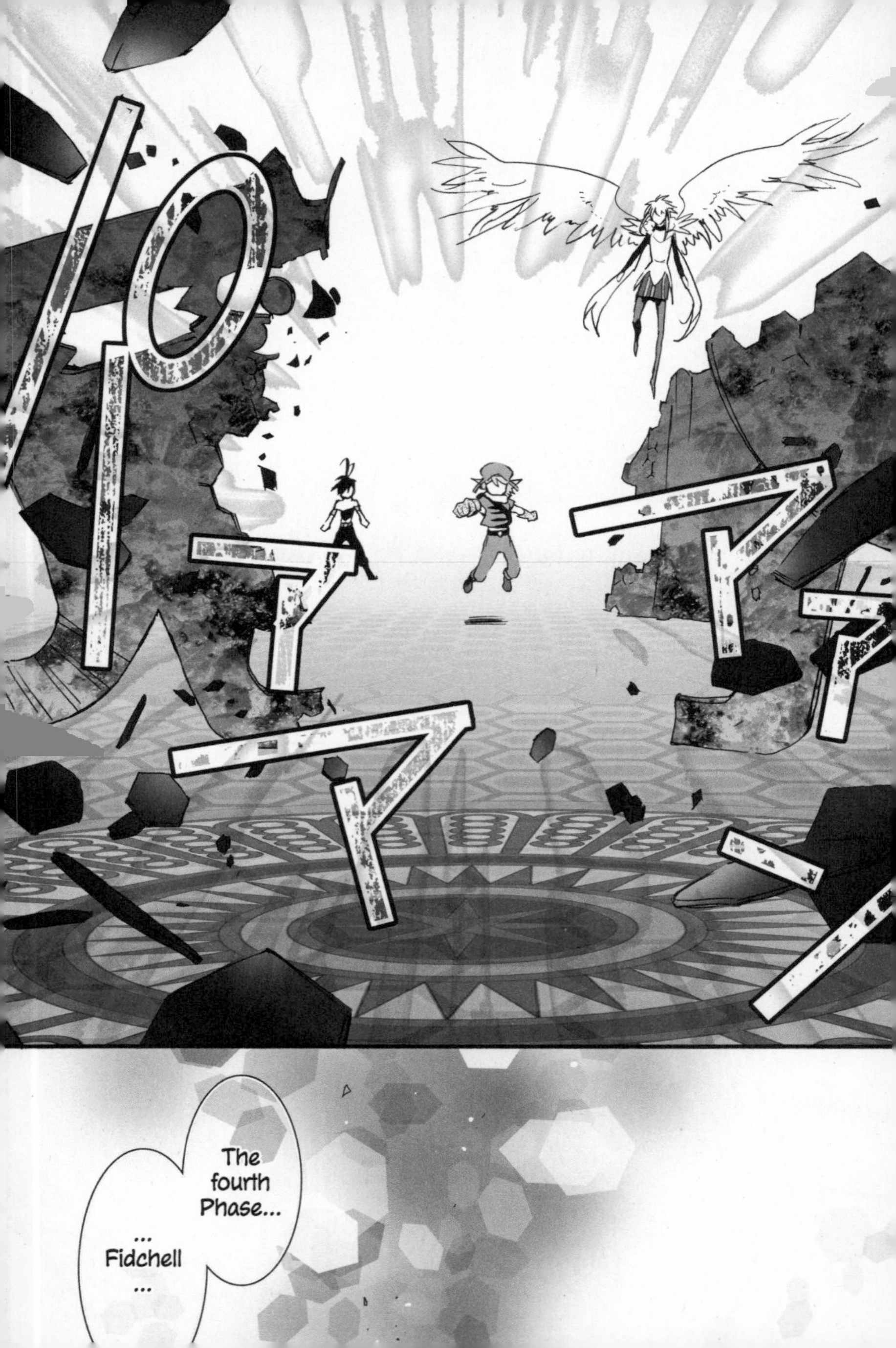
The fourth Phase... ... Fidchell ...

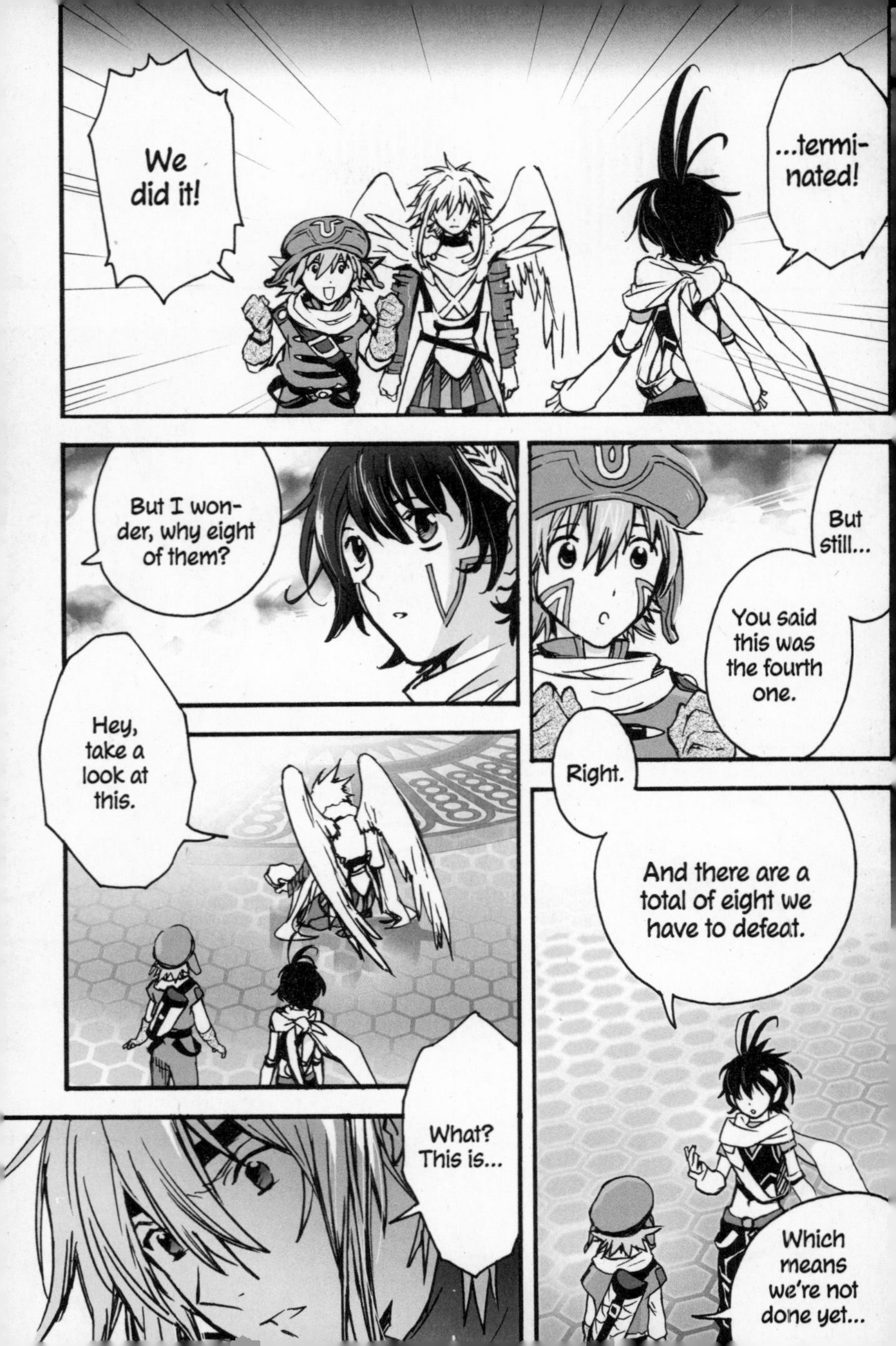
...termi-nated!
We did it!
But still...
You said this was the fourth one.
Right.
And there are a total of eight we have to defeat.
Which means we're not done yet...
But I wonder, why eight of them?
Hey, take a look at this.
What? This is...

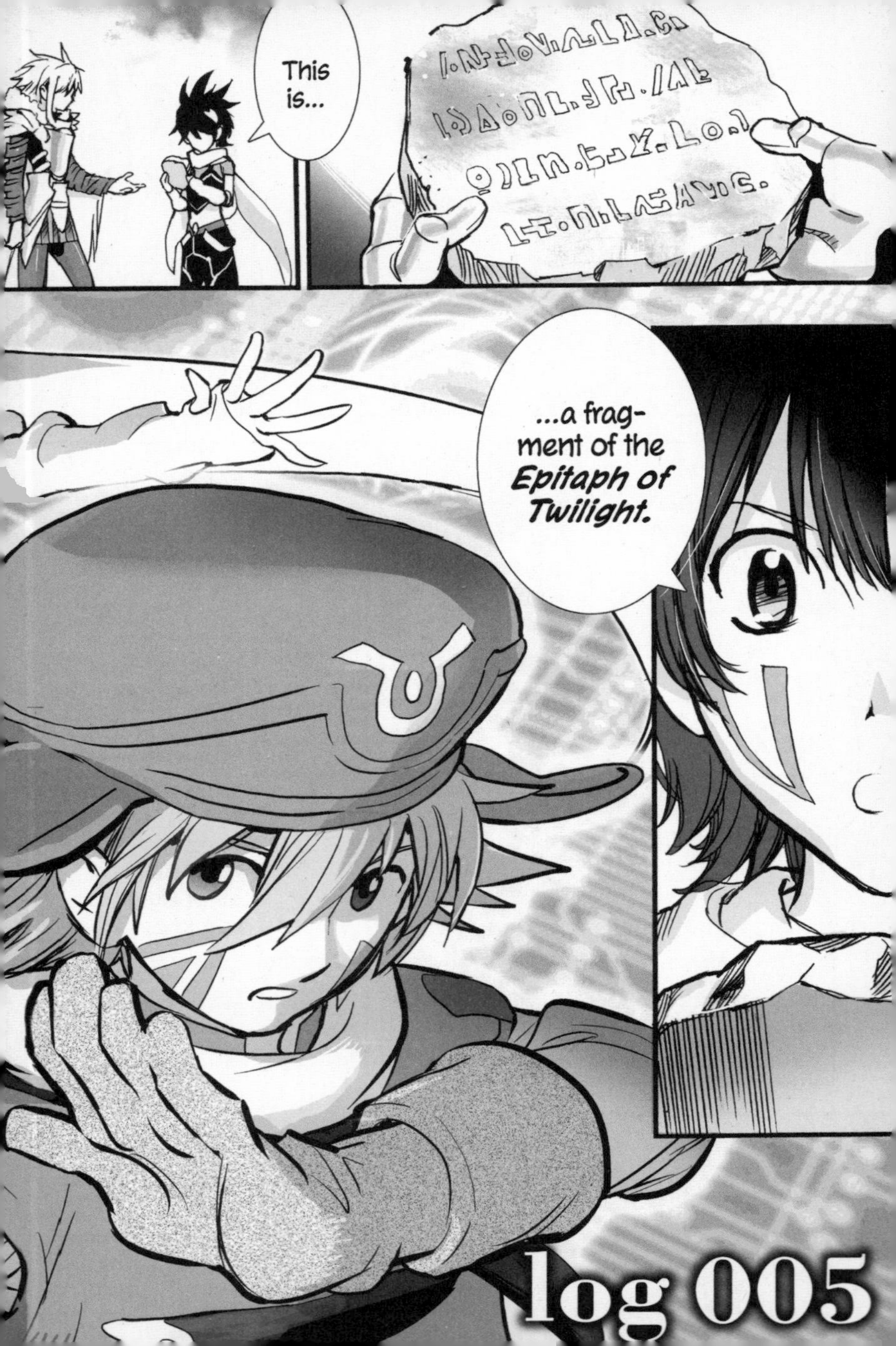
This is...
...a fragment of the *Epitaph of Twilight.*
log 005

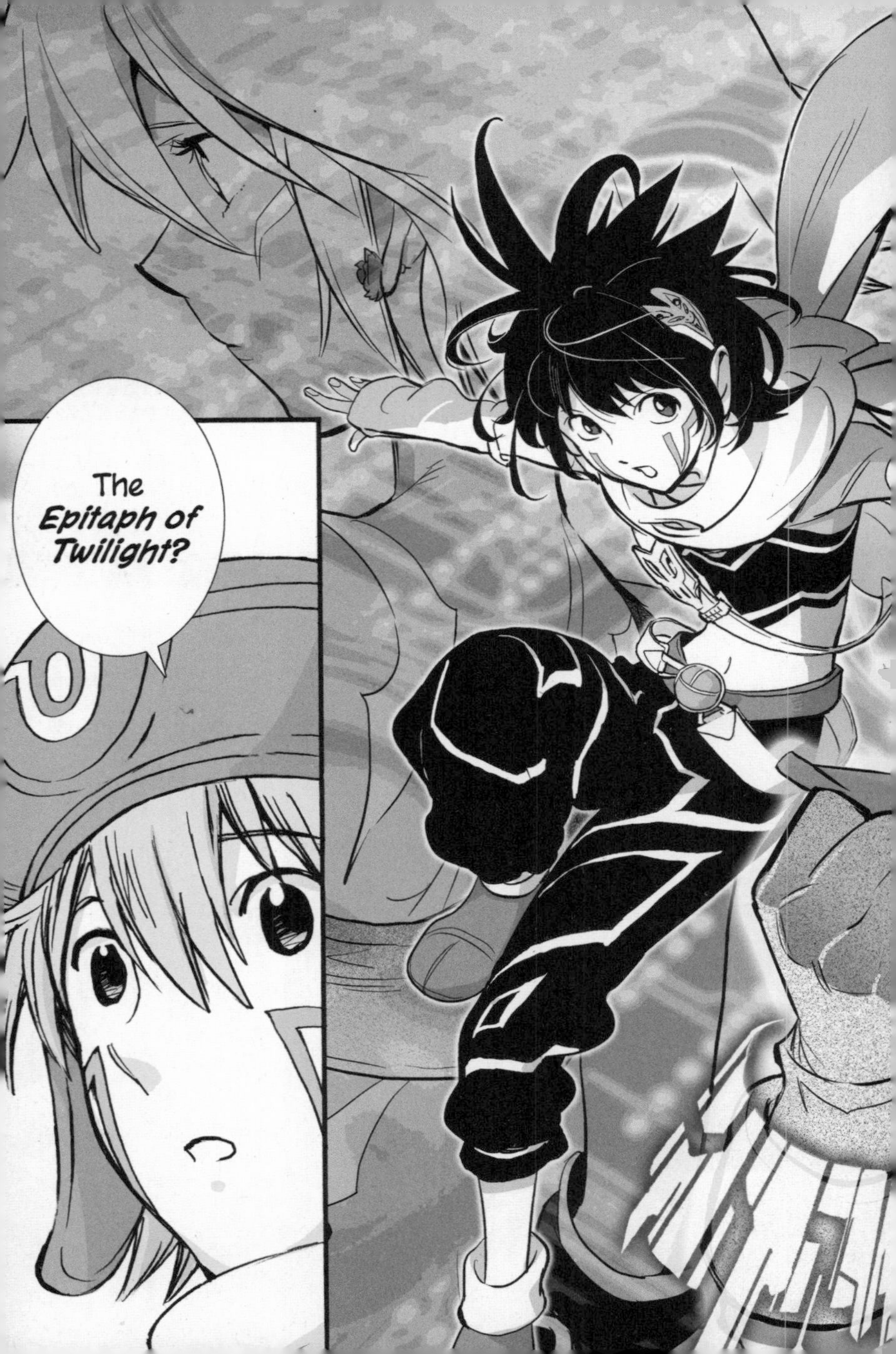
The *Epitaph of Twilight?*

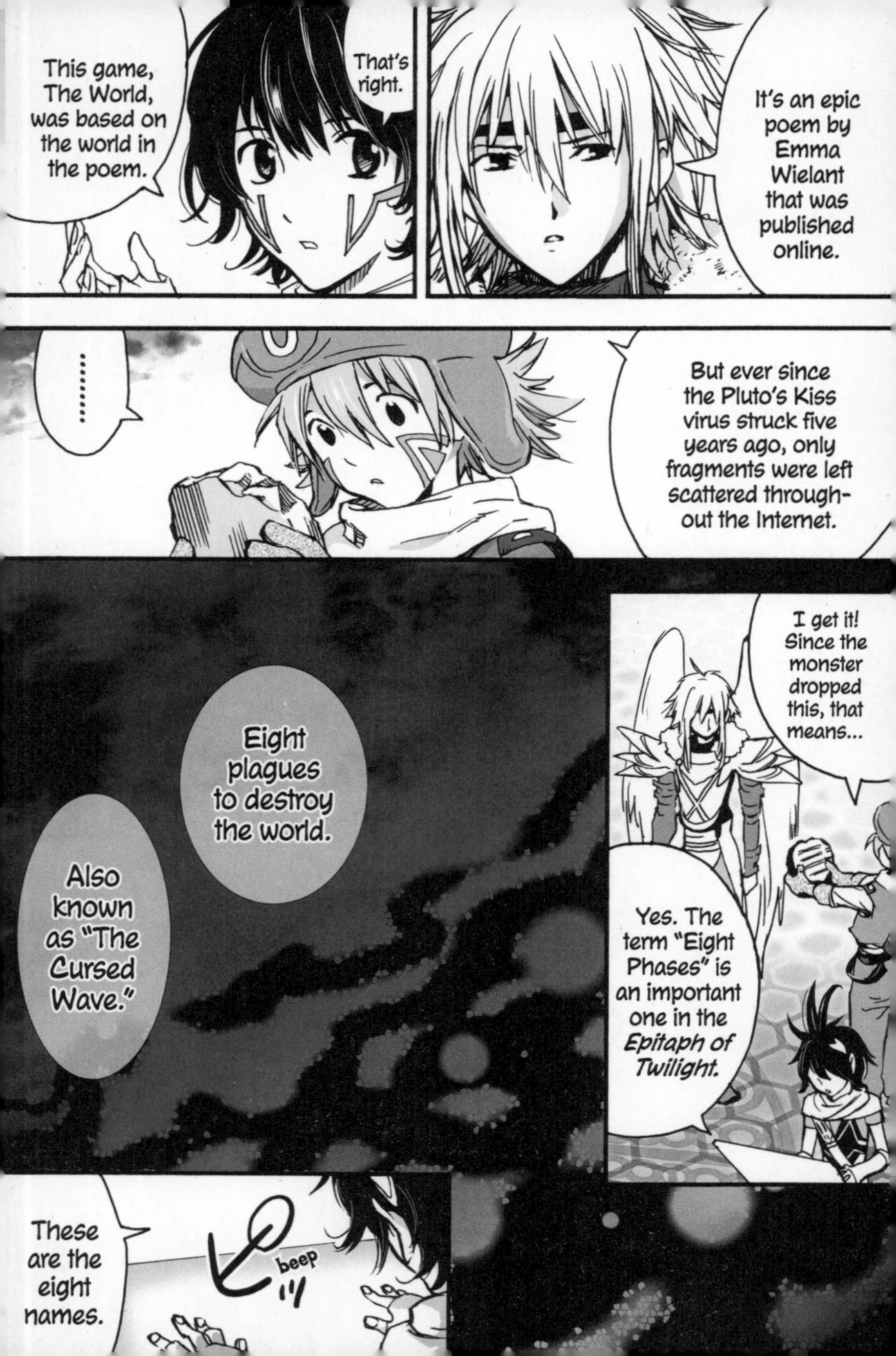
It's an epic poem by Emma Wielant that was published online.
That's right.
This game, The World, was based on the world in the poem.
But ever since the Pluto's Kiss virus struck five years ago, only fragments were left scattered through-out the Internet.
....
I get it! Since the monster dropped this, that means...
Yes. The term "Eight Phases" is an important one in the *Epitaph of Twilight.*
Eight plagues to destroy the world.
Also known as "The Cursed Wave."
beep
These are the eight names.

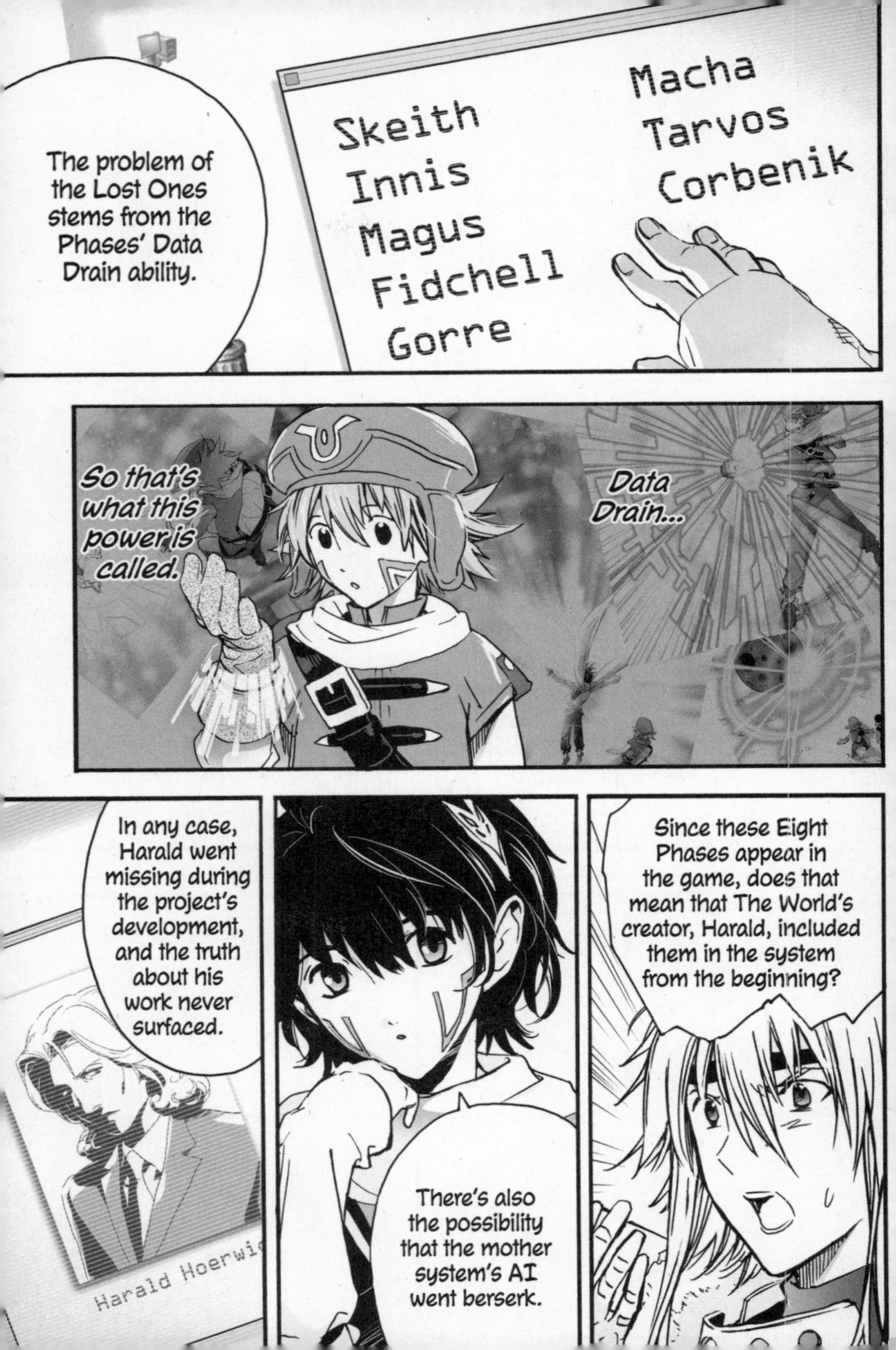
The problem of the Lost Ones stems from the Phases' Data Drain ability.
Skeith
Innis
Magus
Fidchell
Gorre
Macha
Tarvos
Corbenik
So that's what this power is called.
Data Drain...
In any case, Harald went missing during the project's development, and the truth about his work never surfaced.
Harald Hoerwi
Since these Eight Phases appear in the game, does that mean that The World's creator, Harald, included them in the system from the beginning?
There's also the possibility that the mother system's AI went berserk.

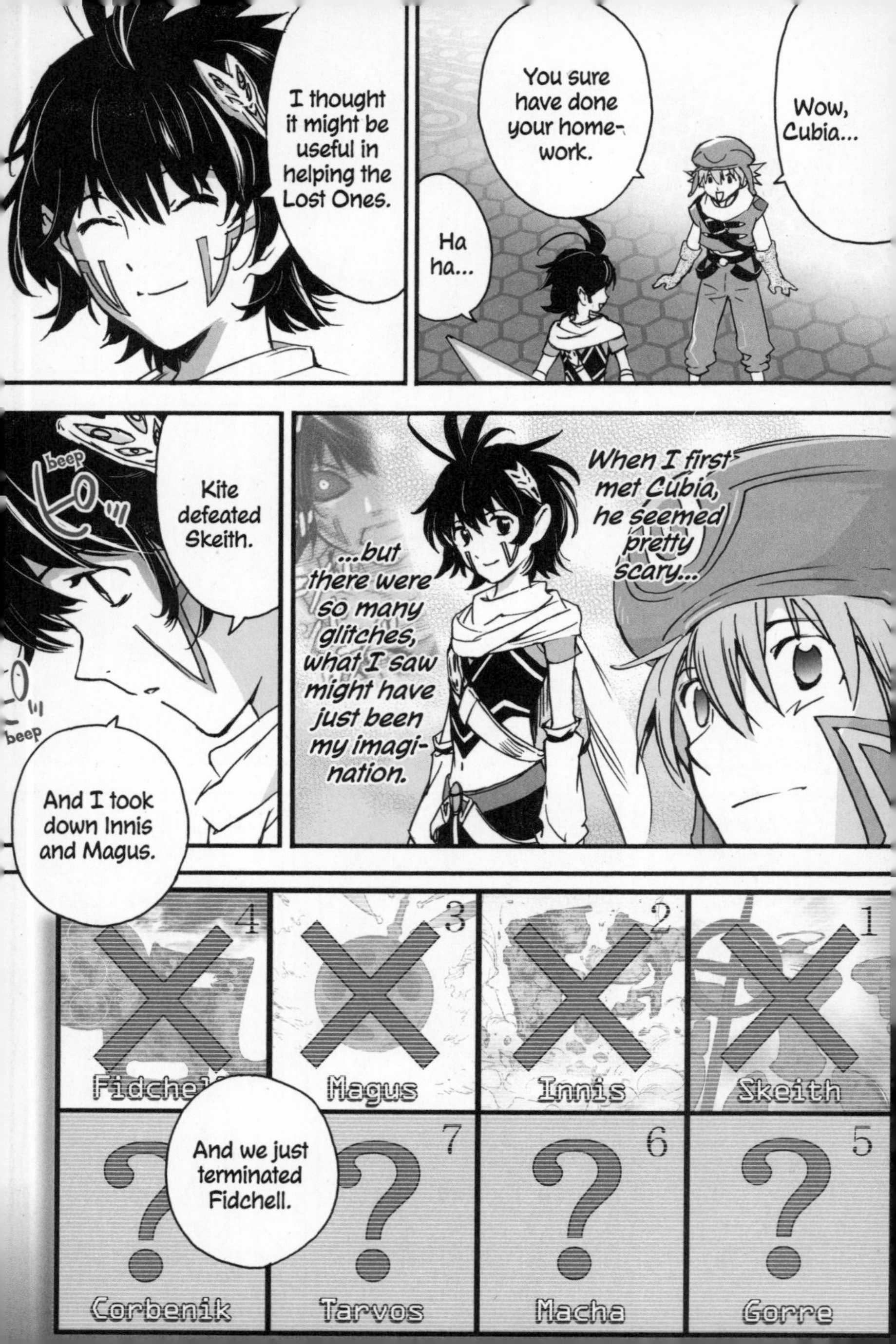
Wow, Cubia...
You sure have done your home-work.
Ha ha...
I thought it might be useful in helping the Lost Ones.
When I first met Cubia, he seemed pretty scary...
...but there were so many glitches, what I saw might have just been my imagination.
beep
beep
Kite defeated Skeith.
And I took down Innis and Magus.
1
Skeith
2
Innis
3
Magus
4
Fidchell
And we just terminated Fidchell.
5
Gorre
6
Macha
7
Tarvos
Corbenik

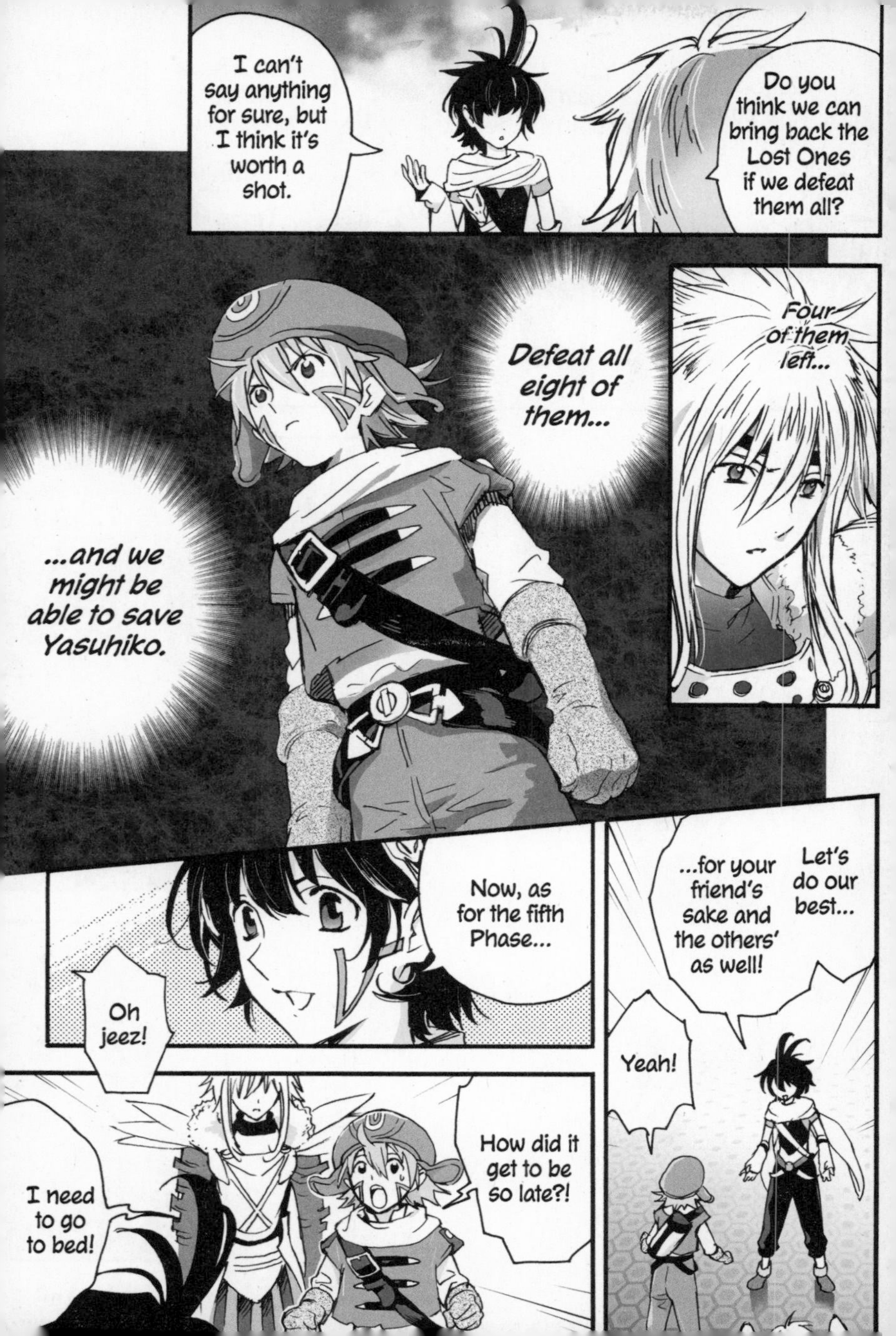
Do you think we can bring back the Lost Ones if we defeat them all?
I can't say anything for sure, but I think it's worth a shot.
Four of them left...
Defeat all eight of them...
...and we might be able to save Yasuhiko.
Let's do our best...
...for your friend's sake and the others' as well!
Yeah!
Now, as for the fifth Phase...
Oh jeez!
How did it get to be so late?!
I need to go to bed!

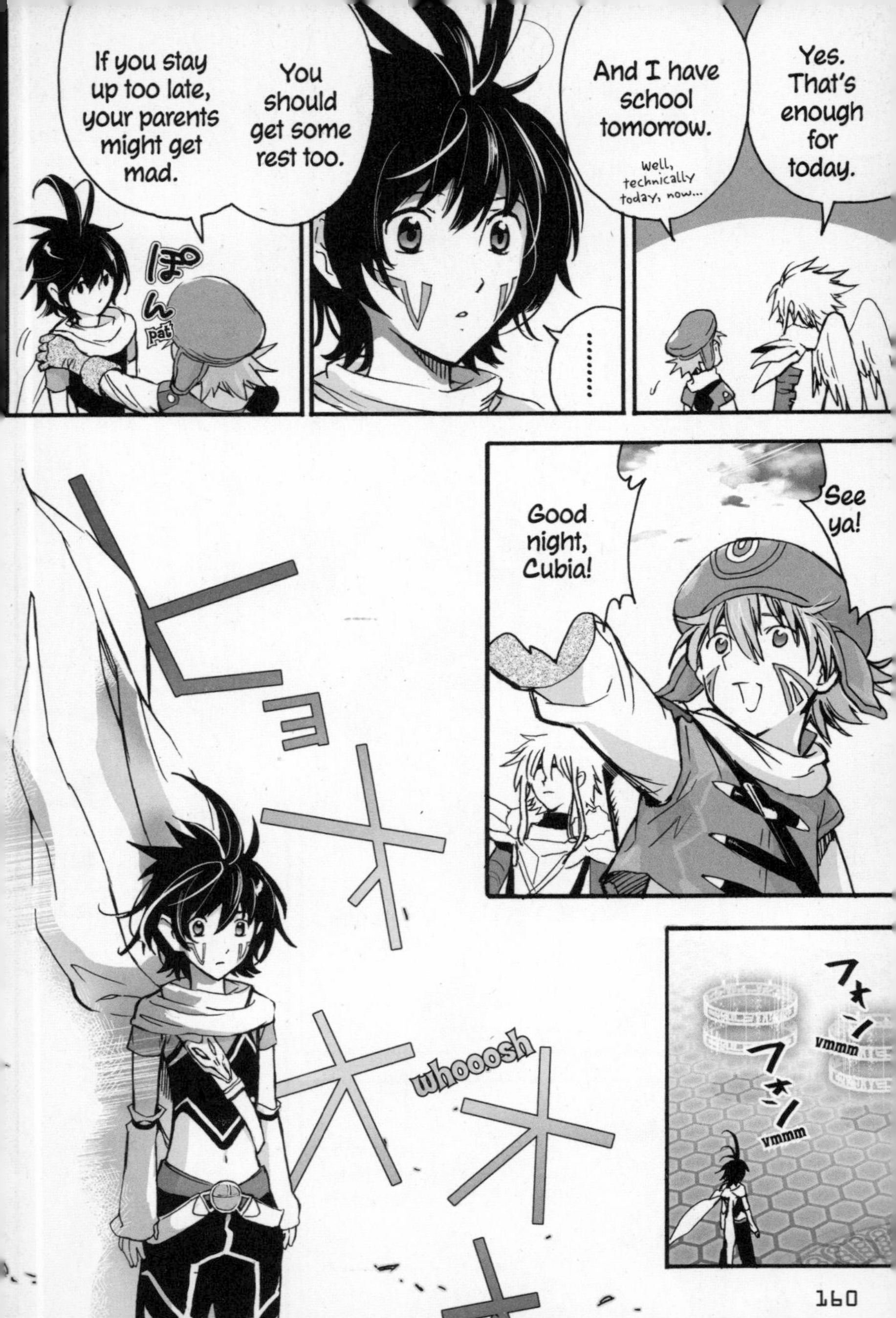
Yes. That's enough for today.
And I have school tomorrow.
Well, technically today, now...
......
You should get some rest too.
If you stay up too late, your parents might get mad.
ぽん
pat
See ya!
Good night, Cubia!
フォン
vmmm
フォン
vmmm
ヒュォォォ
whoooosh

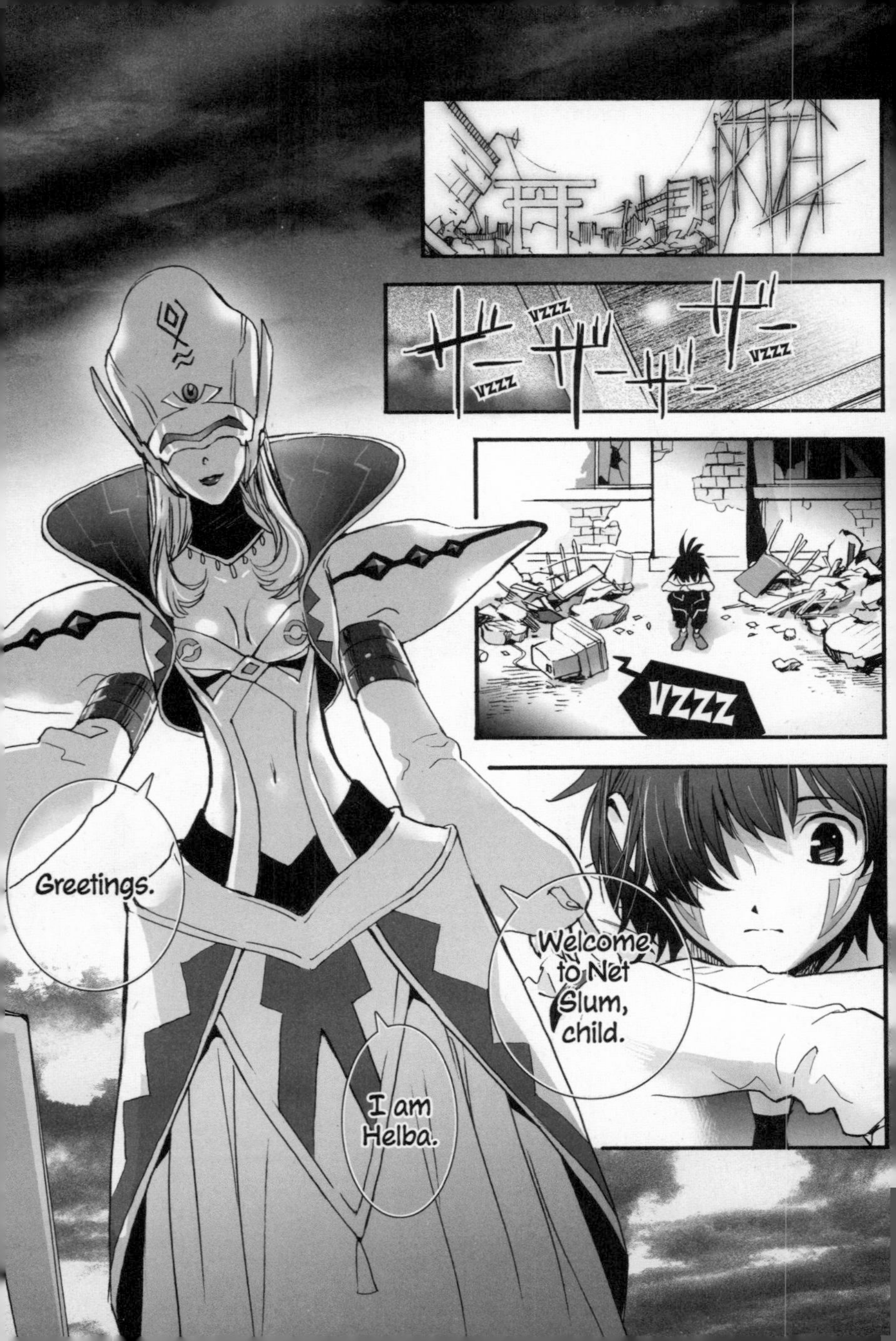
VZZZ
VZZZ
VZZZ
VZZZ
Welcome to Net Slum, child.
Greetings.
I am Helba.

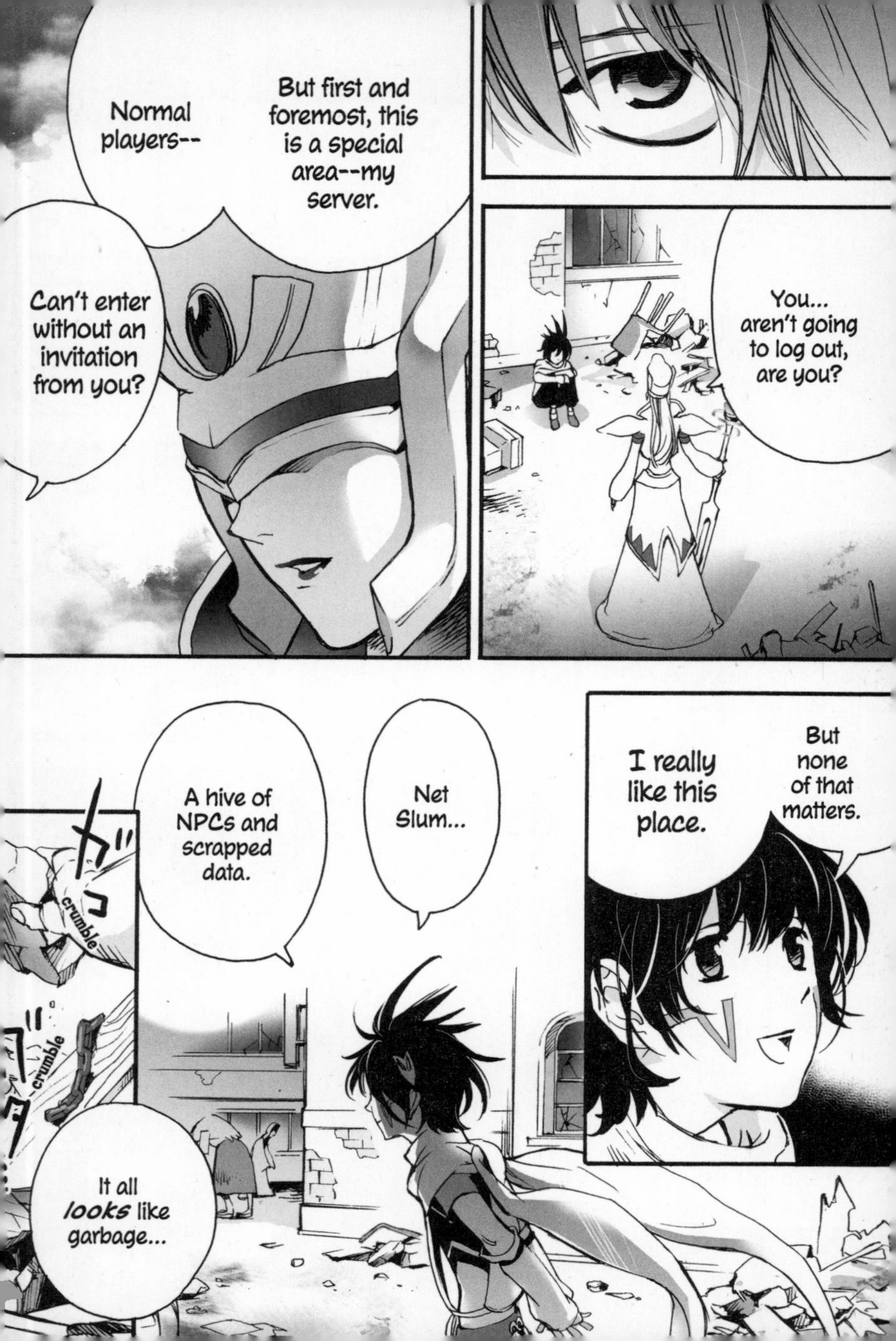

You... aren't going to log out, are you?
But first and foremost, this is a special area--my server.
Normal players--
Can't enter without an invitation from you?
But none of that matters.
I really like this place.
Net Slum...
A hive of NPCs and scrapped data.
crumble
crumble
It all *looks* like garbage...

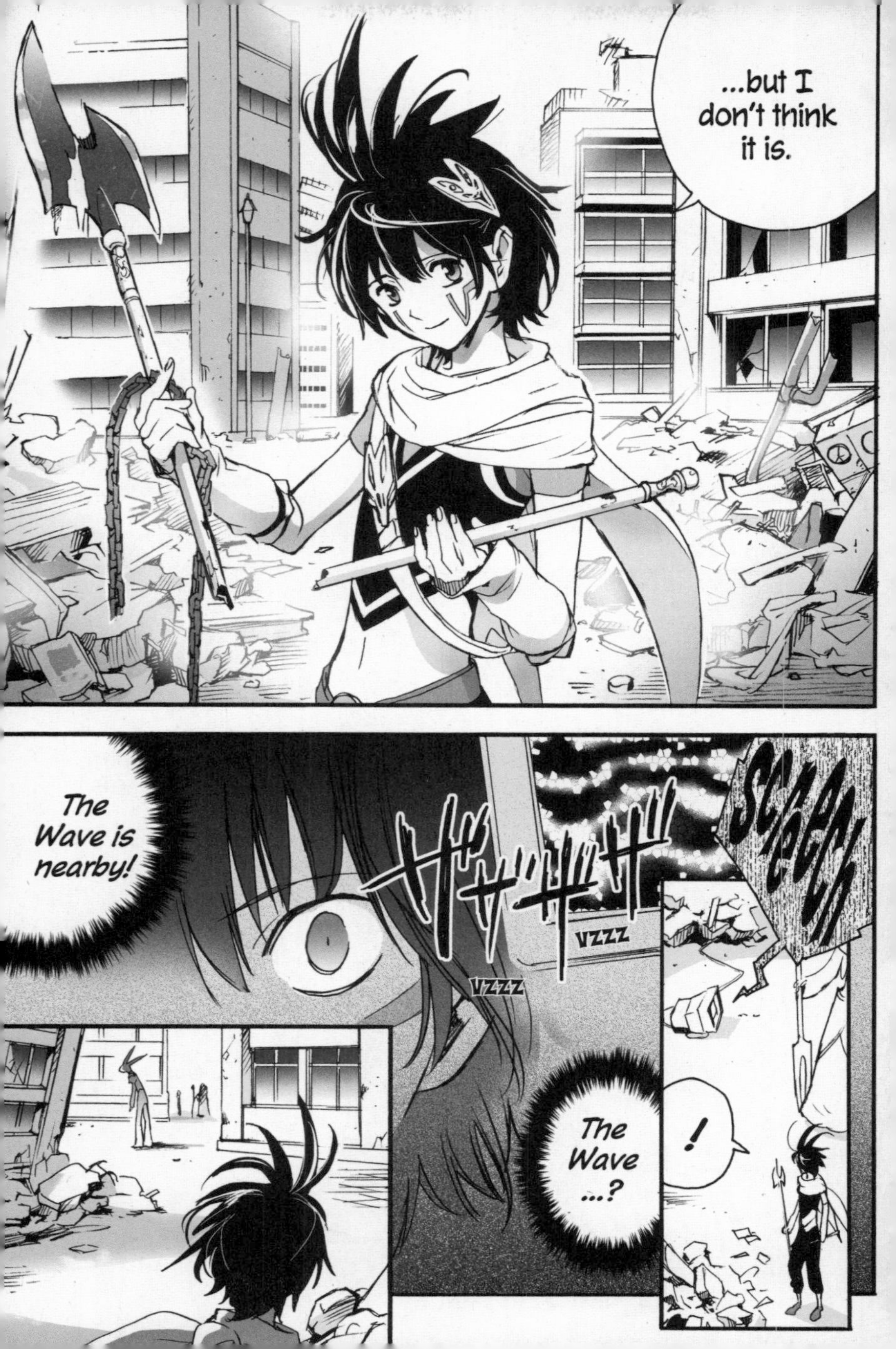
...but I don't think it is.
SCREECH
VZZZ
VZZZZ
The Wave is nearby!
!
The Wave ...?

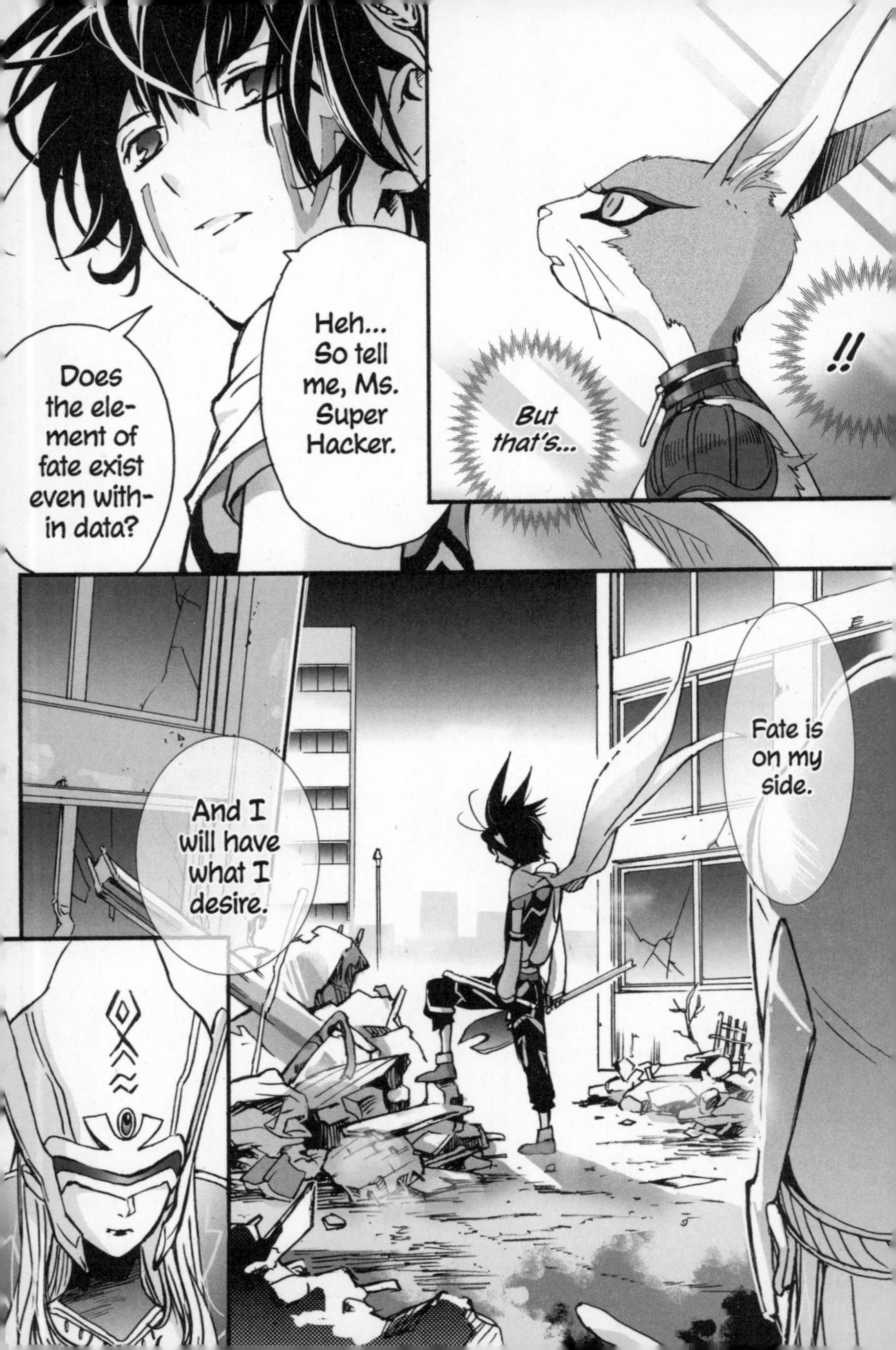
!!
But that's...
Heh... So tell me, Ms. Super Hacker.
Does the ele-ment of fate exist even with-in data?
Fate is on my side.
And I will have what I desire.

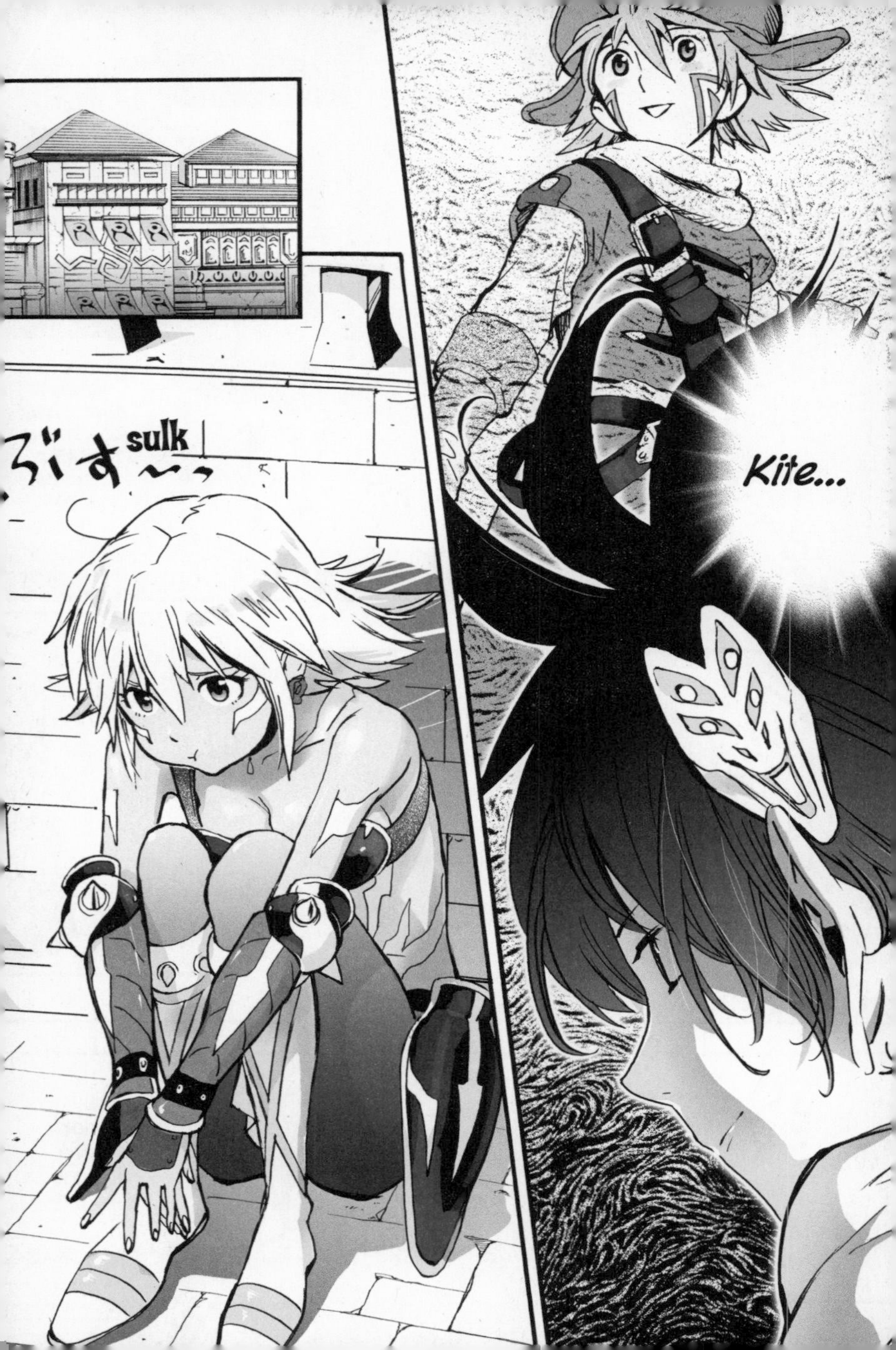
Kite...
ぶいす
sulk

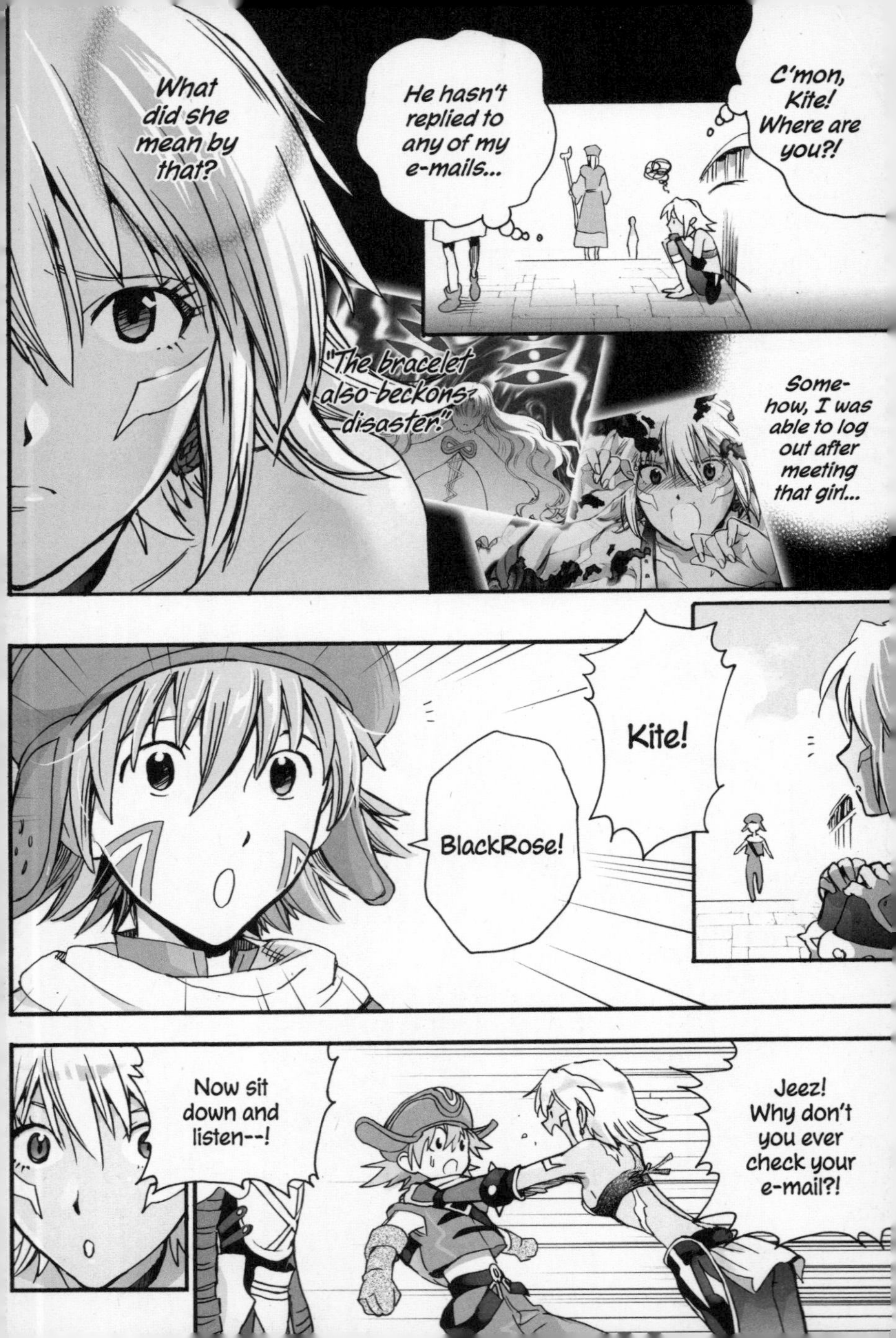

C'mon, Kite! Where are you?!
He hasn't replied to any of my e-mails...
Somehow, I was able to log out after meeting that girl...
"The bracelet also beckons disaster."
What did she mean by that?
Kite!
BlackRose!
Jeez! Why don't you ever check your e-mail?!
Now sit down and listen--!

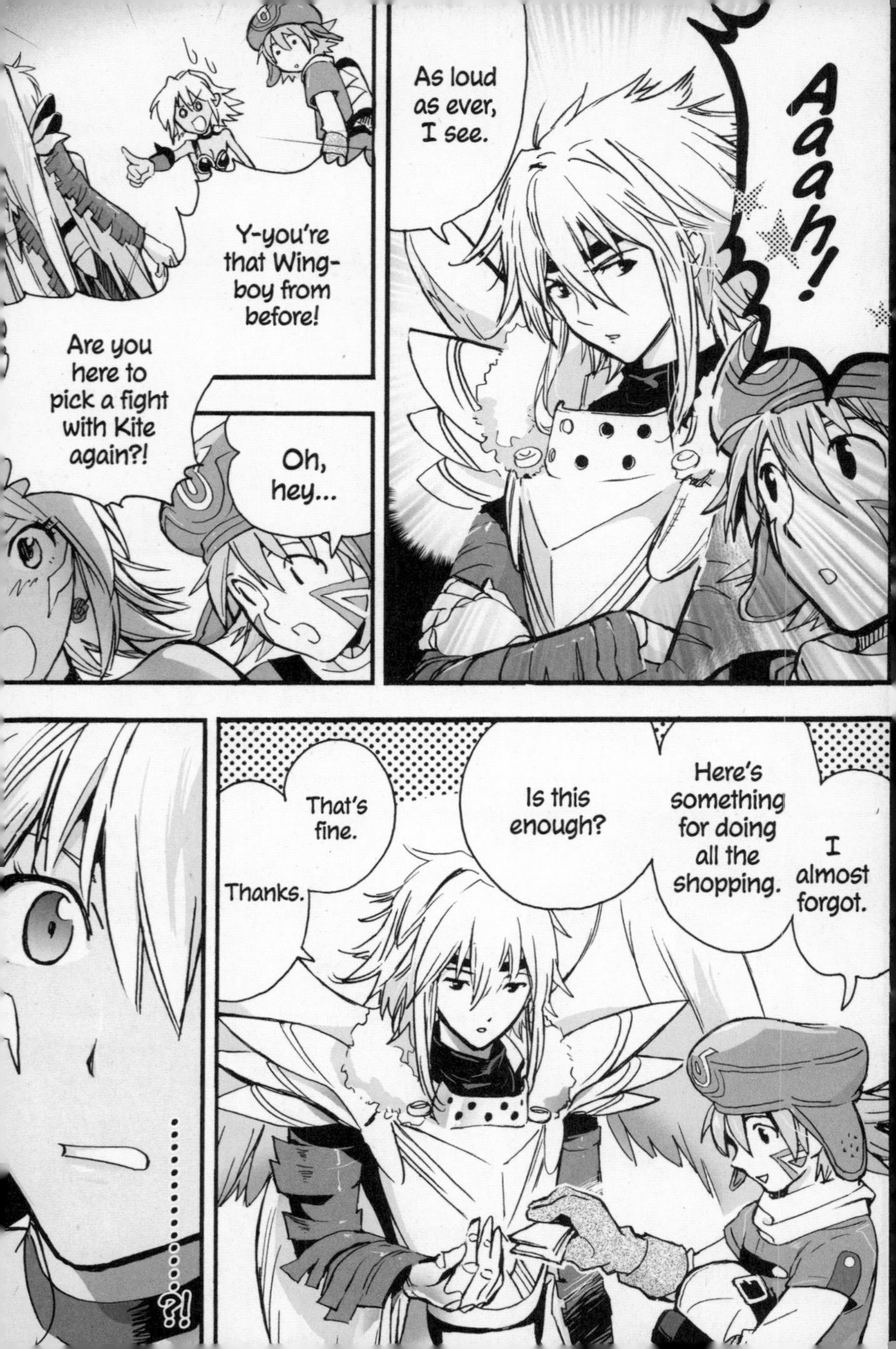
Aaaah!
As loud as ever, I see.
Y-you're that Wing-boy from before!
Are you here to pick a fight with Kite again?!
Oh, hey...
I almost forgot.
Here's something for doing all the shopping.
Is this enough?
That's fine.
Thanks.
..........?!

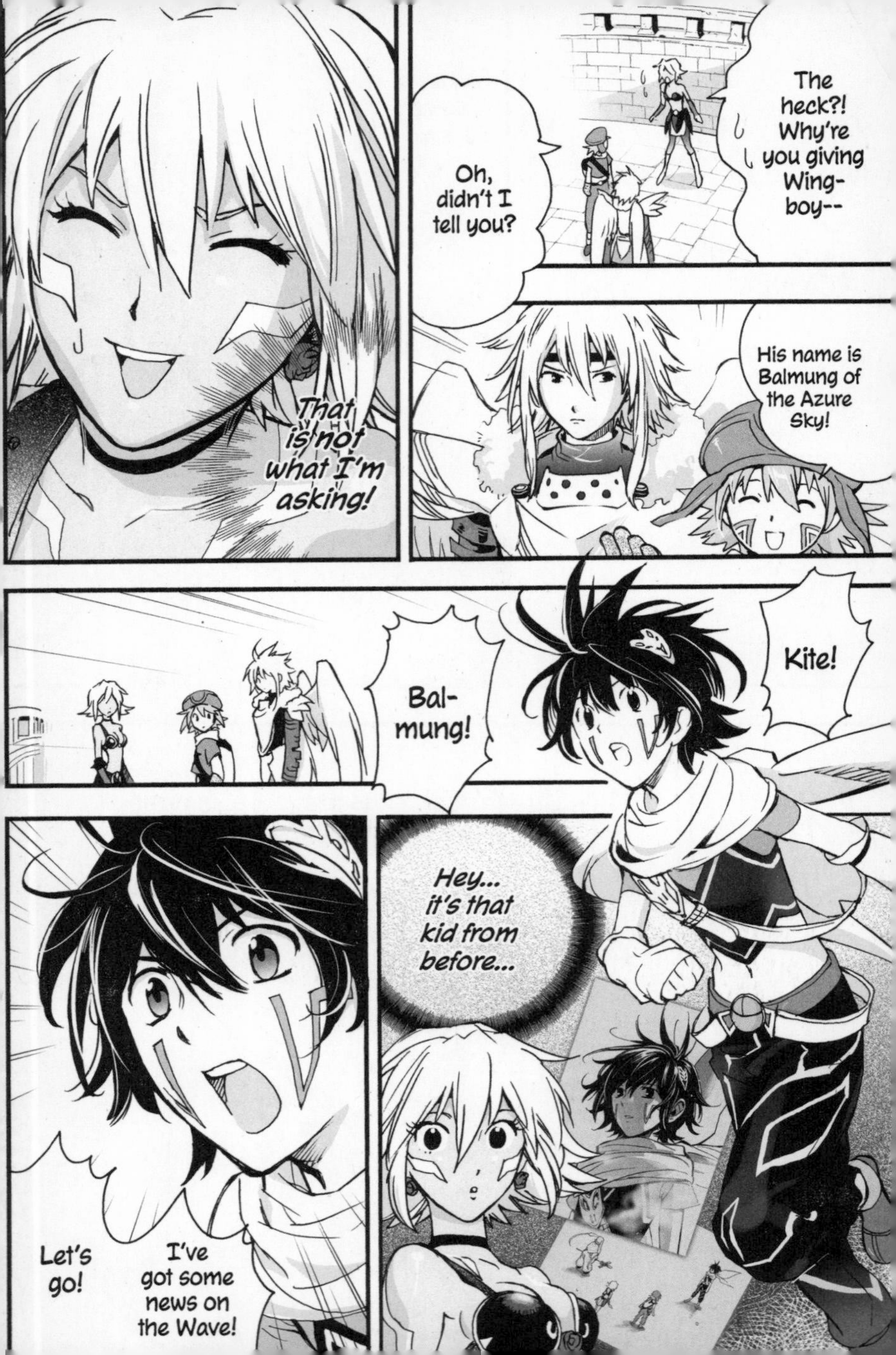
The heck?! Why're you giving Wing-boy--
Oh, didn't I tell you?
His name is Balmung of the Azure Sky!
That is not what I'm asking!
Kite!
Bal-mung!
Hey... it's that kid from before...
I've got some news on the Wave!
Let's go!

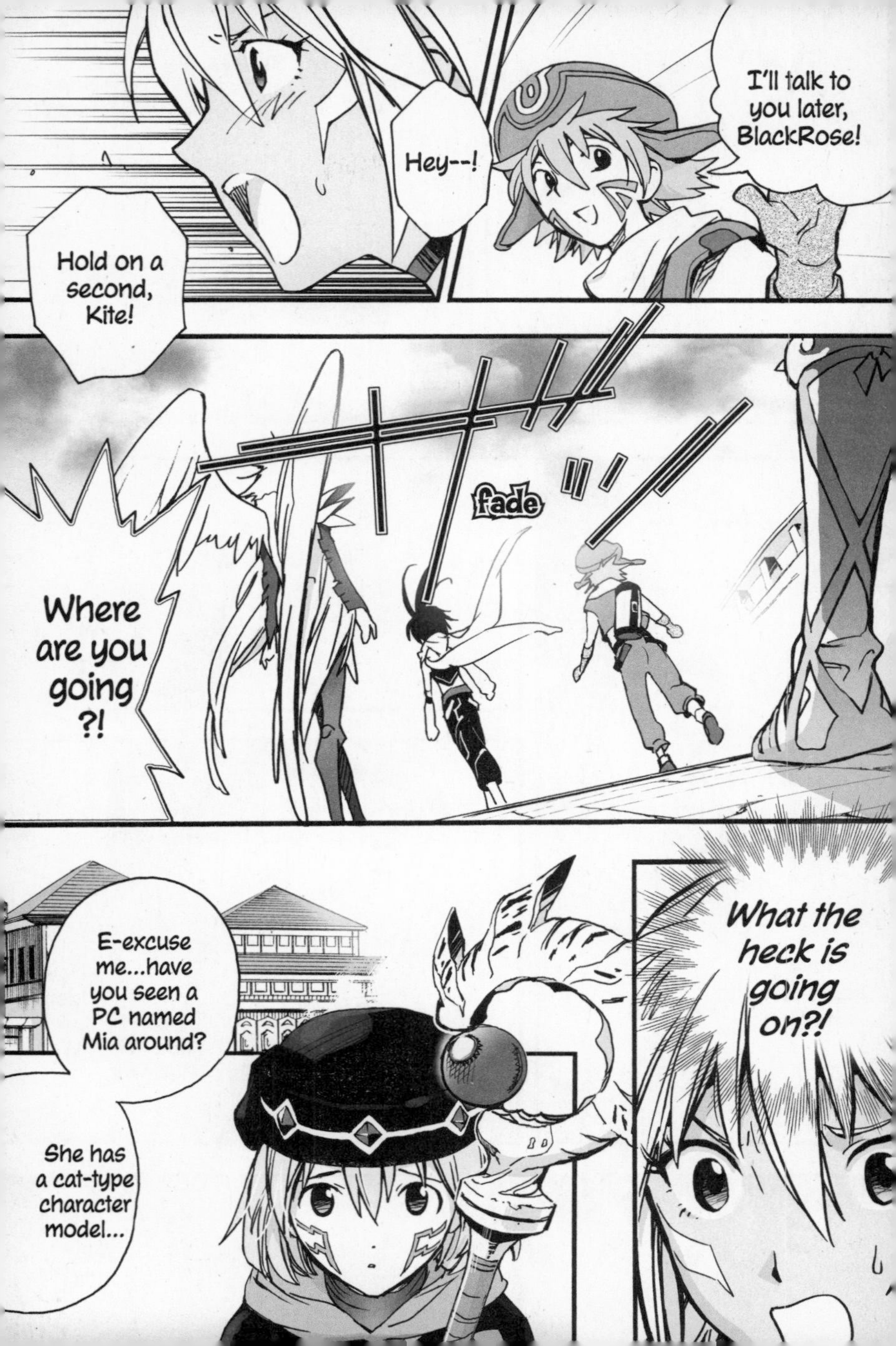

I'll talk to you later, BlackRose!
Hey--!
Hold on a second, Kite!
fade
Where are you going ?!
What the heck is going on?!
E-excuse me...have you seen a PC named Mia around?
She has a cat-type character model...

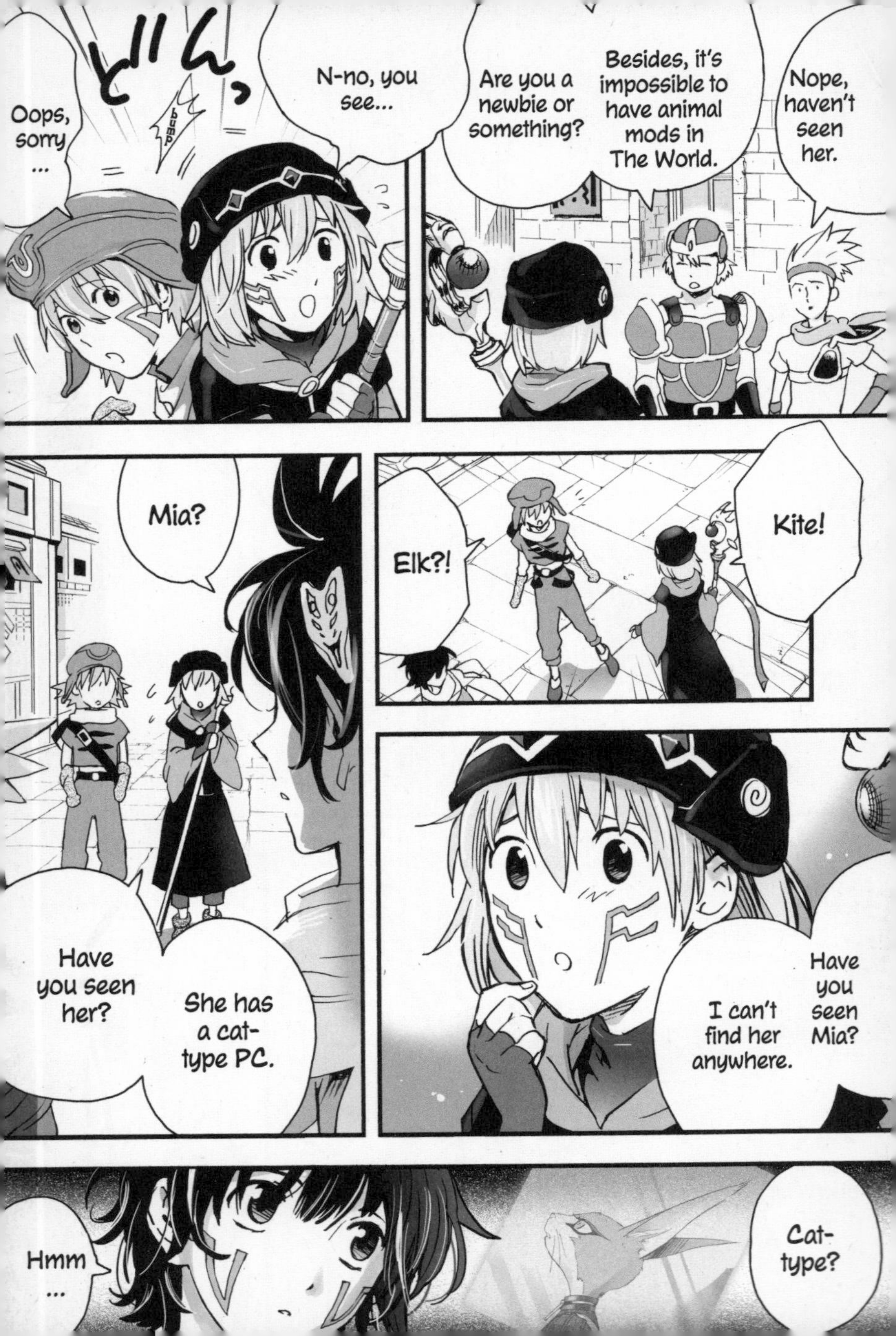
Nope, haven't seen her.
Besides, it's impossible to have animal mods in The World.
Are you a newbie or something?
N-no, you see...
bump
Oops, sorry ...
Kite!
Elk?!
Mia?
Have you seen Mia?
I can't find her anywhere.
She has a cat-type PC.
Have you seen her?
Cat-type?
Hmm ...

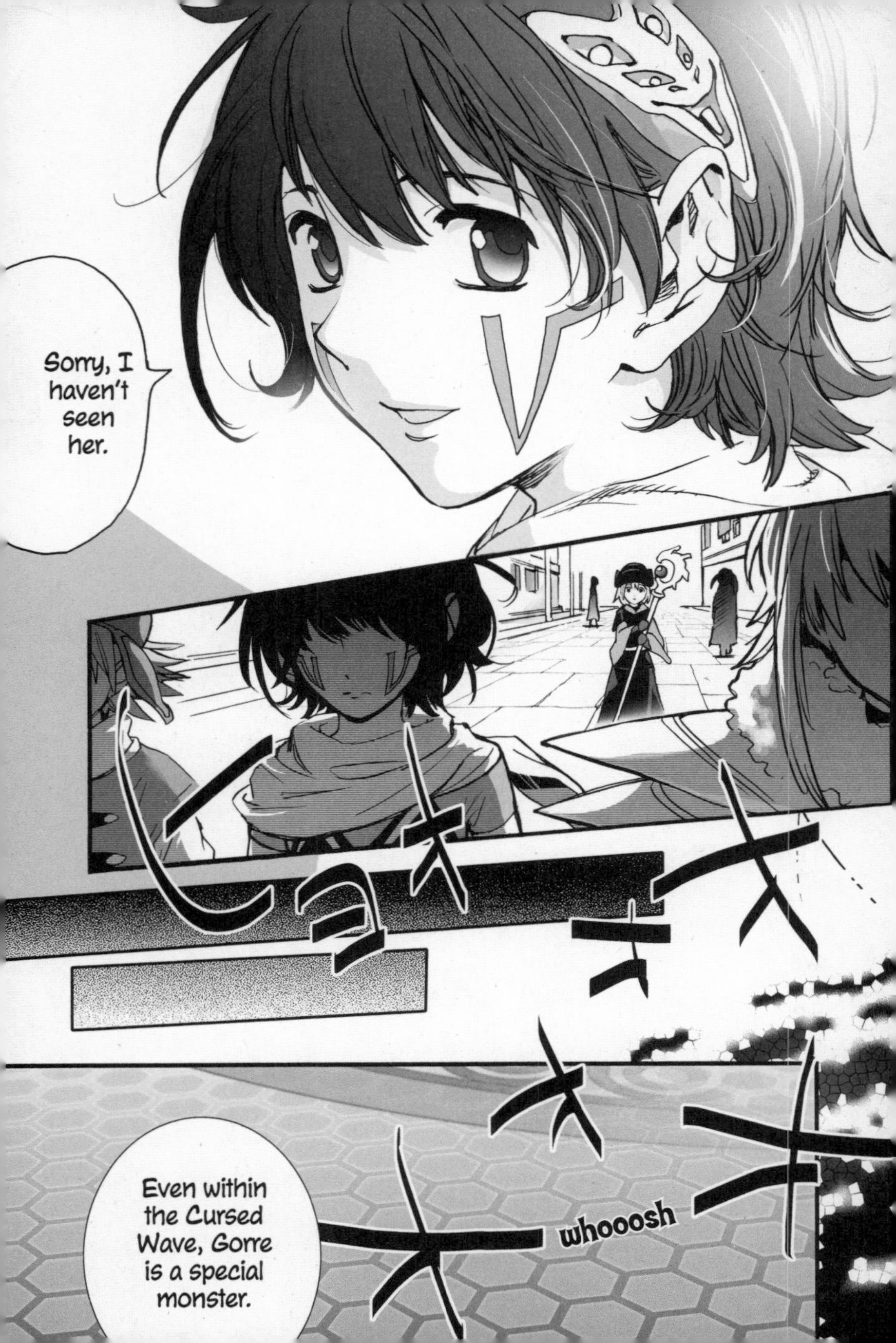
Sorry, I haven't seen her.
whooosh
Even within the Cursed Wave, Gorre is a special monster.

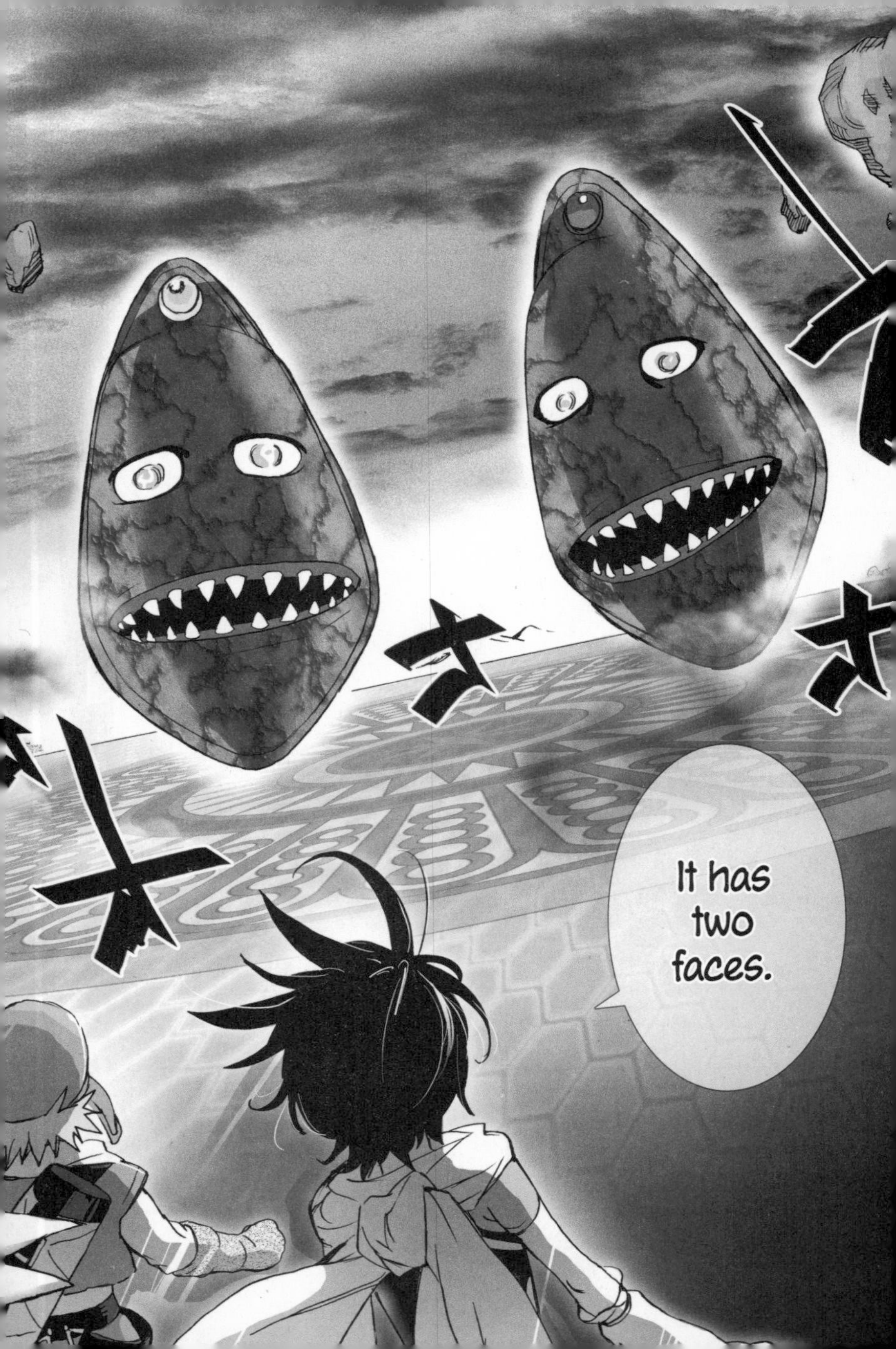
It has two faces.

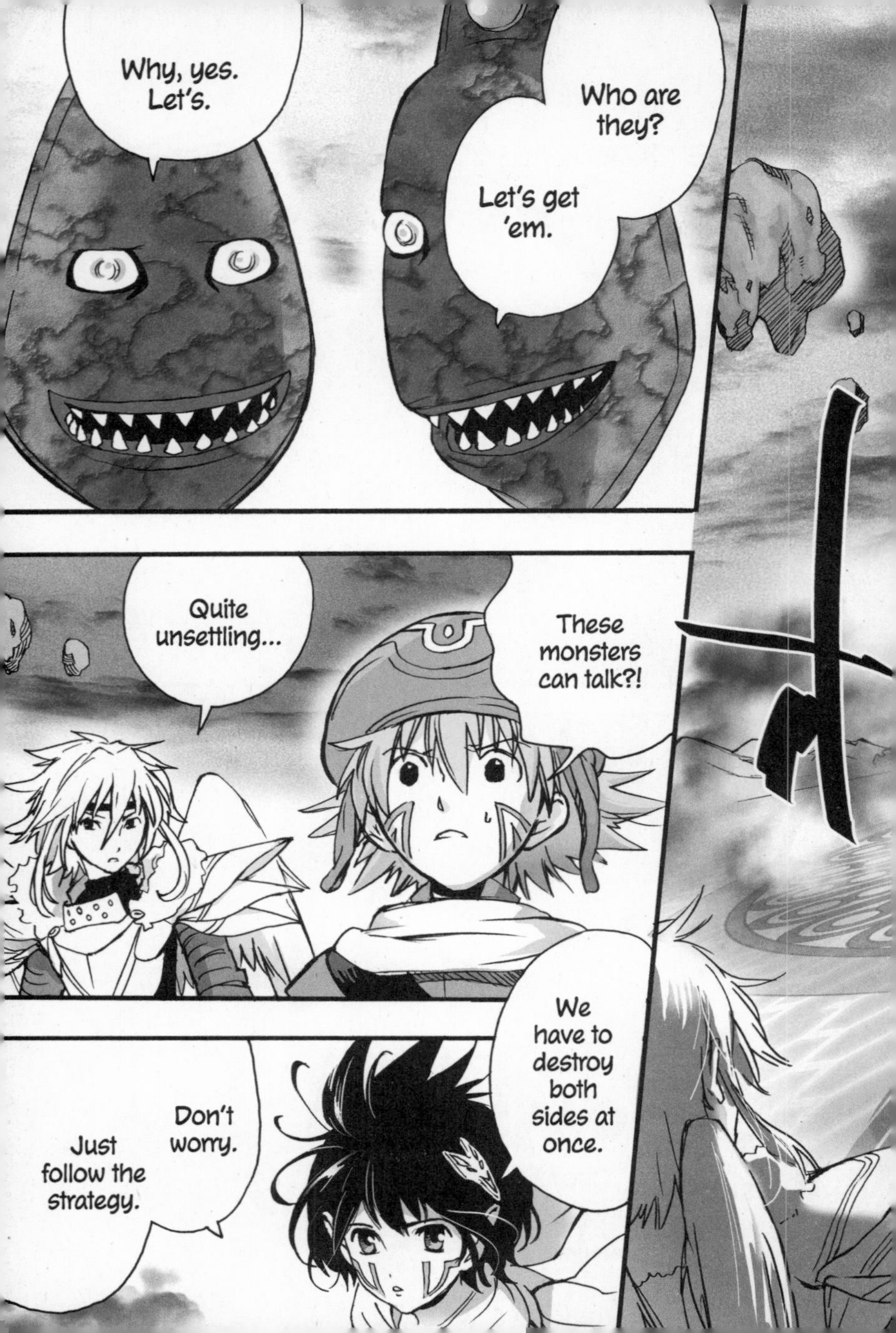
Who are they?
Let's get 'em.
Why, yes. Let's.
These monsters can talk?!
Quite unsettling...
We have to destroy both sides at once.
Don't worry.
Just follow the strategy.

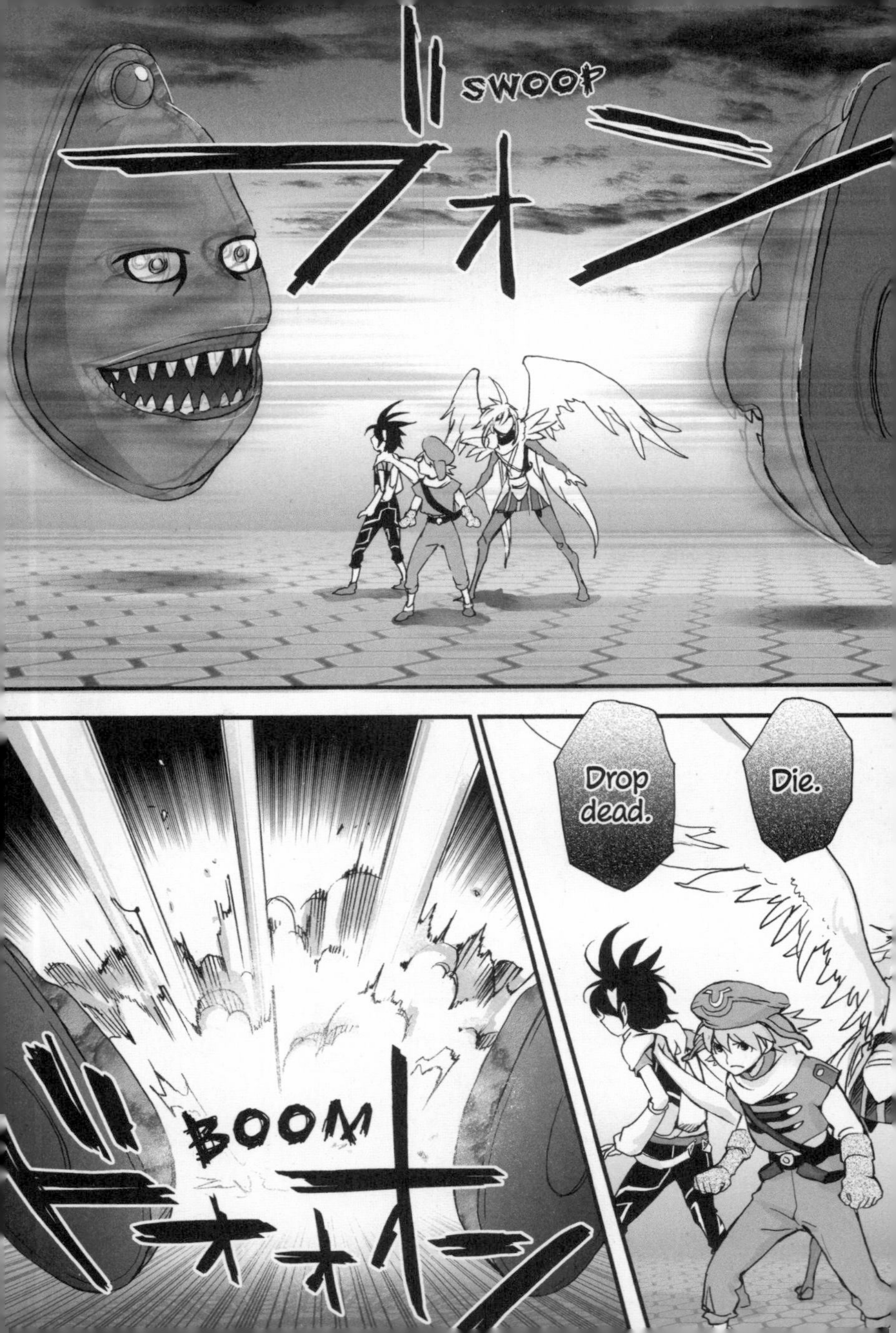
SWOOP
Die.
Drop dead.
BOOM

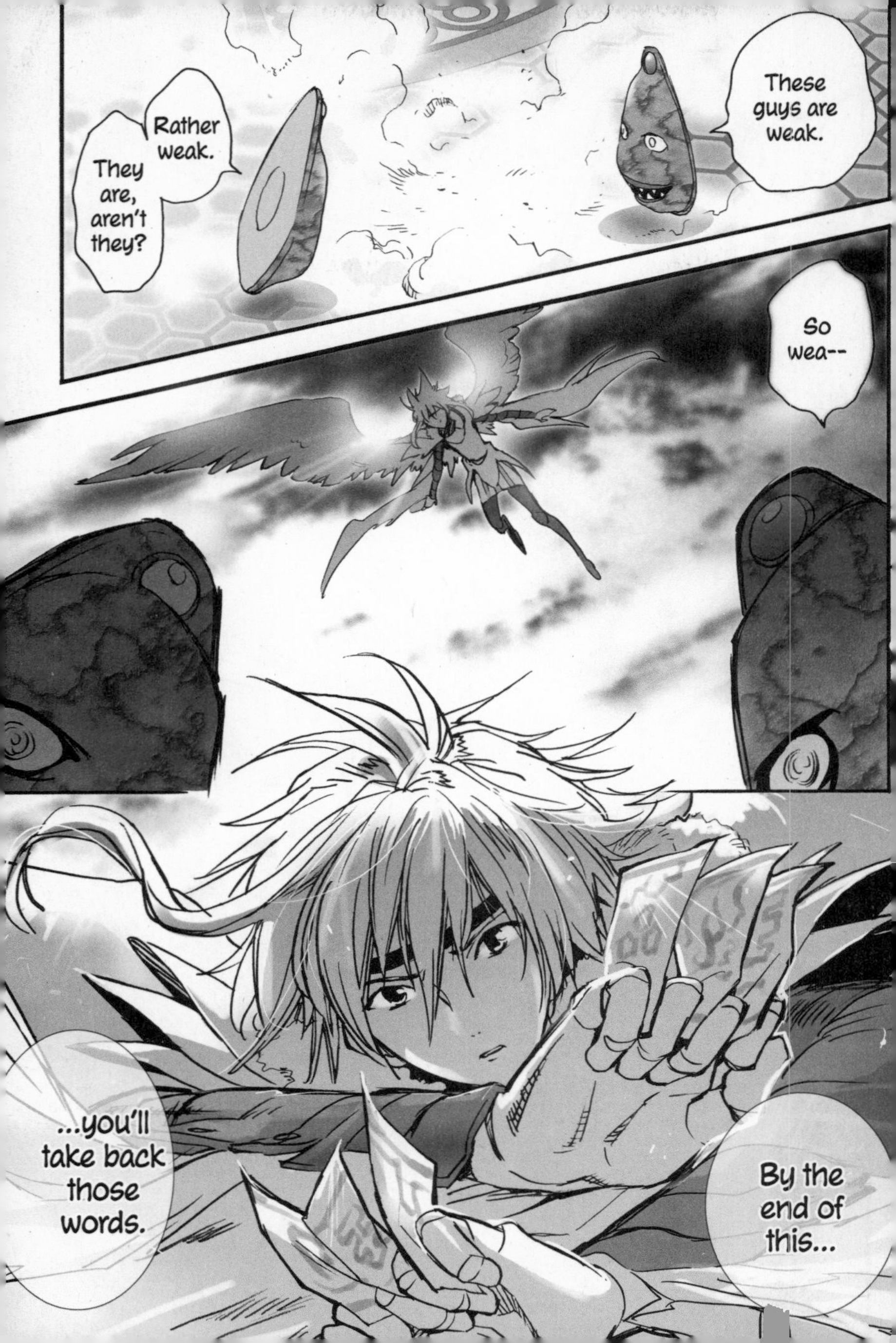
These guys are weak.
Rather weak.
They are, aren't they?
So wea--
By the end of this...
...you'll take back those words.

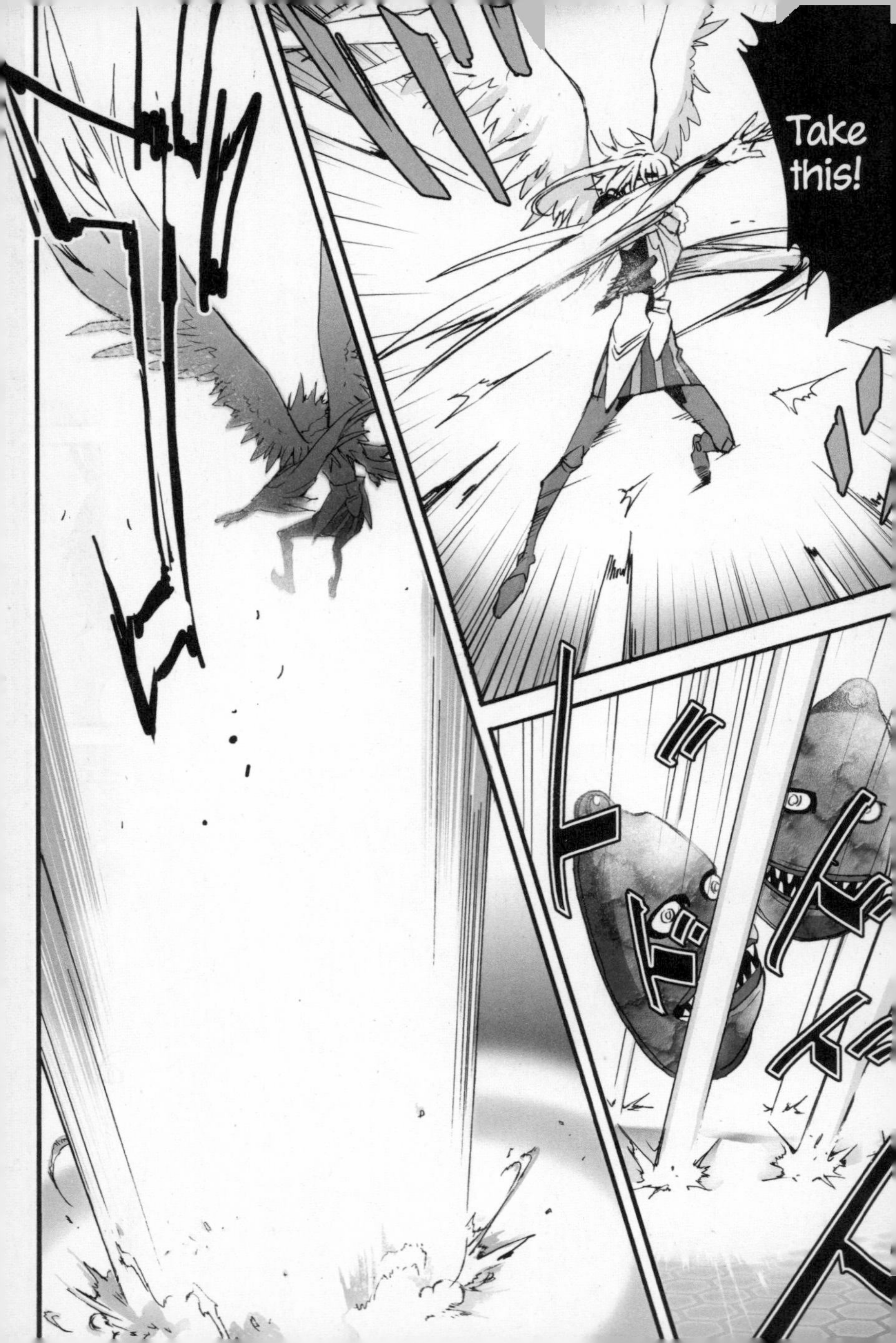
Take this!

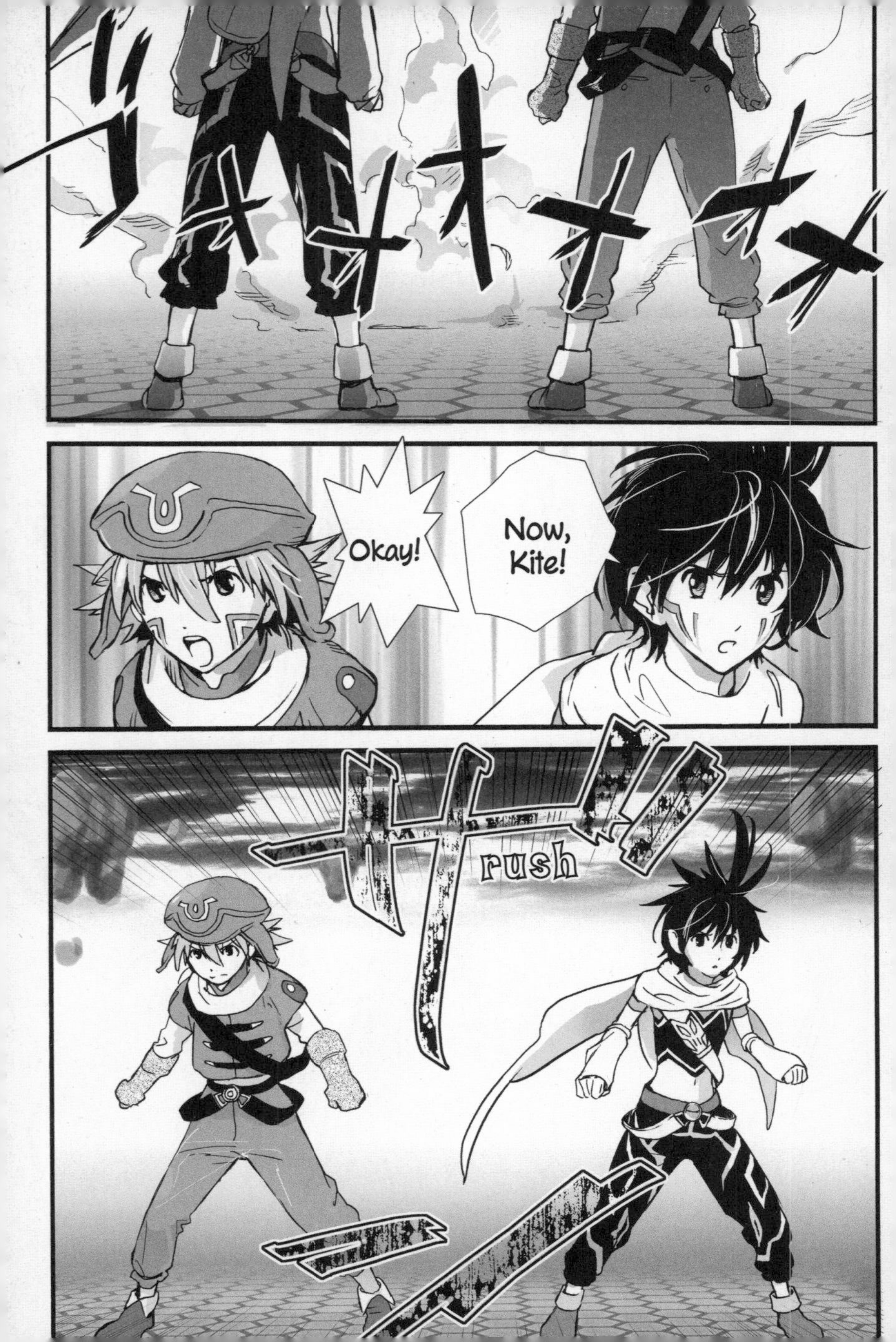
Now, Kite!
Okay!
ザッ!!
rush

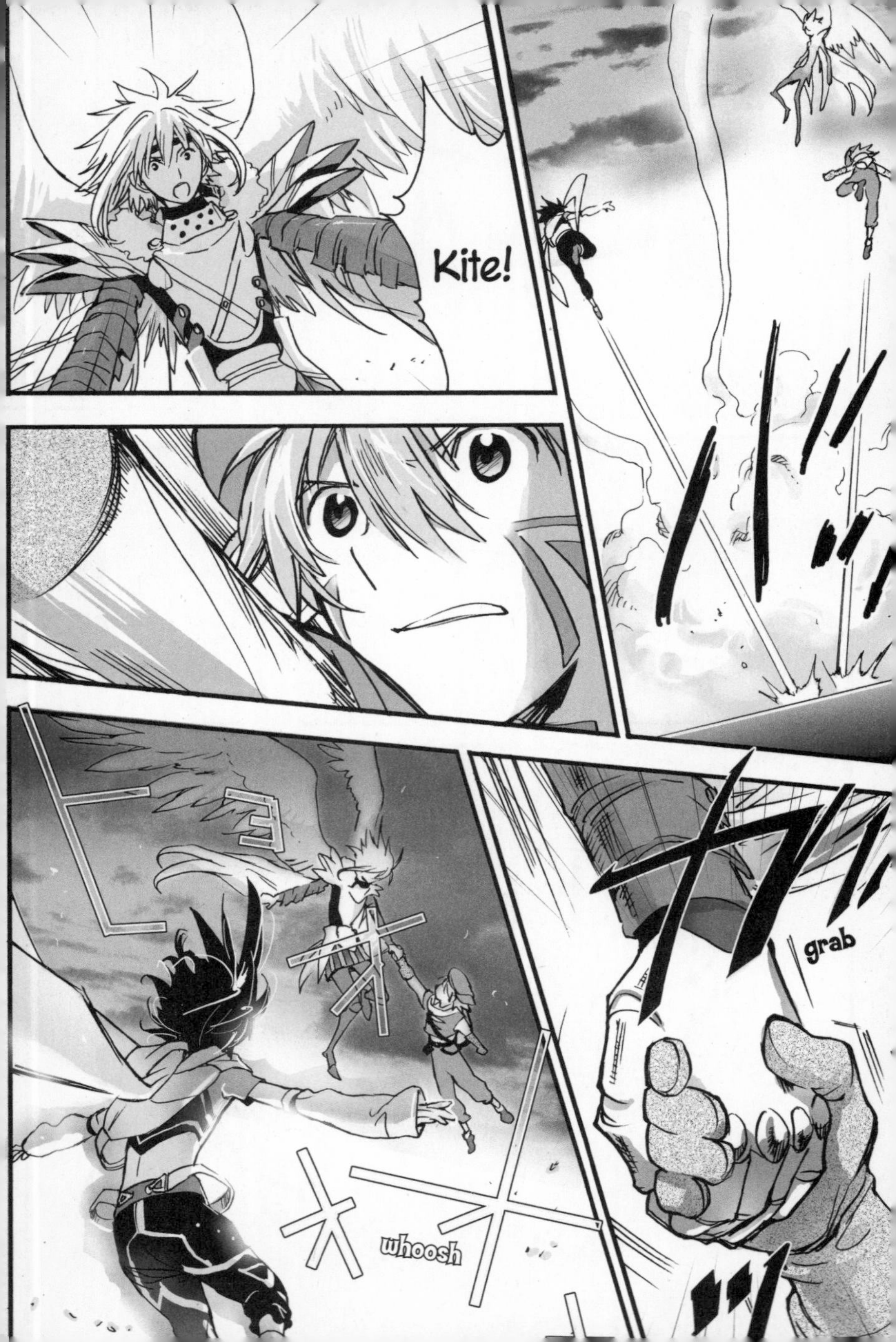
Kite!
grab
whoosh

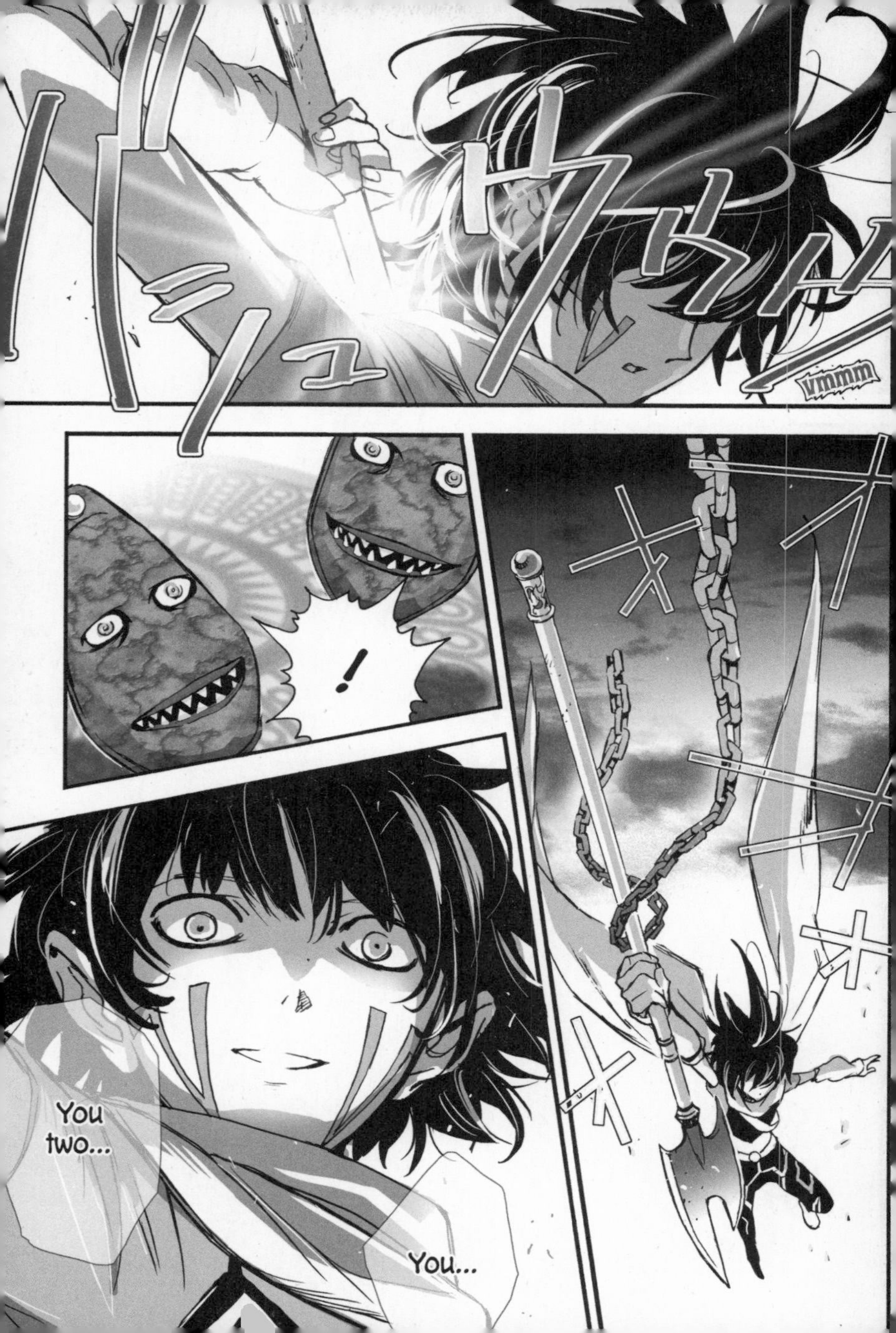
vmmm
!
You two...
You...

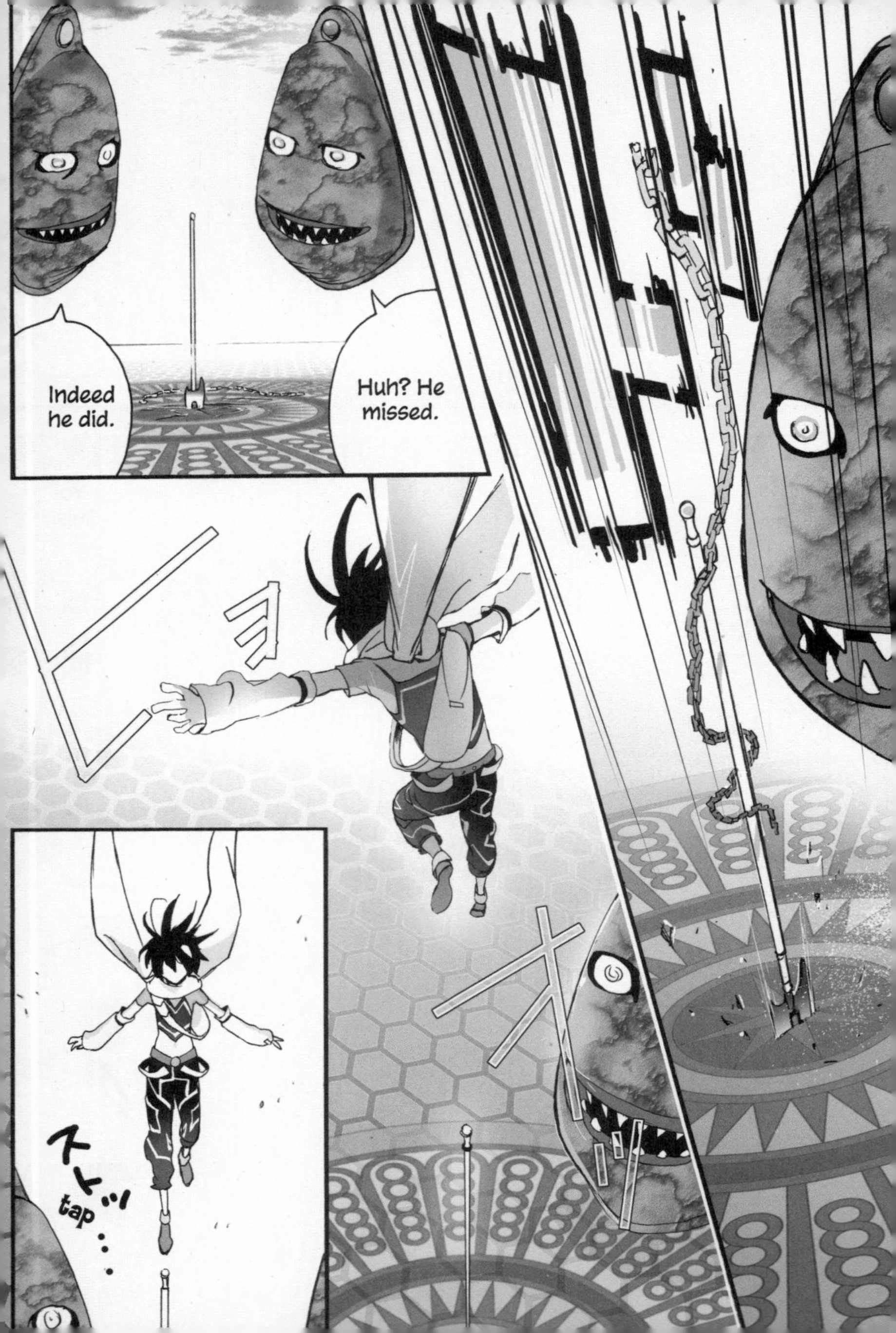
Huh? He missed.
Indeed he did.
ストッ
tap...

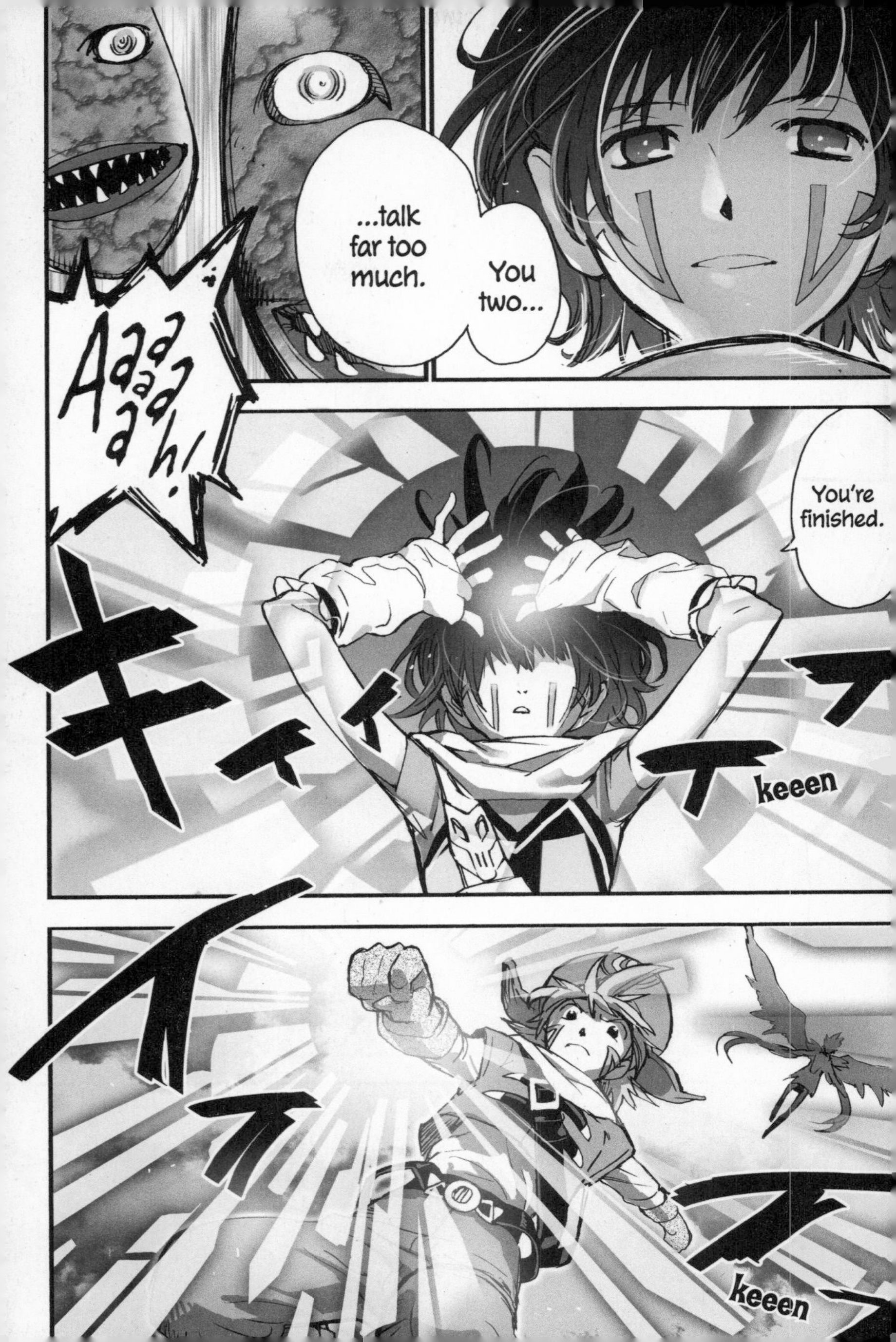
You two...
...talk far too much.
Aaaaaaah!
You're finished.
keeen
keeen

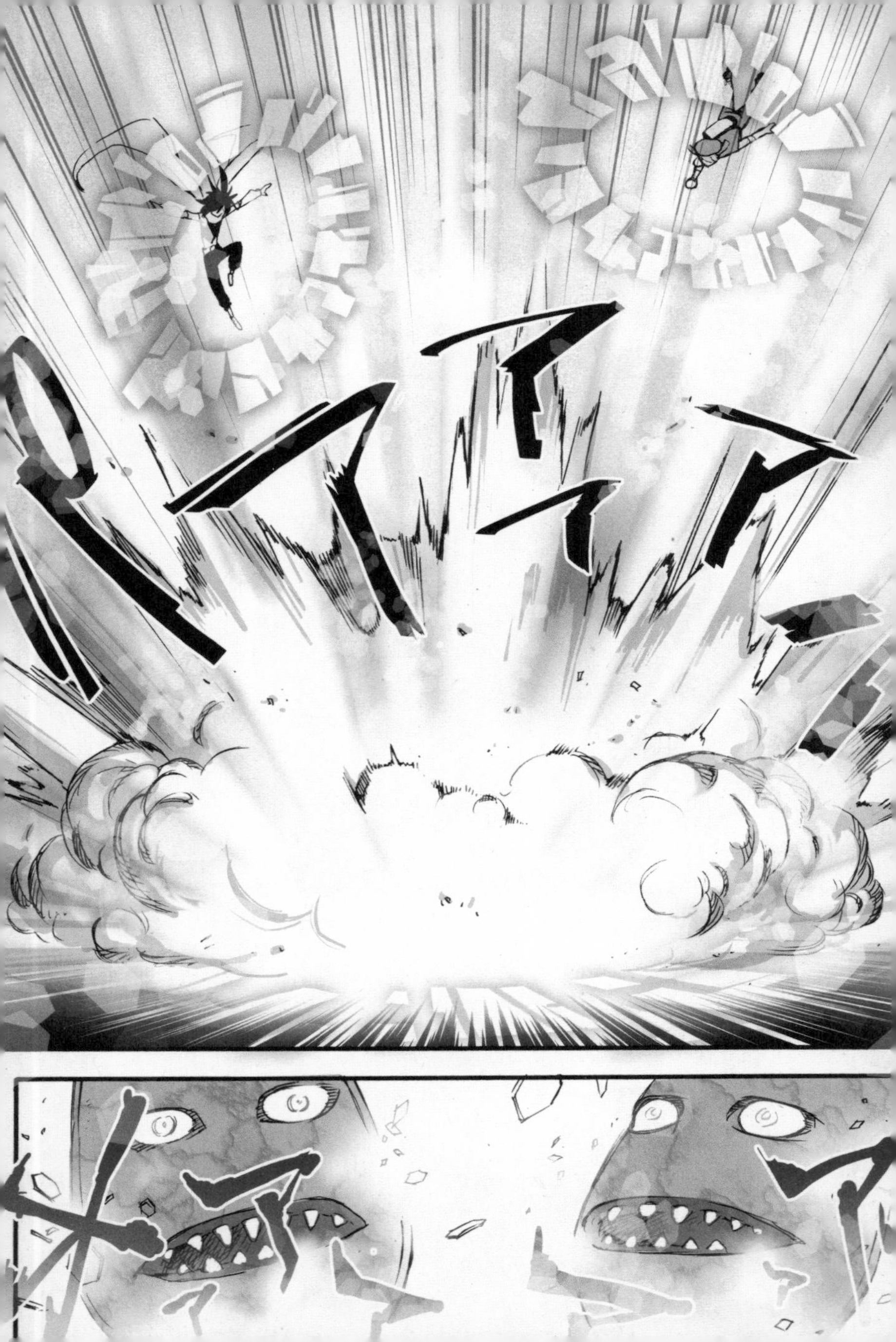

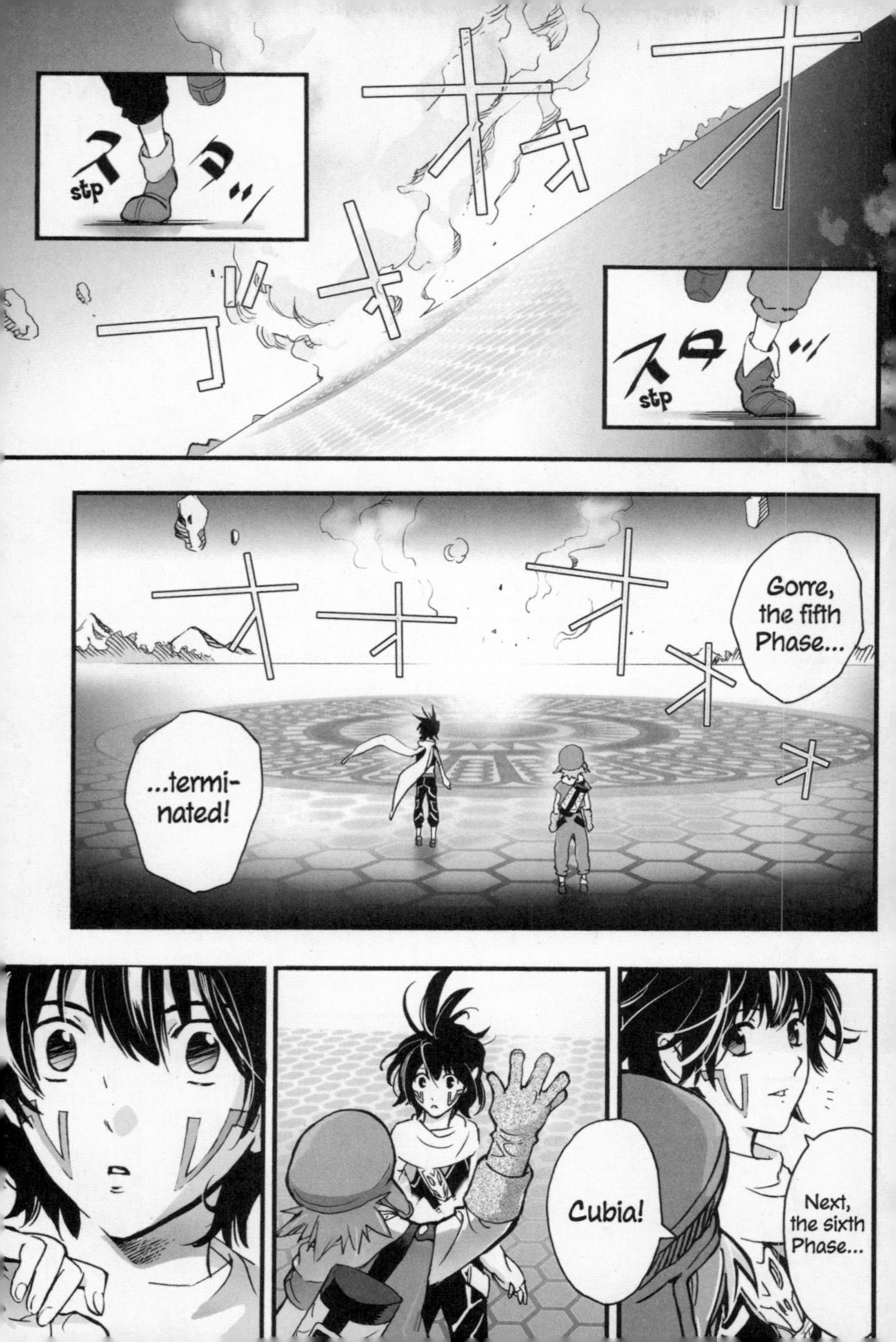

stp
stp
Gorre, the fifth Phase...
...termi-
nated!
Next, the sixth Phase...
Cubia!

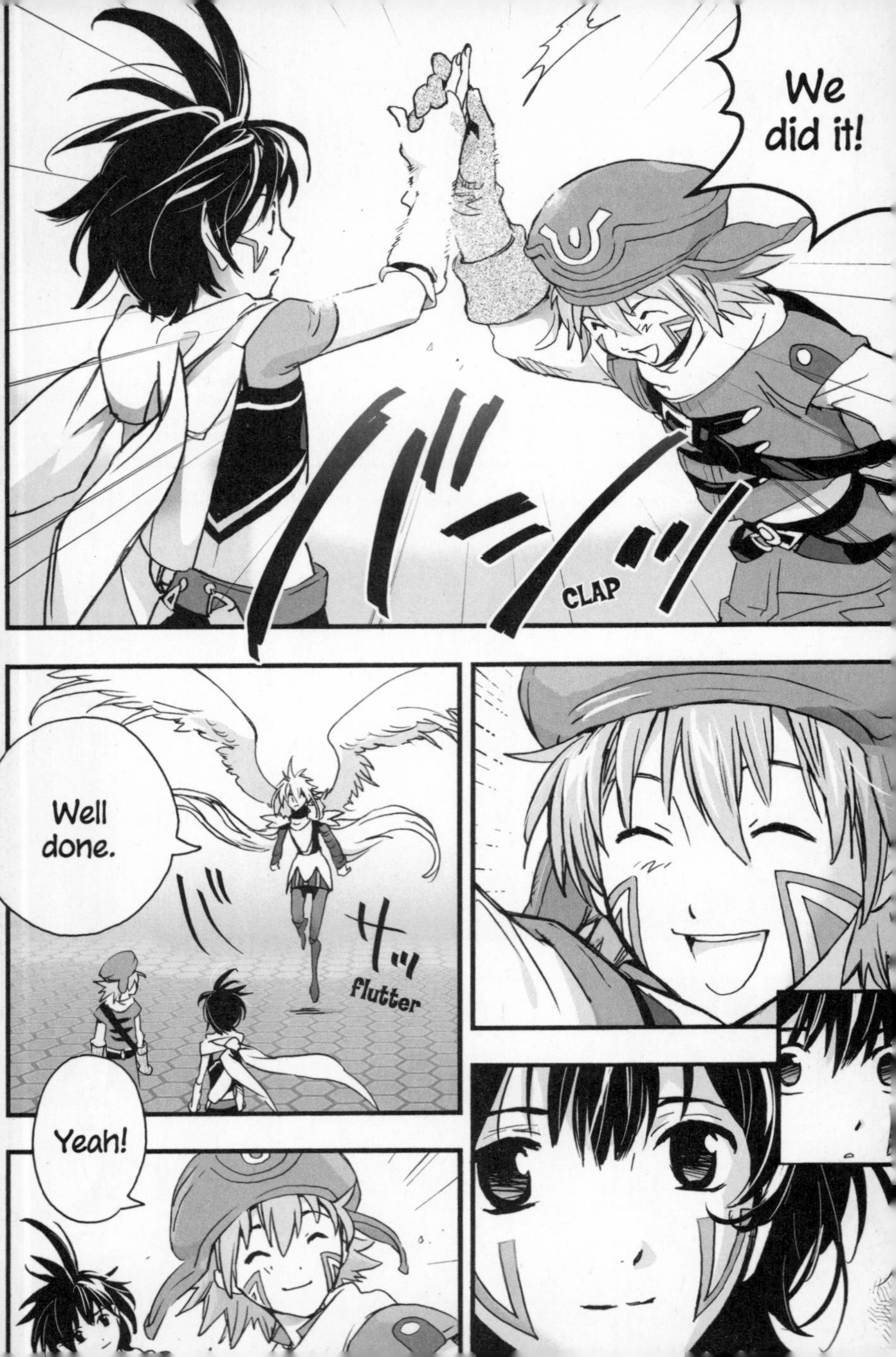
We did it!
バシッ
CLAP
Well done.
サッ
flutter
Yeah!

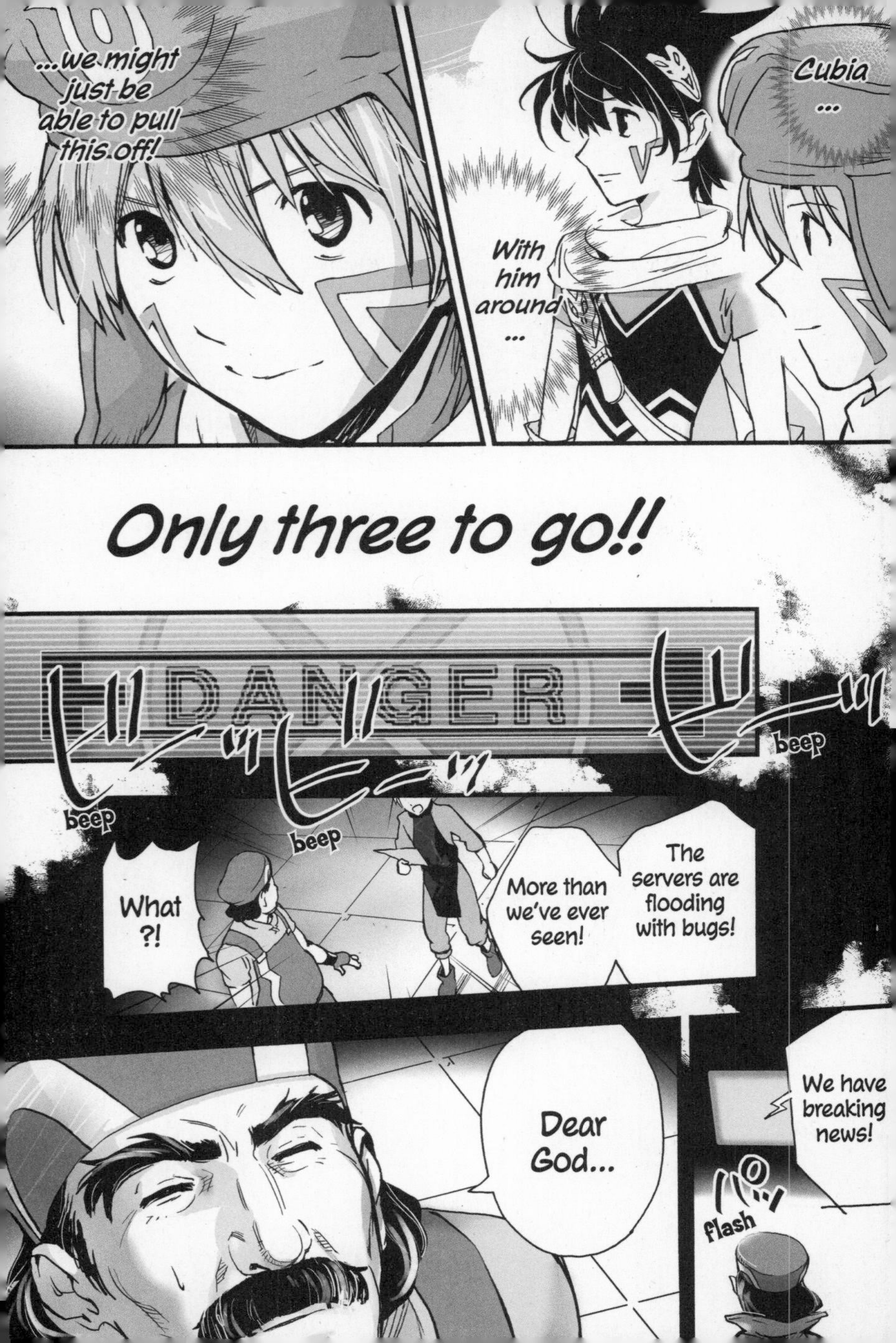
Cubia ...
With him around ...
...we might just be able to pull this off!
Only three to go!!
DANGER
beep
beep
beep
The servers are flooding with bugs!
More than we've ever seen!
What?!
We have breaking news!
flash
Dear God...

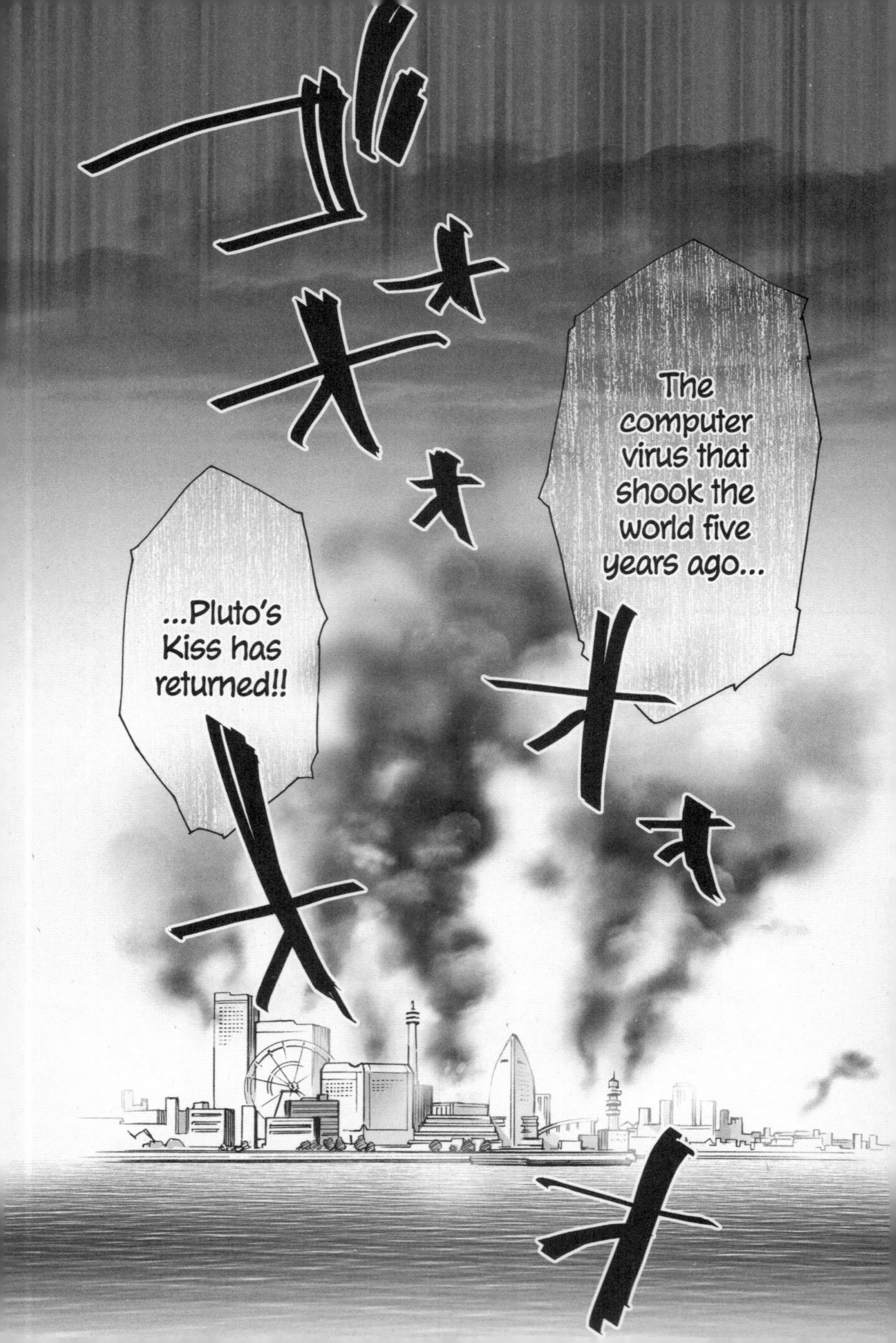
The computer virus that shook the world five years ago...
...Pluto's Kiss has returned!!

.hack//XXXX_OMAKE-page

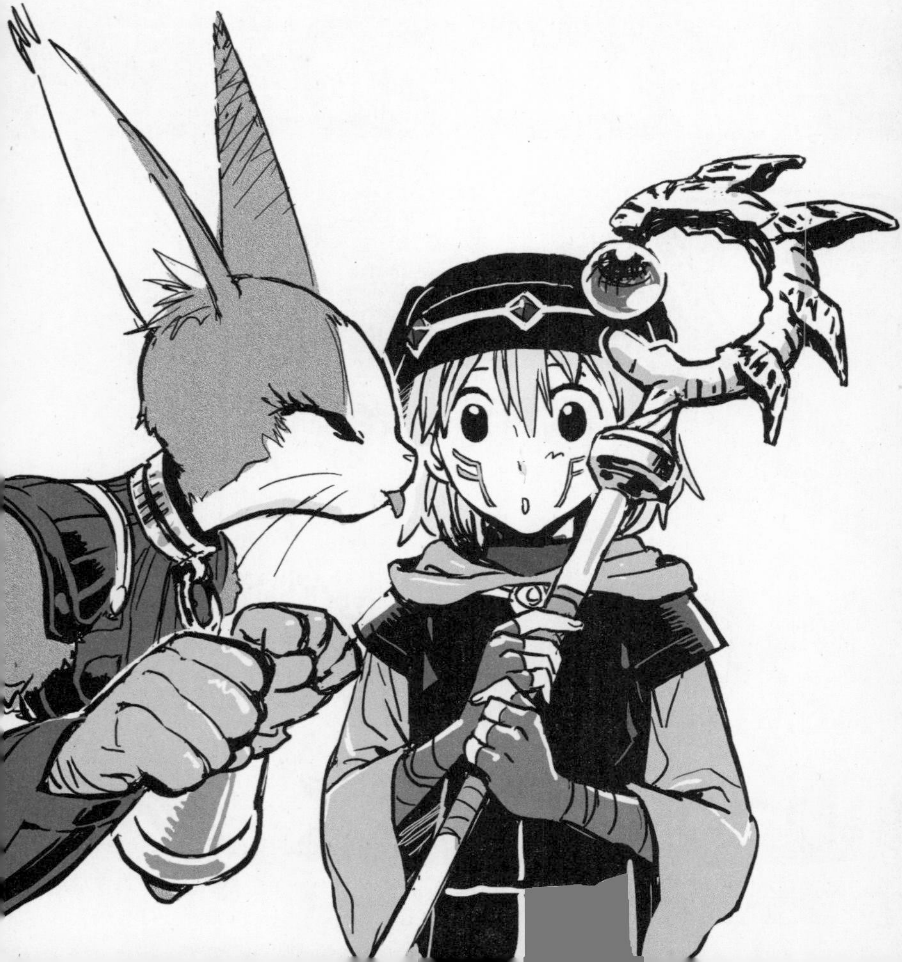

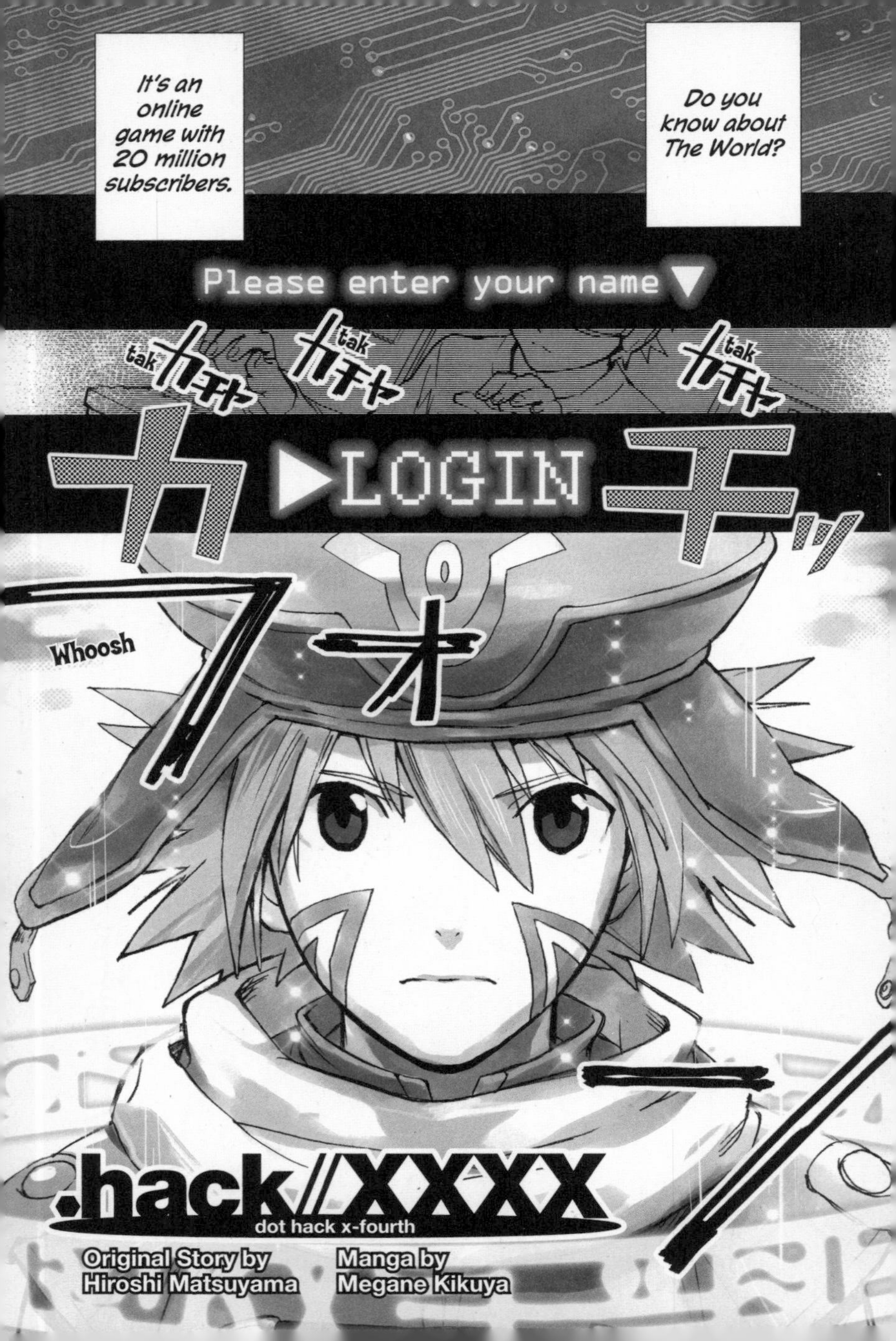

Do you know about The World?
It's an online game with 20 million subscribers.
Please enter your name ▼
tak カチャ
tak カチャ
tak カチャ
カ ▶LOGIN チッ
Whoosh
.hack//XXXX
dot hack x-fourth
Original Story by Hiroshi Matsuyama
Manga by Megane Kikuya

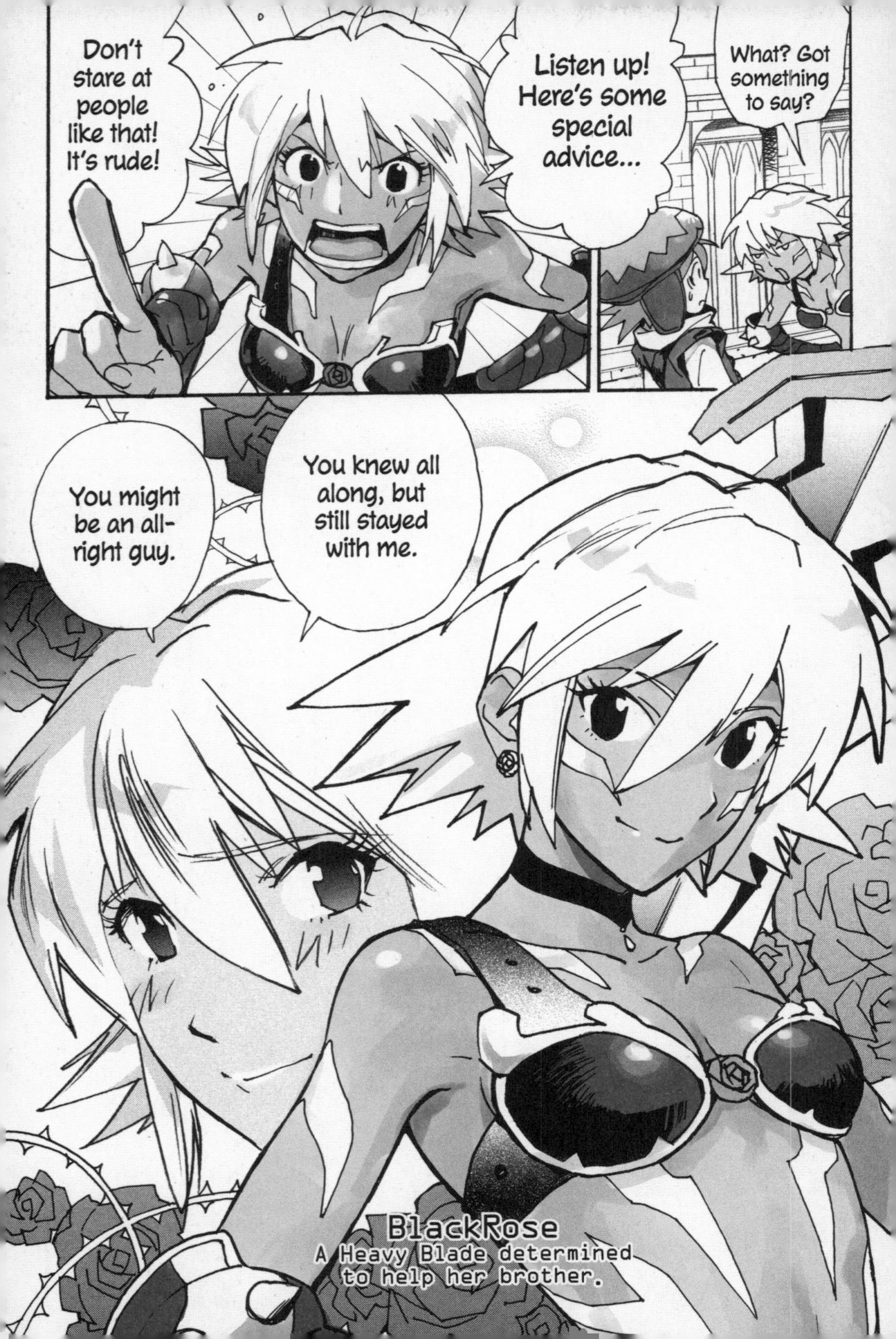
What? Got something to say?
Listen up! Here's some special advice...
Don't stare at people like that! It's rude!
You knew all along, but still stayed with me.
You might be an all-right guy.
BlackRose
A Heavy Blade determined to help her brother.

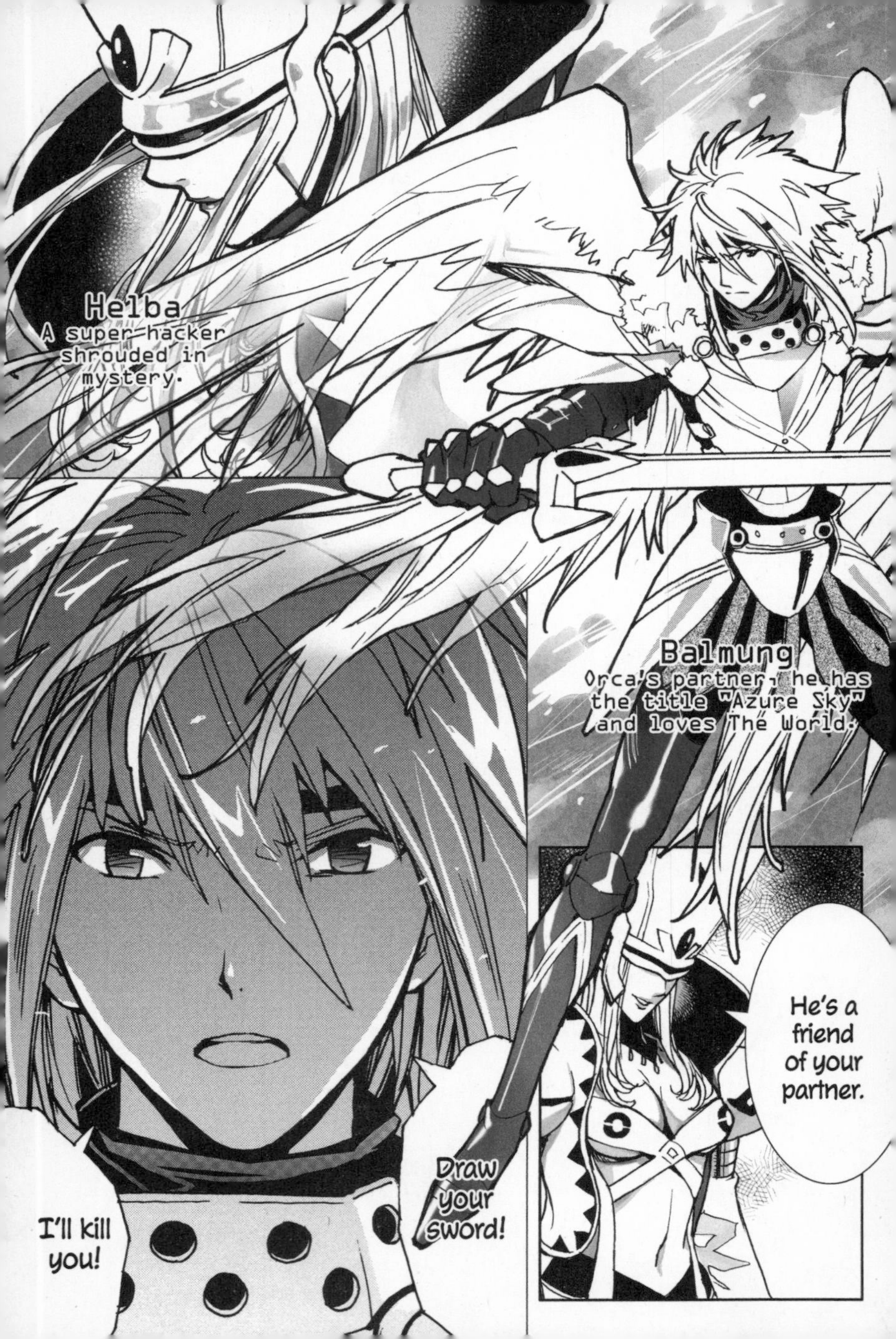
Helba
A super-hacker shrouded in mystery.
Balmung
Orca's partner, he has the title "Azure Sky" and loves The World.
He's a friend of your partner.
Draw your sword!
I'll kill you!

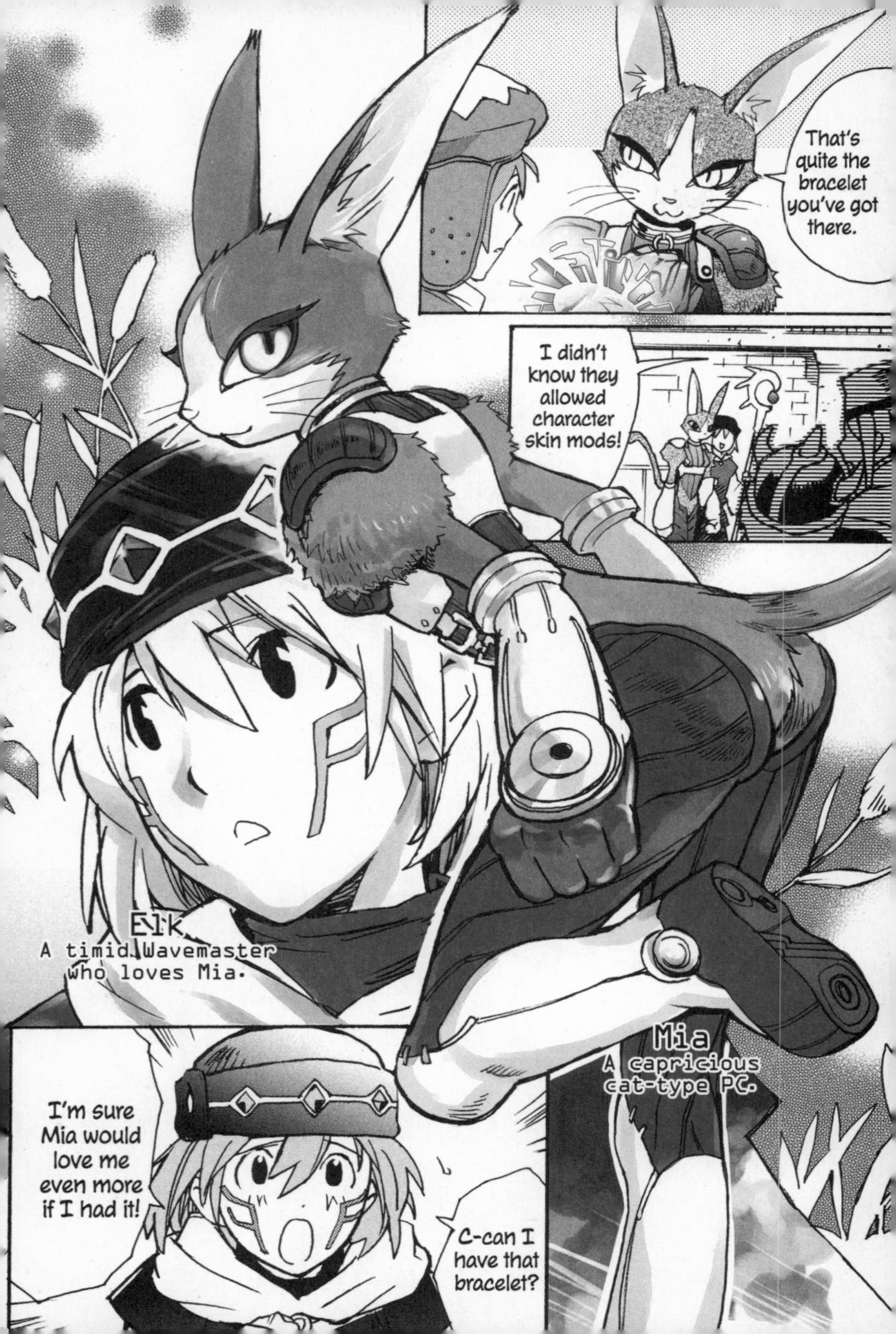
That's quite the bracelet you've got there.
I didn't know they allowed character skin mods!
Mia
A capricious cat-type PC.
Elk
A timid Wavemaster who loves Mia.
C-can I have that bracelet?
I'm sure Mia would love me even more if I had it!

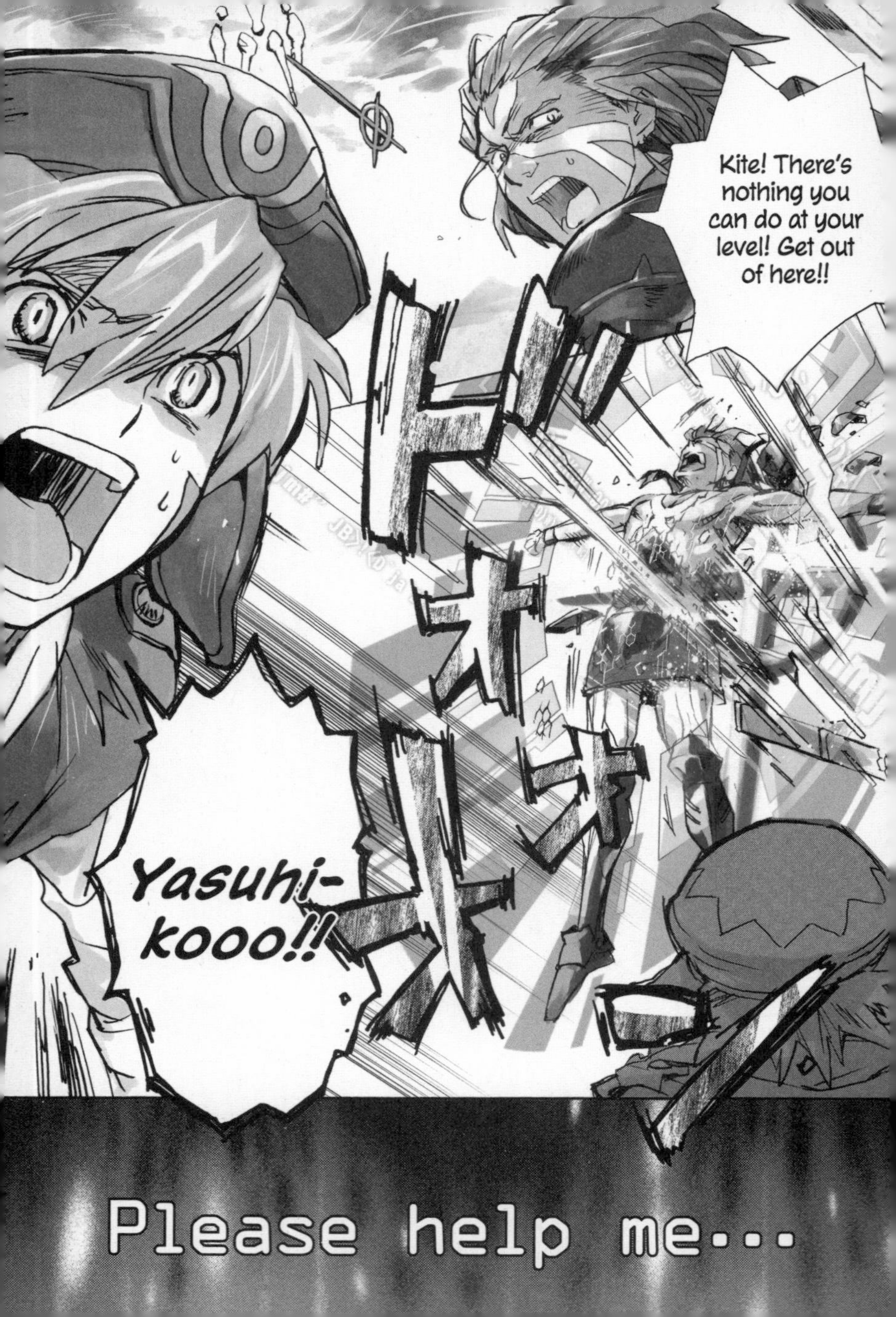
Kite! There's nothing you can do at your level! Get out of here!!
Yasuhi-kooo!!
Please help me...

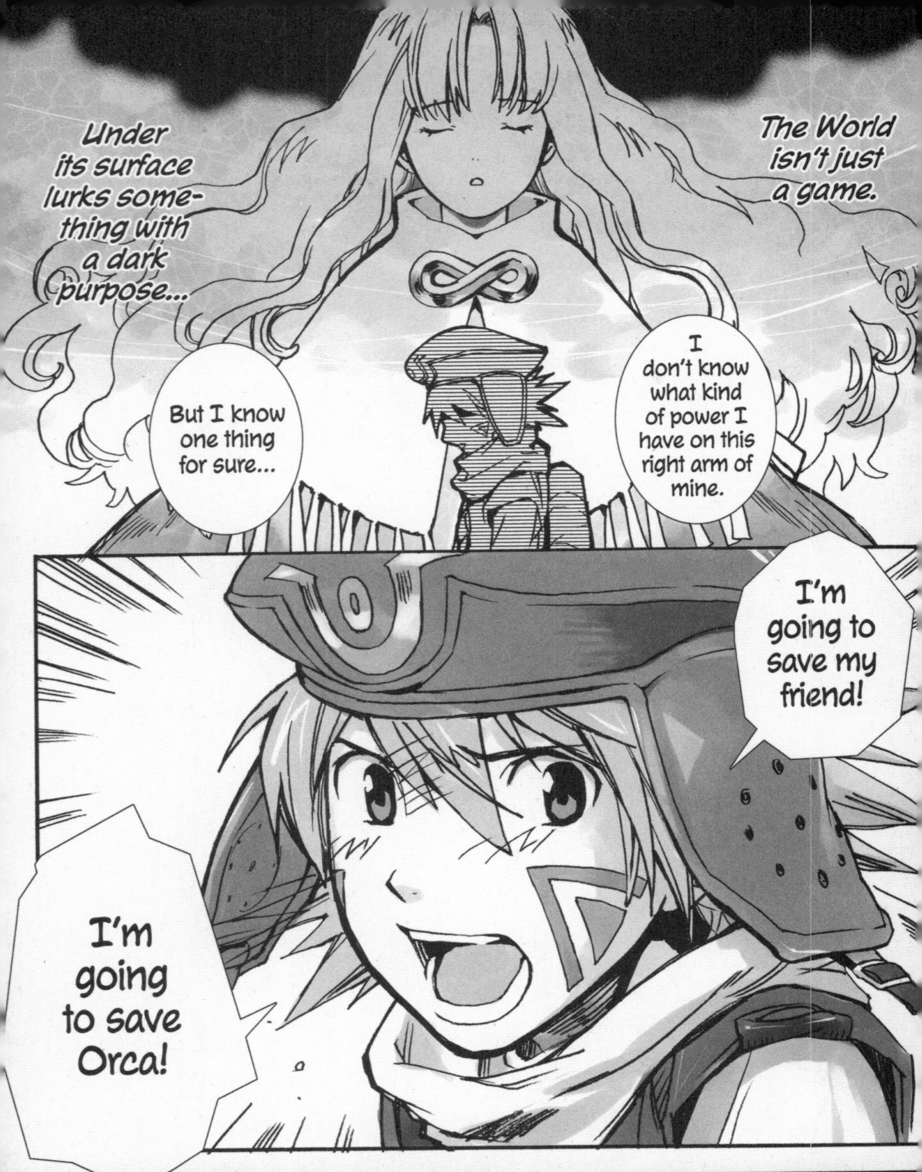
The World isn't just a game.
Under its surface lurks some-thing with a dark purpose...
I don't know what kind of power I have on this right arm of mine.
But I know one thing for sure...
I'm going to save my friend!
I'm going to save Orca!

Vol. 2 coming soon!

.hack//XXXX
ドット ハック イクスフォス

*Incidentally, this background image is a random image from the non-existent manga ALTIMIT XX which .hack//XXXX is simultaneously related to and disconnected from. (CC2: Matsuyama)

What is .hack//XXXX?!

Well, X = Unknown, and that makes this the fourth unknown. Thus the four games from Outbreak to Quarantine, .hack//SIGN, the game tetralogy, .hack//Legend of the Twilight, plus Kite, the Phases, Cubia and Aura that spawned it all, in this new version with four stories in this fourth comic!! That's what this is.

—CyberConnect2
Piroshi Matsuyama

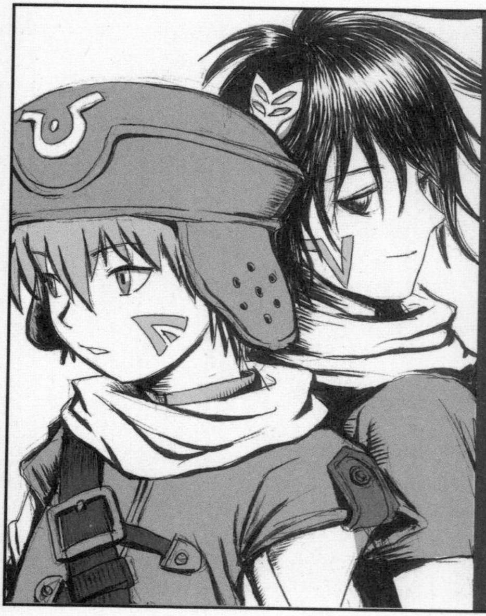

Four years after the games, it's been a long road paved with blood, snot and tears, but Kite has finally been reborn in comic form! The story follows the game for the most part, but there are differences here and there to spice things up and keep readers who played the games from being bored. For example, just look at Boy-Cubia! He's so dark! I just love him!♪

Dear readers, please continue to look over Mr. Popular Kite and the dark lead Cubia!

CyberConnect2

Ninja Blade

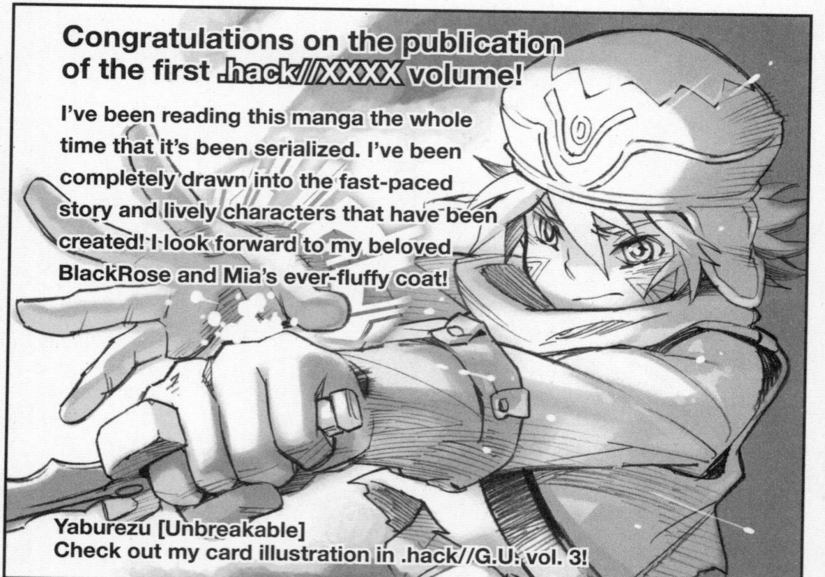
Congratulations on the publication of the first .hack//XXXX volume!
I've been reading this manga the whole time that it's been serialized. I've been completely drawn into the fast-paced story and lively characters that have been created! I look forward to my beloved BlackRose and Mia's ever-fluffy coat!
Yaburezu [Unbreakable]
Check out my card illustration in .hack//G.U. vol. 3!

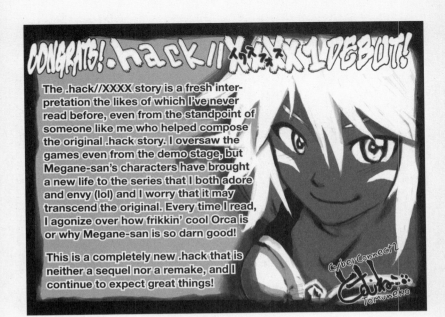

CONGRATS! .hack//XXXX(キサスキサス)1 DEBUT!

The .hack//XXXX story is a fresh interpretation the likes of which I've never read before, even from the standpoint of someone like me who helped compose the original .hack story. I oversaw the games even from the demo stage, but Megane-san's characters have brought a new life to the series that I both adore and envy (lol) and I worry that it may transcend the original. Every time I read, I agonize over how frikkin' cool Orca is or why Megane-san is so darn good!

This is a completely new .hack that is neither a sequel nor a remake, and I continue to expect great things!

CyberConnect2
Gouko
Toruneko

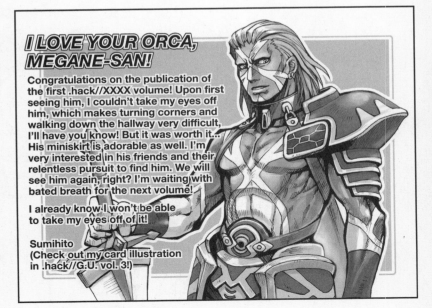

I LOVE YOUR ORCA, MEGANE-SAN!

Congratulations on the publication of the first .hack//XXXX volume! Upon first seeing him, I couldn't take my eyes off him, which makes turning corners and walking down the hallway very difficult, I'll have you know! But it was worth it... His miniskirt is adorable as well. I'm very interested in his friends and their relentless pursuit to find him. We will see him again, right? I'm waiting with bated breath for the next volume!

I already know I won't be able to take my eyes off of it!

Sumihito
(Check out my card illustration in .hack//G.U. vol. 3!)

✿Thank you so much for picking up volume 1 of .hack//XXXX!

This is my first manga ever, and everything feels so new! Thanks to everyone who has to put up with me! I know it's hard when our workspace is the size of a small garage...

It's been my pleasure to rework the story and characters from the games. For people who have entered the world of .hack from the manga, please feel free to play the games! In the games, Kite's got his own little harem going on, as seen below.

Lastly, to all those who have given me comments, I apologize for being busy, but I truly appreciate it! To all the readers, I would love it if we could meet again in volume 2!

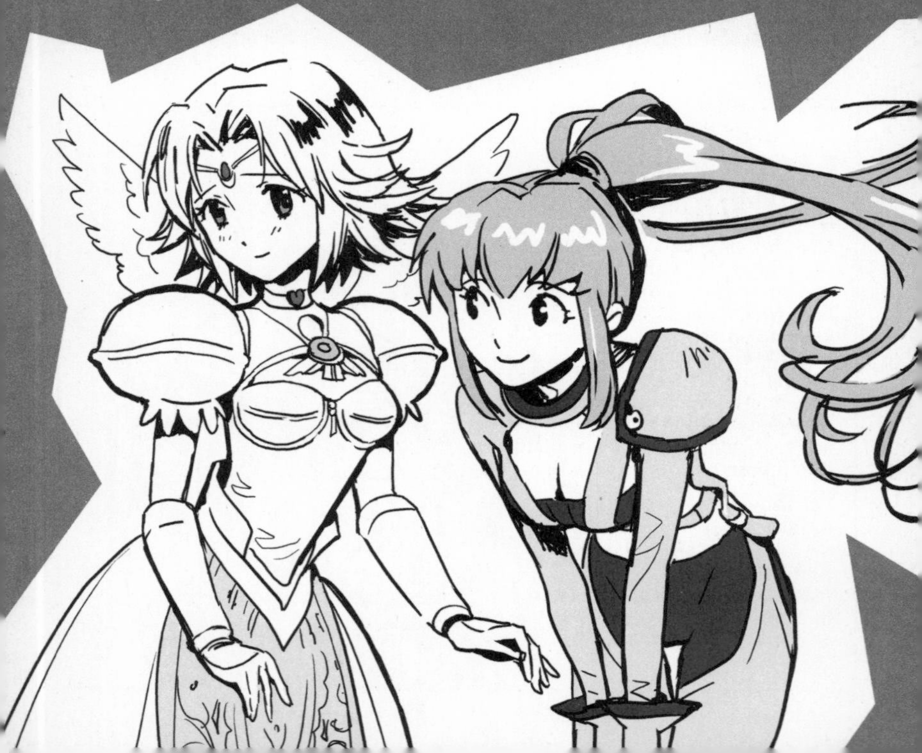

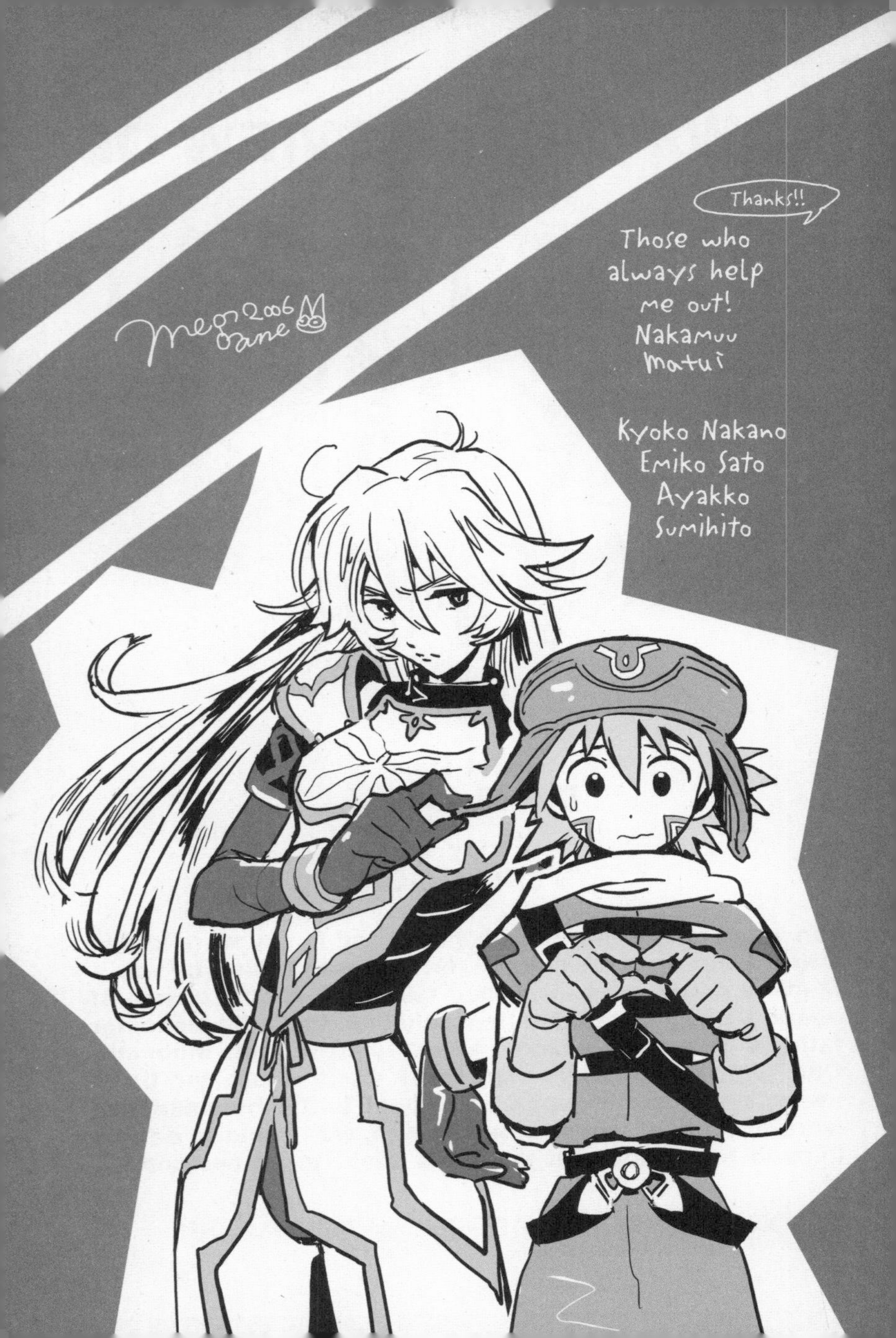
Thanks!!
Those who always help me out!
Nakamuu
Matui
Kyoko Nakano
Emiko Sato
Ayakko
Sumihito

NOW FOR A PREVIEW OF

**Art By
Dat Nishiwaki**

**Story By
TYPE-MOON**

Ten years ago, Shiro Emiya's home and family were lost in a fire. A stranger took him in, later revealing that he was a Magi—a magic user—who had failed to become a Hero of Justice. Shiro swore that he would one day fulfill his foster father's dream and become a hero to protect the innocent. One night, after Shiro has been alone again for three years, he stumbles upon a magical battle between two warriors, one of whom attacks Shiro. He is able to defend himself for a time, but now he's about to be overcome...

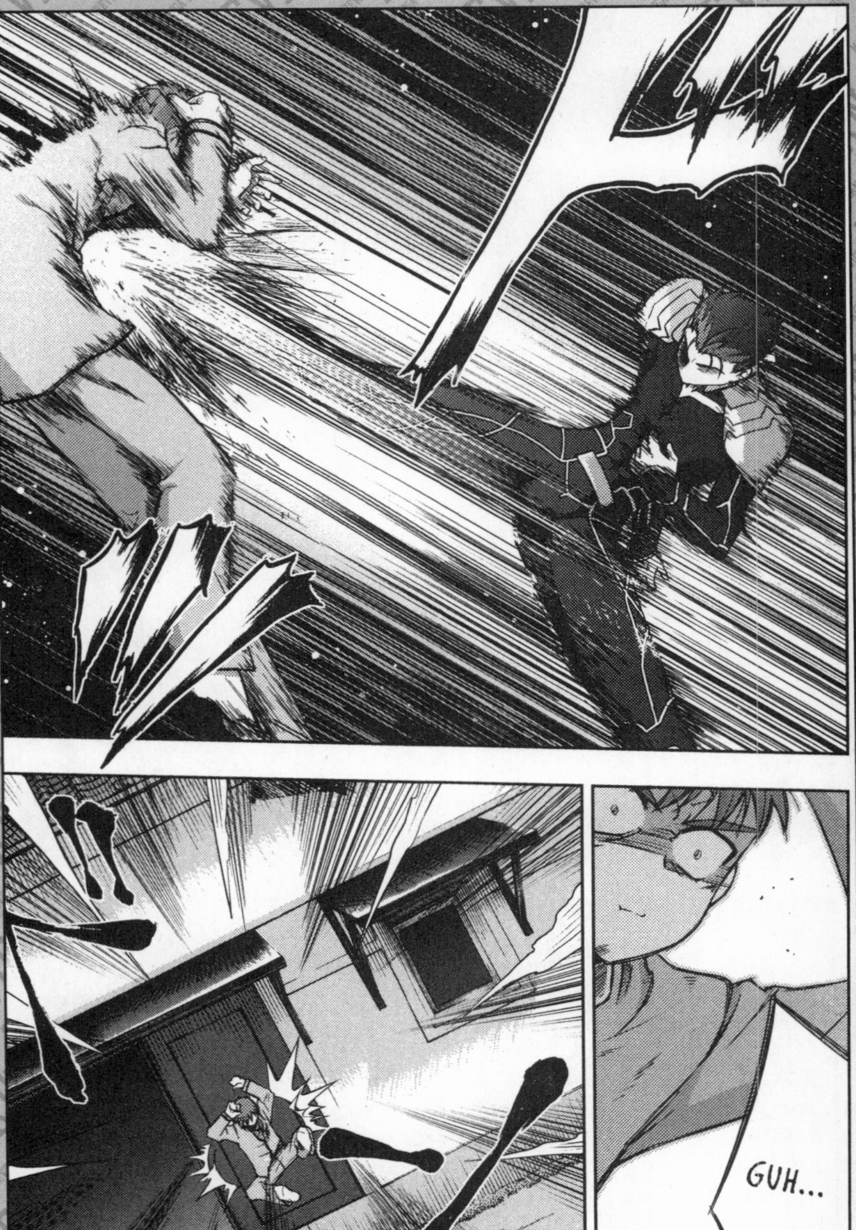
GUH...

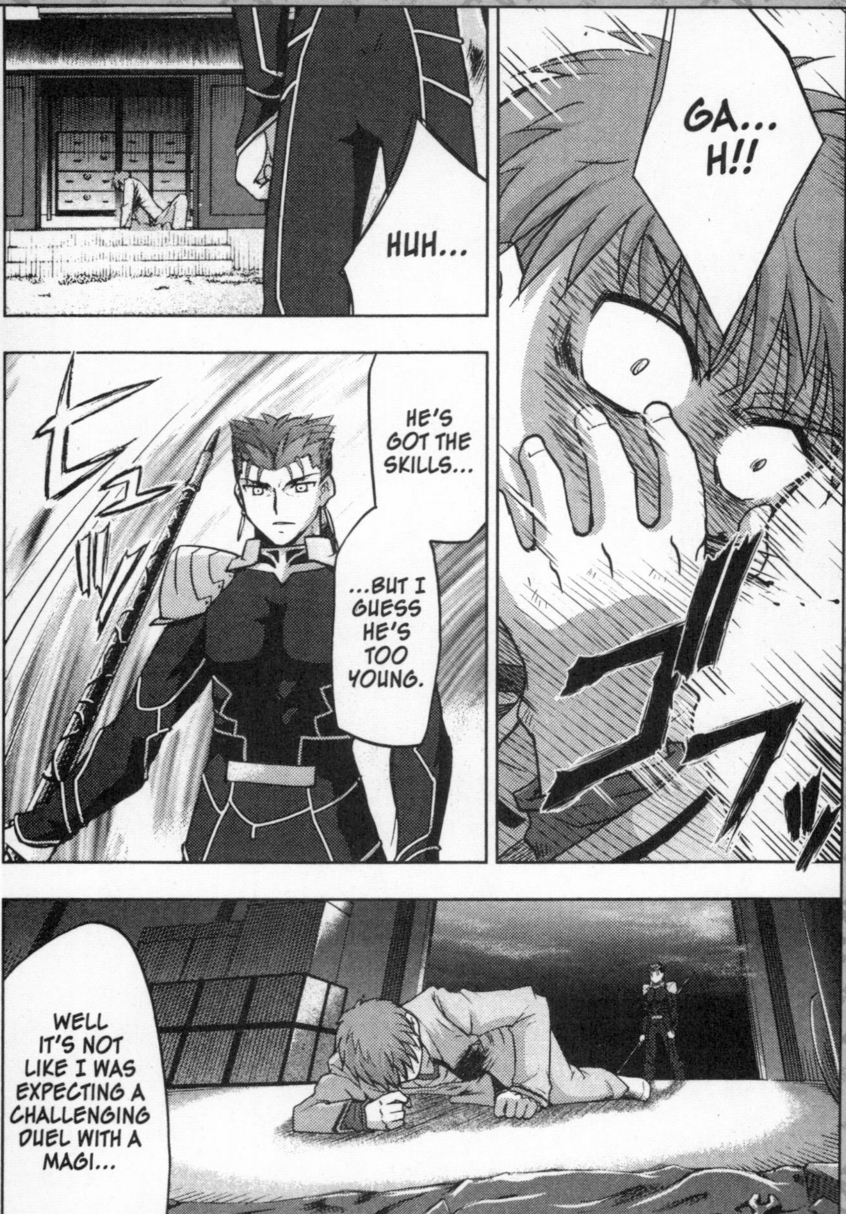
GA... H!!
HUH...
HE'S GOT THE SKILLS...
...BUT I GUESS HE'S TOO YOUNG.
WELL IT'S NOT LIKE I WAS EXPECTING A CHALLENGING DUEL WITH A MAGI...

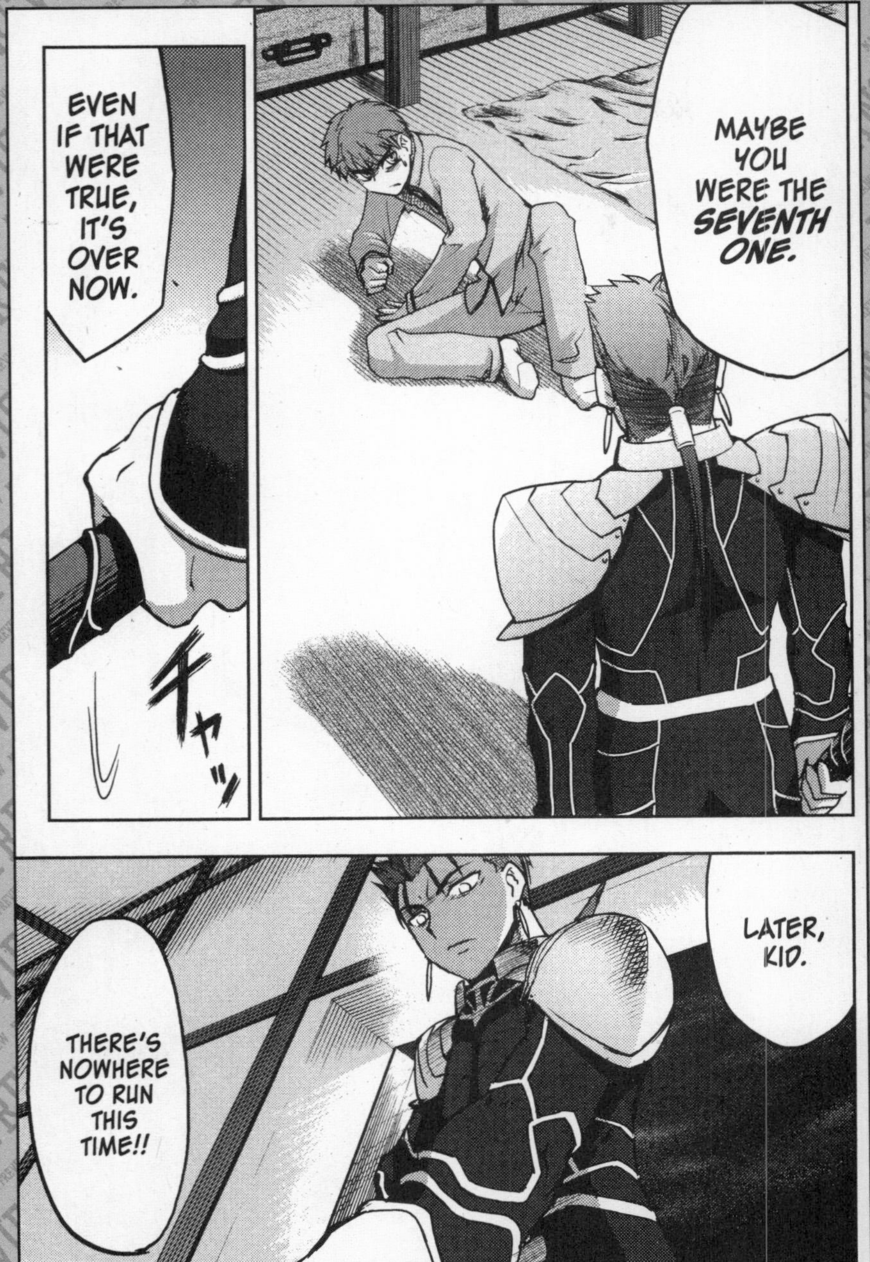
MAYBE YOU WERE THE SEVENTH ONE.
EVEN IF THAT WERE TRUE, IT'S OVER NOW.
チャッ
LATER, KID.
THERE'S NOWHERE TO RUN THIS TIME!!

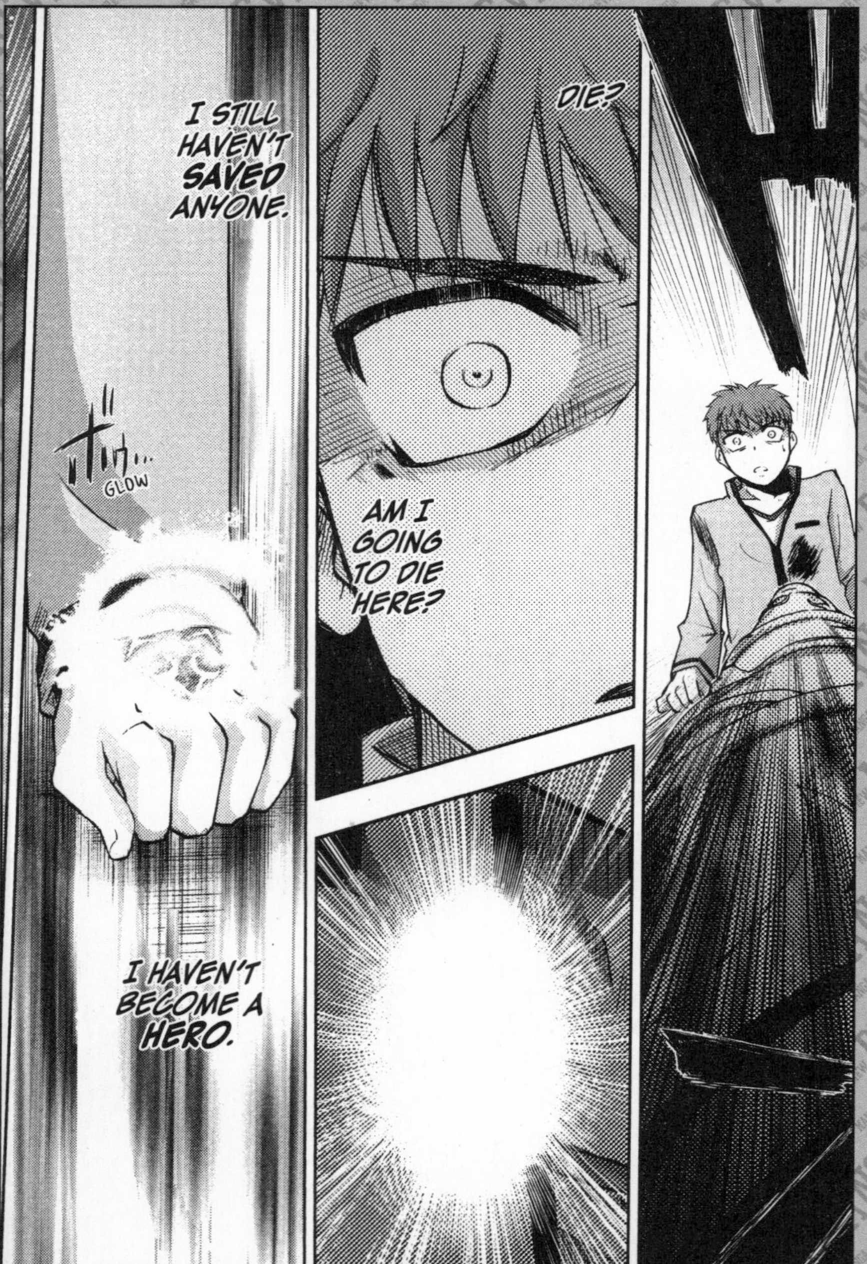
DIE?
AM I GOING TO DIE HERE?
I STILL HAVEN'T SAVED ANYONE.
GLOW
I HAVEN'T BECOME A HERO.

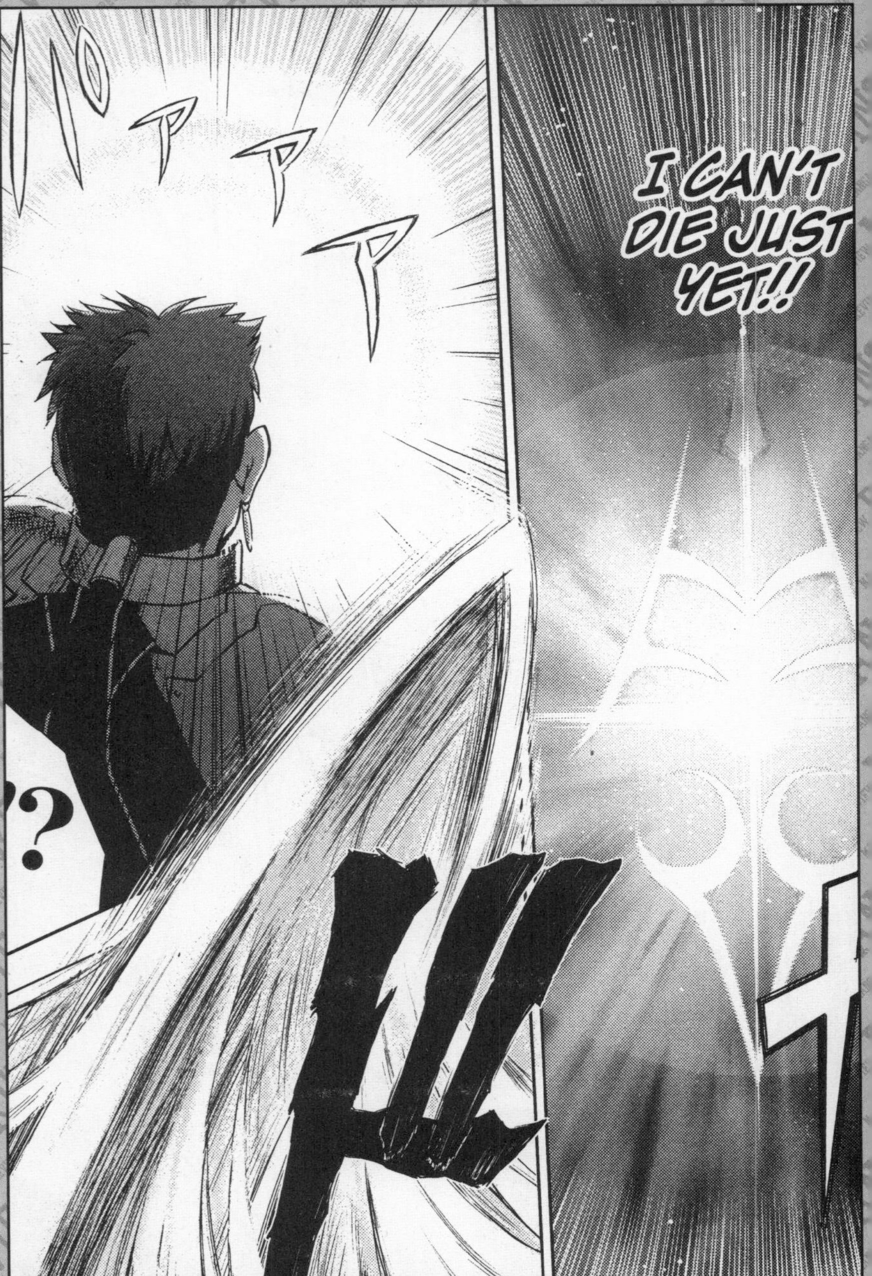
I CAN'T DIE JUST YET!!
??

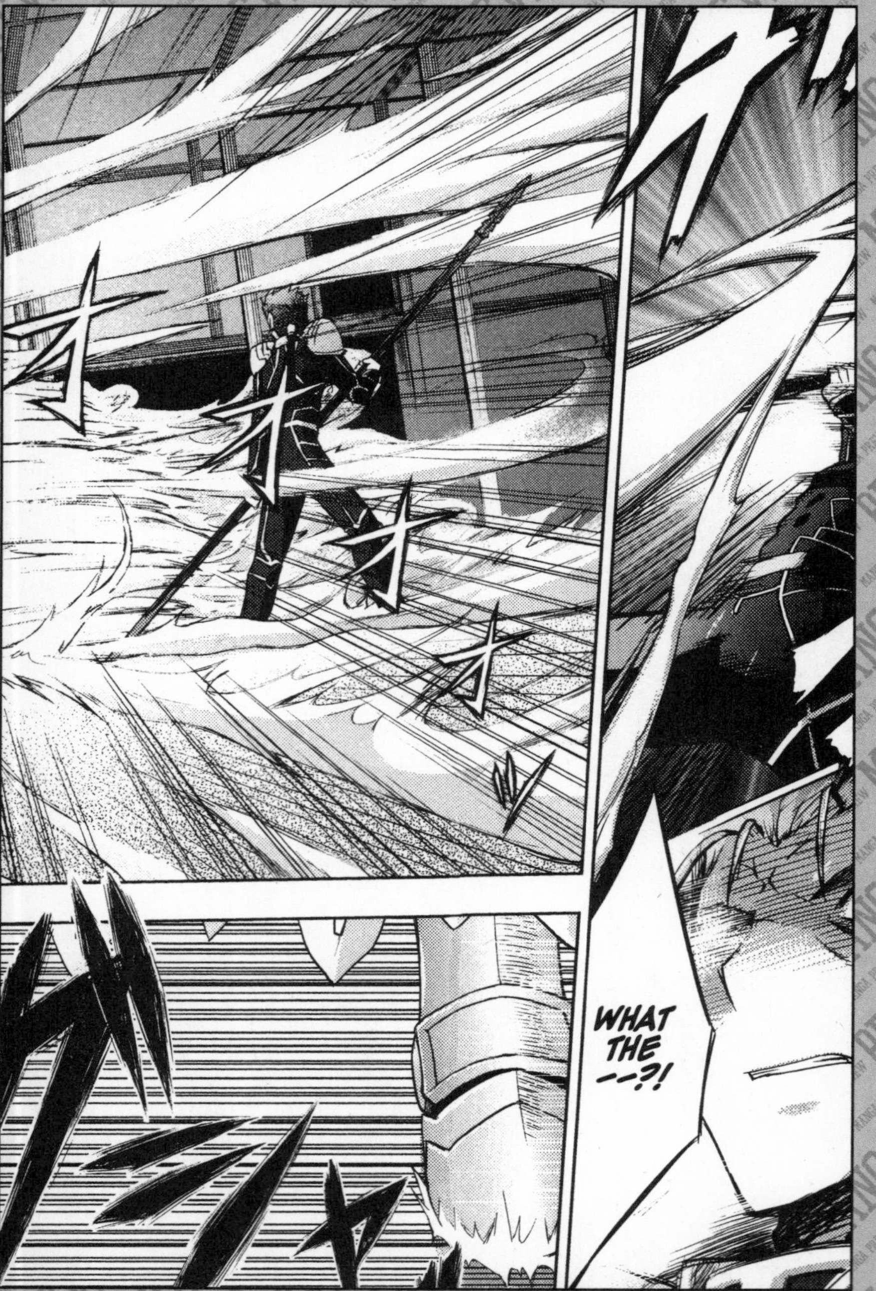
WHAT THE --?!

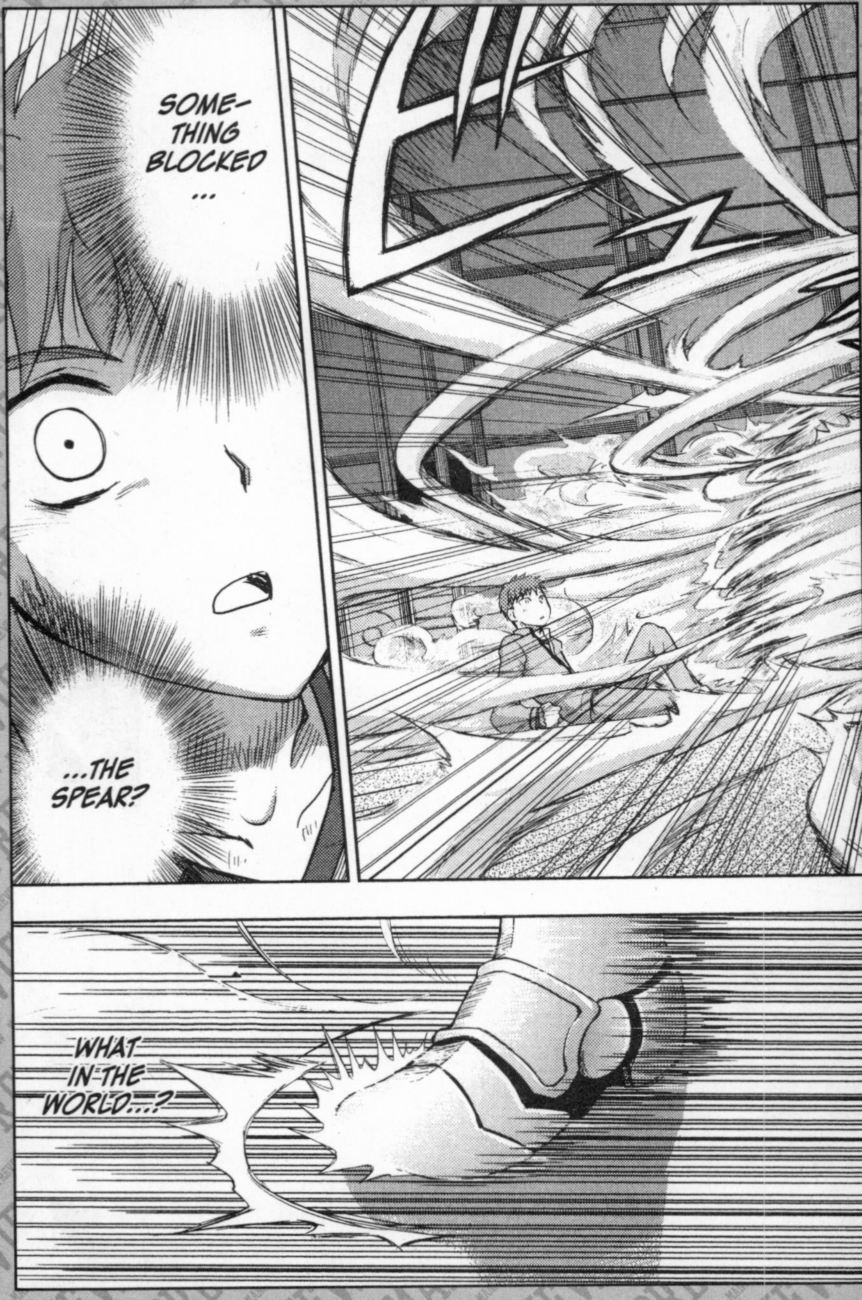
SOME-THING BLOCKED ...
...THE SPEAR?
WHAT IN THE WORLD...?

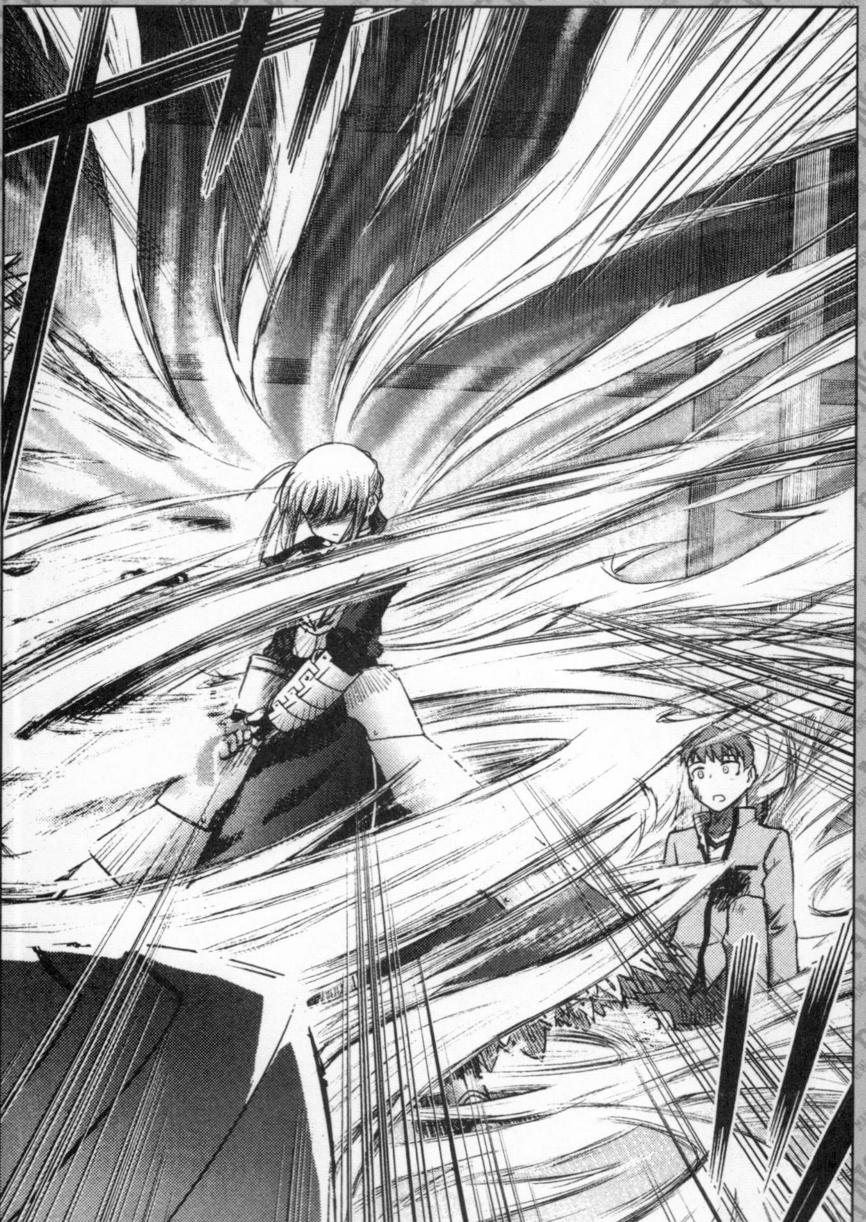

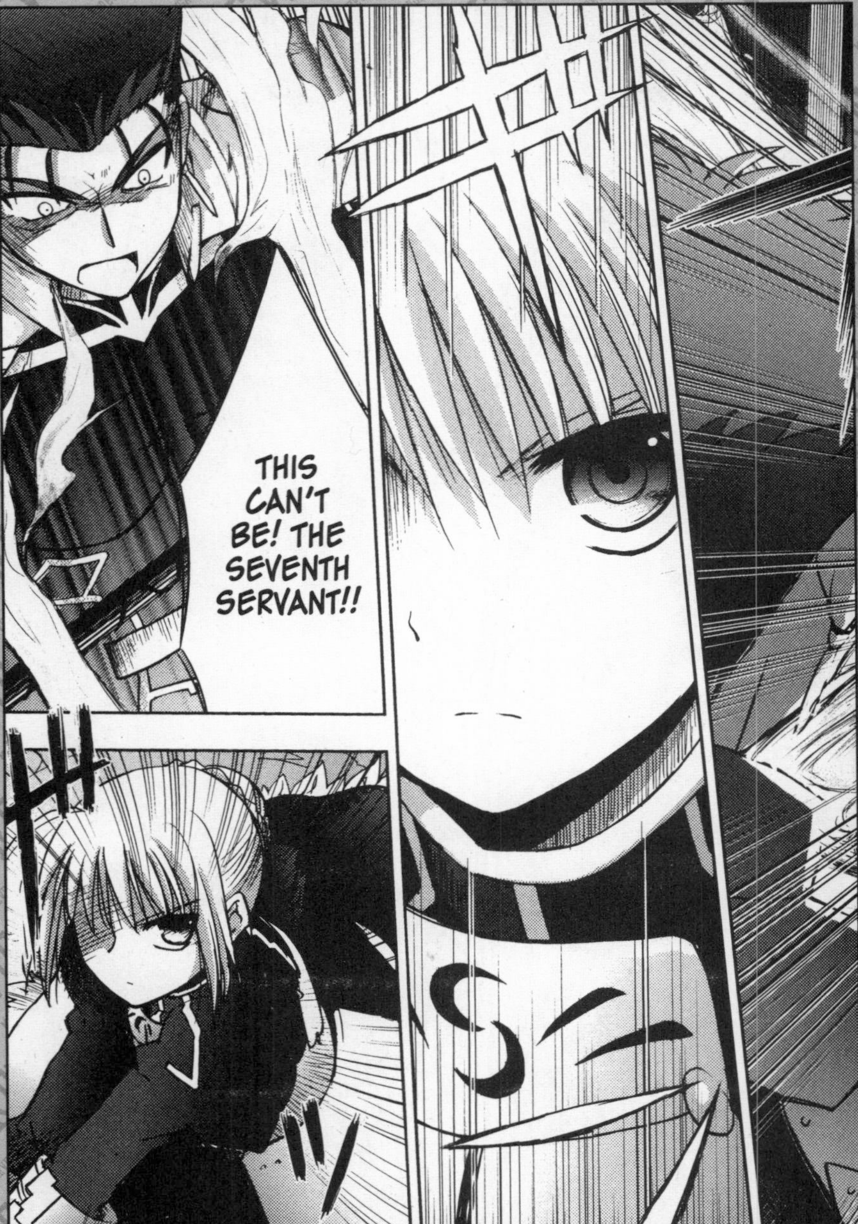
THIS CAN'T BE! THE SEVENTH SERVANT!!

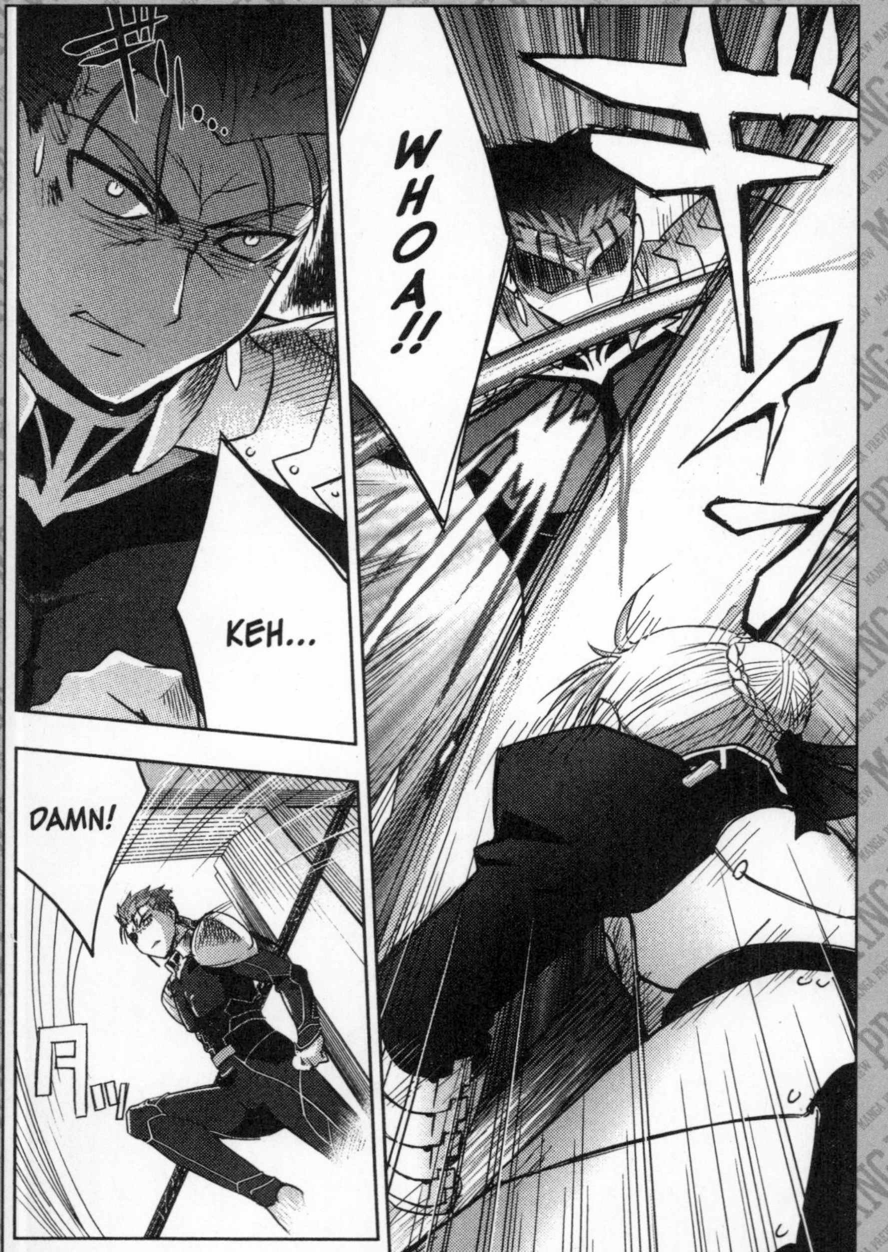
WHOA!!
KEH...
DAMN!

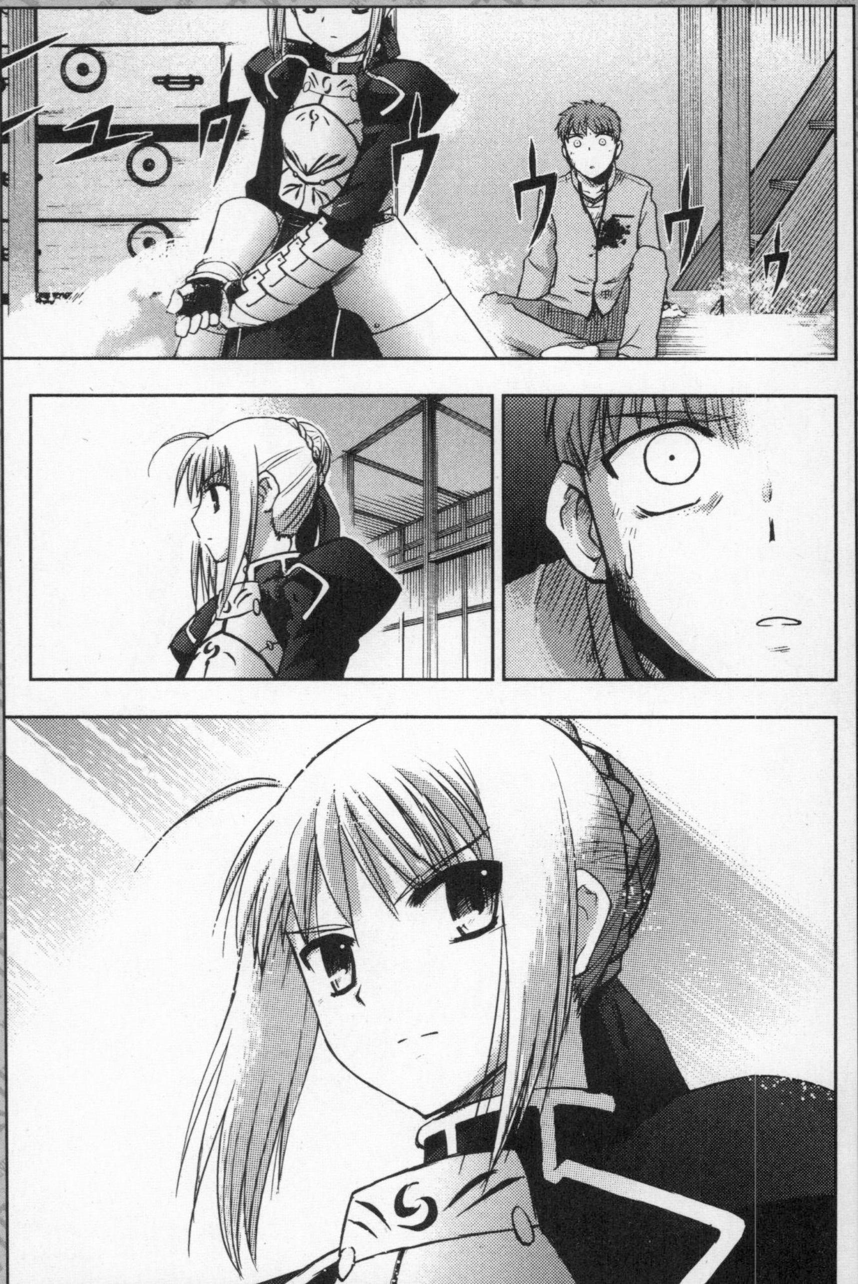

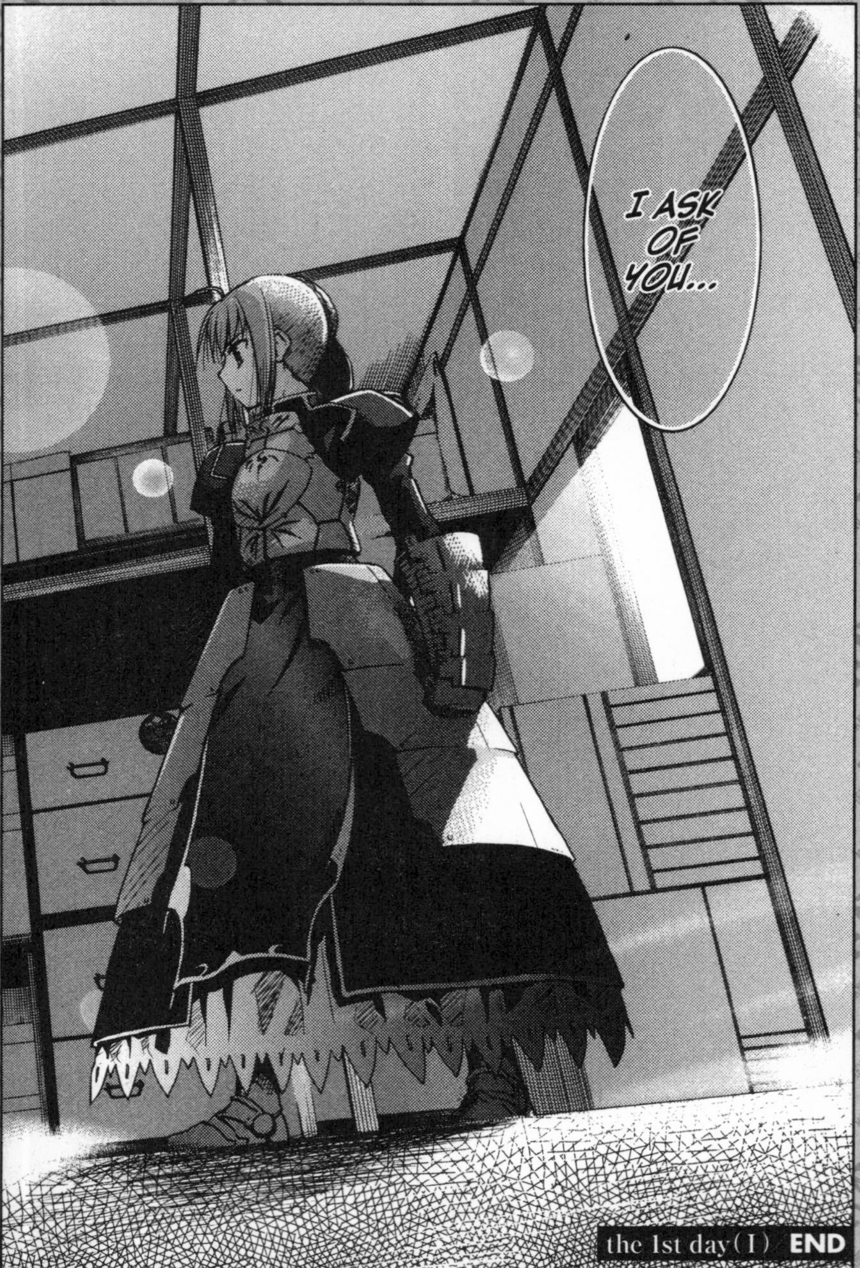
I ASK OF YOU...
the 1st day (I) END

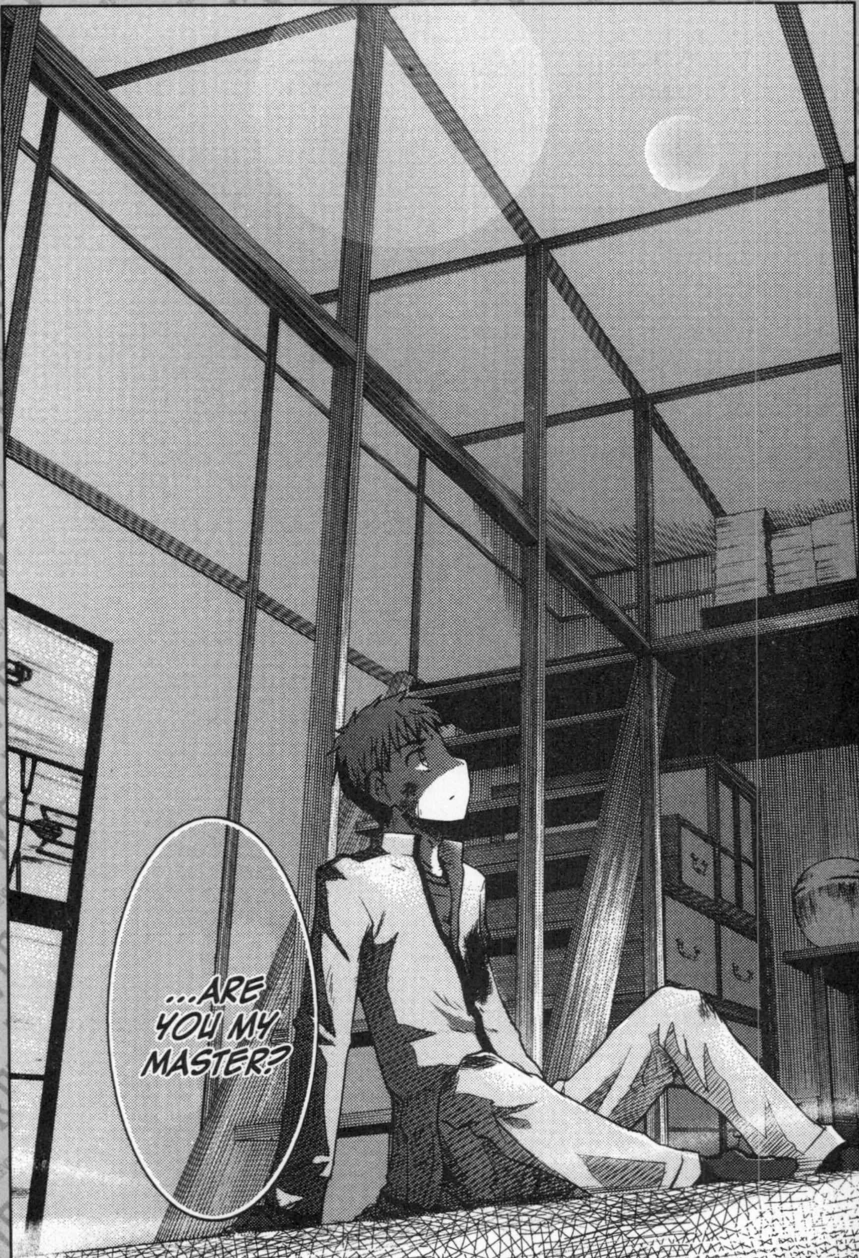
...ARE YOU MY MASTER?

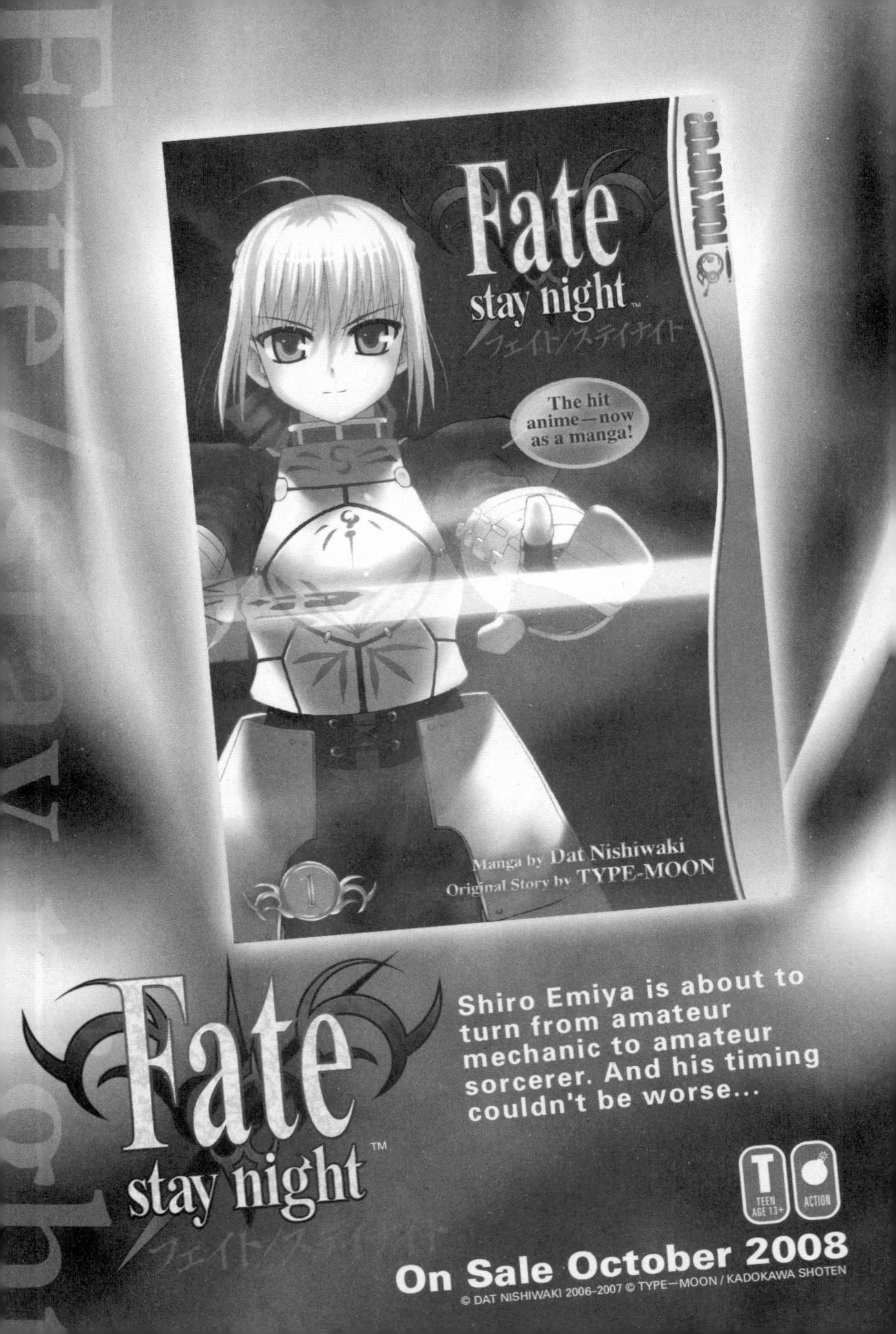
TOKYOPOP
Fate
stay night™
フェイト/ステイナイト
The hit anime—now as a manga!
Manga by Dat Nishiwaki
Original Story by TYPE-MOON
1
Fate
stay night™
フェイト/ステイナイト
Shiro Emiya is about to turn from amateur mechanic to amateur sorcerer. And his timing couldn't be worse...
T TEEN AGE 13+
ACTION
On Sale October 2008
© DAT NISHIWAKI 2006–2007 © TYPE—MOON / KADOKAWA SHOTEN